Diminishing Welfare

Diminishing Welfare

A Cross-National Study of Social Provision

Edited by
Gertrude Schaffner Goldberg
and Marguerite G. Rosenthal

AUBURN HOUSE
Westport, Connecticut • London

Library of Congress Cataloging-in-Publication Data

Diminishing welfare : a cross-national study of social provision / edited by Gertrude
Schaffner Goldberg and Marguerite G. Rosenthal.
   p. cm.
   Includes bibliographical references and index.
   ISBN 0–86569–272–6 (alk. paper)—ISBN 0–86569–311–0 (pbk. : alk. paper)
    1. Public welfare—Cross-cultural studies.   2. Welfare state—Cross-cultural studies.
3. Social policy—Cross-cultural studies. I. Goldberg, Gertrude S. II. Rosenthal,
Marguerite G., 1941–
   HV31.D65 2002
   361.9—dc21   00–069969

British Library Cataloguing in Publication Data is available.

Library of Congress Catalog Card Number: 00–069969
ISBN: 0–86569–272–6
    0–86569–311–0 (pbk.)

First published in 2002

Auburn House, 88 Post Road West, Westport, CT 06881
An imprint of Greenwood Publishing Group, Inc.
www.greenwood.com

Printed in the United States of America

The paper used in this book complies with the
Permanent Paper Standard issued by the National
Information Standards Organization (Z39.48–1984).

10 9 8 7 6 5 4 3 2 1

This book is dedicated to the memory of our parents:

Fredericka Wachtel Schaffner
Alvin A. Schaffner

Ida Leah E. Goldberg
Sarah Shally Goldberg
Irving E. Goldberg

Contents

Acknowledgments

A project of this sort owes a debt to a number of scholars in a number of countries, most especially to our fellow authors, scholars on three continents who gave their considerable talents to the writing of this book.

Several authors of the country studies have acknowledged the experts who reviewed and commented on their chapters. We would like to express special appreciation to Helen Lachs Ginsburg. In addition to co-authoring the chapter on Sweden, she generously shared her knowledge of both full employment and social provision with us throughout the project and carefully read and critiqued three chapters. Mark Kesselman, author of the chapter on France, readily shared his knowledge of European politics and helped us to resolve some of the intellectual dilemmas that we encountered. June Zaccone, Emerita Professor of Economics at Hofstra University, continuously referred important materials to us and also shared her knowledge.

Our thanks also go to the Columbia University Seminars Program and its former director, Dean Aaron Warner, for a grant that helped us to undertake this research.

We thank Solidelle Wasser of the U.S. Bureau of Labor Statistics, who helped us to secure unpublished labor market data for the countries in the study. For those attempting to make cross-national comparisons of social expenditures, labor market conditions, and poverty, the data provided by the Organisation for Economic Co-operation and Development (OECD), the Bureau of Labor Statistics of the U.S. Department of Labor, and the Luxembourg Income Study (LIS) are invaluable. We appreciate the assistance of Kati Foley, Mary Santy, and Koen Vleminckx of the LIS, and of Catherine Duchêne of the OECD in securing and/or interpreting data. We also appreciate the assistance of the reference librarians at the Swirbul Library, Adelphi University, the New Canaan (Connecticut) Library, and the Salem State College Library.

Paul Pierson's theory of welfare state retrenchment raised challenging questions that we sought to answer in this research. Marguerite Rosenthal attended the Social Policy and Citizenship Seminar at the Minda de Gunzburg Center for European Studies, Harvard University, which was under the direction of Professor Pierson. We acknowledge his stimulating contribution to this study.

Diminishing Welfare

Chapter 1

Introduction: Three Stages of Welfare Capitalism

Gertrude Schaffner Goldberg

In the decades following World War II, a permanent and growing social welfare sector seemed a secure, even defining attribute of the "new capitalism." Its "most striking characteristic," wrote British economist Andrew Shonfield, is "the speed with which the advance in national income has been translated into larger benefits for people unable to pre-empt a direct share of the prosperity through their own earnings" (1965, p. 7).

This provision of income support was not the only remarkable characteristic of the "new capitalism." It was also, Shonfield wrote, "the conscious pursuit of full employment"(1965, p. 63). Some writers have even included full employment—along with expansive social policies—in the concept of "welfare statism" (Pfaller with Gough and Therborn, 1991, p. 2). Full employment was part and parcel of post-war welfare states, particularly the most advanced ones (Ginsburg, 1983; Esping-Andersen, 1990). Social policy scholar Arthur Gould (1993, p. 3) uses the term "welfare state" to refer to state provision of a comprehensive range of universal welfare benefits and services *and* a policy of full employment. An earlier definition of the welfare state was "a state democratic in form, interventionist by inclination, and eager to manage the capitalist economy to achieve steady economic growth and maintain full employment" (Logue, 1979, p. 69).

During World War II, Franklin Roosevelt advocated an "economic bill of rights" that would add "freedom from want" to the political and civil liberties guaranteed by the U.S. Constitution in its Bill of Rights. The first economic right was "a useful and remunerative job." In a 1949 lecture, T. H. Marshall (1973) observed that just as civil and political rights were established in the eighteenth and nineteenth centuries, "social" or economic rights to income, irrespective of one's market value, would be secured in the twentieth.[1]

Economic rights did expand in the wealthy capitalist countries during the post-war era, and in contrast to their communist counterparts, civil and political rights held fast, were expanded, or became universal as, for example, through the Civil Rights movement in the United States. To cite another example, France extended the franchise to women and expanded social welfare. The post-war welfare state also differed from the pioneering social insurance program established in Germany in the late nineteenth century by Chancellor Otto von Bismarck. The Iron Chancellor is said to have granted economic rights as an alternative to enlarged political rights and "to preserve the traditional system of political inequality" (Rimlinger, 1971, p. 112).

The welfare state, one of the crowning achievements of the twentieth century, was an unprecedented use of the power of the state to reduce economic insecurity but not at the expense of freedom. The welfare state was not, as an opponent charged, a "road to serfdom" (Hayek, 1944). Indeed, if its humanitarian accomplishments were being emphasized, the twentieth century might be called the century of the welfare state. For a time it seemed that the poor need not always be with us. The "new capitalism" was a good deal less cruel than the old. Winners still took a lot, but losers increasingly were compensated.

THE "CRISIS" OF THE WELFARE STATE

In purely functional terms, the welfare state should be a permanent feature of capitalism for its contribution to political stability. Even after the welfare state had been under assault, Ira Katznelson wrote that "it is impossible to imagine that any capitalist society may achieve stability and continuity without adopting welfare state policies" (1980, p. 118). Or as Claus Offe put it, the welfare state in Western Europe "has . . . become an irreversible structure, the abolition of which would require nothing less than the abolition of political democracy and the unions" (1984, p. 152).

Nonetheless, the welfare state came under attack or severe questioning. This was not an altogether new phenomenon. Even in the 1960s, when the welfare state was expanding, the British historian Asa Briggs believed that it had fallen from the pedestal of the immediate post-war years: "[T]he ideals which inspired the achievement of a 'welfare state' are now no longer universally shared. . . . The switch may be only temporary . . . , but it is a sign that what only recently seemed to be fixed is far from fixed" (1967, p. 26).

One of the earliest Cassandras of the next decade was James O'Connor, who in *The Fiscal Crisis of the State* (1973) held that the two basic functions of the capitalist state, capital accumulation and legitimation—the latter facilitated by social welfare—were incompatible. This was even before the slowdown in economic growth, the stagflation and consequent loss of faith in the Keynesian economic policies that had facilitated both full employment and social welfare programs, and the collapse of the international regulatory institutions that played such an important role in the post-war expansion. In a 1980 article in the *American Economic Review*, Albert O. Hirschman referred to the "so-called 'crisis of the welfare state.' " In contrast to those who diagnosed the problems of the welfare state as structural or fundamental (O'Connor, 1973; Habermas, 1975; Hirsch, 1976), Hirschman considered the troubles temporary growing pains: services had declined in quality owing to their rapid expansion. If, however, the clientele of the welfare state was less satisfied, the continuing and accelerating assault, sooner rather than later in some countries, came primarily from other quarters.

In the 1970s, Britain, under pressure from mounting inflation and the run on the pound, "quickly removed the more expensive (and expansive) elements of the Social Contract. Promises of expanded social provision were jettisoned, and the discussion of industrial and economic democracy was shelved indefinitely" (Krieger, 1991, pp. 51–52). In the United States, the decade had begun with a Republican, Richard Nixon, proposing a guaranteed income for families with children, federalizing and liberalizing benefits for the elderly and disabled poor, and presiding over a 50 percent rise in public assistance expenditures. The 1970s ended with Democrat Jimmy Carter cutting back the job creation program that he had initially expanded, despite continued high unemployment; violating the weak and unenforceable full employment legislation that he had signed; appointing a conservative monetarist to head the Federal Reserve Board; and initiating some of the deregulatory policies and military buildup that mushroomed under his successor, Ronald Reagan—in short, "getting ready for Righty" (Goldberg and Collins, 2001, ch. 6). Stagflation of the U.S. economy meant stagnation of the weak U.S. welfare state. It is said that "the first oil shock heralded the end of the 'Golden Age' of Western capitalism, foreshadowing further expenditure expansion as programmed commitments increased relative to levels of income growth and as the new armies of the unemployed took up their entitlement from the state" (Castles, 1998, pp. 309–310).

Where the welfare state was more costly and more extensive, the dialogue and the policy directions were different. France was soon to turn, if briefly, toward socialism, and Prime Minister Jacques Chirac, who led a subsequent coalition government of the Center and Right, was said to be "far too skilled a politician to take on the welfare state, even if he had been inclined to do so" (Ambler, 1993, p. 25). Sweden's welfare state seemed impregnable in the 1980s, when the welfare state was clearly in trouble elsewhere.

Now, 25 years after O'Connor proclaimed "the fiscal crisis of the state," the decline and perhaps even the fall of welfare states are still predicted.

Nonetheless, the extent to which the welfare state is diminishing remains debatable. The popular consensus is that its growth has been slowing since the 1970s and may now be going into reverse. According to Spanish economist Miren Etxezarreta, "The idea of 'the crisis of the welfare state' is prominent now within the European Union" (1995, p. 31).

When conditions seem to be deteriorating, there is a tendency to glorify the past. Thus, Esping-Andersen refers to the "postwar Golden Age" in which "prosperity, equality, and full employment seemed in perfect harmony"; and he dubs the present period "after the Golden Age." So staunch a proponent of the welfare state as Esping-Andersen (1996) does not reject three diagnoses of the post-Golden Age "crisis," even though he considers them exaggerated: the "market distortion" view that the welfare state stifles the market and incentive; the demographic perspective that focuses on the drain on resources of an aging population and, one might add, the increase in single parenthood; and the consequences of the global economy that "mercilessly punishes profligate governments and uncompetitive economies" (1996, pp. 1–2).

Is the welfare state diminishing? This book answers that question by examining trends in social provision and in employment in nine countries in Europe, North America, and Asia in the last two decades of the twentieth century—France, Germany, Hungary, Italy, Sweden, and the United Kingdom in Europe; Canada and the United States in North America; and Japan in Asia. The remainder of this introductory chapter identifies the salient characteristics and political economies of the two earlier phases of the welfare state, introduces some theoretical and empirical work on welfare state retrenchment, and presents a rationale for the selection of the countries in this cross-national investigation.

THE INITIAL PHASE

Various forms of social insurance—protection against industrial accidents, sickness, unemployment, and old age—were invented and inaugurated in the countries of Western Europe in the last third of the nineteenth century (Flora and Alber, 1981).[2] As Heclo (1981, p. 389) points out, the social insurance programs in the early phase of the welfare state were seen as deviations from established economic doctrines, and few saw them as good economics. Bismarck, whose political motivations have already been noted, regarded the social insurance programs that he introduced as insurance against socialism (Pflanze, 1990, pp. 145–184). The fact that these programs were seen as economically unsound, even if politically necessary, reminds us that currently the welfare state is regarded as a drag on the economy.

The model of social insurance of the experimental era, known as the Bismarckian model, contrasts with the approach advocated by Sir William

Beveridge in England in the early 1940s. In the Bismarckian approach, existing hierarchies were maintained, with more privileged groups such as civil servants garnering more favorable treatment in social insurance. One of its objects was "to consolidate divisions among wage-earners by legislating distinct programs for different class and status groups, each with its own conspicuously unique set of rights and privileges which was designed to accentuate the individual's appropriate station in life" (Esping-Andersen, 1990, p. 24). In this tradition, the civil service was particularly privileged and rewarded for its loyalty to the state. This approach persists in the countries of Central Europe—France, Germany, Austria, Italy—that have been designated conservative or "corporatist" (Esping-Andersen, 1990).[3] Mann (1987, pp. 344–349), who places Germany, Austria, Russia, and Japan in the corporatist camp, traces the origin of this "divide-and-rule" approach to the tradition of absolutism or authoritarian monarchy. From the perspective of conservative rule, division of the working class and allegiance to the state are double gains of Bismarckian policy.

In the early era of the welfare state, the United States exhibited its traditional exceptionalism. Prior to the 1930s, it initiated only a state workmen's compensation program—first for federal employees in 1908, followed by the adoption of insurance programs against industrial injury in 43 states between 1909 and 1920 (Lubove, 1968). Theda Skocpol (1992) has made the case that pensions for Civil War veterans can be compared to social insurance programs adopted by some European nations in this period, but these were not social insurance and lasted only as long as the veterans and their dependents lived. The existence of these veterans' benefits probably reduced pressure for a permanent system of old age insurance just as extensive provisions for World War II veterans may have retarded liberalization of benefits for the general population. France, though initiating social insurance early (Flora and Alber, 1981, p. 59), was much slower than some other European countries, notably, Germany and the United Kingdom, to cover most of its population with public pensions.

At the very end of the period, amid the economic and political crisis of the Great Depression that led to the mobilization of the unemployed, labor, and the elderly, the United States adopted federal Old Age Insurance and a program of state-federal Unemployment Insurance. The United States provides pensions in relation to former earnings, thereby carrying income differences into social welfare, although a weighted benefit formula in Old Age Insurance results in higher income replacement rates for lower-wage recipients. While it treats all occupational groups equally once they are in the system, Old Age Insurance—and for that matter, Unemployment Insurance—initially excluded whole occupational sectors, notably, agriculture and domestic service, in which women and the black population were disproportionately employed.

How serious a problem was unemployment during the experimental phase of the welfare state? Although unemployment had been known but not called by that name from early times, it became increasingly important with the advent of wide-scale wage labor and a more serious problem as the laboring classes lost access to resources other than their wages, particularly under industrialism. Historian John Garraty (1978, p. 121) refers to unemployment as a "burning issue" during the severe depression that afflicted a number of industrialized countries in the 1880s. William Beveridge recognized its importance but wrote that before World War I, unemployment was "an evil calling for remedy," not the foremost problem of the era (1945, p. 105). Nonetheless, Beveridge observed that in Britain the conditions for full employment existed for only a few years between 1883 and 1914 (p. 108). As for the Continent, "extensive unemployment . . . wracked Europe in the mid-1880s and early 1890s" (Alber, 1981, p. 152).

World War I did demonstrate to observers like Sidney and Beatrice Webb in England that what was regarded as a surplus population could be employed and that most classified as unemployable could be "usefully and even profitably put to work" (Webb and Webb, cited in Garraty, 1978, p. 146). However, there was little systematic economic thinking on which to base continuance of wartime full employment. There was a will but not a way. For example, a clause guaranteeing every German the right to employment was included in the Weimar Constitution of 1919 (Stachura, 1986), but, as mass unemployment in the next decades proves, this was hardly an enforceable right. This early, experimental phase of what would later be called the welfare state ended in mass unemployment. It had been anything but a full employment state.

WELFARE STATISM: THE FULL EMPLOYMENT WELFARE STATE

The welfare state expanded in the third quarter of the twentieth century under highly unusual political and economic conditions, often differing among countries. The memory of mass unemployment and its consequences played a role. Hot and cold wars were political factors that created powerful rationales for reform and enlightened policies, including the decision of the United States to contribute large sums to finance European recovery. The end of the Cold War and the passing of leadership to a post-Depression generation thus removed some powerful rationales for welfare state expansion.

War and Interventionist Government

To finance the war, governments "inadvertently" adopted the methods of John Maynard Keynes: unbalanced budgets, heavy public investments, and low interest rates (Garraty, 1978, pp. 229–230). In so doing, they eliminated unemployment. Continuance of activist government during peacetime played an important role in economic expansion and job creation, even where policymakers did not follow Keynesian methods in the immediate post-war years. Although Shonfield (1965, p. 106) holds that Keynesian thought was not generally accepted on the Continent after World War II, Garraty (1978, pp. 230–231) provides evidence of conversion on the part of policymakers in France, Britain, Canada, and the United States.[4] During a small recession in the 1960s, Germany adopted Keynesian policies (Shonfield, 1965, pp. 287–288; Schmid, 1988; Ginsburg, 1993). In one way or another and to varying degrees most capitalist nations attempted to maximize employment. The United Nations Charter of 1945 pledged member states to action in support of full employment, and the Universal Declaration of Human Rights, adopted unanimously in 1948, proclaimed, "Everyone has the right to work" (Article 23).

Keynes, who had written a scathing critique of the post–World War I settlements, participated in establishing the international institutions that facilitated the implementation of his call for government intervention and regulation to stimulate consumer demand and economic growth. It was his strong desire to make world currency arrangements serve the purposes of high domestic demand and employment instead of the reverse (Lekachman, 1966, p. 181). Whether or not a country adopted full employment policies or Keynesian methods, its economic expansion and recovery were stimulated by the Bretton Woods international agreements. In Germany, for example, the continuing boom in world trade that was fostered by these post-war agreements was one of the foremost factors that stimulated its economy and employment even when domestic demand fluctuated (Shonfield, 1965).

War and the Post-war Welfare State

War mobilization demanded a solidarity and a commitment on the part of the British working class, who, having suffered a deep depression, might otherwise have had limited motivation to make the necessary sacrifices. Under the auspices of the British wartime government, William Beveridge (1942) proposed a program for post-war income security that included comprehensive social insurance and national assistance programs, a children's allowance, and a national health service as well as maintenance of employment and prevention of mass unemployment. Beveridge's—and we assume the government's—rationale for making these plans at that time was that "each individual citizen is more likely to concentrate upon his war effort if he feels that his Government will be ready in time with plans for that better world" (1942, p. 171). In his report, Beveridge called attention to the Atlantic Charter, declaring the desire of the American and British leaders "to bring about the fullest collaboration between all nations in the economic field, with the object of securing for all improved labour standards, economic advancement, and social security" (p. 171). According to T. H. Marshall (1965, p. 76), the social welfare plans were for a post-war society that was to be "governed by the same principles of pooling and sharing that governed the emergency measures of the war."

Beveridge's principles departed from earlier social policies, notably, the Bismarckian model, in at least two important respects: insurance was to be universal, compulsory, and contributory, and benefits were to be at the same flat, subsistence rates for all (Beveridge, 1942). A third and integrally related principle was that statutory benefits should be supplemented by voluntary saving, which was to be encouraged by positive measures included in this scheme. Means-tested assistance for the poor was to continue but to be reduced with the onset of widespread insurance coverage (pp. 141–145). The emphasis on universalism fitted the need for solidarity. Writing particularly of social security reforms in post-war Germany, Gaston Rimlinger (1971, p. 149) observed that the Beveridge Report of 1942 "became a landmark in the development of social security thought; its influence has extended to every major country in the world."

For Beveridge, the "spectacular achievement" of the "planned war economy" demonstrated the possibility of full employment (1945, pp. 117–118, 120). As the American economist Robert Lekachman observed, "Our wishes sometimes are granted in unpleasant ways. It was World War II, a gigantic experiment in the macroeconomics of aggregate demand, that finally convinced the universe of the validity of Keynes' emphasis upon the symbiosis between employment and total spending" (1976, p. 259). According to New Deal historian William Leuchtenburg (1963, p. 347), spending the money required for full employment had been helped along by the war, which had "freed the government from the taboos of a balanced budget and revealed the potentialities of spending." Instead of rolling back taxes to nearly pre-war levels, Western democratic governments maintained the high levels of taxation that the war had made politically possible (Steinmo, 1994, citing Peacock and Weisman, 1961).

Full employment was important in the Beveridge scheme for several important reasons. First, he recognized that it would be easier to finance the welfare state with full employment because "larger benefits in terms of money can be provided for materially lower contributions by all parties concerned" (1945, p. 160). When more people work and pay taxes, treasuries expand, and at the same time fewer benefits are needed to pay for the direct and indirect costs of unemployment. Nevertheless, Beveridge held that "maintenance of employment is wanted for its own sake and not simply to make a Plan for Social Security work more easily" (p. 17). Full employment alone would make it possible "to ensure to the people the first condition of happiness—the opportunity of useful service" (p. 122). This emphasis on the "opportunity of useful service" is one of the central components of the Beveridge approach to both the welfare state and full employment. "Idleness," wrote Beveridge, "is not the same as Want, but a separate evil, which men [and it was largely men and male breadwinners on his mind] do not escape by having an income. They must also have the chance of rendering useful service and of feeling that they are doing so" (p. 20).

Like Beveridge, Swedish policymakers, who pursued full employment policies from the mid-1930s on, thought that full employment meant much more than economic security. The concept of normalization was fundamental to the Swedish social welfare system, and work was the key to a normal life, a means of reducing isolation, loneliness, and alienation (Ginsburg, 1983, p. 123). Socially useful jobs were preferable to income maintenance for persons of working age who were not caring for the young and the frail in their families, but full employment did not obviate their need for social welfare, even in economies with adequate wages. It required a different kind of welfare state, particularly as both parents became employed and as many women became single parents. The Swedes did not require the motivation of the war to expand social policies and reduce unemployment, but they were aided by the arms race in the late 1930s and the war. Indeed, Ginsburg observes that "during the war it was no longer necessary to pursue an active full-employment policy through expansionary programs. Labor scarcities were prevalent, as in the United States" (Ginsburg, 1983, p. 112).

Americans on the home front were free of enemy attack and benefiting from wartime prosperity. Yet, many who fought for the American way of life were part of the "third of a nation" that was, in Roosevelt's famous phrase, "ill-fed, ill-clothed, ill-housed." In 1944, an election year, FDR proposed his Economic Bill of Rights with its prospect of a far fairer life than in the pre-war years.

Cold War and Domestic Policies

During the Cold War, Western capitalist countries had another reason to expand social welfare: to compete with Communism's combination of full employment and comprehensive benefit systems (Mishra, 1996). A more general reflection on the exigencies of the Cold War is that "The political conditions of Europe, in which powerful communist parties threatened to harness the frustrations of the working class into an irresistible revolutionary movement, helped concentrate even the most cynical minds on the importance of reform" (Mead, 1988–1989, p. 4). A 1962 German government report proposing Keynesian instruments for control of the business cycle called attention to the disastrous effects of the Weimar government's inability to master unemployment and concluded that "in the light of the East–West conflict," public policy must ensure against a similar failure (quoted in Shonfield, 1965, p. 288).

In an unusual example of enlightened self-interest and bipartisan agreement, the United States, the only great power to emerge economically unscathed from the war, facilitated a post-war economic expansion that did, in fact, do much to rebuild European economies, pay for reconstruction, finance their welfare states, and halt the spread of Communism. Post-war reconstruction, like war itself, stimulated employment. Through the Marshall Plan, the U.S. government made extensive loans to the devastated Western European countries, allowing them to reindustrialize and creating markets for U.S. products. U.S. policies were partly based on anti-Communism and on the premise that the United States would prosper more rather than less, if it helped its allies and former enemies to recover their purchasing power (Mead, 1988–1989, p. 3).

If the Cold War pushed European domestic policy and U.S. foreign aid policy in a progressive direction, it had the opposite effect on U.S. domestic policy. Seeking to turn back newly won labor rights and reduce interventionist government—legacies of the New Deal and the war experience—conservatives seized on the communist threat to attack the left-leaning and more progressive unions and to discredit social reform. Major extensions of the welfare state were stalled. Unable to achieve universal, public programs like those being established in Europe, unions bargained for health care and other services as private occupational benefits for their members (Stevens, 1990).

The Policies in Tandem

The relationship between social welfare as employment and as income transfers is complex. Transfers complement and substitute for market income when workers suffer involuntary unemployment, low wages, incapacity, or forced retirement. In fact, "decommodification," or breaking the tie between market status and access to essential goods and services, has been seen as a primary function of advanced welfare states (Esping-Andersen, 1990). In his definition of the welfare state, the English historian Asa Briggs (1967, p. 29) includes among three goals of the welfare state "guaranteeing individuals and families a minimum income *irrespective of the market value of their work or their property*" (emphasis added). Yet, the welfare state works best and is most secure when everyone who wants a job has one and earns an adequate wage. According to John Myles, "A generous welfare state is sustainable only if most people do not rely on it most of the time" (1996, cited in Bakker, 1999, p. 62).

Perhaps paradoxically, decommodification went furthest in those countries where the full employment ideal came closest to being realized. Decommodification, of course, was never complete. Even in Sweden, where services and income transfer programs have been most generous and less contingent on market achievement than elsewhere, benefits such as parental leave required a prior work history as a condition of eligibility (Marklund, 1988).

The welfare state generated employment, both directly and indirectly, and served as an economic stabilizer. Where social services were extensive, as in the Nordic countries, large numbers of people, primarily women, were employed as child-care workers, home health aides, and other service providers (Esping-Andersen, 1990; Alestalo, Bislev, and Furåker, 1991). The welfare state was recognized as an economic stabilizer, keeping up consumption when unemployment increased and helping to prevent a 1930s-style depression. Government spending on stabilizers such as unemployment compensation and social assistance increases when national income declines. The post-war welfare state was considered good economics with economic and social policy integrally related (Heclo, 1981, p. 389). "In the light of the Keynesian doctrine of economic policy," wrote Offe (1984, p. 148), "the welfare state came to be seen not so much as a burden imposed upon the economy, but as a built-in economic and political stabilizer which could help to regenerate the forces of economic growth and prevent the economy from spiraling downward to deep recessions." Has this stabilizing function of the welfare state changed? Or is it only public perceptions that have altered?

Commitment to Full Employment

In the period of welfare statism, the wealthy capitalist countries differed in their commitment to full employment, in their overall spending, and in the range and generosity of social welfare benefits. "Full employment has become an orthodox objective of policy" in Britain, wrote an outstanding English economist in the early 1960s (Robinson, 1962, p. 96). In the mid-1940s, however, the U.S. Congress rejected a policy of full employment in favor of maximum employment compatible with price stability. Along with the United States, Italy and Canada did not achieve full employment in the post-war decades, but their unemployment levels were considerably lower in the 1960s than in the following decades (except for the United States in the late 1990s). In the 1960s, the unemployment rate, adjusted to U.S. concepts, averaged around 2 percent or under in France, West Germany, Japan, and Sweden and under 3 percent in the United Kingdom and in the first five years of the 1970s was under 3 percent in France, West Germany, Japan, and Sweden (U.S. Department of Labor, 2000, table 2). (For five-year averages for all countries, 1960–1999, see Chapter 11, Table 11.4). Observing unemployment in the G-7 countries, British economist Sir John Eatwell (1995) wrote that "it is not unreasonable to talk of a period of 'full' employment," to which he, too, applied the label "Golden Age."

The achievements of the Golden Age, though impressive, often failed to measure up to Beveridge's definition of full employment. To Beveridge, full employment was not simply a low unemployment rate. It meant "always having more vacant jobs than unemployed men [*sic*], not slightly fewer jobs" (1945, p. 18). An employer who had trouble filling a vacancy was inconvenienced, but to the worker who cannot find a job, it is a "personal catastrophe," for he is told that "he [*sic*] is of no use" (p. 23). Full employment, however, was never truly achieved. Low official unemployment statistics conceal considerable amounts of hidden unemployment, especially among women, because they do not include involuntary part-time workers and those who do not look for work because they have become discouraged. Work for less than a living wage was also prevalent in some of these countries, and such jobs are a form of underemployment.

Women and Full Employment

In one important respect, the achievements of the welfare state exceeded the visions of the 1940s. As Beveridge's formulation made clear, the concept of full employment was initially a gendered one. In the 1960s, when nearly full employment was reached in a number of countries, the labor force participation of women, though varied, was low in all of them. The average for eight of the countries in this study (all but Hungary) was 41 percent in 1969, compared to 79 percent for men (U.S. Department of Labor, 2000, table 4).

Even when women were included, full employment was not sufficient for vulnerable groups of working-age women to escape poverty or share in prosperity through their earnings. In the late 1980s, many single mothers and their families in all of these countries needed income transfers (Smeeding and Rainwater, 1991, table 7). In Sweden, which had an unemployment rate of 2.5 percent in 1981 and 2.2 percent in 1987, the pre-transfer poverty rates for single-parent families were nonetheless 35.2 percent and 29.1 percent, respectively (Smeeding and Rainwater, 1991, table 7). In West Germany, the pre-transfer poverty rate for single parents was 26.1 percent in 1981, when its unemployment rate was 4.0 percent. These were high rates of pre-transfer poverty, albeit considerably lower than in the United States, Canada, the United Kingdom, and the Netherlands, where market income alone meant that half or more of single-parent families were poor. In the early 1980s, income transfers were reducing the poverty rates of single-parent families by 75 percent in Sweden and 93 percent in the Netherlands. It took income transfers to break the relationship between family composition and poverty that is often taken for granted in nations with less comprehensive and adequate income transfers than Sweden or the Netherlands.

Social Expenditures

As our discussion suggests, commitments to social welfare as well as to full employment varied. The United States, the richest of the capitalist countries, was among the least beneficent, and much writing on the welfare state has attempted to explain what is still another example of American "exceptionalism" (Skocpol, 1992; Piven and Cloward, 1993; Pierson, 1994). Nonetheless, even in the United States, social welfare programs expanded. By the mid-1960s, social welfare in the United States was sufficiently great and widely enough dispersed among the population to be considered a form of wealth or a "new property" (Reich, 1964). In Japan, private occupational welfare and the family system remained as substantial sources of provision, but the state, though less active in social welfare than in other developed nations, nonetheless passed an Unemployment Insurance Law (1947), a National Health Insurance Law (1958), and other forms of social provision, albeit ones that remained minimal by European standards (Axinn, 1990; Gould, 1993, pp. 35–54). Although some observers have pointed out that hidden or disguised unemployment is very high in Japan (Takahashi, 1997), its official unemployment rates were very low throughout the period.

The more developed welfare states of Western Europe were, as is well known, far more extensive. In 1980, Sweden was spending about 30 percent of its resources on social welfare; West Germany and France, nearly one-fourth; and Italy and the United Kingdom, just under one-fifth, which was about average for the eight capitalist countries in this study. This was also close to the mean for 18 OECD (Organisation for Economic Cooperation and Development) countries for which 1980 data were available (OECD, 1988, pp. 16–17). On average, the eight countries in the study were spending an additional 5.6 percent of their resources on education (OECD, 1988, 16–17). Even the low spenders like the United States and Japan expended considerable sums on social welfare, 9.9 and 13.4 percent of gross domestic product (GDP), respectively.

Poverty Reduction

During the Golden Age, poverty reduction varied among the welfare states. Some came close to eradicating it, while others did much less well. Around 1980, at the end of this period, overall poverty, as measured by the relative standard used by the Luxembourg Income Studies (LIS),[5] ranged from 16.4 percent in the United States to 5.6 percent in Sweden. Elderly poverty was under 3 percent (2.7) in Sweden, compared to between 21 and 25 percent in Canada, the United Kingdom, and the United States, with France and Germany around 10 percent (Smeeding, 1997, appendix table A-4). Market income alone left many households behind, between 13 and 18 percent in Canada, France, Sweden, the United Kingdom, and the United States but just under 7 percent in Germany (Smeeding and Rainwater, 1991, table 7). Income transfers reduced non-aged poverty by nearly 60 percent in Sweden. France nearly halved its poverty rates through transfers, and the United Kingdom reduced pre-transfer poverty by one-third. The United States, by contrast, barely trimmed its pre-transfer poverty rates for these non-aged households (a reduction of 3.1 percent).

In the mid-1980s, those regimes that were most encompassing or social democratic and that continued to pursue full employment (Finland, Norway, Sweden) had mean overall poverty rates of 4.2 percent for the total population and 2.6 percent for the elderly. The Gini coeffficients of these three Nordic countries averaged .226. Inequality and poverty were higher in the countries with less encompassing transfer systems, although elderly poverty rates were very low in France and the Netherlands as well as in the Nordic countries (Korpi and Palme, 1998, table 2, using data from the LIS).[6] Toward the end of the middle phase, as Francis Castles pointed out, Scandinavian welfare states achieved a fundamental improvement in the conditions of the working classes, if not a fundamental transformation of the reward structure of capitalism (1978).

THE THIRD PHASE

This volume explores the extent to which welfare and well-being were diminishing in the last years of the century that held out the promise of guaranteeing social and economic rights. The contributors examine social and economic policies in nine developed countries in Asia, Europe, and North America. We ask first whether and to what extent retrenchment has occurred in their social welfare programs since 1980. We probe the question of whether the economic changes partially subsumed by the phrase "globalization of the world economy" reduce the capacity to finance social welfare or primarily provide a rationale for cutbacks. Or, are the countries considered here still developing and administering their social welfare programs primarily on the basis of their internal histories, politics, and established structures? Are the losses, whatever their extent, temporary or permanent? Will the losses themselves reduce support for the welfare state, particularly among those more politically engaged non-poor groups that benefited from higher benefits and higher replacements of former earnings? Is it possible to regain whatever ground has been lost? How well can nations do with less social welfare? Will a reduced stimulus from social welfare make it easier for chronic declines in the business cycle to descend from recession to depression? What have been the political consequences of welfare cutbacks thus far? What are they likely to be?

Conceptualizing Retrenchment

Paul Pierson (1994, 1996) is one scholar who has brought both theory and data to the issue of retrenchment. Pierson maintains that welfare retrenchment is not a mere playback or reversal of welfare state development. Therefore, the welfare state is not necessarily doomed because the forces that contributed to its rise, such as trade unions and labor parties, have been weakened. Power resource theory, which holds that the mobilization of labor or the working class and its ability to form coalitions with other classes are key variables determining differences in welfare state development among advanced nations (Korpi, 1978; Esping-Andersen and Korpi, 1984; Olsen and O'Connor, 1998), would not, in this view, explain retrenchment. Some writers contend that retrenchment has proceeded less where labor and working-class parties have remained strong (Piven, 1991; Garrett, 1998).

Pierson's thesis is that the welfare state creates powerful constituencies in the form of beneficiaries who are able to protect entitlements against attack. "Retrenchment advocates must operate on a terrain that the welfare state itself has fundamentally transformed" (Pierson, 1994, p. 2). Pierson's explanatory concept, "policy feedback," draws on E. E. Schattschneider's insight that "new policies create new politics." Policy feedback refers to "the ways in which previous policy choices influence present political processes"(Pierson 1994, p. 39, citing Schattschneider, 1935, p. 288). Though they differ as to which political interests are critical in resisting retrenchment, both of these approaches emphasize politics and political structures, not technological change or economic development, in accounting for welfare state development and decline.

Pierson identifies criteria for both programmatic and systemic retrenchment of the welfare state. The former results from spending cuts or reshaping social welfare programs, while the latter involves policy changes that alter the context of future spending decisions. Pierson's three measures of programmatic state retrenchment are (1) significant increases in means-tested benefits (as opposed to universal benefits); (2) a major shift of responsibility for social provision from the public to the private sector; and (3) dramatic changes in benefit and eligibility rules that indicate a qualitative change in the nature of a particular program (1996, p. 157). Using these criteria, along with expenditure levels, Pierson concluded that significant retrenchment had not taken place under the Thatcher and Reagan administrations in the United Kingdom and the United States in the 1980s (1994) or in those countries as well as Germany and Sweden through the mid-1990s (1996).

Regardless of whether Pierson is accurate in minimizing welfare state reduction or is perhaps premature in his conclusions, his criteria are useful for determining whether programmatic retrenchment has occurred. The Canadian switch from a universal children's allowance available to all families regardless of income to one that is means-tested is an example of the first. Privatization, as exemplified by the spectacle of large corporations like Lockheed bidding to run the restructured public assistance programs in the United States (Bernstein, 1996), is an example of the second criterion. Radically changed rules and loss of entitlement status in public assistance for single-mother families in the United States corresponds to the third.

Social expenditures as a percent of GDP are often used to show general trends and commitment to social welfare (e.g., Pierson, 1996, pp. 157–159). Gross statistics like these, of course, can be misleading. A rise in social spending could reflect the greater costs of services like health care, as in the United States, where there was a 104.2 percent rise between 1980 and 1995. Technological and administrative costs rose steeply, but coverage, in fact, declined sharply during those years. Or, expenditures that remain stable or even increase may result from changes in demography, economic conditions like unemployment, or even a catastrophe such as a deadly epidemic rather than from increased or even consistent commitment to meeting social need. Moreover, policy changes that ultimately result in reduced expenditures may not show up in spending data (Pierson, 1994, pp. 14, 143). With these caveats, we will consider trends in social expenditures to get a general idea of where welfare states are wending.

Since full employment and social welfare were twin peaks of welfare state policies during the Golden Age, we ask: What is the status of full employment? It appears that retrenchment may have proceeded further in employment than in social policies. Having been cut back for a time, mass unemployment has returned to the capitalist landscape (International Labour Organization [ILO], 1995; Ginsburg et al., 1997). Whereas the Bretton Woods system, which followed the Keynesian principles of intervention and growth, made employment a high priority, not so its successors. The General Agreement on Tariffs and Trade (GATT) regarded free trade not as an end but as a means to promote high spending and full employment (ILO, 1995, p. 195). The Maastricht Treaty, for one, subordinates other economic goals, including full employment, to price stability (Huffschmid, 1997). The World Trade Organization (WTO), which replaced GATT, extends free movement to capital whatever the consequences to the environment, employment, or wages.

Is this third stage similar to the first, not only in regarding social programs as a burden rather than a boon to the economy but in its failure to make employment opportunity an entitlement available to all who seek work? Since the early 1970s unemployment, contingent work, and/or low wages have increased in the developed countries, thereby potentially increasing the need for income transfers (ILO, 1995; Eatwell, 1995; Ginsburg et al., 1997). Ethan Kapstein of the influential and politically moderate Council on Foreign Relations has observed, "Just when working people are most in need of the nation-state as a buffer from the world economy, it is abandoning them" (1996, p. 16). The English poor law "reform" of the nineteenth century—with its severe restrictions in relief to able-bodied workers at the height of the Industrial Revolution—has been similarly described: "At the very time when society was imposing unprecedented strains on the mass of its members, the concept of the need of the individual for group support was being lost" (Checkland and Checkland, 1974, p. 21, cited in Handel, 1982, p. 121).

In this time of global economic change, are welfare states likely to do what England did during the Industrial Revolution? Or what major American cities did later in the century when the Industrial Revolution arrived in the Western Hemisphere (Mohl, 1983)? The United States has already done something similar to people of working age: cutting unemployment benefits and the assistance programs that are the recourse for the long-term unemployed and those who do not establish a steady foothold in the labor market. Increased unemployment in many countries and declining real wages in others are recent changes in social conditions that increase the need for social provision. If these new or greater needs are not met, then social welfare loses ground in its goal of reducing poverty and inequality, even if spending levels remain constant.

Whereas employment policy in the initial stage of welfare states was more a matter of economics or lack of knowledge of instruments for achieving full employment, politics may be uppermost in this era. I say this despite the fact that the no-confidence verdict regarding Keynesian methods is frequently cited as a reason for the changes. For example, Joel Krieger, referring to Britain in the late 1970s, writes: "Keynesianism is everywhere in retreat, and with it the class compromise-welfarist ethic that it had intellectually legitimated throughout the postwar period" (1991, p. 53). Yet, modified Keynesian methods continued to maintain the welfare state and low levels of unemployment in Sweden (Ginsburg, 1996). The power relations between the interests served by full employment and livable wages and those who prefer price stability and looser labor markets shifted sooner or later during these decades. If retrenchment includes decreased commitment to full or maximum employment, then the constituencies served include the beneficiaries not only of social programs or income transfers but of full employment. The advocates for full employment have tended to be the backers of the most advanced welfare states—namely, unions and working-class parties—that are believed to have lost power in recent decades (Piven, 1991; for a dissenting view, see Garrett, 1998).

Retrenchment is not simply a matter of inputs—either employment opportunity or changes in programs or expenditures. It is important to look at outcomes or achievement of the goals of the welfare state. The reduction of poverty is an important goal of welfare states, and in some, though not all, the aim is to reduce inequality, not simply to raise the incomes of the very poor. Thus, in assessing retrenchment, we examine the outcomes of social policies, such as trends in poverty and income distribution, not simply inputs such as changes in programs or expenditures.

It is important to determine which groups are experiencing social exclusion or impoverished social relationships. It could be argued that working-age people who are denied employment opportunities can experience non-monetary deprivations even if they have access to public benefits. Paugam's research (1996) has found that precariousness in the labor market results in impoverished social relationships in some countries, for example, France, Germany, and the United Kingdom, though not in Denmark, Italy, Spain, and the Netherlands.

When to study the phenomenon is a question that should be considered by students of retrenchment. Esping-Andersen concluded that "in most countries what we see is not radical change, but rather a 'frozen' welfare state landscape" (1996, p. 24), but this statement was published in the same year that the United States repealed its entitlement to assistance for women and children and severely cut back benefits to legal immigrants. The fate of its social security program remains undecided. Canada compensated for its high unemployment and deteriorating wages until the mid-1990s but has reduced its commitment to welfare since then. On the other hand, it is possible to ask whether Sweden's pullback in the early 1990s was a temporary detour or a permanent reversal. The risks of studying retrenchment in medias res must be borne in mind.

CHOICE OF COUNTRIES

Comparative studies of social welfare have become an important area of inquiry in the last decade (Esping-Andersen, 1990, 1996, 1999; Goldberg and Kremen, 1990; Gould, 1993; Pierson, 1994, 1996; McFate, Lawson, and Wilson, 1995; Mishra, 1996). The countries considered in this book include the most powerful economies on three continents, Asia, Europe, and North America. There are, moreover, exemplars of each of the three "welfare state regimes"—liberal, conservative, and social democratic—that constitute Esping-Andersen's (1990) well-known typology.[7] At the same time, a number of these welfare states have been considered exceptional, from the standpoint of either the paucity or abundance of provision, the timing of development, or the forces that gave rise to or expanded them.

The United States and Canada

The United States and Canada are the two North American countries in the sample. The United States is the largest economy and one of the world's wealthiest and, in the wake of communist demise, increasingly a model for Europe. These make it an obvious subject for this study. Retrenchment may be less unexpected in the United States, at best a "semi-welfare state" (Katz, 1986). Race has played a role in stunting the welfare state in the United States (Quadagno, 1994) and has divided the constituencies that have mobilized on behalf of social welfare in some other countries. With its heavy reliance on means-tested programs that are mean as well, its greater faith in the ability of the market to provide, its weaker labor unions, its ethnic as well as racial divisions, and a system of government that is fragmented vertically and horizontally, the United States might be less likely than other advanced industrial nations to maintain its commitment to social welfare. On the other hand, as noted, Pierson (1994, 1996) concluded that retrenchment had not proceeded far under the popular, conservative regime of Ronald Reagan. My own appraisal at the beginning of the 1990s was not dire: that the U.S. welfare state had been "diminished but not dismantled" (Goldberg, 1991a, pp. 1–2).

Canada, like the United States and Britain, is classified by Esping-Andersen (1990) as a "liberal" welfare state regime but nevertheless differs considerably from its giant neighbor in population and power, in some areas of social provision, particularly health, in ethnic and racial diversity, and in state structures. Canada is a federation with a relatively weak central government, but unlike the federal system to the south, its central government is a unitary, parliamentary system. Despite its reputation for more generous social welfare provision and higher expenditures than the United States, its meager provision for poor women and children drew the description "bordering on the feminization of poverty" (Goldberg, 1990). Some of its recent changes in family policy (Evans, 1995) and its persisting high unemployment also recommended Canada for this study of diminishing welfare. Unemployment has been very high in the two decades under consideration and, in fact, exceeded the average for the other countries in this sample during every five-year interval since 1960.

Sweden

The choice of Sweden is easy to justify. Sweden, though a small economy, has been the epitome of the so-called Scandinavian or social democratic welfare state model, the most advanced of the welfare state regime types with a commitment to services and to gender equality (Esping-Andersen, 1990). Its recent changes, such as abandonment of centralized labor bargaining, rising unemployment, and retractions in social welfare benefits, add support to the view that welfare state retrenchment may be inevitable, particularly in the light of economic globalization and the country's decision to join the European Community (Marshall, 1996; Olsen, 1999). Although recognized as a world leader in universal benefits, Sweden relies more heavily on income-tested programs than is generally acknowledged (Rosenthal, 1990). In the mid-1990s, Pierson wrote that despite a fiscal crisis and a conservative bourgeois coalition, "there was no sign that the welfare state would be radically restructed" (1996, p. 171). However, the big change in Sweden was its high unemployment rates. Has the quintessential full employment state abandoned a 50-year commitment to jobs for all, or merely put it aside for a time?

The United Kingdom

The United Kingdom is the star witness in Pierson's argument for downplaying retrenchment. The Conservative governments of Thatcher and Major may have sought to jettison the welfare state, but Pierson concludes that the social sector was not cut substantially (Pierson, 1994, 1996). Yet, the numbers of unemployed Britons who are ineligible for national insurance benefits and who have recourse only to means-tested and lower-paying assistance programs have increased in recent years (Millar, 1995). According to Arthur Gould (1993, pp. 158–159), state collectivism in the provision of welfare was reduced in the 1980s, although not commensurate with the libertarian rhetoric of the government. The fact that interpretations have varied adds interest to a study of the extent of retrenchment in Britain. Further, the "new" Labour leadership of Tony Blair provides an opportunity to examine emerging trends in an altered political environment.

France

Observers differ as to whether France, perhaps the most advanced welfare state among the larger industrial economies, is closer to the Scandinavian model or to that of the more patriarchal and "corporatist" (or conservative) European states (Esping-Andersen, 1990, 1999; Goldberg, 1991b). As a principal partner in the European Community but a country with significant employment strains, France is notable for its political volatility and social protest, though not from a highly unionized base. Its labor density is even lower than that of the United States (Rothstein, 1998, p. 293), although coverage (percent of workers covered de facto) under collective bargaining agreements is high (Esping-Andersen, 1999, table 2.1, p. 20, using Visser [1996, table 2] as a source). The political context for the expansion of social welfare policies is also anomalous. One study of 17 nations in the two decades preceding 1980 found that France was "the only nation in which social spending was highly developed in spite of domination of the government for several decades by various coalitions of conservative parties" (Cameron, 1993, pp. 66–67; see also Ross, 1991).

Owing to popular protest, France has held on to the benefits and services of welfare statism. Late in 1995, French government workers, with strong support from students and the general public, staged a massive general strike and successfully fended off the government's threat to cut their pensions. Yet, only five months later, the threat of retrenchment reappeared in what one reporter (Whitney, 1996, p. A5) described as "the most far-reaching [proposed] changes in 50 years in the state-run health-care system." To recognize these threats in the area of pensions and health is not to overlook the fact that as recently as 1994, French family policies, among the most comprehensive in the world, continued to enjoy broad, national support despite increasing pressures on the social budget (Sparrow, 1994). Political mobilization against cutbacks has remained substantial in France. So has unemployment. One wonders why this aspect of welfare statism has been abandoned so much faster than benefits and services and why the resistance to retrenchment in the employment sphere has been either weaker or unable to prevail. What are the positive or negative consequences for a nation-state that is obliged by popular demand to remain steadfast in its commitment to social welfare?

Germany

For a number of reasons Germany is important to this study: the size and strength of its economy; the effect of its restrictive monetary policies on social spending in other European nations, including its dominance in the European Union; and the conservative, patriarchal nature of its substantial welfare state. Also of interest is its absorption of a former, Soviet-style state that, though it denied political and civil rights, extended considerable economic rights—full employment for women as well as men and very extensive social provision (Goldberg, 1991b; Rudolph, Appelbaum, and Maier, 1991).

As in France, Germany's workers and electorate are politically engaged. For instance, when former Chancellor Helmut Kohl proposed to cut $5 billion from the German welfare state—including reductions in sick pay and unemployment benefits and a postponement of scheduled increases in children's allowances—thousands of protesters streamed into Bonn. The ensuing demonstration, estimated at 300,000 people, was almost equal in size to the population of the city itself (Cowell, 1996a, 1996b). Welfare cuts were not new in Germany. The welfare state, according to German economist Jörg Huffschmid (1997), has been trimmed for 20 years. Reflective of changing ideologies and reinforcing neoliberalism in Germany and elsewhere is the Maastricht Treaty of the European Union, with its strict targets for government deficit and debt reduction and consequent restraints on government spending by member countries. In its 1998 elections Germany turned moderately to the Left, to its Social Democratic Party. The latter, like Britain's Labour Party (Crewe, 1991), Sweden's Social Democratic Party, and the U.S. Democratic Party, has become more conservative. Acknowledging that demographic and budgetary pressures that "assure . . .

an atmosphere of austerity will continue to surround the German welfare state," Pierson, nonetheless, concludes that "a fundamental rethinking of social policy seems a remote possibility" (1996, p. 170).

Italy

Including two other nations on the Continent, one in Southern and the other in Central Europe, broadens this study of retrenchment. Italy, though classified as a Continental, conservative welfare state (along with Spain and Portugal) by Esping-Andersen (1999) and as an example of the Christian Democratic tradition (Navarro, 1999), is also described by the term "Mediterranean model" (Leibfried, 1993; Ferrera, 1996). Occupational welfare is an important facet of social policy in Italy, while many social and economic supports that are provided by either the market or the state in other countries are instead the responsibility of the family, principally women. Women's unpaid labor averages about 45 hours a week in Italy and Spain, compared to 31 and 25 in the United States and Denmark (Esping-Andersen, 1999, p. 58).

Overall welfare spending in Italy is at the median for OECD countries but tilted very heavily toward support of the elderly (OECD, 1999). Italy, like other Southern European countries, still has a high level of agricultural employment and a persisting low level of industrial employment (in the south), a very low rate of female participation in the labor market, and very high youth and female unemployment (Pugliese, 1995). Italy's high unemployment is made more serious than in a country like Britain, which has a comparable level, by its territorial concentration (Pugliese, 1996). Yet, unemployment is less likely to lead to social exclusion in Italy than in some other countries (Paugam, 1996). The "deep-rooted dualism" of Italy is said to be reflected in the different social problems prevailing in the two regions. "Whereas in central and northern Italy the needs of the elderly are at the fore, in the south poverty and unemployment definitely take priority" (Fargion, 1997, p. 137).

Hungary

In contrast to Germany, which provides an example of the unification of a former socialist country and a Western capitalist nation—or, perhaps more accurately stated, the absorption of the former by the latter—other countries in Central Europe are independently making the transition or return to capitalism. The former communist states are excluded from most analyses of welfare state regimes, although they combined full employment and a wide array of income transfers. In their post-communist stages, they have had to contend with unemployment, poverty, and provision for those unable to work. The break with the past was quite sudden.

Hungary offers an example of an industrialized, former Soviet satellite that, in its transition period, is experiencing considerable unemployment and substantial pressures to cut back its previous array of social provisions. In other words, Hungary is experiencing strains similar to those in Western Europe and North America, but with fewer and diminishing total resources (Baxandall, 1995). There was an 18 percent drop in Hungary's GDP in the five years prior to 1996 (Baxandall, 1996). The rapid expansion of poverty was evident very soon after beginning its transition to capitalism (Ferge, 1990). Hungary provides an intriguing example of changing welfare state activity in a political and economic context different, in important respects, from that of the other countries being considered here.

Japan

The most powerful economy in Asia and among the world's top three, Japan has, until recently, consistently maintained very low official unemployment rates—2.9 percent in 1994, compared to an average of 9.7 percent for the European and North American countries in the sample (excluding Hungary) (U.S. Department of Labor, 2000, table 2). Family income is less unequally distributed than in other capitalist countries (Atkinson, Rainwater, and Smeeding, 1995), even though social welfare spending is low (OECD, 1999). Yet one scholar finds it surprising that Japan's social welfare policies are as large as they are, given the absence of factors that have promoted them elsewhere: "The paradox is that without strong vested interests and social welfare movements, without social democratic government led by parties backed by organized labor and without political commitments to a welfare state, Japan supports substantial social policies" (Anderson, 1993, p. 1).

Japan, considered a variant of the conservative welfare state (Esping-Andersen, 1999), has traditionally relied upon the male earner, with the wife providing unpaid social support for the other family members, not only children but the elderly and, when male breadwinners are employed outside the large firms, as part of a peripheral workforce. In its dependence on the services of women and in both the monopoly of spending for the elderly and the minimal public support of social services, Japanese social policy bears some resemblance to the Italian. In Japan, women experience more inequality and lower pay than elsewhere (Axinn, 1990). Official rates of unemployment have been very low by international standards, but owing to substantial amounts of latent unemployment, low unemployment has been deemed a myth (Takahashi, 1997, pp. 57–58).

Current changes are undoubtedly causing strains in an economic and social culture that has relied heavily on long-term attachments to a particular employer for a substantial proportion of workers and in which occupational welfare schemes play an important role. Japan, like most of the other countries included here, has a rapidly expanding elderly population, and this is one area where the government has taken a more active role in social welfare policy development. The poor of all ages and the mentally ill are seriously neglected (Gould, 1993, p. 86), and for those persons under 65 who do not meet very stringent definitions of disability, the system can be extremely harsh (Kristof, 1996).

Although it is hard to assess future trends accurately, our study of these nine countries enables us to conclude whether, in fact, the welfare state is diminishing at this time. We hope that this systematic, cross-national comparison may also contribute to an understanding of the process of retrenchment and perhaps even shed additional light on the development of the welfare state.

NOTES

The author wishes to thank Helen Lachs Ginsburg and Marguerite Rosenthal for their careful reading, critiques, and editorial suggestions.

1. Marshall's formulation pertains specifically to Britain, although it has been applied more widely. Of course, nowhere were women accorded either political or civil rights until the twentieth century. Jill Quadagno (1994), in discussing Marshall's work, points out the suppression of freedom for African Americans in the United States and also that the United States followed a different or idiosyncratic path from that of Europe—precocious in providing civil and political liberties to white males at an early date but slower than the others to develop a national welfare state. British sociologist Anthony Giddens (1982, p. 172) is critical of Marshall on several grounds, among them his tendency to regard the expansion of citizenship rights as an evolutionary process rather than "the active endeavors of concrete groups of people." Finally, Michael Mann (1987) deems Marshall's theory of citizenship as not only evolutionist but Anglocentric. The latter, however, seems unfair in view of Marshall's limiting his discussion to Britain.

2. By the outbreak of World War I, 12 countries had some kind of workmen's compensation schemes, 10 had introduced either compulsory or subsidized voluntary sickness insurance programs, 8 provided for old age, and 5 had some kind of unemployment insurance. At the start of World War II, most had compulsory accident and sickness insurance, all had some kind of unemployment insurance, and all but 1 provided for old age (Flora and Alber, 1981).

3. The term "corporatist" is somewhat confusing because writers also refer to "social democratic corporatism" in countries where powerful left-wing parties are allied with broad and centrally organized labor movements. See, for example, Garrett (1998).

4. Commenting on the influence of Keynes in Canada, the United States, and Britain in the 1940s and citing a number of sources, including his own earlier work, Keynesian economist Harold Chorney (1999) writes:

Thus in all three countries stabilization policy inspired by Keynes' ideas was in the process of becoming the dominant approach to public policy. But even at this early stage there was a watering down of the commitment to full employment as opposed to high employment and a certain vulgarization of Keynes' ideas with regard to the problem of inflation and the role of public intervention in the area of investment.

The United States, it should be noted, adopted a policy that has been designated as "military Keynesianism" in which defense spending is used to bolster demand.

5. The LIS uses a relative standard of 50 percent of the median disposable income, adjusted for family size.

6. Korpi and Palme were specifically interested in the extent to which social insurance institutions in these countries were targeted or universal. Their findings were roughly categorized according to the regime types identified by Esping-Andersen. Ramesh Mishra (1996, p. 323) describes Germany as committed to social welfare "but more from the viewpoint of security and stability than equality."

7. The term "liberal" is usually equated with "progressive" in the United States and with intervention on the part of the state to reduce inequality and poverty—a meaning that it took on in the 1930s under the New Deal, which bore some resemblance to social democracy. This was a switch from the earlier, classical meaning of the term in the United States and what it continues to mean elsewhere in the world, namely, anti-statism and laissez-faire. In the United States, conservatism is associated with what is called liberalism elsewhere. The liberal model refers to the English-speaking countries, and "liberal" is used in the classical sense.

REFERENCES

Alber, J. (1981). "Government responses to the challenge of unemployment: The development of unemployment insurance in Western Europe." In P. Flora and A. J. Heidenheimer, eds., *The Development of Welfare States in Europe and America*. New Brunswick, NJ: Transaction Books, pp. 151–183.

Alestalo, M., S. Bislev, and B. Furåker. (1991). "Welfare state employment in Scandinavia." In J. E. Kolberg, ed., *The Welfare State as Employer*. Armonk, NY: M. E. Sharpe, pp. 3–35.

Ambler, J. S., ed. (1993). *The French Welfare State: Surviving Social and Ideological Change*. New York: New York University Press.

Anderson, S. I. (1993). *Welfare Policy and Politics in Japan: Beyond the Developmental State*. New York: Paragon House.

Andor, L. (1999). "East Europe sinking." *Dollars and Sense* 226 (November/December): 47.

Andrews, E. L. (1996). "New hard line by big companies threatens German work benefits." *New York Times*, October 1, pp. A1, D4.

Atkinson, A., G. L. Rainwater, and T. M. Smeeding. (1995). *Income Distribution in OECD Countries*. Paris: Organisation for Economic Co-operation and Development.

Axinn, J. (1990). "Japan: A special case." In G. S. Goldberg and E. Kremen, eds., *The Feminization of Poverty: Only in America?* New York: Praeger, pp. 91–105.

Bakker, I. (1999). "Globalization and human development in the rich countries: Lessons from labour markets and welfare states." In *Globalization with a Human Face*, Background Papers, vol. 2, Human Development Report 1999. New York: United Nations Development Programme, pp. 29–80.

Banting, K. (1987). *The Welfare State and Canadian Federalism*, rev. ed. Montreal: McGill–Queen's University Press.

Baxandall, P. (1995). "The privatization myth: Disillusionment follows free markets in Hungary." *Dollars and Sense* 197 (January/February): 22–25, 41–42.

———. (1996). *Reinventing Unemployment in Hungary: The Legacy of Politics, Pensions, and Patterns of Work*. Paper presented at the 1996 Annual Meeting of the American Political Science Association, San Francisco, August 29–September 1.

Bernstein, N. (1996). "Giant companies entering race to run state welfare programs." *New York Times*, September 15, pp. 1, 26.

Beveridge, W. H. (1942). *Social Insurance and Allied Services*. New York: Macmillan.

———. (1945). *Full Employment in a Free Society*. New York: W. W. Norton.

Briggs, A. (1967). "The welfare state in historical perspective." In C. Schottland, ed., *The Welfare State*. New York: Doubleday, pp. 25–45.

Cameron, D. R. (1993). "Continuity and change in French social policy: The welfare state under Gaullism, liberalism, and socialism." In J. S. Ambler, ed., *The French Welfare State: Surviving Social and Ideological Change*. New York: New York University Press, pp. 58–93.

Castles, F. G. (1978). *The Social Democratic Image of Society*. London: Routledge and Kegan Paul.

———. (1998). *Comparative Public Policy*. Cheltenham, England: Edward Elgar.

Checkland, S. G., and E.O.A. Checkland, eds. (1974). *The Poor Law Report of 1834*. Harmondsworth, England: Penguin Books.

Chorney, H. (1999). *Unemployment in Canada, 1974 to 1999: A Case Study of Monetarism in Action*. Paper presented at the Columbia University Seminar on Full Employment, New York, December 6.

Cowell, A. (1996a). "Germans stage huge protest on budget plan." *New York Times*, June 16, p. 8.

———. (1996b). "Kohl offers plan for big cuts in the German welfare state." *New York Times*, April 27, pp. 1, 4.

Crewe, I. (1991). "Labor force changes, working class decline, and the Labour vote: Social and electoral trends in postwar Britain." In F. F. Piven, ed., *Labor Parties in Postindustrial Societies*. New York: Oxford University Press, pp. 20–46.

DePalma, A. (1996). "Protesters take to streets to defend Canada's safety net." *New York Times*, October 26, p. 3.

Eatwell, J. (1995). *Disguised Unemployment: The G7 Experience*. Paper based on a report to UNCTAD. Cambridge: Trinity College.

Esping-Andersen, G. (1990). *Three Worlds of Welfare Capitalism*. Princeton, NJ: Princeton University Press.

———, ed. (1996). *Welfare States in Transition: National Adaptations in Global Economies*. London: Sage Publications.

———. (1999). *Social Foundations of Postindustrial Economies*. Oxford: Oxford University Press.

Esping-Andersen, G., and W. Korpi. (1984). "Social policy as class politics in postwar capitalism: Scandinavia, Austria, and Germany." In J. H. Goldthorpe, ed., *Order and Conflict in Contemporary Capitalism.* Oxford: Clarendon Press, pp. 179–208.

Etxezarreta, M. (1995). *The welfare State: Alternatives to Social Cuts and Deregulation.* Notes for discussion presented at the Workshop on Alternative Economic Policies for Europe: Approaches and Perspectives. Bremen: Arbeitsgruppe Alternative Wirtschaftspolitik.

Evans, P. M. (1995). *The Claims of Women: Gender, Income Security, and the Welfare State.* Paper presented to the Seventh Conference on Canadian Social Welfare Policy, Vancouver, B.C., June 25–28.

Fargion, V. (1997). "Social assistance and the North-South cleavage in Italy." In M. Rhodes, ed., *Southern European Welfare States: Between Crisis and Reform.* London: Frank Cass, pp. 135–154.

Ferge, Z. (1990). "The fourth road: The future for Hungarian social policy." In B. Deacon and J. Szalai, eds., *Social Policy in the New Eastern Europe: What Future for Social Welfare?* Aldershot: Avebury, pp. 103–118.

Ferrera, M. (1996). "The Southern model of welfare in social Europe." *Journal of European Social Policy* 6(1): 17–37.

Flora, P., and J. Alber. (1981). "Modernization, democratization, and the development of the welfare state in Europe." In P. Flora and A. J. Heidenheimer, eds., *The Development of Welfare States in Europe and America.* New Brunswick, NJ: Transaction Books, pp. 37–80.

Garraty, J. (1978). *Unemployment in History: Economic Thought and Public Policy.* New York: Harper & Row.

Garrett, G. (1998). *Partisan Politics in the Global Economy.* Cambridge: Cambridge University Press.

Giddens, A. (1982). *Profiles and Critiques in Social Theory.* Berkeley: University of California Press.

Ginsburg, H. (1983). *Full Employment and Public Policy: The United States and Sweden.* Lexington, MA: Lexington Books.

———. (1993). "With Jobs for All: Rhetoric and Reality in the United States, Germany, and Sweden." Unpublished manuscript. Department of Economics, Brooklyn College, City University of New York.

———. (1996). "Whatever happened to Sweden?" *In These Times,* December 23, pp. 21–23, 36.

Ginsburg, H. L., J. Zaccone, G. S. Goldberg, S. D. Collins, and S. M. Rosen. (1997). "The challenge of full employment in the global economy." *Economic and Industrial Democracy: An International Journal* 18(1): 5–34.

Goldberg, G. S. (1990). "Canada: Bordering on the feminization of poverty." In G. S. Goldberg and E. Kremen, eds., *The Feminization of Poverty: Only in America?* New York: Praeger, pp. 59–89.

———. (1991a). *Government Money for Everyday People: A Guide to Income Support Programs,* 4th ed. Lexington, MA: Ginn Press and Adelphi University School of Social Work.

———. (1991b). "Women on the verge: Winners and losers in German unification." *Social Policy* 22 (Fall): 35–45.

Goldberg, G. S., and S. D. Collins. (2001). *Washington's New Poor Law: Welfare "Reform" and the Roads Not Taken, 1935 to the Present.* New York: Apex Press.

Goldberg, G. S., and E. Kremen, eds. (1990). *The Feminization of Poverty: Only in America?* New York: Praeger.

Gould, A. (1993). *Capitalist Welfare Systems: A Comparison of Japan, Britain & Sweden.* London: Longman.

Greenstein, R. (1991). "Universal and targeted approaches to relieving poverty: An alternative view." In C. Jencks and P. E. Peterson, eds., *The Urban Underclass.* Washington, DC: The Brookings Institution, pp. 437–459.

Habermas, J. (1975). *Legitimation Crisis.* Trans. T. McCarthy. Boston: Beacon Press.

Handel, G. (1982). *Social Welfare in Western History.* New York: Random House.

Hayek, F. (1944). *The Road to Serfdom.* London: G. Routledge and Sons.

Heclo, H. (1981). "Toward a new welfare state?" In P. Flora and A. J. Heidenheimer, eds., *The Development of Welfare States in Europe and America.* New Brunswick, NJ: Transaction Books, pp. 383–406.

Hirsch, F. (1976). *Social Limits to Growth.* Cambridge, MA: Harvard University Press.

Hirschman, A. O. (1980). "The welfare state in trouble: Systemic crisis or growing pains?" *American Economic Review* 70 (May): 112–116.

Huffschmid, J. (1997). "Economic policy for full employment: Proposals for Germany." *Economic and Industrial Democracy* 18(1): 67–86.

International Labour Organization. (1995). *World Employment Report.* Geneva: ILO.

Kapstein, E. (1996). "Workers and the world economy." *Foreign Affairs* 75 (May/June): 16–37.

Katz, M. B. (1986). *In the Shadow of the Poorhouse: A Social History of Welfare in America.* New York: Basic Books.

Katznelson, I. (1980). "Accounts of the welfare state and the new mood." *American Economic Review* 70 (May): 117–122.

Korpi, W. (1978). *The Working Class in Welfare Capitalism: Work, Unions, and Politics in Sweden.* London: Routledge and Kegan Paul.

Korpi, W., and J. Palme. (1998). "The paradox of redistribution and strategies of equality: Welfare state institutions, inequality, and poverty in the Western countries." *American Sociological Review* 63 (October): 661–687.

Krieger, J. (1991). "Class, consumption, and collectivism: Perspectives on the Labour Party and electoral competition in Britain." In F. F. Piven, ed., *Labor Parties in Postindustrial Societies.* New York: Oxford University Press, pp. 47–70.

Kristof, N. D. (1996). "Welfare as Japan knows it: A family affair." *New York Times*, September 10, pp. A1, A14.

Leibfried, S. (1993). "Towards a European welfare state? On integrating poverty regimes into the European community." In C. Jones, ed., *New Perspectives on the Welfare State in Europe.* London: Routledge, pp. 133–156.

Lekachman, R. (1966). *The Age of Keynes.* New York: McGraw-Hill.

———. (1976). *Economists at Bay.* New York: McGraw-Hill.

Leuchtenburg, W. E. (1963). *Franklin D. Roosevelt and the New Deal, 1932–1940.* New York: Harper.

Logue, J. (1979). "The welfare state: Victim of its success." *Dissent* 108(4): 69–88.

Lubove, R. (1968). *The Struggle for Social Security, 1900–1935.* Cambridge, MA: Harvard University Press.

Mann, M. (1987). "Ruling class strategies and citizenship." *Sociology* 21 (August): 339–354.

Marklund, S. (1988). *Paradise Lost? The Nordic Welfare States and the Recession 1975–1985.* Lund: Arkiv.

Marshall, M. (1996). "The changing face of Swedish corporatism: The disintegration of consensus." *Journal of Economic Issues* 30 (September): 843–858.

Marshall, T. H. (1965). *Social Policy in the Twentieth Century.* London: Hutchinson University Library.

———. (1973). *Citizenship and Social Development.* Westport, CT: Greenwood Press.

McFate, K., R. Lawson, and W. J. Wilson, eds. (1995). *Poverty, Inequality, and the Future of Social Policy: Western States in the New World Order.* New York: Russell Sage.

Mead, W. R. (1988–1989). "From Bretton Woods to the Bush team." *World Policy Journal* (Winter): 1–45.

Millar, J. (1995). "Women, poverty and social security." In C. Hallett, ed., *Women and Social Policy.* Brighton, England: Harvester/Wheatsheaf, pp. 52–64.

Mishra, R. (1996). "The welfare of nations." In R. Boyer and D. Drache, eds., *States against Markets: The Limits of Globalization.* London and New York: Routledge, pp. 316–333.

Mohl, R. (1983). "The abolition of public outdoor relief, 1870–1900: A critique of the Piven and Cloward thesis." In W. I. Trattner, ed., *Social Welfare or Social Control: Some Historical Reflections on* Regulating the Poor. Knoxville: University of Tennessee Press, 1983, pp. 35–50.

Myles, J. (1996). "Public policy in a world of market failure." *Policy Options* 17 (July–August): 14–19.

Navarro, V. (1999). "The political economy of the welfare state in developed capitalist countries." *International Journal of Health Services* 29(1): 1–50.

O'Connor, J. (1973). *The Fiscal Crisis of the State.* New York: St. Martin's Press.

OECD. (1988). *OECD in Figures: 1988 Edition.* Paris: Author.

———. (1991). *Solo Women in Europe.* Brussels: European Commission, V/1368/91-EN.

———. (1999). *OECD Social Expenditure Database, 1980–1996.* Paris: Author.

Offe, C. (1984). *Contradictions of the Welfare State.* J. Keane, ed. London: Hutchinson.

Olsen, G. M. (1999). "Half empty or half full? The Swedish welfare state in transition." *Canadian Review of Sociology and Anthropology* 36(2): 241–267.

Olsen, G. M., and J. S. O'Connor. (1998). "Introduction: Understanding the welfare state: Power resources theory and its critics." In J. S. O'Connor and G. M. Olsen, eds., *Power Resources Theory and the Welfare State: A Critical Approach.* Toronto: University of Toronto Press, pp. 3–33.

Paugam, S. (1996). "Poverty and social disqualification." *Journal of European Social Policy* 6(4): 287–303.

Peacock, A., and J. Weisman. (1961). *The Growth of Public Expenditures in the United Kingdom.* Princeton, NJ: Princeton University Press.

Pfaller, A., with I. Gough and G. Therborn. (1991). "The issue." In A. Pfaller, I. Gough, and G. Therborn, eds., *Can the Welfare State Compete? A Comparative Study of Five Advanced Capitalist Countries*. London: Macmillan, pp. 1–14.

Pflanze, O. (1990). *Bismarck and the Development of Germany*, vol. 3. Princeton, NJ: Princeton University Press.

Pierson, P. (1994). *Dismantling the Welfare State? Reagan, Thatcher, and the Politics of Retrenchment*. Cambridge: Cambridge University Press.

———. (1996). "The new politics of the welfare state." *World Politics* 48 (January): 143–179.

Piven, F. F., ed. (1991). *Labor Parties in Postindustrial Societies*. New York: Oxford University Press.

Piven, F. F. and R. A. Cloward. (1993). *Regulating the Poor: The Functions of Public Relief*, updated ed. New York: Pantheon.

Pollitt, K. (1996). "French lessons." *The Nation* 262 (February 19): 9.

Pugliese, E. (1995). "Special measures to improve youth unemployment in Italy. In K. McFate, R. Lawson, and W. J. Wilson, eds., *Poverty, Inequality, and the Future of Social Policy: Western States in the New Social Order*. New York: Russell Sage, pp. 439–460.

———. (1996). *Models of Unemployment in Europe*. Paper presented at the Tenth Conference of the Europeanists, Chicago, March 14–16.

Quadagno, J. (1994). *The Color of Welfare: How Racism Undermined the War on Poverty*. New York: Oxford University Press.

Reich, C. A. (1964). "The new property." *Yale Law Journal* 72: 1347–1360.

Rimlinger, G. (1971). *Welfare Policy and Industrialization in Europe and America*. New York: Wiley.

Robinson, J. (1962). *Economic Philosophy*. Garden City, NY: Doubleday.

Rosenthal, M. G. (1990). "Sweden: Promise and paradox." In G. S. Goldberg and E. Kremen, eds., *The Feminization of Poverty: Only in America?* New York: Praeger, pp. 129–155.

Ross, G. (1991). "The changing face of popular power in France." In F. F. Piven, ed., *Labor Parties in Postindustrial Societies*: New York: Oxford University Press, pp. 71–100.

Rothstein, B. (1998). "Labour-market institutions and working-class strength." In J. S. O'Connor and G. M. Olsen, eds., *Power Resources Theory and the Welfare State: A Critical Approach*. Toronto: University of Toronto Press, pp. 283–311.

Rudolph, H., E. Appelbaum, and F. Maier. (1991). *Beyond Socialism: The Ambivalence of Women's Perspective in the Unified Germany*. Berlin: Wissenschaftszentrum Berlin.

Schattschneider, E. E. (1935). *Politics, Pressures, and the Tariff*. New York: Prentice-Hall.

Schmid, G. (1988). *Labour Market Policy in Transition: Trends and Effectiveness in the Federal Republic of Germany*. Stockholm: EFA—The Delegation for Labour Market Policy Research, Swedish Ministry of Labour, EFA Report, No. 17.

Shonfield, A. (1965). *Modern Capitalism*. New York: Oxford University Press.

Skocpol, T. (1992). "State formation and social policy in the United States." *American Behavioral Scientist* 35(4/5): 559–584.

Smeeding, T. M. (1997). *Financial Poverty in Developed Countries: The Evidence from LIS.* Working Paper No. 155. Syracuse, NY: Maxwell School of Citizenship and Public Affairs, Syracuse University.

Smeeding, T. M., and L. Rainwater. (1991). *Cross National Trends in Income, Poverty and Dependency: The Evidence for Young Adults in the Eighties.* Working Paper No. 67. Syracuse, NY: Maxwell School of Citizenship and Public Affairs, Syracuse University.

Smothers, R. (1996). "Farewell, welfare state." *New York Times*, October 13, p. E5.

Sorrentino, C. (1995). "International unemployment indicators, 1983–93." *Monthly Labor Review* 118 (August 1995): 31–49.

Sparrow, D. G. (1994). "French family policy: Impacts on low-income families." Unpublished paper, Boston.

Stachura, P. (1986). *Unemployment and the Great Depression in Weimar Germany.* New York: Macmillan.

Steinmo, S. (1994). "The end of redistribution? International pressures and domestic tax policy choices." *Challenge* (November–December): 9–17.

Stevens, B. (1990). "Labor unions, employee benefits, and the privatization of the American welfare state." *Journal of Policy History* 2(3): 233–260.

Takahashi, Y. (1997). "The labor market and lifetime employment in Japan." *Economic and Industrial Democracy: An International Journal* 18 (February): 55–66.

U.S. Department of Labor, Bureau of Labor Statistics. (2000). "Comparative civilian labor force statistics: Ten countries, 1959–1999." Unpublished data, Washington, DC, April 17. Available on the Internet at ftp://ftp.bls.gov/pub/special.requests/ForeignLabor/flslforc.txt.

Visser, J. (1996). "Union trends revisited." Mimeo, University of Amsterdam.

Webb, S., and B. Webb. (1963). *English Poor Law History*, Vol. II. New York: Acheson.

Whitney, C. R. (1996). "In France, socialized medicine meets Gallic version of H.M.O." *New York Times*, April 25, p. A5.

Chapter 2

More than Reluctant:
The United States of America

Gertrude Schaffner Goldberg

In 1965, Harold Wilensky called the United States a "reluctant welfare state." In the previous year, President Lyndon Johnson had declared "unconditional war" on poverty and Congress had just enacted two major entitlement programs, Medicare and Medicaid. Nonetheless, Wilensky wrote, "We move toward the welfare state, but we do it with ill grace, carping and complaining all the way" (1965, p. xvii). The epithet "reluctant welfare state" stuck (e.g., Jansson, 1997). Since then, the United States has been accused of making war not on poverty, but on welfare, and so the designation "reluctant welfare state" may now be an understatement. The welfare state, which has a positive connotation in most countries, tends to be a pejorative term in the United States, even though individual programs are valued by the public.

Throughout the history of the United States, most political and economic elites have been wary of the state, although the nation has perhaps been more inclined toward "affirmative government" than is usually conceded (Schlesinger, 1986).[1] In the last two decades leading politicians have repudiated the "big government" of the New Deal and post-war eras—which was large in the perspective of U.S. history but not by international standards. It is hardly surprising that Ronald Reagan would refer to government as "the problem" instead of "the solution," but it is striking that Bill Clinton, a Democrat and putative heir to the New Deal, has declared that "the era of big government is over," adding at the same time that "we must not go back to an era of 'every man for himself'" (Clinton, 1996, p. 90). What that has meant may become clearer as the record of Clinton and his immediate predecessors is explored.

The Reagan and succeeding Bush administrations employed fiscal, mon-

etary, and regulatory policies to change the balance of economic and political power. Under the banners of inflation control and capturing global
markets, the federal government pursued policies that weakened a labor
movement already on the defensive, gave greater rein to business, and abetted a growing chasm between the rich and the rest of society that can be
compared only to earlier periods of "capitalist overdrive" (Phillips, 1991).
A moving force behind the greatly increased influence of capital was the
political mobilization of the U.S. business community in the 1970s—a tre-
mendous expansion in the number of firms maintaining Washington lobbyists as well as the development and financing of a campaign to
promulgate neoliberal[2] ideas through right-wing think tanks, television programs, newspaper ads, school curricula, and funding of university chairs
(Goldberg and Collins, 2001, ch. 5). Conservative administrations also left
their stamp on the third powerful branch of the divided American government, the judiciary. With appointees of Ronald Reagan, George Bush, and
Richard Nixon, the Supreme Court has been expanding states' rights at the
expense of the individual.

THE ROOTS OF RELUCTANCE AND THE LIKELIHOOD
OF RETRENCHMENT

Significant policy change, either progressive or conservative, is infrequent
in the United States. Major change is inhibited by the U.S. political structure, particularly its division of authority both within the national government and between the national government and the 50 states. Indeed, it
has been argued that progressive policy change must be preceded by structural changes, including "modifying the U.S. Constitution's excessive separation of powers between the legislative and executive branches" (Phillips,
1994, p. 188). A number of interrelated characteristics of American society,
moreover, either impede progressive policy change or contribute to welfare
state retrenchment: persistent, entrenched individualism; deep racial and
ethnic cleavages; marked regional differences; and a labor movement that
is relatively weak and, for much of the post–World War II period, ideologically conservative.

Divided Authority

Because the U.S. Constitution deliberately divided authority within the
national government, significant change is largely confined to periods of
crisis when the legislative and executive branches are forced to act in con-
cert to reduce unrest and upheaval. Even so, change was constrained during
one of these periods, the Great Depression, by the opposition of an independent and conservative judiciary, the third of the divided powers established by the Constitution. Moreover, federal control of new social

programs was limited in deference to conservative legislators, primarily representatives of the low-wage agrarian economy of the South. Members of the Democratic Party who had captured the White House and a huge majority in Congress, these southern legislators struck from the bill that became the Social Security Act of 1935 the requirement that federally aided public assistance provide "a reasonable subsistence compatible with decency and health."

The Social Security Act established federal Old Age Insurance, required states to levy a payroll tax on employers and employees that would be used to establish state unemployment insurance programs, and shared with the states the cost of public assistance to the aged, blind, and dependent children in single-mother families. Assistance was largely confined to the unemployable population, single mothers being excused from the breadwinner role at the time. A number of occupations, notably, agricultural and domestic work, in which 70 percent of the black population was then employed, were initially excluded from the insurance programs.

During the 1940s and 1950s, social welfare expanded incrementally, not significantly. The exception was the extensive benefits for veterans under the G.I. Bill of Rights, but this was a temporary measure and confined to a select group of exceptionally "worthy" recipients. During the 1940s and 1950s, political leaders, including Republican president Dwight Eisenhower—"a conservative caretaker of the welfare state"—basically accepted the premises of the Social Security Act. Franklin Roosevelt's vice president and successor, Harry Truman, tried to implement more of the New Deal agenda and achieved some modest improvements in benefits and coverage, but Congress turned back the proposals for national health insurance, full employment, and federal support to all of the needy (rather than confined to specific categories like the aged or dependent children). Alliances between federal bureaucrats and key congressional leaders contributed to incremental change—notably, the extension of both public assistance and social insurance to the disabled.

A second period of significant social welfare expansion, the 1960s, witnessed the enactment of Medicare (health insurance for the elderly and, later, disabled workers and certain of their dependents), Medicaid (health care to certain categories of the poor), food stamps, a federal anti-poverty program pledged to making "unconditional war on poverty," and increased commitment to public housing. African Americans gained civil and political rights long denied them in the American democracy, and women began a second drive for liberation. This, too, was a period of social and political, though not economic, upheaval—riots in many of the nation's cities and a massive mobilization on behalf of civil rights that evoked a violent response and state resistance to federal authority. For a short time the White House, the Congress, and the Supreme Court were dominated either by progressives or by Democrats who felt impelled to go along with progressive changes. In such periods, moderates like Presidents Franklin Roosevelt, John F. Kennedy, and Lyndon Johnson have been pushed leftward. In the 1960s, the Democratic Party attempted to absorb the Civil Rights movement, but, however necessary, that proved divisive, given the party's strong base in the white South at that time.

The federal anti-poverty program, a response to the unrest as well as a political debt owed to urban blacks for critical electoral support of the Democratic Party, put pressure on the local welfare bureaucracies that had denied assistance to countless eligible applicants, disproportionately people of color. Despite the administration's declared preference for a "hand-up" instead of a "handout," its anti-poverty program, often employing and co-opting civil rights and other protesters, provided resources for the organization of recipients that contributed measurably to a welfare explosion—the addition of millions to the welfare rolls—in a time not of depression, but of economic expansion. Subsequent proposals by Presidents Nixon and Carter to federalize public assistance and extend it to all families never got through Congress. Although Nixon lost interest in his Family Assistance Plan, a modest guaranteed income for families with children, southern senators, protective of their low-wage labor market, dealt critical blows to the proposal, which would, inter alia, have reduced the political isolation of single-mother families.

Cutting and ultimately destroying the welfare state were goals of the Reagan administration, the most conservative since the 1920s. Reaganites attempted to destroy legal services for the poor and, presaging devolution of federal responsibility in the next decade, succeeded in changing programs such as public social services (Title XX of the Social Security Act) from more tightly controlled federal grants-in-aid to block grants that give more leeway to the states. However, the Reagan revolution was stopped or slowed when Congress stood up for social security in the first year of his first term, but not before painful cutbacks such as denying Survivors' Insurance to students in post-secondary education or training programs. The low-income programs at first lost ground, but by the end of the 1980s, a Democratic Congress and welfare advocates, largely outside the government bureaucracies, had succeeded in protecting them and even making some gains. Divided government, this time preventing significant retrenchment, was one factor, and the strong constituent support of social security, another. Nonetheless, the Reagan administration, with the assent of a Democrat-controlled House of Representatives, enacted tax cuts and stepped up defense spending with a resultant budgetary deficit that was to render increased social spending fiscally irresponsible.

Powers Behind the Welfare State

The powerful working-class parties associated with the development and flowering of welfare states in some other countries are not a feature of the

American political landscape. The New Deal Democratic Party, through the Wagner Labor Act of 1935—the Magna Carta of labor—gave government sanction and protection to collective bargaining rights for workers and as a result cemented labor's allegiance to the Democratic Party and with it a source of financial support independent of business and powerful economic interests. However, little more than a decade after the passage of the Wagner Act, the trade union movement was stripped of some of those rights by the Taft-Hartley Act, the work of a conservative Congress. Despite the efforts of President Harry Truman to expand the welfare state with the support of labor, Congressional conservatives were able to prevail, and in the wake of this defeat labor bargained for occupational benefits for its members, leaving large substantial numbers of the workforce without such coverage (Stevens, 1990). Organized labor lost its more progressive elements in post-war anti-communist purges that were abetted by that legislation. Labor's decline in numbers and vision and its drift toward the Center deprived the Democratic Party of potential, progressive strength. The deep ethnic and racial divisions in American society contribute to the weakness of working-class movements and to the failure to establish a working-class party.

If not organized labor and working-class parties, what were the interest groups that championed social welfare? The birth of a permanent welfare program in 1935 was, in considerable measure, a response to the mass mobilization of the elderly and the unemployed in a time of economic and political crisis (although the Social Security Act fell far short of their demands and was a step backward from temporary relief measures). Organized labor had not been an advocate of social welfare, preferring to gain its benefits through workplace bargaining, but the movement, itself being challenged by the more progressive industrial unions, did lend its support to the Social Security Act. In 1935, there were few advocates of aid to mothers and children, and its potential beneficiaries were voiceless. Leaders of a federal bureaucracy, the U.S. Children's Bureau, used their strategic position to tie Aid to Dependent Children (later Aid to Families with Dependent Children [AFDC]) to the coattails of the popularly supported programs for the elderly and unemployed.

Though not the perpetrators of the riots that swept the urban landscape during the 1960s or the force behind the widespread civil rights protests, the well-organized elderly, aided this time by labor in the case of health care, were once again able to turn crisis to their advantage. They were major beneficiaries of Medicare and Medicaid and also of a federalized public assistance program, Supplemental Security Income (SSI).

Aid to Dependent Children, greatly expanded during and immediately following the War on Poverty, was nonetheless under attack since the late 1960s. Benefits increased by about one-third in the 1960s, but inflation eroded the purchasing power by about that amount from the mid-1970s to the mid-1990s. AFDC's beneficiaries, though mounting a short-lived welfare rights movement in the 1960s, when government and private donors provided them with resources of money and skill, were almost voiceless 30 years later, just as they had been in 1935. Potential allies in labor, civil rights, and the women's movement were either weak or without strong commitment to the program. Two other important contributors to the repeal of the 60-year-old program that had become an entitlement for poor, single-parent families are the capture of both houses of Congress by the Republican Party for the first time in 50 years—and by conservative elements in the party; and ideological change in the Democratic Party with the "New Democrat" in the White House campaigning in 1992 to "change welfare as we know it."

How does Paul Pierson's thesis (1994)—that policy creates politics or that the beneficiaries of the welfare state defend it even if its original advocates are weakened—fit the United States? Does the repeal of the entitlement for women and children prove him wrong? For all the furor and agonizing that it caused, AFDC was a relatively small program, spending only 1/18th the amount of Old Age Insurance. Pierson (1994, p. 166), though hypothesizing that welfare states are hard to retrench because social welfare programs create vested interests or constituents who resist the loss of their benefits, recognizes that means-tested programs with marginalized beneficiaries have to rely primarily on public interest groups and providers. In the case of AFDC, these were weak or non-supportive. Old Age Insurance or social security is another matter. First, the prime beneficiaries and advocates of social security are the same and remain strong. Many others who are not current recipients support social security because they will become elderly themselves or because they have elderly relatives. Time will tell whether this strong constituency will, as Pierson would predict, be able to defend its programs against the powerful economic interests that are attacking it and that have gained ground with the narrow and bitterly contested election of President George W. Bush.

ECONOMIC WELFARE: POVERTY AND INEQUALITY

Poverty

This discussion of poverty uses two measures, one absolute and the other relative. The former is the official U.S. poverty standard developed over 30 years ago by the Social Security Administration (SSA). The SSA standard is meager and flawed,[3] but voluminous data collected annually by the Census Bureau are presented in terms of this threshold. For cross-national comparisons, data from the Luxembourg Income Study (LIS) are used.[4]

This discussion of U.S. trends in absolute poverty is based on figures for the first and last years for which data are available (1959 and 1999) as well for the three peak years in the business cycle in the intervening

Table 2.1
Poverty Rates (SSA standard) for the Total U.S. Population and Subgroups,
Selected Years

	All People	Children	Elderly	Couples with Children	Single-Mother Families	Black	Hispanic
1959	22.4	27.3	35.2	(NA)	59.9	55.1	(NA)
1973	11.1	14.4	16.3	(NA)	43.2	31.4	21.9
1979	11.7	16.4	15.2	6.1	39.6	31.0	21.8
1983	15.2	22.3	13.8	10.1	47.1	35.7	28.0
1989	12.8	19.6	11.4	7.3	42.8	30.7	26.2
1993	15.1	22.7	12.2	9.0	46.1	33.1	30.6
1999	11.8	16.9	9.7	6.3	35.7	23.6	22.8

Source: U.S. Bureau of the Census (2000b), tables B-1, B-2, B-3.

period (see Table 2.1). Although not necessarily the peak of the current cycle, 1999 was the seventh year of recovery following the last recession.

The U.S. poverty rate was cut in half between 1959 and 1973, an interval including a number of years of high economic growth and relatively low unemployment, some of it war-induced. Thereafter, the poverty rate rose to highs of just over 15 percent in 1983 and 1993, both low points in the business cycle. In 1999, with the unemployment rate well below what mainstream economists had considered "natural" or compatible with price stability only a few years earlier, the official U.S. poverty rate was nonetheless not quite down to the 1973 mark. In interpreting U.S. poverty rates, it is important to bear in mind the meagerness of the official standard. According to a study for the Joint Economic Committee of Congress (Ruggles, 1990), a standard 150 percent of the SSA threshold would achieve the criterion of minimal adequacy. A 150 percent standard would have meant much higher poverty rates: 21 percent of the total population and 28 percent of U.S. children in 1999 (U.S. Bureau of the Census, 2000b, table 2). During the years when the offical poverty rate was climbing, the number of people who were very poor or in "deep poverty"—with incomes of less than 50 percent of the poverty line for their size families—rose much more (Mishel, Bernstein, and Schmitt, 1999, p. 290, using U.S. Bureau of the Census data). "Deep poverty" remains well above the 1979 mark: almost two-fifths of the poor in 1999, compared to about one-third 20 years earlier.

After the longest peacetime expansion since World War II, the poverty rates of children in the world's wealthiest nation, though down from the rates early in the decade, were 17 percent greater than a quarter century earlier (1973). Other vulnerable population groups have become less poverty-prone. Elderly poverty is 40 percent lower than in 1973. Hispanic poverty is about what it was in the 1970s, and black poverty has dropped. Nonetheless, nearly one in four persons in both groups is poor.

While some categories of single-mother families are less likely to be poor than previously, poverty remains feminized in the sense that families supported by single women predominate among the poor. In 1999, single-mother families made up three-fifths (60.8 percent) of all poor families with children. More than two-thirds (69.7 percent) of the elderly poor are women, a figure reflecting both their labor market disadvantages and their greater longevity. Here, too, U.S. poverty remains feminized.

Among countries in the Luxembourg Income Study, the United States ranks highest on two measures that ought to be negatively related: wealth and poverty. According to the LIS standard, the U.S. overall poverty rate in the mid-1990s was nearly 20 percent, more than double the 17-country average (Smeeding, 1997, table 2). A few years earlier, Germany, France, Sweden, and Italy had poverty rates below 8 percent. For children, the United States again did the worst—about one-fourth of its next generation was poor. The U.S. child poverty rate was twice Japan's, over three times France's, and nearly three times that of Germany; less than 5 percent of children in Finland, Norway, Belgium, and Sweden were poor (Smeeding, 1997, table 3). In the mid-1990s, three-fifths of U.S. children in single-parent families were poor. Rates in the United Kingdom, Germany, and Canada were also high (40–45 percent) (Bradbury and Jäntti, 1999, table 3.4).

The fact that the United States ranks highest in the rate of child poverty is not simply a function of the relative poverty standard used by the LIS. In fact, U.S. children in the bottom quintile had lower *real* incomes than their counterparts in 16 countries (Rainwater and Smeeding, 1995, figure 3).[5] As Rainwater and Smeeding (p. 22) conclude, "every other nation has produced better results in fighting child poverty than has the United States." An LIS finding that illustrates the egregious inequality in the United States is the fact that U.S. children in the top quintile had higher real incomes than children in any of the other 16 countries.

The United States has substantially reduced the proportion of poor among the elderly. Once the most impoverished age group, older Americans are now less prone to poverty than the population as a whole. However, the official poverty rate masks the numerous elderly who often live in destitution just above the poverty threshold. For many married elderly women, a life of poverty lies just around the corner, the inevitable result of their spouse's death (and consequent loss of a sizable portion of their combined social security benefits) (Callahan, 1999). Moreover, seniors in the United States do not do as well as their counterparts in other rich nations. The average rate of poverty for the elderly in 17 countries was 11.7 percent, compared to the U.S. figure of 19.6 percent (Smeeding, 1997, table 3). Only the United Kingdom and Australia left higher proportions of elderly people impoverished.

Inequality

"Created equal" is part of the American creed, but extreme economic inequality is one of the defining characteristics of the world's first modern democracy. The American creed traditionally applies to equal political and civil rights, but these are surely jeopardized when access to economic resources is severely limited or when wealth becomes even more concentrated. Indeed, when money can influence the political process to the extent that it does in the United States—in financing its protracted and exceedingly expensive election campaigns and in monopoly of the media—then democracy is seriously compromised.

In 1973, one of the most egalitarian years on record, the 20 percent of households with the highest aggregate incomes had 10 times as much as the lowest quintile. In 1999, the ratio was over 13 to 1. In 1997, the Gini ratio was the highest of any year since 1967 (the earliest year for which it was calculated), and in 1999, it was only slightly lower. Together, the lowest two quintiles—40 percent of the population—had only 12.5 percent of total income. Since 1989, the bottom four quintiles lost ground, while the already bloated top quintile became fatter (U.S. Bureau of the Census, 2000a, tables B-3, B-6). A report issued by the Economic Policy Institute reviewed the evidence on income inequality and concluded that "despite recent improvements, a longer-term view of the economy reveals that income inequality has grown substantially from 1979 to the present" and that "the income gap between those at the top, middle, and bottom of the income scale has expanded over time" (Bernstein, Mishel, and Brocht, 2000, pp. 2, 10).

Income distribution hardly tells the whole tale of economic inequality. Wealth or net worth (household assets minus debts) is much more unequally divided than income. More than four-fifths of assets (83 percent) were held by the top fifth, with almost half of that appropriated by the richest 1 percent of U.S. families (Mishel, Bernstein, and Schmitt, 2001, table 4.2, p. 260). Even more important than the trend, which is toward somewhat larger shares for the rich, is persistent, gaping inequality.

WELFARE OR MARKET FAILURE?

According to popular wisdom, the welfare state is in decline. During the same period market income also declined for many Americans. This section asks whether deficiencies in the welfare state or in the labor market, a combination of the two, or some other factor such as demography account for persisting, high poverty rates.

Around 1990, about one-third of all U.S. households had market (pre-transfer) income less than one-half of the median (adjusted for family size). The range for various population groups was from over three-fourths of single, elderly persons to about one in eight for childless couples. Three-fifths of lone parents were poor before cash transfers, compared to about one-fifth of couples with children (Bradshaw and Chen, 1996, table 2). U.S. pre-transfer poverty rates for all households were about average for 20 countries in Europe, North America, and Asia.

The poverty-reduction effects of the U.S. welfare state, however, were below the 20-country average in all population categories, substantially so in most. For the U.S. population as a whole, income transfers reduced poverty by just under one-third (31.0 percent), compared to the 20-country average of almost twice that proportion (57.9 percent). Using the SSA poverty standard and counting the value of Medicare and Medicaid as well as cash benefits, Mishel, Bernstein, and Schmitt (2001, table 5.15, p. 312) found that pre-transfer or market poverty worsened slightly in the 1979 to 1998 period and that the effectiveness in reducing poverty of taxes and transfers, though greater in 1998 than in 1989, was about the same as in 1979. Whereas elderly poverty was reduced by a larger amount in 1998 than in 1979, the effect of transfers declined for families with children, both single-parent and married-couple. This occurred despite the growth of the Earned Income Tax Credit for families with children.

THE LABOR MARKET

Interpreting the U.S. economic performance in the 1990s is a complex task. The recovery from the recession early in the decade was less impressive than is generally believed but long-lasting and continuing at least into early 2001, when unemployment was in the 4 percent range. Depending on the choice of starting date, economic growth either has been the slowest on record or, at best, resembles the post-war norm. The recovery of the 1990s does not compare with the expansion of the 1960s; job growth has been slow by historical standards; and unemployment, though the lowest in 30 years, is still not as low as it was then (Galbraith, 1998). Relatively low unemployment, however, has been accomplished without the aid of war or a military buildup. There is, of course, no commitment on the part of political leaders to keep unemployment low, and the Federal Reserve Board has stood poised to raise interest rates and unemployment at the slightest hint of inflation. Unemployment rates that held steady the first quarter of 2001, when other economic signs were darkening, may be lagging indicators in an economy that had Wall Street as well as more reliable forecasters worried.

One of the most disturbing developments in the last 30 years was the rise of what sociologist William Julius Wilson (1996) called "jobless ghettos," where, in contrast to the situation in the 1950s and 1960s, the majority of adult males were not employed during the average week. Thus, it is important and encouraging to observe that sustained low levels of unemployment are reaching the ghettos (Johnson, 1999; Nasar, 1999a). In mid-1999, black and Hispanic unemployment rates were at historic lows, and teenage unemployment had dropped 16 percent since the beginning of the year. However, declining unemployment rates can mask falling rates of labor force participation since those who drop out are not counted as unemployed. Had the labor force participation of black men remained at its 1992 levels, their unemployment rate would have still been double-digit—10.5 percent instead of 8.5 percent—and had their participation rate been the same as for white men, unemployment would have been a staggering 18.1 percent (Cherry, 1998). Further, U.S. incarceration, which grew threefold in the last two decades of the twentieth century, removed able-bodied, working-age men from the labor force and lowered the unemployment rate by an estimated two percentage points in the mid-1990s (Western and Beckett, 1999). Also, it is important to bear in mind that even in the best of times, there are several job seekers for every job (Harvey, 1997). According to a report of the U.S. Department of Housing and Urban Development (1999), one in six U.S. cities has chronically high unemployment rates despite the general decline in unemployment.

One reason that the job recovery was allowed to continue so long is that it did not bring about a commensurate wage recovery. For every year between 1959 and 1973, real, hourly wages rose, even during recessions (*Economic Report of the President*, 1998, table B-47; Tilly, 1998). Reflecting the significant shifts in economic and political conditions and power already noted, wages took a "U-turn" after 1973 (Harrison and Bluestone, 1988). By 1996, the real average weekly earnings of production and nonsupervisory workers were still 14.2 percent below their 1973 level (Mishel, Bernstein, and Schmitt, 1999, table 3.3, p. 126). In 1999, real average weekly earnings were 11 percent below the 1973 level, and real average hourly earnings, 4.8 percent below (Mishel, Bernstein, and Schmitt, 2001, table 2.4, p. 120). While median hourly wages for women rose 11.7 percent between 1973 and 1999, men's were down 8.3 percent (ibid., table 2.9, p. 128). Over one-fourth of all U.S. workers earned poverty-level wages. Poverty-level wages are defined as less than the poverty level for a family of three or $13,290 for full-time, year-round work in 1999. Poverty-level wages were the lot of one-third of all U.S. women, two-fifths of black women, and just over half of Hispanic women (ibid., tables 2.11–2.13, pp. 133–135).

The widening of the wage gap between highly and poorly educated male workers played a role in increasing economic inequality. The conventional explanation is that technological change created a mismatch of skills or that competition from low-wage countries eliminated many unskilled jobs in the United States. However, the low-wage share of employment increased sharply between 1979 and 1989, and the number of college graduates outstripped the creation of jobs requiring a college education (Howell, 1994). Indeed, by the 1990s, entry-level, college-educated workers, both men and women, suffered a sharp decline in wages (Mishel, Bernstein, and Schmitt, 1999, p. 162).

An alternative explanation for the collapse in wages for the low-skilled and one compatible with the fact that low-wage workers have upgraded their skills without commensurate wage increases is "the new confrontational approach adopted by many employers in the 1980s and a simultaneous shift by government toward laissez-faire public policies" (Howell, 1998). Among the latter are application and administration of labor laws in a manner unfavorable to labor and refusal to raise the minimum wage, resulting in a decline in its value and anti-poverty effect—from 120 percent of the three-person poverty level for full-time, year-round work in the late 1960s to 70 percent in 1989, and despite four increases in the 1990s, still only 78 percent in 2000. Union density declined from 24 percent of wage and salary workers in 1973 to 14 percent in 1999 (Hirsch and MacPherson, 1998; U.S. Department of Labor, 2000b). Responding to the tendency of policymakers to emphasize technology-driven increase in demand for "educated and skilled workers," Mishel and his colleagues (1999, pp. 197–207) point out that the impact of technology on the wage and employment structure was no greater in the 1980s and 1990s than in the 1970s and that its growth does not explain the increasing wage inequality in those decades.

The effect of globalization on the American workforce is subject to debate. On the one end are pessimists who argue that expansion and changing patterns of trade among the developing countries have hurt unskilled workers in the developed countries (Wood, 1994). Three years after the implementation of the North American Free Trade Agreement, research by six policy research organizations concluded that it had put downward pressure on wages and living standards in the United States as well as Mexico and Canada (Economic Policy Institute, 1997), thus adding to conditions already contributing to such an effect.[6] A later report (Scott, 1999) concluded that between 1994 and 1998, growth in the net export deficit with Mexico and Canada had destroyed 440,172 jobs, and the imbalance in the U.S. trade deficit attributable to NAFTA had led to even more job losses.

Others provide evidence that international trade has had little net impact on the size of the manufacturing sector and that the United States continues to buy the bulk of its imports from other advanced countries, not from developing countries with cheaper labor (Krugman and Lawrence, 1994). The International Labour Organization (1995) also downplays the job-destroying effects of imports and of relocation of production to developing countries and points, among other things, to benefits of foreign direct investment to the capital-exporting country. Even an emphasis on negative consequences for employers in the capital-exporting countries suggests several feasible solutions: expanding the supply of skilled workers through education or training—if it is needed; creating more unskilled jobs on projects to improve infrastructures or in community work; and supplementing the incomes of low-wage workers (Wood, 1994). In other words, the welfare state could step in to subsidize low wages with health insurance and earnings supplements, so that production costs are kept competitive. The United States is subsidizing low wages with the Earned Income Tax Credit (EITC) (see below for more on the EITC).

Mass immigration—18 million legal newcomers and 3–3.5 million undocumented aliens—is concurrent with the downturn in wages and high average levels of unemployment in the 1970s, 1980s, and early 1990s. The consequences of this wave of newcomers are hotly debated among experts and politicians on both sides of the political spectrum. On the one hand, the return of sweatshops, those notorious companions of earlier immigration, seems a telltale phenomenon. Some scholars have written that native groups, particularly minorities, suffer from competition with immigrants for the declining number of low-skilled jobs that provide a livable income (Briggs, 1990). Some studies of specific cities or industries with large numbers of immigrants have concluded that the result has been job displacement and declining pay in secondary labor markets (North, 1994; Beck, 1996). On the other hand, Maria Enchautegui's (1993) research found that the wages of vulnerable groups such as black men are not negatively affected by immigration. Indeed, much empirical evidence points to the conclusion that increased immigration has, to date, no overall effect on the unemployment of native-born workers (DeFreitas, 1998, 1999) and that immigrants, many of them self-employed, generate jobs through their businesses and personal consumption. The conclusion of an expert panel convened by the National Research Council (Smith and Edmonston, 1997, p. 7) is that: "immigration has had a relatively small adverse impact on the wage and employment opportunities of competing native groups." Nonetheless, the National Research Council did point out that the one group that appears to suffer substantially from new waves of immigrants is immigrants from earlier waves, for whom the recent immigrants are close substitutes in the labor market. The conclusions of David Howell and Elizabeth Mueller (1998), which pertain to the New York metropolitan area, are less sanguine than those from most other empirical studies: they state that "a higher share of recent immigrants in New York metropolitan area jobs is clearly associated with lower native-born earnings in both 1979 and 1989; similarly, a growing concentration of recent immigrant workers in jobs is strongly linked to lower rates of earnings growth over the 1980s." In any case, it seems fair to ask whether, in the absence of mass immigration, there would have been greater pressure on the educational system and on employers to train and upgrade native, unskilled workers.

THE STATE OF SOCIAL WELFARE

The welfare edifice is still standing even in the quintessential liberal welfare state. Yet, nearly all major programs have suffered cutbacks, major structural change, or the threat of it.

Earned Income Tax Credit (EITC)

The one notable exception is the Earned Income Tax Credit (EITC), which, beginning modestly in 1975, now spends more federal money than was budgeted for AFDC in the late 1990s or than its successor, Temporary Assistance for Needy Families (TANF), is actually using. A refundable tax credit (i.e., providing benefits regardless of whether beneficiaries pay income taxes), the EITC functions as a wage supplement, largely for working-poor families with children. It raised more children out of poverty in 1996 than all other government programs combined (Greenstein and Shapiro, 1998), reducing childhood poverty about 14 percent to 21 percent (U.S. SSA standard) (Liebman, 1998). This reduction, however, may say more about the meagerness of the American welfare state than about the anti-poverty power of the EITC. In 1998, the EITC raised hourly income by 40 percent for families with two or more children to a maximum of $3,756 (by 34 percent for one-child families to a maximum of $2,271). After earnings reach $12,260 (about three-fourths of the four-person poverty level), the EITC is gradually phased out.

Unlike traditional public assistance, the EITC provides less money to the very poor than to families in the maximum earnings range and offers nothing to those without earnings. Critics of the EITC are also concerned lest it reduce workers' incentives to press for higher wages. Not surprisingly, employers are said to like the EITC because it raises employee earnings "without any cost to their employers, easing the pressure to raise wages" (Perez-Peña, 1998, p. B24). In 1998, the combined value of the maximum EITC and year-round, full-time earnings at the minimum wage was just equal to yearly earnings at the minimum wage in 1968 (constant dollars). Thus, the EITC has functioned more to offset the decline in wages than to better workers' conditions (Cherry and Goldberg, 2000).

Social Security

The cover of the November 1998 issue of *Social Policy* magazine featuring "The Social Security Crisis Fraud" pictured Franklin Roosevelt with a tear running down his cheek. Although not without its critics, social security enjoyed widespread popular support and gave Ronald Reagan the first defeat in his halcyon days—the Senate's unanimous rejection of large, proposed cuts in the summer of 1981 (although Congress did assent to some cuts both in 1981 and in 1983 that worked hardships on vulnerable groups and made its financing more regressive but did not alter the structure of the program). Since social security is the "centerpiece of the American welfare state" and its largest program ($399.5 billion in 1999), this defeat played a critical part in what the administration's budget director referred to as "stop[ping] the Reagan Revolution dead in its tracks" (Stockman, 1986, pp. 184–228).

When told that payroll taxes for his Old Age Insurance program were regressive, Roosevelt said that their purpose was to give contributors a legal, moral, and political right to collect their benefits.[7] "With those taxes in there," said FDR, "no damn politician can ever scrap my social security program" (Schlesinger, 1958, p. 309). In the summer of 1981, when social security alone stood in the way of the Reagan revolution, Roosevelt seemed prophetic. However, Old Age, Survivors, and Disability Insurance (the latter two added in 1939 and 1956) as well as health insurance (Medicare, enacted in 1965) have to be cut back significantly if the attack on big government is to succeed. The strategy of the campaign is to exaggerate both the long-term financial problems caused by the increasing longevity of the population and U.S. economic stagnation in the twenty-first century in order to justify cutbacks and investment of the trust funds in stocks with higher yields than current investments. In other words, if the program can be discredited and shown to be in crisis, then it can be cut and carved up for private consumption.

Despite its popularity, social security has been under attack for some time and declining in value since the early 1980s. Political repercussions have been muted by changes that seem technical, that are incremental, or that affect future, rather than present, beneficiaries (Pierson, 1994). Amendments passed in 1977 during the administration of Jimmy Carter altered the basis of calculating benefits. As a result, average earners reaching the age of 65 in 1981, before these amendments went into effect, were eligible for benefits replacing 54.4 percent of former earnings, compared to 43.0 percent in the year 2000. In the same interval, low earners' replacement rates fell from 72.5 to 57.8 percent, and those of maximum earners, from 33.4 to 25.4 percent (U.S. House of Representatives, 1998, table 1–17, p. 27). Taxation of the benefits of higher-income recipients, a selective benefit cut, was instituted by the 1983 amendments proposed by the Reagan-appointed, but bipartisan, National Commission on Social Security Reform. Such changes could lead middle- and higher-income groups, particularly, to withdraw support for a direct social welfare program and to seek alternative, private forms of protection (Skocpol, 1991; Korpi and Palme, 1998). However, as replacement rates were declining in social security, the proportion of full-time workers in medium-sized and large establishments covered by employer-provided, defined benefit pension plans was shrinking substantially—from 82 percent in 1984 to 50 percent in 1997—and from 1992 to 1996, such coverage in small, private establishments, very low to begin with, fell from 22 to 15 percent (U.S. Department of Labor, 1999, table 45, p. 195, table 46, p. 196). Previously, the Reagan administration, in a move both shortsighted and punitive, had removed survivor benefits for post-secondary students between the ages of 18 and 22. Gradual increase of the full-benefit retirement age from age 65 to 67, between 2000 and 2027, was another benefit reduction in the 1983 amendments that may have appeared more benign.

Social security has been under attack for a number of years, but the current assault is distinguished by a well-financed campaign of Wall Street and corporate America to have all or part of the trust funds invested in the stock market or other private assets instead of government bonds.[8] Some of these privatization proposals would establish a system of individual retirement accounts over which beneficiaries would have a strong degree of personal ownership and control. As the accounts build up, existing benefits would be scaled back through a variety of adjustments, including an increase in the retirement age. According to an estimate by actuarial consultant David Langer (cited by Darby and Celarier, 1999), putting only 5 percent of social security funds in the market could earn the finance industry $240 billion in fees in little more than 10 years.

Demography is no bigger problem for the United States than for other wealthy nations that do not consider their systems in crisis. In fact, of 13 such nations in 1993, only Australia, Canada, and Japan had smaller proportions of their populations 65 or older (DuBoff, 1997, citing United Nations figures). Richard DuBoff argues that the total dependency ratio— the proportion of children *and* elderly in the population, divided by the population aged 20 to 64—is the true measure of the burden on the working population, and when the baby boomers retire, that ratio will be lower than when they were being educated. The ratio of all dependents to working-age people is projected to reach 79 percent in 2030, compared to an average of 89 percent between 1960 and 1975—a time when U.S. resources were considerably less than they will be in the twenty-first century.

While they exaggerate the burden of demography, critics underestimate the size of the social security trust funds. Indeed, if the economic forecasts are as dire as prophets of doom foresee, social security will be the least of the economic worries of the United States in the new millennium. Former president of the American Economic Association Robert Eisner (1997) pointed out that the "somber intermediate projections" on which the social security trustees base their conclusion that the system will run out of funds are less promising than past and present performance of the U.S. economy. Even the largely ignored but less pessimistic "low-cost projections" of the trustees are not as good as current economic indicators. Interestingly, the growth, unemployment, and inflation projections in the 1999 federal budget were considerably more optimistic than those being used to anticipate the future of the social security trust funds (Spitz, 1998). In any case, minor adjustments proposed by a number of experts would avert the alleged shortfall (Eisner 1997; Spitz, 1998).

Privatization advocates point out that over the past century the inflation-adjusted rate of return to stocks has averaged around 7 percent per year and that for most future retirees the return on their payroll contributions will be less than half as much. President George W. Bush complains of the low returns from social security. It is true that returns to stocks have averaged 7 percent over the long run, but there were 22, 20-year periods between 1900 and 1998 when returns were less than 2.5 percent (DuBoff, 1999). Also to be reckoned are the costs of managing the funds, which, according to former social security commissioner Robert M. Ball, would reduce revenues by 20 percent or more over 40 years (cited by Spitz, 1998). As James Galbraith has said, the social security, Medicare, and budget "crises" of recent years rest on specious claims, seek to legitimate cutbacks and privatization, and enjoy support from financial and commercial elites (1998, pp. 4–5).

In early 1999, proponents of privatization came closer than ever before to achieving their goals. The president, most Democrats in Congress, labor unions, and several liberal policy institutes favored investment of some social security funds in the stock market. Powerful members of the Republican-controlled Congress and Senate, including some prominent Democrats, favored more privatization—investment accounts owned by individual workers. Responding to opinion polls that found the public skeptical over altering a "popular program," Republican leaders announced that they would abandon the idea of making fundamental changes in social security before the next election but did not give up, and indeed Republican President George W. Bush has perpetuated the idea that unless personal savings accounts are established, social security will not be available for today's young. Indeed, Bush is so ideologically committed to a social security "crisis" that he interpreted projected official extensions of Social Security and Medicare trust funds as indications of "only so many years to get the systems back on track." In the words of the *New York Times* reporter, he "took what appeared to be good news and made it sound like bad news" (Pear, 2001, p. A18). Distinguished experts, including former social security commissioner George Ball, contend that Bush's privatization plan would drain about $1 trillion out of the social security trust funds in the next 10 years for individual accounts. Since Bush has offered no plan for replacing this money, his plan is assumed to cause a shortfall that would necessitate benefit cuts (Social Security Information Project, 2000). The Democratic standard-bearer, Vice President Al Gore, opposed privatization and favored subsidizing individual savings accounts set up apart from social security but, given the pressure from Wall Street, might well have proposed partial privatization (Uchitelle, 2000, p. C8). Stock market volatility and descent may well prove to be the most formidable enemies of privatization.

It is true that a popular, universal program was proving more resistant to major change than the program for poor, single mothers, many of them women of color, but the fight is not over. A strong economy fattened the trust funds—extending the system's solvency by three years between 1997 and 1998 and by another three years in the following year. A weak economy could do just the opposite. Neither political leaders nor powerful nongovernmental organizations like organized labor, including those trying to preserve social security and opposing privatization, seriously challenge the premises of the social security "crisis."

Health Insurance

Health reform fared badly in the last two decades. Late in the Reagan presidency, Washington enacted the Medicare Catastrophic Care Act, which liberalized coverage of hospital, nursing home, and physicians' fees and paid for outpatient prescription drugs—only to repeal it in the first year of the Bush presidency. In the 1990s, a Democratic president backed universal coverage but could not persuade a Congress controlled by his own party to enact it. One of the paradoxes of the health issue is that the United States fails to cover a substantial minority of its population but, nevertheless, spends a higher proportion of its resources on health care than any other OECD country, indeed, nearly twice the average (OECD, 1998a, pp. 50–51).

High on President Clinton's first-term agenda was universal health care. The Clinton Health Security Act would have covered everyone but maintained costly insurance intermediaries instead of adopting the single-pay approach characteristic of government insurance programs in other countries and, for that matter, the U.S. Medicare program. The 1,300-page Clinton proposal was complicated and difficult to explain to the public, and its scheme for controlling costs was unconvincing. It was compromised by political leaders' unwillingness to take on powerful elements of what has been called the "medical/industrial complex" and, as Skocpol (1997) emphasizes, by catering to the anti-government ethos of the Reagan years. According to two professors at Harvard Medical School who helped found Physicians for a National Health Program, the Clinton plan would have "guarantee[d] more bureaucracy, less consumer choice and a health system owned by a few insurance giants" (Woolhandler and Himmelstein, 1994). An important reason for the lack of strong popular support for a universal program is that, although a sizable minority of the population is uninsured, over 80 percent of the U.S. population is covered by some form of private or public health plan.

Still a minority, the proportion of persons without health coverage throughout the year rose from 12.9 percent in 1987 to 16.1 percent in 1997 (U.S. Bureau of the Census, 1988; Bennefield, 1998), partly owing to reduced workplace coverage and, in recent years, loss of Medicaid for those being pushed off the welfare rolls. Some recipients have lost health along with disability benefits, many of them still eligible for Medicaid but either uninformed or, in violation of federal regulations, denied benefits by state and local authorities. The proportion of children without health coverage rose from 13.8 percent in 1995 to 15.0 percent in 1997 (Bennefield, 1997, 1998). To ameliorate this problem, Congress and President Clinton agreed to a Child Health Insurance Program (CHIP) in 1997, which was intended to expand coverage to up to 5 million children in families whose incomes are low but above the level for Medicaid. However, the states had enrolled only 1 million children by mid-1999, and in many states the increase is less than the decrease in Medicaid coverage (Pear, 1999).

Discontent among consumers and providers who *are* covered by health insurance is rising over "managed care"—that is, organizations that regulate the price, utilization, or site of health care services. Managed care has restricted physicians' choice of the type and length of service and drastically reduced hospital stays—for bypass surgery, hip replacements, mastectomies, and childbirth (dubbed "drive-through deliveries"). A major form of managed care, health maintenance organizations (HMOs)—prepaid plans combining insurance and delivery of health care—are increasingly profit-making enterprises (Fein, 1998). With increasing discontent over out-of-pocket costs as well as delivery-of-care issues, the majority who have health insurance may exert pressure that could be channeled in the direction of a universal system.

For the time being, the thrust is on legislation regulating managed care, especially HMOs. All states have passed at least some patient protection laws, for example, requiring appeal procedures to challenge denial of benefits, banning restrictions on doctor–patient communications, and prohibiting compensation of doctors for ordering less care than is medically necessary. But at the federal level, "the parties remain split . . . about how extensively the Federal Government should regulate insurers, who are poised to marshal at least as many millions of dollars and hundreds of lobbyists to block the legislation as they have in the past" (Bruni, 1999). Still another sign of discontent with HMOs is increased unionization among doctors.

Another problem in health care is the financing of Medicare. The unfavorable demographic and economic forecasts that have been used to undermine social security can be made against health insurance. Fiscal problems can also be viewed as a product of program successes in providing added years of quality life to the elderly and disabled (Fein, 1998). According to health finance expert Marilyn Moon (1998), Medicare's biggest problem is that health care costs tend to rise faster than payroll. One contributor is the heavy overhead costs in private insurance, which is still responsible for over half of U.S. health expenditures (OECD, 1998a). Overhead for private insurance is 14 percent, compared to 4 percent in Medicaid and 2 percent in Medicare (Woolhandler and Himmelstein, 1994).

Owing to provisions of the Balanced Budget Act of 1997 that transferred fee-for-service to prospective payment systems for a number of services and increased mechanisms for reducing error and fraud, Medicare growth in 1998 was the slowest in its history. The cuts are said to be reducing the quality of service and jeopardizing the future of teaching hospitals. Spending for home health care, all the more critical with declines in length of hospital stays, plummeted 45 percent from 1997 to 1999 (Pear, 2000, p. A1). It appears, even to some proponents of the 1997 Balanced Budget Act, that it is not only fat but bone that has been cut.

The 1997 legislation made other changes that weakened the protection of vulnerable groups. It allowed Medicare patients choice among competing health plans and limited Medicaid's obligation to cover Medicare co-payments for the poor elderly, thus fragmenting what was formerly a single insurance pool that spread risks among the full population. The Balanced Budget Act of 1997 is said to have initiated a system of competing health plans that "poses a challenge to the principles of risk spreading, redistribution and government responsibility on which Medicare rests" (Feder and Moon, 1999, p. 58).

Congress passed a bill in 1995 that would have transformed Medicare from a *defined benefit* to a *defined contribution* (from a guarantee of specified benefits to a fixed-dollar amount or voucher for purchasing private insurance). President Clinton vetoed the measure, but the threat did not end there. The full voucher plan was only narrowly defeated in 1999, when a 17-member federal advisory commission fell just 1 vote short of the 11 needed to approve a final report. In addition to a voucher plan, the commission report also recommended raising Medicare eligibility from age 65 to 67.

Democrats and Republicans differ on the approach to Medicare. As presidential candidate, George W. Bush proposed a sweeping overhaul of the Medicare program: the creation of a system in which private insurers compete with government to provide coverage. Instead of defined health benefits, the Bush plan would offer subsidies that elderly people could use to buy government-approved health insurance plans (Mitchell, 2000, p. A1). By contrast, his rival proposed to shore up the current Medicare system with additional funds. As president, Bush greeted news of the longest period of projected solvency in the program's history (a 30-year extension of the life of the Medicare Trust Funds between 1993 and 2001) with continued pessimism about its future. Democrats, on the other hand, saw this report of the Medicare trustees as a chance to add prescription drug benefits without making radical changes in the structure of the program. According to Pete Stark, ranking Democrat on a health subcommittee of Congress, "The trustees' report makes clear that Republican claims about Medicare's so-called financing crisis are simply an excuse to raid the Medicare surplus to pay for tax breaks for the wealthy" (Pear, 2001, p. A18).

Unemployment Insurance

Cutbacks in Unemployment Insurance (UI), a federal-state program, have taken the form of discontinuing the automatic extension of benefits by Washington when unemployment is high. Virtual dismantling of this Extended Benefits (EB) program in 1980 and 1981, during the Carter and Reagan regimes, substantially reduced the proportion of the unemployed who get benefits during recessions. Enacted in 1970, the EB program automatically extended compensation for up to 13 weeks when national or state unemployment rates reached specified levels for designated periods of time. By the 1990s, the EB program was defunct, and complicated temporary emergency extensions were the means of dealing with high levels of unemployment. The added insecurity for the unemployed is indicated by the fact that before Emergency Unemployment Compensation was enacted in 1991, the Bush administration had vetoed several earlier extensions (Woodbury and Rubin, 1997).

The EB program and temporary additional extensions made it possible for UI to provide up to 65 weeks of compensation during the severe recession of the mid-1970s instead of the typical state duration of 26 weeks. It also provided benefits to three-fourths and two-thirds of the unemployed during the two years of highest unemployment, respectively (Woodbury and Rubin, 1997). With unemployment nearly 10 percent during 1982 and 1983, the highest since the Great Depression, less than half the unemployed (about 45 percent) received benefits (Shapiro and Nichols, 1992). In three subsequent recession years in the 1980s, with unemployment 7 percent or more, only one in three was covered. In 1992, the year of highest unemployment in the last recession, coverage improved following enactment of an emergency extension but was still only 50 percent.

Unlike a number of other nations, the United States has no means-tested program for UI claimants who exhaust their benefits. Available instead for the long-term unemployed or those who do not establish a foothold in the labor market are public assistance programs, either the federal-state program Aid to Families with Dependent Children, which was largely for single-parent families (succeeded in 1996 by TANF), or, for childless individuals or couples, meager state general assistance programs. Not only are both of these more demeaning than programs directly tied to unemployment, but in recent years, UI and these backup programs have become stingier in tandem. The following section deals at some length with AFDC, in which average monthly benefits dropped 37 percent from the mid-1970s to the mid-1990s (U.S. House of Representatives, 1996, p. 467). As for general assistance, in 1991, the state of Michigan had a 9.2 percent unemployment rate, and with only 41 percent of its unemployed workers covered by UI, it virtually eliminated its general assistance program. With similar proportions of their unemployed not covered by UI, Illinois and Ohio made comparable cutbacks (Shapiro and Nichols, 1992).

Accompanying the rise of unemployment and the reduction of general assistance were higher rates of conviction of accused offenders and stiffer sentences for crime. By midyear 1998, an estimated 1.8 million persons were incarcerated in U.S. prisons and jails, more than twice the number in 1985 (Gilliard, 1999). Crime and imprisonment are heavily concentrated among Hispanic and, especially, black minorities whose unemployment and poverty rates are also disproportionately high. One statistical analysis of the factors responsible for the increase in incarceration between 1974 and 1986 found that the largest factor, accounting for more than half the change, is higher imprisonment rates (Langan, 1991). Longer sentences also contribute to the higher imprisonment rates.

FEDERAL AND FEDERAL-STATE ASSISTANCE PROGRAMS

Beginning in the 1930s, the federal government assumed varying degrees of responsibility for cash and in-kind programs for the poor. Although most of these have been cut in recent decades, only Aid to Families with Dependent Children has been repealed.

Family Assistance

Under the Social Security Act, Washington matched state assistance expenditures for the elderly, blind (later all of the disabled), and dependent children, up to a stipulated maximum and, in return, held the states accountable to certain standards—that benefits be in cash, that hearings be held when benefits were denied, and that recipients maintain certain citizenship rights that had been denied them under the poor laws. States, for their part, had important powers, notably, the right to establish benefit levels, thus permitting low-wage jurisdictions, particularly in the South, to keep assistance levels even lower. As a result, benefits, though inadequate in all 50 states, varied widely. In the 1970s, the assistance programs for adult unemployable persons (aged, blind, disabled) were combined and federalized (Supplemental Security Income), with states being given an option to supplement the basic benefit guaranteed by Washington. As noted, Congress refused to do the same for families with dependent children.

The 1996 repeal of Aid to Families with Dependent Children, Title IV of the Social Security Act of 1935, is the most significant retrenchment of the U.S. welfare state to date. Never generous, benefits had been falling for 20 years (largely because states failed to raise them in response to inflation). Federal work requirements, entirely absent for the custodial parent until 1967, were gradually increased until, in 1988, only mothers with children under age three (or at state option, under one) were exempt from work or training requirements. Yet, the Personal Responsibility and Work Opportunity Reconciliation Act of 1996 (PRWORA) goes much further. Not only does the new law state specifically that the AFDC successor, Temporary Assistance for Needy Families (TANF), is not an entitlement in the sense of being available to all who meet eligibility criteria, but it no longer requires that benefits must be in cash; in fact, PRWORA permits states to transfer money from cash assistance to various non-cash media such as vouchers and subsidies to employers or service providers. Most indicative of change is a five-year lifetime limit on the receipt of benefits for parents and their children, regardless of whether or not jobs are available for those who exhaust their benefits.

Low benefits and restrictive eligibility requirements, particularly prior to 1960, kept AFDC from its stated goal of freeing single mothers from the breadwinning role so that they could assume the nurturing role. PRWORA's strict work requirements, with their absence of any federal exemption for mothers of very young children, accords no value to the traditional work of women or to parental care of their own children. In a reversal of the trend toward state patriarchy (Boris and Bardaglio, 1983), women are to depend on themselves or on men, but not on the state.

The new law also has strict work requirements for recipients while they are on relief, sometimes forcing them to enroll in "workfare" programs to work off their benefits under conditions that often violate labor laws and pay them no more than their welfare checks. Although states are strictly bound to meet work requirements for specified portions of their caseloads, the new legislation is in the devolution mode since it consists of block grants that leave open to lower levels of government many decisions regarding eligibility, use of federal funds, and types of benefits that were formerly specified by the federal government under the previous, grant-in-aid structure of AFDC. Moreover, TANF is a fixed-sum grant based on states' average spending in the years prior to repeal. Thus, while increased AFDC spending by a state usually increased the size of the federal grant, there is no such incentive under TANF. In fact, most states refused to spend all the federal money available to them in 1998. TANF has operated during a period of economic expansion, but its fixed-grant structure means that, unlike the AFDC entitlement, funds will not automatically expand with a rising caseload. There is less money available for such a contingency than the increase in welfare costs during the last recession. Even without a recession, the Congressional Budget Office estimated that the amount of money available to the states through TANF would, over the next six years, fall $12 billion short of what will be necessary to meet its work requirements, not including child care costs (Super et al., 1996).

Along with the demise of AFDC and its replacement with TANF, the new law repeals federal Emergency Assistance for Families and the Jobs Opportunity and Basic Skills (JOBS) program, enacted less than a decade earlier to encourage states to provide employment and training to welfare recipients. PRWORA also imposes work requirements for food stamp recipients who are neither elderly, disabled, nor raising dependent children— a restriction that could deny aid to half a million people. Stricter definitions of childhood disability could result in the loss of SSI benefits by over 100,000 children. Legal immigrants are barred for five years from receiving food stamps or SSI, and although subsequent legislation rescinded restrictions for some legal immigrants who were receiving benefits or were eligible for them at the time when PRWORA was passed, the basic ban persists. Total funding losses resulting from PRWORA were estimated at nearly $55 billion for the four years following its passage (Super et al., 1996).

In a press briefing in May 1998, the secretary of Health and Human Services bragged that the welfare rolls, which had dropped about 45 percent from 1994 through 1998, had not been so low since 1969. Neither had unemployment. But is reducing the rolls the issue? The AFDC caseloads were far less static than welfare bashers claimed; most families received AFDC for two years at a time or less (Garfinkel and McLanahan, 1986; Bane and Ellwood, 1994; Pavetti, 1995). History amply demonstrates that relief authorities are perfectly capable of reducing the rolls. Indeed, removal for violating welfare rules and fudging statistics and deterrent practices that keep the needy from applying contribute to the touted roll reductions. The real issue is not dependency, as the welfare "reformers" frame the problem, but poverty. Both the scarcity of jobs, particularly when unemployment is higher, and the wages that they pay mean that many welfare leavers will remain impoverished.

In nine state studies compiled by the National Governors' Association and other organizations, 40 to 50 percent of families who left TANF did not have a job, and a New York state study reported that 71 percent of former TANF recipients did not have employer-reported earnings (Sherman et al., 1998). Further, most did not earn wages sufficient to keep them out of poverty and were increasingly unable to pay for food and rent. Not surprisingly, several studies, covering recipients in 13 states, have found that although former recipients tended to work more than 30 hours a week, they were earning less than the poverty level for a family of three, continued to depend on public benefits like food stamps and subsidized child care, and returned to welfare within a few years (Parrott, 1998). A Tufts University Study (1998) found that two-thirds of the states implemented policies that made families worse off than under the old welfare system. Funds for the TANF block grants expire in Fiscal Year 2002, and reauthorization of the new welfare law will be considered by the 107th Congress, which was sworn in in January 2001.

Child Care

One of the assumptions of welfare "reform" is that employment outside the home is preferable to work in the home, even if it means leaving very young children without proper care, which is in short supply in the United States. In 1971, Congress passed the Comprehensive Child Care Act, which would have provided billions of federal dollars to fund preschool, day-care, nutritional, and other programs, but President Nixon, despite including work requirements for mothers in his welfare reform proposal, vetoed the measure, which would have served many of the non-poor, claiming that it would diminish parents' authority and involvement with their children.

AFDC guaranteed child-care assistance for families on welfare and, for one year, for those "transitioning off." Providing no such assurance, PRWORA consolidates four federal child-care programs and increases total funding by $4 billion over six years—an estimated $1.4 billion less than needed (Children's Defense Fund, 1997, p. 38). Although many states have increased their own spending in order to draw down federal matching funds and are using surplus money from their reduced welfare rolls, the money will not be adequate to serve all the families that meet eligibility criteria (Long et al., 1998, p. 11). Before welfare repeal, two-thirds of the 1.5 million children in federally subsidized child care were from working-poor families, but as more welfare recipients are forced to go to work, they will compete with these families for the insufficient day-care slots available. (This is one of several features of the new policy that exacerbate divisions between welfare recipients and the working poor.) With no guarantee of child care for those not on public assistance, welfare recipients who exhaust their time limits will also face a child care deficit (Preston, 1996). The U.S. Department of Health and Human Services has estimated that only 1 in 10 potentially eligible low-income families actually gets the child-care assistance that it needs (Sherman et al., 1998, p. 28). The idea of child care as a universal right—one that, like education for older children, should be a public responsibility—has never taken hold in the United States.

The child care problem is not only quantitative. Many states are solving the shortage by paying TANF mothers to care for other recipients' children in their own homes. While some states provide training, licensing, and supervision of such "family day-care providers," many have found it expedient to pay for informal arrangements in which a relative, friend, or neighbor agrees to take care of the children. A study of unregulated care in four cities found that only 9 percent of the households examined provided what was rated as "good quality care," and more than a third of the care was determined to have adversely affected the children's developmental progress (Sexton, 1996). Day-care advocates fear that as the need expands, more states will resort to such informal arrangements, since they cost about a third as much as day-care centers and about half of what states pay to licensed, family providers (Kilborn, 1997). With need likely to increase and services deficient in both quantity and quality, the Bush administration was planning to cut federal child care funds in the first budget it submits to Congress.

Housing Assistance

Although the United States has had a public housing program since 1937, programs that provide public housing or vouchers for subsidized units have always fallen far short of the number of people who are eligible for them. Never adequate, spending on low-income housing began to be reduced in the 1970s. In the next decade, the Reagan administration dealt a deadly blow to affordable housing when it slashed the low-income housing budget by 75 percent, even as poverty was rising (Atlas and Dreier, 1989). In 1970, affordable housing units (defined as costing less than 30 percent of an annual income roughly equivalent to the three-person poverty level) exceeded low-income renters; by 1995, there was an affordable housing gap of 4.4 million units (Daskal, 1998). More than three-fifths of low-income renters spend over half of their incomes on rent and utilities, undoubtedly stinting on other necessities as a result. Another result is homelessness, estimates of which ranged widely, from a low figure of 228,000 to as many as 3 million in the early 1990s (Karger and Stoesz, 1998, p. 407).

Unequal treatment of the poor and the better-off is exemplified by the difference between federal tax expenditures on housing, that is, deductions for mortgage interest and state and local property taxes on owner-occupied homes, and direct outlays for housing for lower-income groups. In 1999, the treasury provided an estimated $78.1 billion in fiscal welfare to homeowners (U.S. Congress, Congressional Budget Office [CBO], 2000, table 5–1, p. 109), largely middle-income or above and, according to the CBO, spent only $27.0 billion in direct outlays for housing and homeless programs for lower-income groups.

PRIVATIZATION OF SERVICE DELIVERY

Assessing privatization "mainly depends on the point of departure—the prior public–private balance previously struck in a particular domain" (Starr, 1989, p. 15). Private investment of taxes collected for social security has already been discussed. This section takes up some different points of departure and destinations in the privatization of service delivery.

The United States already depends heavily on the private sector to deliver health and welfare services, usually with direct government financing in the case of Medicare and Medicaid or indirect support through the tax system for employer-provided health insurance. With Medicare and Medicaid, government reimburses the largely private providers of care, including for-profit hospitals, home health, and nursing home establishments. Medicare and Medicaid involved a vast increase in government spending and public financial responsibility for a major function that was formerly private, usually paid for by individuals and families (including insurance), or neglected. The choice was to reimburse private providers rather than for government to deliver the service itself, as is done in the United Kingdom and Sweden. With Medicare and Medicaid, private delivery of a service was concurrent with a major expansion of government financial responsibility.

The 1967 amendments to the Social Security Act authorized the states to purchase services from non-profit providers, and so did several other important pieces of legislation. In the last quarter century government purchase of social services became widespread (Smith and Lipsky, 1993; Gibelman and Demone, 1998). Here, as with Medicare and Medicaid, government financing of private service delivery represented a sizable increase in social provision.

Privatization of two services formerly financed and delivered by the states was a consequence of the practice known as deinstitutionalization or reduced reliance on traditional institutions for the care of populations such as the mentally ill or retarded (Lerman, 1982).[9] With services almost entirely underwritten by state purchase-of-service contracts, voluntary organizations already providing services to the developmentally disabled expanded in order to meet increased demands for community living arrangements. Currently, 14 states have some state-operated group homes in residential communities, but the overwhelming majority of group homes and associated day programs are privately operated (Hanlon, 1999). Here, too, privatization and service expansion went together.

That has not been the case for the mentally ill, who are frequently without appropriate care at all. The states, though relieved by SSI, Disability Insurance (DI), Medicare, and Medicaid of 50 to 100 percent of the costs of maintaining the mentally ill in institutions, failed to replace these hospitals with outpatient services or community care. Many of the mentally ill elderly ended up in nursing homes where, unlike the situation with mental hospitals, Washington shared the costs with the states. Many younger mental patients landed on the streets. This turn of events, referred to as deinstitutionalization, "was not a policy mandated by statutory law" but "an unforseen outgrowth of a series of federal entitlement programs having little to do with the severely mentally ill" (Grob, 1997, p. 55). Under the banner of this non-policy, many of the severely mentally ill were either reinstitutionalized or neglected. Their problems were exacerbated in the 1980s, when the Reagan administration reviewed eligibility for SSI and DI and succeeded in denying the applications and removing from the rolls thousands of people, many of them mentally ill. According to a 1998 national study, fewer than half of Americans with schizophrenia receive adequate care, and the Bazelon Center for Mental Health Law estimates that spending by the 50 states on treatment for the seriously mentally ill is a third less today than it was in the 1950s (Winerup, 1999).

One reason that states were more inclined to pay for services to the developmentally disabled than to the mentally ill is that a well-organized lobby and voluntary services existed earlier for the former than for the latter. By the time families of the mentally ill came together in an advocacy organization (National Alliance for the Mentally Ill, or NAMI) in 1979, the times were less friendly to financing social services.

Homelessness and imprisonment have been among the frequent results of state neglect of the mentally ill. There are currently more mentally ill persons in jails and prisons than in state hospitals, and it has been estimated that many homeless persons in New York City are mentally ill (Winerup, 1999). It is possible to reduce the number of patients in mental hospitals just as it is possible to purge relief rolls. To reduce poverty or improve the quality of life for the mentally ill is quite different from what passes for welfare "reform" or "community care."

Welfare "reform" is accelerating privatization of services (Gibelman, 1998). The route here is often from public to private, for-profit auspices. Unlike Medicare and Medicaid, which greatly extended public financial responsibility, the new welfare law (PRWORA) gives preference to community-based organizations but cuts funding for social services by 15 percent (U.S. Congress, 1996, Title IX, sec. 908). This form of privatization or "profitization" has already taken place in prison management, with nearly every state in the country either having one or more private prisons or sending inmates to such institutions in other states (Belluck, 1999).

The new welfare law permits TANF funds to be used in any manner that is reasonably calculated to accomplish the purposes of the program for needy families. Prior to the passage of PRWORA, many states were contracting with private companies for tasks such as child support enforcement and job training (Mannix et al., 1996, p. 5). Now they can contract out the administration of the TANF block grant, TANF-related services, and the administration of child-care funds. Private firms are lobbying to take over what had been a governmental function at least since 1935: the determination of eligibility for assistance and the amounts of benefits paid. The law allows states to contract not only with voluntary and proprietary organizations to provide the services that accomplish its purposes but with religious bodies as well.

Even before the new welfare law went into effect, corporations like Lockheed Martin (a defense contractor), IBM, Unisys, Andersen Consulting, and Ross Perot's Electronic Data Systems were providing services in 49 states. In Texas, Governor George W. Bush had asked the federal government for a waiver so that private firms could take over the eligibility determination not only for TANF but for food stamps and Medicaid as well (Hartung and Washburn, 1998). Corporations are eager to lay their hands on a new stream of money, approximately $28 billion, that government now spends to administer welfare programs.

Privatization often substitutes lower-paid staff for better-paid, government workers. Typically the latter are unionized, whereas those in the private sector are not. A 1996 study by the Chicago Institute on Urban Poverty found that in 7 out of 10 public service categories in that city, privatization drove the wages of entry-level workers below the poverty level (Hartung and Washburn, 1998, pp. 14–15). So privatization is a strike against workers and against the labor movement. It complements other policies to weaken the power of workers.

The unionization of 74,000 public health care workers in Los Angeles County—the largest organizing victory since the United Auto Workers' win at General Motors in 1937—is likely to enhance the quality of services as well as improve the wages of home-care aides (Greenhouse, 1999). Raising their wages is expected to reduce the 40 percent annual turnover among these workers, thereby increasing the security of the elderly or disabled clients who depend on them. Moreover, it is anticipated that the union and the county authorities will provide training for these workers. The 10,000 home-care workers in Los Angeles County who work for private agencies will not be unionized.

One critique of government purchase of services from the voluntary, non-profit sector is that it cedes state power for the control of vulnerable populations to private agencies and that it may be difficult to hold them accountable (Smith and Lipsky, 1993). If this is the case, how much more risky is it for the state to give away responsibility for such populations to profit-making organizations? Corporate prison managers have been known to skimp on food, activities, staffing, and surveillance devices, thereby abetting violence or endangering public safety by their "savings" (Bates, 1998; Belluck, 1999). City and state officials attempting to build tighter controls into contracts with prison companies believe that private prisons may not be subject to the same regulations and oversight as public ones. Largely due to understaffing, the private nursing home industry, "the nation's longest-running experiment in privatization," has been responsible for such blatant violations of patients' rights that legislators who ordinarily come down on the side of "free enterprise" have begun to advocate for government standards (Bates, 1999). As heavy contributors to federal and state candidates for public office, the nursing home industry is well positioned to resist government regulation and requirements for accountability.

What of the claim that volunteers or the private, non-profit sector will assume responsibilities that government sheds? According to Richard Steinburg, professor of economics and philanthropy at Indiana University, each one-dollar cut in government aid to the poor is made up by no more than 35 cents or less from private charities (Kilborn, 1997). With cuts in the food stamp budget and state time limits on receipt of public assistance already starting to kick in, private charities and non-profits are struggling to keep the shredding safety net together. In 1996, in the midst of a recovery, the U.S. Conference of Mayors reported that 18 percent of requests for emergency food assistance went unmet (Tufts University, 1997). Second Harvest, the nation's largest distributor of donated food to emergency food providers, projects a shortfall from 1997 to 2002 of 24,558 billion tons of food, or the equivalent of three meals a day for 3.24 million low-income people for an entire year. To make up for this loss, they estimate that they will have to expand their collection and distribution activities by more than 425 percent over their 1995 capacity and maintain this expanded level throughout the six-year period. Yet despite this quantum leap in demand, the companies that donate food are now providing less than they were, in part because of streamlined business methods that result in less leftover food (Cook and Brown, 1997; Revkin, 1999).

The United States is noted among industrial nations for the amount of time that its people spend in volunteer activities, but the kind of sustained, intensive work that is needed by troubled children and families is in short supply.[10] There has been a long and impressive tradition of self-help among economically oppressed groups, particularly African Americans, but black leaders have become increasingly concerned over their capacity to meet the multidimensional needs of the people in their communities (Stafford, 1997). When President Clinton took his plea for more voluntary care to New York, one African American chief executive officer (CEO) delivered this response:

Black businesses and the black church are doing more than their fair share in picking up the slack . . . [after] more than a decade of cuts in services to the urban poor by Federal, state and local governments. It is unrealistic and unfair to expect the private sector in general—and black businesses in particular—to sacrifice profit margins in order to do the government's job. (Nagourney, 1997)

DIMINISHING WELFARE IN THE UNITED STATES

If any country in the world has the resources to reduce poverty, inequality, and their attendant ills, it is the United States of America. The GDP per capita of the United States more than doubled since 1960, when it was already a rich nation, and grew by nearly 50 percent (47.3 percent) between 1980 and 1998 (U.S. Department of Labor, Bureau of Labor Statistics, 2000a). The United States is proof positive that a bigger pie does not necessarily mean a larger slice for everyone.

Welfare has diminished in the United States. The average poverty rate for the 1990s was 13.8 percent, compared to 11.8 percent for the 1970s (when the poverty standard itself was less deficient in relation to the median income than it is today). Income inequality is the highest in the post-war era. Tax cuts favoring the rich and high on the agenda of the Republicans who captured the White House and control Congress, would only widen the gap. Despite the lowest unemployment rates in 30 years and six years of economic expansion, wages are still below their 1973 level. Downsizing continues to threaten the security of workers, even in years of economic boom. The welfare state is doing less to cushion the losses of retirement and unemployment and has withdrawn a partial entitlement to income support for families with dependent children. Indeed, the changes in public assistance not only entail benefit losses but undermine communal principles that have been part of the U.S. welfare state, however reluctant, for more than 60 years. Threatened changes in social insurance would go much further in this direction. Another trend, devolution to lower levels of government, may uphold federalist principles for some but has traditionally permitted lower standards of care, particularly for minorities (Schlesinger, 1986). The proportion of the population not covered by public or private health insurance has risen nearly 25 percent since 1987. The provision of necessities to the poor and the immigrant has also diminished. The United States was already more privatized in health and welfare services than other countries, and now Washington is turning over additional responsibilities to the private, often for-profit, sector. Services are shorter on quantity and quality. With George W. Bush in the White House the push for privatization accelerated, in keeping with a general, renewed drive for deregulation and almost unthinkable cutbacks in child care, health programs for the uninsured, and other vital services. The hotly contested presidential election resulted in the defeat of the candidate more supportive of social welfare and in favor of some liberalization of Medicare and a hands-off approach to social security.

For all this, the welfare state has not been dismantled. The repeal of AFDC has not meant the end of aid to needy families, although such support has become "temporary," hence, less secure. The universal insurance programs, though less appealing to the non-poor and stingier to all, have nonetheless been resistant so far to the well-financed campaigns to discredit and conjure up non-existent crises. Less desirable than some other strategies for raising the incomes of the poor, the Earned Income Tax Credit has overtaken federal funding for family assistance and measurably boosts the incomes of working-poor families. Although not immune to political criticism, the EITC aids, hence, potentially unites more of the working class than conventional public assistance and has grown under Republicans and Democrats in a time generally unfavorable to low-income programs. Yet, it offers scant aid to the very poor, disappears with unemployment, subsidizes low-wage, including sweatshop, employers, and may reduce the drive to increase wages. Preferable but politically unlikely are public employment funds in which government money subsidizes the vital services that are in such short supply.

Progressive political mobilization is perceptible, but barely. In a labor movement that seemed moribund a decade ago, there are signs of strength, recovery, and a concern that transcends the direct needs of its membership—particularly its mobilization of women and workers of color in the tertiary sector and its campaign to raise the minimum wage. The right-wing takeover of Congress, though responsible, along with the New Democrat in the White House, for repeal or retrenchment in social welfare, experienced too great popular resistance to remove from office a twice-elected president, albeit one who may anger his Republican opponents precisely because he so successfully co-opted some of their platform. Devolution of the major public assistance program for families has forced relatively powerless advocates to fight on 50 separate fronts but at the same time has stimulated some state and local action to create jobs and limit the abuses of workfare. The strict work requirements and time limits of the new welfare law have led welfare advocates to think more about job creation and have increased public consciousness of the deficiencies of the low-wage labor market. Most states have passed legislation to protect patients' rights, and 17 cities and counties, including Los Angeles and Chicago, have enacted living wage ordinances requiring that firms doing business with city government pay all their employees a prescribed living wage (Pollin and Luce, 1998). Indeed, *New York Times* economics analyst Louis Uchitelle referred to this push for wage laws as a "movement" (Uchitelle, 1999, p. C1), although its effects are confined to employees of local governments and those who do business with the municipalities. Campus activism may be picking up as students, in a revival of the "ethical-consumption" principles of the Progressive era in the early decades of the twentieth century, mobilize to resist purchase of supplies produced in sweatshops in the United States and abroad.

It is too early to tell whether devolution will not only divide and conquer but stimulate and unite the grass roots. This, however, can be forecast. Democrats will be more like Republicans, and the latter will continue in "capitalist overdrive" unless popular movements like those of the 1930s and the 1960s—marching to different songs and under different banners—force officials to act as if they are democratically elected. Such movements, however, have yet to be born.

NOTES

1. Moreover, even when ecomonic and political elites were pledging allegiance to laissez-faire, government often intervened on the side of business; for example, with large land grants to the railroads and in support of business in labor disputes.

2. The term "liberal" is usually equated with "progressive" in the United States and with intervention on the part of the state to reduce inequality and poverty—a meaning that it took on in the 1930s under the New Deal, which bore some resemblance to social democracy. This was a switch from the earlier meaning of the term in the United States and what it means elsewhere in the world, namely, anti-statism and laissez-faire. In the United States, conservatism is associated with what is called liberalism elsewhere.

3. The SSA standard is based on an "economy food plan" that was intended "for temporary use when funds are low" (Orshansky, 1965, p. 5). For families of three or more, the food plan is multiplied by three, the amount by which total costs are assumed to exceed food expenses—a figure too small to encompass the high costs of housing. The standard is indexed to the cost of living but has not been raised in real terms in over 35 years.

4. The LIS uses a relative poverty standard of less than half of each country's median income, adjusted for family size.

5. Only Ireland and Israel, two much less wealthy countries, ranked lower.

6. The Institute for Policy Studies (IPS) (1999) cited a *Wall Street Journal* report that unemployment in U.S. counties bordering Mexico rose from 10.4 percent in 1994 to 13.5 percent in 1998, despite the overall decline in unemployment. According to the IPS, employers hold down wages or fight unions by threatening to move to Mexico or other low-wage countries.

7. All covered earners pay the same proportions of their earnings for social security, up to a maximum, after which no more taxes are paid. Thus, participants with incomes above the cutoff ($76,200 in 2000) pay smaller proportions of their incomes than those below the maximum.

8. According to a cover story in the *Investment Dealers' Digest*, Wall Street made sure that it shaped the debate on privatization of social security by "quietly bankrolling think tanks, research and public policy forums, in addition to spending millions of dollars in Congressional political contributions" (Darby and Celarier, 1999, p. 2). The source of data on political contributions from the securities industry and on contributions from Wall Street to members of Congress who oversee social security and have supported partial privatization is the well-respected, Washington-based public interest group Common Cause. According to Darby and Celarier, Wall Street became less enthusiastic when the details of privatization became clearer, notably, that managing the assets associated with partial privatization may well entail low fees and high costs. However, Wall Street continues to lobby for privatized social security accounts (Uchitelle, 2000).

9. Deinstitutionalization has complex, intertwined roots, including shifts in professional ideology (i.e., preference for community over institutional care); enactment of federal entitlement programs that provided support for disabled populations outside state institutions or in non-traditional institutions; state officials' seizing these opportunities to shed all or part of the costs of care; psychoactive

drugs that made it possible for formerly institutionalized persons to live in the community; and judicial rulings extending the civil rights of disadvantaged groups and attempting to correct the flagrant abuse of vulnerable populations in state institutions (Lerman, 1982; Johnson, 1990; Johnson and Surles, 1994; Grob, 1997; Karger and Stoesz, 1998).

10. Big Brothers and Big Sisters programs, which have reported success in reducing alcoholism and truancy among youth, have a waiting list of 30,000 children and estimate that as many as 15 million could benefit from the kind of mentoring services that they provide (Gerson et al., 1997).

REFERENCES

Atlas, J., and P. Dreier. (1989). "America's housing crisis: A grasssroots strategy and policy agenda." *Social Policy* 19 (Winter): 25–38.

Bane, M. J., and D. Ellwood. (1994). *Welfare Realities—From Rhetoric to Reform.* Cambridge, MA: Harvard University Press.

Bates, E. (1998). "Private prisons." *The Nation* 268 (January 5): 11–17.

———. (1999). "The shame of our nursing homes." *The Nation* 266 (March 29): 11–19.

Beck, R. (1996). *The Case against Immigration: The Moral, Economic, Social, and Environmental Reasons for Reducing U.S. Immigration Back to Traditional Levels.* New York: W. W. Norton.

Belluck, P. (1999). "As more prisons go private, states seek tighter controls." *New York Times,* April 15, pp. A1, A24.

Bennefield, R. L. (1997). "Health Insurance Coverage: 1996." Current Population Reports, P60–199. Washington, DC: U.S. Bureau of the Census, September.

———. (1998). "Health Insurance Coverage: 1997." Current Population Reports, P60–202. Washington, DC: U.S. Bureau of the Census, September.

Bernstein, J., L. Mishel, and C. Brocht. (2000). *Any Way You Cut It: Income Inequality on the Rise Regardless of How It's Measured.* Washington, DC: Economic Policy Institute.

Boris, E., and P. Bardaglio. (1983). "The transformation of patriarchy: The historical role of the state." In I. Diamond, ed., *Families, Politics, and Public Policy.* New York: Longman, Green.

Bradbury, R., and M. Jäntti. (1999). *Child Poverty across Industrialized Nations.* Working Paper no. 205, Luxembourg Income Study. Florence: UNICEF International Child Development Centre; Syracuse, NY: Maxwell School of Citizenship and Public Affairs, Syracuse University.

Bradshaw, J., and J. Chen. (1996). *Poverty in the UK: A Comparison with Nineteen Other Countries.* Working Paper no. 147, Luxembourg Income Study. Syracuse, NY: Maxwell School of Citizenship and Public Affairs, Syracuse University.

Briggs, V., Jr. (1990). "The changing nature of the workforce: The influence of U.S. immigration policy." Washington, DC: National Planning Association, December.

Bruni, F. (1999). "Curbs on managed care still divide two parties." *New York Times,* March 17, p. A18.

Callahan, D. (1999). "Still with us." *American Prospect* (July–August): 74–77.

Cherry, R. (1998). "Black men still jobless." *Dollars and Sense* (November/December): 43.

Cherry, R., and G. S. Goldberg. (2000). "The Earned Income Tax Credit: What it does and doesn't do." In R. Baiman, H. Boushey, and D. Saunders, eds., *Political Economy and Contemporary Capitalism: Radical Perspectives on Economic Theory and Policy*. Armonk, NY: M. E. Sharpe, pp. 294–301.

Children's Defense Fund. (1997). *The State of America's Children Yearbook 1997*. Washington, DC: Author.

Clinton, B. (1996). *Between Hope and History: Meeting America's Challenges for the 21st Century*. New York: Random House.

Cook, J. T., and J. L. Brown. (1997). *Analysis of the Capacity of the Second Harvest Network to Cover the Federal Food Stamp Shortfall from 1997 to 2002*. CHPNP Working Paper Series FSPSF-070197-1. Medford, MA: Center on Hunger, Poverty and Nutrition Policy, Tufts University School of Nutrition Sciences and Policy, July.

Council of Economic Advisors. (1999). *Economic Indicators*. Washington, DC: U.S. Government Printing Office, January.

Dalaker, J. (1999). *Poverty in the United States: 1998*. Current Population Reports, P60–207. Washington, DC: U.S. Government Printing Office.

Dalaker, J., and B. D. Proctor. (2000). *Poverty in the United States: 1999*. Current Population Reports, P60–210. Washington, DC: U.S. Government Printing Office.

Darby, R., and M. Celarier. (1999). "Where's the payoff?" *Investment Dealers' Digest* (August 9): 2–8.

Daskal, J. (1998). *In Search of Shelter: The Growing Shortage of Affordable Rental Housing*. Washington, DC: Center on Budget and Policy Priorities.

DeFreitas, G. (1998). "Immigration, inequality, and policy alternatives." In D. Baker, G. Epstein, and R. Pollin, eds., *Globalization and Progressive Economic Policy*. Cambridge: Cambridge University Press, pp. 337–356.

———. (1999). "Fear of foreigners: Immigrants as scapegoats for domestic woes." In R. Albelda, ed., *Real World Micro*, 8th ed. Somerville, MA: Dollars and Sense, pp. 77–82.

DuBoff, R. B. (1997). "The welfare state, pensions, privatization: The case of social security in the United States." *International Journal of Health Services* 27: 1–23.

———. (1999). "Social security is not in 'crisis.' " *Uncommon Sense*, no. 21 (February). New York: National Jobs for All Coalition, unpaged.

Dunlea, M. (1996–1997). "The poverty profiteers privatize welfare." *CAQ* (Winter): 6–10.

Economic Policy Institute. (1997). *The Failed Experiment: NAFTA at Three Years*. Washington, DC: Author.

Economic Report of the President. (1998). Washington, DC: U.S. Government Printing Office.

Eisner, R. (1997). *The Great Deficit Scares*. New York: The Century Foundation Press.

Enchautegui, M. (1993). *The Effects of Immigration on the Wages and Employment of Black Males*. Washington, DC: Urban Institute.

Feder, J., and M. Moon. (1999). "Can Medicare survive its saviors?" *American Prospect* (May–June): 56–60.

Fein, R. (1998). "The HMO revolution." *Dissent* (Spring 1998): 29–36.

Galbraith, J. K. (1998). *Created Unequal: The Crisis in American Pay.* New York: Free Press.

Garfinkel, I., and S. S. McLanahan. (1986). *Single Mothers and Their Children: A New American Dilemma.* Washington, DC: Urban Institute Press.

Gerson, M. J., et al. (1997). "Do do-gooders do much good? Most volunteers aren't solving care problems." *U.S. News & World Report* (April 28): 26–30.

Gibelman, M. (1998). "Theory, practice, and experience in the purchase of services." In M. Gibelman, M. and H. W. Demone, Jr., eds., *The Privatization of Human Services: Policy and Practice Issues*, vol. 1. New York: Springer, pp. 1–52.

Gibelman, M., and H. W. Demone, Jr., eds. (1998). *The Privatization of Human Services: Policy and Practice Issues*, vol. 1. New York: Springer Publishing Company.

Gilliard, D. K. (1999). "Prison and jail inmates at midyear 1998." *Bureau of Justice Statistics Bulletin.* Washington, DC: U.S. Department of Justice, March.

Goldberg, G. S., and S. D. Collins. (2001). *Washington's New Poor Law: Welfare "Reform" and the Roads Not Taken, 1935 to the Present.* New York: Apex Books.

Greenhouse, S. (1999). "In biggest drive since 1937, union gains a victory." *New York Times*, February 26, A1, A18.

Greenstein, R., and I. Shapiro. (1998). *New Research Findings on the Effects of the Earned Income Tax Credit.* Washington, DC: Center on Budget and Policy Priorities.

Grob, G. N. (1997). "Deinstitutionalization: The illusion of policy." *Journal of Policy History* 9: 48–73.

Hanlon, M. D. (1999). "Running on two tracks: The public and private provision of human services." *New Labor Forum* (Queens College, City University of New York) (Spring/Summer): 100–109.

Harrison, B., and B. Bluestone. (1988). *The Great U-Turn.* New York: Basic Books.

Hartung, W. D., and J. Washburn. (1998). "Lockheed Martin's new empire: Targeting welfare dollars." *The Nation* 266 (March 2): 11–16.

Harvey, P. (1997). "How many jobs are there? The need for a job vacancy survey." *Uncommon Sense*, no. 17. New York: National Jobs for All Coalition, unpaged.

Hirsch, B. T., and D. A. MacPherson. (1998). *Union Membership and Earnings Data Book: Compilations from Current Population Survey (1998 Edition).* Washington, DC: Bureau of National Affairs.

Howell, D. (1994). "The skills myth." *American Prospect* (Summer): 81–90.

———. (1998). "The collapse of low-skill wages: Technological change or institutional failure?" *Uncommon Sense*, no. 13. New York: National Jobs for All Coalition, unpaged.

Howell, D., and E. D. Mueller. (1998). "Immigration and native-born male earnings: A jobs-level analysis of the New York City metropolitan area labor market, 1980–90." New York: Robert J. Milano Graduate School, New School University, March.

Institute for Policy Studies. (1999). *Five Years under NAFTA*. Washington, DC: Author.

International Labour Organization. (1995). *World Employment 1995*. Geneva: Author.

Jansson, B. S. (1997). *The Reluctant Welfare State: American Social Welfare Policies: Past, Present, and Future*, 3rd ed. Pacific Grove, CA: Brooks/Cole Publishing Company.

Johnson, A. B. (1990). *Out of Bedlam: The Truth about Deinstitutionalization*. New York: Basic Books.

Johnson, A. B., and R. C. Surles. (1994). "Has deinstititionalization failed?" In S. A. Kirkand and S. D. Einbinder, eds., *Controversial Issues in Mental Health*. Boston: Allyn and Bacon, pp. 214–226.

Johnson, D. (1999). "Facing shortage, builders and labor court workers." *New York Times*, March 13, p. A1.

Karger, H. J., and D. Stoesz. (1998). *American Social Welfare Policy: A Pluralist Approach*, 3rd ed. New York: Longman.

Kilborn, P. T. (1997). "Child-care solutions in a new world of welfare." *New York Times*, June 1, p. A1.

Korpi, W., and J. Palme. (1998). "The paradox of redistribution and strategies of equality: Welfare state institutions, inequality, and poverty in Western countries." *American Sociological Review* 63 (October): 661–687.

Krugman, P. R., and R. Z. Lawrence. (1994). "Trade, jobs, and wages." *Scientific American* 270 (April): 44–49.

Langan, P. A. (1991). "America's soaring prison population." *Science* 251 (March 29): 1568–1573.

Lerman, P. (1982). *Deinstitutionalization and the Welfare State*. New Brunswick, NJ: Rutgers University Press.

Lieberman, T. (1997). "Social insecurity: The campaign to make the system private." *The Nation* (January 27): 11ff.

Liebman, J. (1998). "The impact of the Earned Income Tax Credit on incentives and income distribution." In J. Poterba, ed., *Tax Policy and the Economy*, vol. 12. Cambridge, MA: MIT Press.

Long, S. K., G. G. Kirby, R. Kurka, and S. Waters. (1998). *Child Care Assistance under Welfare Reform: Early Responses by the States*. Occasional Paper no. 15. Washington, DC: Urban Institute, September.

Mannix, M. R., H. A. Freedman, M. Cohan, and C. Lamb. (1996). *Implementation of the Temporary Assistance for Needy Families Block Grant: An Overview*. New York: Center on Social Welfare Policy and Law, November.

Mishel, L., J. Bernstein, and J. Schmitt. (1999). *The State of Working America, 1998–99*. Ithaca, NY: ILR Press.

———. (2001). *The State of Working America 2000–01*. Ithaca, NY: Cornell University Press.

Mitchell, A. (2000). "Bush spells out major overhaul in Medicare plan." *New York Times*, September 6, pp. A1, A22.

Moon, M. (1998). *Medicare, Medicaid, and the Health Care System*. New York: Century Foundation.

Nagourney, A. (1997). "In surprise confrontation during visit, president is criticized on welfare law." *New York Times*, February 19, p. B6.

Nasar, S. (1999a). "More groups are sharing in job growth: Blacks and teen-agers showed gains in April." *New York Times*, May 8, pp. C1, C14.

———. (1999b). "Unemployment falls again, but job growth is moderating." *New York Times*, June 5, pp. C1, C14.

North, D. S. (1994). "Enforcing the minimum wage and employer sanctions." *Annals of the American Academy of Political and Social Science* 534 (July): 58–68.

OECD (1998a). *OECD in Figures: 1998 Edition*. Paris: Author.

———. (1998b). *OECD Social Expenditure Database*. Paris: Author.

Orshansky, M. (1965). "Counting the poor: Another look at the poverty profile." *Social Security Bulletin* 28 (January): 3–29.

Parrott, S. (1998). *Welfare Recipients Who Find Jobs: What Do We Know about Their Employment and Earnings?* Washington, DC: Center on Budget and Policy Priorities, November.

Pavetti, L. A. (1995). "Who is affected by time limits?" In I. A. Sawhill, ed., *Welfare Reform: An Analysis of the Issues*. Washington, DC: Urban Institute Press, pp. 31–34.

Pear, R. (1999). "Many states slow to use children's insurance fund." *New York Times*, May 9, pp. 1, 22.

———. (2000). "Medicare spending for care at home plunges by 45%." *New York Times*, April 21, pp. A1, A20.

———. (2001). "Trustees extend solvency estimates for 2 benefits." *New York Times*, March 20, p. A18.

Perez-Peña, R. (1998). "Tax credit rise urged for poor in New York." *New York Times*, March 2, p. B24.

Phillips, K. (1991). *The Politics of Rich and Poor: Wealth and the American Electorate in the Reagan Aftermath*. New York: HarperPerennial.

———. (1994). *Arrogant Capital: Washington, Wall Street, and the Frustration of American Politics*. Boston: Little, Brown.

Pierson, P. (1994). *Dismantling the Welfare State? Reagan, Thatcher, and the Politics of Retrenchment*. Cambridge: Cambridge University Press.

Pollin, R., and S. Luce. (1998). *The Living Wage: Building a Fair Economy*. New York: New Press.

Preston, J. (1996). "Welfare rules intensify need for day care." *New York Times*, November 11, pp. B1, B7.

Rainwater, L., and T. M. Smeeding. (1995). *Doing Poorly: The Real Income of American Children in Comparative Perspective*. Working Paper no. 127, Luxembourg Income Study. Syracuse, NY: Maxwell School of Citizenship and Public Affairs, Syracuse University.

Revkin, A. C. (1999). "As need for food grows, donations steadily drop." *New York Times*, February 27, pp. A1, B7.

Ruggles, P. (1990). *Drawing the Line: Alternative Poverty Measures and Their Implications for Public Policy*. Washington, DC: Urban Institute Press.

Schlesinger, A. M., Jr. (1958). *The Coming of the New Deal*. Boston: Houghton Mifflin.

———. (1986). *The Cycles of American History*. Boston: Houghton Mifflin.

Scott, R. E. (1999). *NAFTA's Pain: Job Destruction Accelerates in 1999*. EPI Briefing Paper. Washington, DC: Economic Policy Institute, November.

Sexton, J. (1996). "Welfare mothers and informal day care: Is it up to par?" *New York Times*, October 14, pp. B1, B2.

Shapiro, I. (1987). *No Escape: The Minimum Wage and Poverty.* Washington, DC: Center on Budget and Policy Priorities.

Shapiro, I., and M. E. Nichols. (1992). *Far from Fixed: An Analysis of the Unemployment Insurance System.* Washington, DC: Center on Budget and Policy Priorities.

Sherman, A., C. Amey, B. Duffield, N. Ebb, and D. Weinstein. (1998). *Welfare to What: Early Findings on Family Hardship and Well-Being.* Washington, DC: Children's Defense Fund and National Coalition for the Homeless, December.

Skocpol, T. (1991). "Targeting within universalism: Politically viable policies to combat poverty in the United States." In C. Jencks and P. E. Peterson, eds., *The Urban Underclass.* Washington, DC: Brookings Institution, pp. 441–446.

———. (1997). *Boomerang: Health Care Reform and the Turn against Government.* New York: Norton.

Smeeding, T. M. (1997). *Financial Poverty in Developed Countries: The Evidence from LIS.* Working Paper no. 155, Luxembourg Income Study. Syracuse, NY: Maxwell School of Citizenship and Public Affairs, Syracuse University.

Smith, J. P., and B. Edmonston, eds. (1997). *The New Americans: Economic, Demographic, and Fiscal Effects of Immigration.* Washington, DC: National Academy Press.

Smith, S. R., and M. Lipsky. (1993). *Nonprofits for Hire: The Welfare State in the Age of Contracting.* Cambridge, MA: Harvard University Press.

Social Security Information Project, Campaign for America's Future (2000). Reports from the Project on Social Security. Available on the Internet at http://www.ourfuture.org., May 15, June 23, July 10, September 8, October 6.

Spitz, G. N. (1998). "Social Security doesn't need saving." *Social Policy* 29 (Fall): 19–28.

Stafford, W. W. (1997). *Black Civil Society and the Black Family in New York City: A Struggle for Inclusion in Decision-Making.* New York: Black Family Task Force/Manhattan Borough President's Office.

Starr, P. (1989). "The making of privatization." In S. B. Kamerman and A. J. Kahn, eds., *Privatization and the Welfare State.* Princeton, NJ: Princeton University Press, pp. 15–48.

Stevens, B. (1990). "Labor unions, employee benefits, and the privatization of the American welfare state." *Journal of Policy History* 2: 233–260.

Stevenson, R. W. (1999). "Wage growth in '99 below expectations." *New York Times*, April 30, pp. C1–C2.

Stockman, D. (1986). *The Triumph of Politics: Why the Reagan Revolution Failed.* New York: Harper and Row.

Super, D., A. Super, S. Parrott, S. Steinmetz, and C. Mann. (1996). *The New Welfare Law.* Washington, DC: Center on Budget and Policy Priorities.

Tilly, C. (1998). "Reversing the spread of lousy jobs." *Uncommon Sense*, no. 20. New York: National Jobs for All Coalition, unpaged.

Tufts University Center on Hunger, Poverty and Nutrition Policy. (1997). *Analysis of the Capacity of the Second Harvest Network to Cover the Federal Food Stamp Shortfall from 1997 to 2002*. Medford, MA: Author, July.

———. (1998). *Are States Improving the Lives of Poor Families? A Scale Measure of State Welfare Policies*. Medford, MA: Author, February.

Uchitelle, L. (1999). "Minimum wages, city by city." *New York Times*, November 19, pp. C1, C19.

———. (2000). "A retirement plan that Wall Street likes." *New York Times*, November 12, pp. C1, C8.

U.S. Bureau of the Census. (2000a). *Money Income in the United States: 1999*. Current Population Reports, P60–209. Washington, DC: U.S. Government Printing Office.

———. (2000b). *Poverty in the United States: 1999*. Current Population Reports, P60–210. Washington, DC: U.S. Government Printing Office.

U.S. Bureau of the Census, Housing and Household Economics, Statistics Division. (1988). Current Population Reports, CPS Supplement. Washington, DC, March.

U.S. Congress. (1996). Public Law 104–193. "Personal Responsibility and Work Opportunity Reconciliation Act of 1996," August 22.

U.S. Congress, Congressional Budget Office. (2000). *Budget of the United States Government: Fiscal Year 2000, Analytic Perspectives*. Washington, DC: U.S. Government Printing Office.

U.S. Department of Housing and Urban Development. (1999). *Now Is the Time: Places Left Behind in the New Economy*. Washington, DC: Author.

U.S. Department of Labor. (1999). *Report on the American Workforce*. Washington, DC: Author.

U.S. Department of Labor, Bureau of Labor Statistics. (2000a). "Comparative real gross domestic product per capita and per employed persons: Fourteen countries, 1960–1998," Unpublished data. Washington, DC, March 30. Available on the Internet at ftp://ftp.bls.gov/pub/special.requests/ForeignLabor/flsgdp.txt (visited May 2, 2000).

———. (2000b). "Union members in 1999." Washington, DC, January 19, unpublished report. Available on the Internet at ftp://146.142.4.23/pub/news.release/union2.txt (visited March 30, 2000).

U.S. House of Representatives, Committee on Ways and Means. (1996). *1996 Green Book: Background Material and Data on Programs within the Jurisdiction of the Committee on Ways and Means*. Washington, DC: U.S. Government Printing Office.

———. (1998). *1998 Green Book: Background Material and Data on Programs within the Jurisdiction of the Committee on Ways and Means*. Washington, DC: U.S. Government Printing Office.

Western, B., and K. Beckett. (1999). "How unregulated is the U.S. labor market? The penal system as a labor market institution." *American Journal of Sociology* 104 (January): 1030–1060.

Wilensky, H. L. (1965). "Introduction to the paperbound edition: The problems and prospects of the welfare state." In H. L. Wilensky and C. N. Lebeaux, *Industrial Society and Social Welfare*. New York: Free Press, pp. v–liii.

Wilson, W. J. (1996). *When Work Disappears: The World of the New Urban Poor*. New York: Vintage Books.

Winerup, M. (1999). "Bedlam on the streets." *New York Times Magazine*, May 23, pp. 42–49, 56, 65–66, 70.

Wood, A. (1994). *North-South Trade, Employment and Inequality*. Oxford: Clarendon Press.

Woodbury, S. A., and M. A. Rubin. (1997). "The duration of benefits." In C. J. O'Leary and S. A. Wandner, eds., *Unemployment Insurance in the United States: Analysis of Policy Issues*. Kalamazoo, MI: W. E. Upjohn Institute for Employment Research.

Woolhandler, S., and D. U. Himmelstein. (1994). "Universal care: Not from Clinton." *New York Times*, March 11, p. A31.

Chapter 3

Downloading the Welfare State, Canadian Style

Patricia M. Evans

INTRODUCTION

T. H. Marshall (1964) characterized the twentieth century as the era of struggle for the social rights of citizenship, comparing it to the struggles in the eighteenth and nineteenth centuries to entrench civil and political rights. "Welfare capitalism" captured the reality of a reasonably interventionist state that accepted some measure of responsibility for ensuring a social safety net to soften the fallout from a free market economy. As Esping-Andersen (1996, p. 1) suggests, "The modern welfare state became an intrinsic part of capitalism's postwar 'Golden Age,' an era in which prosperity, equality, and full employment seemed in perfect harmony." Although the semblance of "perfect harmony" may be overstated, the so-called Keynesian welfare state appeared to marry, in principle at least, the broad objectives of capitalism and social protection with a fair degree of compatibility.

However, the gilt is rapidly wearing thin on that Golden Age. Economic problems, sparked by the oil crisis in the mid-1970s, disrupted the pattern of stable post-war growth, fueled government debt and deficits, and eased the emergence of neoliberal governments in the 1980s. The rapidly escalating concerns about the increasing competitiveness of the "global economy" in the 1990s, have, some suggest, transformed the "welfare" state into the "farewell" state. Rather than viewed as the solution to the problems of production and distribution in a capitalist economy, the welfare state is now targeted as the problem.

Canada, along with the United Kingdom, the United States, Australia, and New Zealand, has been classified as a "liberal welfare-state regime"

(Esping-Andersen, 1990). This version of the welfare state has a distinctly residual cast, with a heavy reliance on means testing while offering few, if any, universal programs, compared to its counterparts in Western Europe and Scandinavia. However, there are also important differences in national social welfare provision among the liberal bloc of welfare states.

In comparison to the United States, Canada's social safety net has captured a broader section of the population, covered a more comprehensive set of risks, and delivered higher levels of benefits. As a result, Canadian unemployment, welfare, and pension benefits traditionally have been more effective in buffering the impact of the growing inequalities in market incomes (Blank and Hanratty, 1993; Myles, 1996; Banting, 1997). Between 1984 and 1993, years in which income inequality rose sharply in the United States, the share of income belonging to Canadian families in the lowest income quintile actually increased, and improvements in government transfers helped to offset a 32 percent drop in earnings (Lochhead and Shalla, 1996; Banting, 1997). However, as this chapter makes clear, the Canadian social safety net is now considerably more fragile.

Canada is a rich country, and in this study only the United States surpasses its standard of living (gross domestic product [GDP] per capita). It devotes a relatively high proportion of the GDP to public spending and, among the 29 Organisation for Economic Co-operation and Development (OECD) countries, ranks eighth, along with Germany (OECD, 1997b, p. 45). However, the proportion that is spent on social protection falls below that of all of the major OECD countries, except the United States, Australia, and Japan (OECD, 1997a, p. 65). Between 1992 and 1998, federal expenditures on health, social services, and education fell by 23 percent.[1] Despite the surplus and the spending increases announced in the 2000–2001 budget, federal program spending, as a percentage of the GDP, fell to the lowest level since the 1950s (Canadian Labour Congress, 2000). The federal government's presence in social welfare is disappearing, the traditional protection offered by transfer payments has declined, and the only universal program that remains is Medicare, Canada's health insurance program.

All levels of government have pursued an aggressive deficit-reduction agenda that has curtailed the public sector and imposed significant cuts to social programs. The impacts of these cuts have fallen disproportionately on low-income Canadians, who are most vulnerable to decreases in income transfers and other social services. The cuts also fall heavily on women, who not only lose an important source of employment as the public sector declines but must increase their unpaid caring work as services are reduced (Luxton and Reiter, 1997). While the downward trend in social spending has been reversed in 1999 and 2000 with slight improvements in spending, the social welfare landscape has been radically altered.

This chapter explores the Canadian version of welfare state retrenchment, which Pierson (1994, p. 1) describes as a "distinctive and difficult political enterprise." The first section discusses several aspects of Canadian distinctiveness that are important in understanding the economic and political landscape of retrenchment. The remaining sections explore the extent and nature of changes in Canadian welfare provision that have occurred in response to the pressures of globalization, changing labor markets, and the "hollowing out" (Jessop, 1993) of the nation-state.

THE LANDSCAPE OF RETRENCHMENT

Geography, Identity, and Trade

One of Canada's prime ministers wryly commented that some countries have "too much history, but Canada's problem is too much geography" (cited in Lipset, 1990, p. 56). Canada's geography has, indeed, featured prominently in shaping its social and economic landscape. Canada's population (30 million) is about one-tenth of the population of the United States, but its landmass is second only to that of the former Soviet Union. Because much of the land is inhospitable, most Canadians live within a 150-mile belt stretched out along the U.S. border, creating a powerful north–south axis. The fragility of Canadian nationhood is further complicated by the linguistic and cultural divisions that were so very evident in the breathtakingly close vote on Quebec separation in the 1995 referendum.[2] Nonetheless, some part of a Canadian identity is reflected in the self-image of a more compassionate country than its neighbor to the south. Canada's universal health care system is perhaps the most obvious point of contrast and reflects what is generally regarded as a more collectively oriented and interventionist state (Lipset, 1990; LeClerc, 1991; O'Connor, Orloff, and Shaver, 1999).[3]

Canada's abundant natural resources have been the traditional staple of foreign trade; conversely, manufacturing was later to develop than in England or in the United States and remains comparatively weak. It is exceptionally vulnerable to the ebbs and flows of the U.S. market, and over 80 percent of exports are shipped across the southern border, making it more dependent upon a single market than any other G-7 country (Banting and Simeon, 1997). One of the consequences is that New York's bond market evaluation of Canada's deficit has nearly as much influence on budgetary policy as the Toronto Stock Exchange (Albo and Jenson, 1997, p. 217).

The Canada–United States Free Trade Agreement (FTA) of 1989 and the inclusion of Mexico into the North American Free Trade Agreement (NAFTA) in 1994 expand and tighten these economic ties, raising concerns about a downward pressure on social benefits. Wiseman (1996, p. 123) suggests that the "most powerful and most disturbing explanation for the severity of the assault on Canada's welfare state tradition is the downward pressure on wages, working conditions and social programs arising from the internationalization of the Canadian economy and, in particular, the impact of so-called free trade agreements."

Inequality and the Labor Market

While the employment picture in virtually all the OECD countries has deteriorated since the mid-1970s, the Canadian labor market has been described as offering the worst of both worlds, a combination of "European-style unemployment levels and American-style polarization" (Betcherman, 1996, p. 251). Headlines such as, "Unemployment Up despite Rise in Jobs" (cited in Swift, 1997, p. 35) attest to the fragile linkages among economic growth, job creation, and increased earnings. Unemployment averaged 7.6 percent in 1999, and this was the fifth consecutive year that the rate fell below the double-digit levels that characterized the early 1990s. However, the declining unemployment rate has resulted in only a very slight improvement in the proportion of the population actually employed.[4] The explanation appears to be an increase in the number of "discouraged" workers who are not actively looking for work. In 1989, 21 percent of the unemployed had not worked in the preceding 12 months; by 1997 this number had grown to 38 percent (Little, 1998).

Gaps in market income are also widening for those who are employed: as the hourly wages of younger workers decline, fewer workers are full-time and full-year, and higher-paid workers are working longer weeks (Glenday, 1997). Canadians with low earnings did not simply lose out relative to higher-paid workers; they lost out in absolute terms. The earnings of those in the bottom fifth of family income distribution fell by 32 percent between 1984 and 1993, although, as noted earlier, increases in transfer payments helped to maintain their overall share of total income (Lochhead and Shalla, 1996).

There has been a narrowing of the gender gap in earnings, employment participation, and job tenure, but these improvements in women's labor market position must be viewed in the context of the changing economy. Some of these gains are attributed to the deteriorating conditions of men's work and the "feminizing" of the labor market as it "harmonizes down" in the global economy (Armstrong, 1996a). Women whose earnings improved generally had benefited from good jobs in health, education, and social services. But between 1992 and 1996, public sector jobs, typically unionized, were lost, while private sector employment increased slightly, and self-employment increased significantly.[5] In 1995, almost two-thirds of private sector women workers and 70 percent of self-employed women earned less than $20,000 a year; this was true for less than one-third of the women who worked in the public sector (Scott and Lochhead, 1997).

Membership in Canadian unions has not shown the decline that has occurred in the United States. Approximately 30 percent of the Canadian workforce remains unionized. This is double the proportion of unionized workers in the United States, and differences in union coverage are attributed, in part, to a highly unionized and larger Canadian public sector (Banting, 1997).[6] Collective bargaining, however, has weakened in the traditional sectors of mining, manufacturing, and construction. In addition, the traditionally strong union presence in the public sector has not prevented considerable downsizing at both federal and provincial levels.

Although the recovering economy produces new jobs, the jobs are frequently short-term and part-time. Recent evidence suggests that the gap between rich and poor is now widening, and government transfers are not offering the same degree of income protection against losses in earnings. Statistics Canada (1998) reported an increase in after-tax income inequality in 1996 due in part to deteriorating levels of income support.[7] Although poverty declined slightly from 1996 to 1997, the rates remain stubbornly high despite improvements in the economy. The poverty rate in 1997 was 17.5 percent, down .4 percent from 1996. However, 20 years earlier, the 1977 rate stood at 13.3 percent, or 24 percent lower (Battle, 1999). Between 1989 and 1997, the low-income population had expanded by 39 percent (Statistics Canada, 1999). As Morisette, Myles, and Picot (1995, p. 24) suggest, "Rising inequality in the labor market means more work for the welfare state or, alternatively, rising poverty and a decline in aggregate social welfare."

The Restructuring Discourse

Rising inequality in the labor market has not meant that the Canadian welfare state has assumed more responsibilities. Rather, Canada has followed the lead of the OECD (1994) and is responding to the competitive global market by efforts to increase labor market "flexibility" and a concerted program of deficit reduction. This has led to severe cuts in unemployment insurance at the federal level, deteriorating levels of social assistance payments across most of the 10 Canadian provinces, and cutbacks in funding for social services. The economic, political, and social bases of the welfare state are changing. Spending on social welfare, no longer viewed as producing positive counter-cyclical effects such as maintaining purchasing power in a relatively sheltered economy, is now seen as a drag on the ability of a nation-state to compete in an increasingly internationalized economy.

Canadian politics in the 1980s did not produce the strong neoliberal discourse that was spearheaded by Thatcher in Britain or Reagan in the United States. Nonetheless, the Conservative government of Brian Mulroney, elected in 1983 and remaining in power for a decade, made important incursions into the Canadian social welfare landscape while speaking of social programs as a "sacred trust" (Evans, 1994). These inroads have deepened and widened since the 1993 election of the Liberal government of Jean Chrétien. Despite an election platform that promised gradual deficit reduction, his government has been more successful in promoting a radical and rapid deficit-reduction agenda than could have been imagined during the Mulroney years. The victories of neoliberal provincial governments in Alberta (1992) and Ontario (1995) and the ascendance of the populist, right-wing (at least in the Canadian context) Reform Party as the federal official opposition have helped to solidify a discourse that appears to have succeeded in altering Canadians' expectations of their government's role in social welfare. Polling data suggest that no more than 13 percent of Canadians thought that deficit reduction should be an important governmental priority during the Conservative years; shortly before the 1995 Liberal budget, this had risen to 48 percent (Maslove and Moore, 1997). Even traditionally social-democratic-leaning Quebec has cut back significantly on social spending.

No one would argue that Canada's deficit has not been a problem. In 1993, it was second only to Italy's among the G-7 countries (Canada, 1994). However, the evidence suggests that the deficit was not caused by dramatic increases in social spending but resulted from decreases in government revenue, effects of high interest rates, and tight monetary policy that dampened economic growth and led to higher levels of unemployment (see, e.g., Cohen, 1997; Maslove and Moore, 1997). The Chrétien government has moved consistently ahead of its deficit-reduction targets. The 1998 budget announced an elimination of the deficit that had stood at $19 billion, while the 1999 and 2000 budgets were in surplus, some of which has been allocated to increased spending. However, as this chapter suggests, the hardships imposed on Canadians were severe. The political consequences of aggressive deficit reduction also became apparent. A later section of the chapter details the recent injections of funds into health care budgets to allay the escalating concerns of Canadians about overcrowding, waiting lists, and a deterioration in nursing care.

The process of restructuring "involves a complex displacement of the state power and political terrain once occupied by the welfare state" (Brodie, 1996, p. 389). The restructuring discourse portrays less government spending in general and a reduced welfare state in particular as the inevitable, necessary, and desirable "adaptations" to forces that are considered beyond the control of individuals and nations. While deficit reduction was more prominent in the early 1990s, the need to compete in the globalizing economy became a more important rationale for cutbacks that occurred in the mid-1990s. At the end of the decade, we began to see some reinvestments in targeted areas such as health care. But even if this signals a general loosening of spending restraint, an important transformation of the Canadian welfare state has taken place. The particular nature of Canadian welfare state retrenchment and the impacts on its people are the subjects of the remainder of this chapter. The next section considers the declining role of the federal government in social programs that have traditionally been viewed as important instruments of nation-building in the Canadian federation.

THE DISAPPEARING FEDERAL PRESENCE

The Canadian version of federalism is far more decentralized than its U.S. counterpart, and federal–provincial relations represent a significant and continuing impediment to Canadian policy making. The government in Ottawa has never possessed the power and influence that characterize the relationship between Washington and the 50 states; the 10 provinces, together, spend and collect more than the federal government (Simeon and Willis, 1997). Regional, linguistic, and cultural divisions intersect and reinforce the influence of the provinces and constitute the cleavages (similar to race within the United States) that factor significantly into the politics of social policy. Provincial influence is most apparent in the case of Quebec, whose governments have consistently fought for maximum control over its own policies.

The combined authority of the executive and the legislature in a parliamentary system has nonetheless facilitated an important federal presence in Canadian social policy (Simeon and Willis, 1997). In the past, the federal government exerted considerable influence, spearheading universal programs such as Old Age Security, Family Allowances, and Medicare. Throughout the 1960s, Canada responded to the growing issue of poverty with a "transfer-intensive" strategy, which included a major expansion in unemployment insurance and social assistance, as well as the initiation of contributory pensions and an income-tested supplement for the elderly.

The role of the federal government in social programs has changed, however. The 1980s were characterized by a steady and relatively quiet erosion of the welfare state, accomplished by a series of technical and incremental changes (Mishra, 1990; Lightman and Irving, 1991; Evans, 1994). Paul Pierson (1994) suggests that this obfuscating strategy reduces the visibility of policy changes and plays a key role in diminishing the political resistance to retrenchment. The Canadian tradition of "social policy by stealth" (Battle, 1990), so dominant in the 1980s, was taken over in the 1990s by a highly explicit and articulated program of social spending cuts and restructuring that followed on the heels of the 1993 Liberal electoral victory. As the federal government retreats from social programs, it also distances itself from the immediate implications of changes in the economy, changes that will have increasing repercussions for the provinces (Rice, 1995). The diminishing presence of the federal government is illustrated in the next section through several interrelated trends: downloading the costs of social programs, significant shifts in funding for health and child care, damaging cuts to income support programs, including social assistance and unemployment insurance, and the elimination of universality in favor of increased targeting in child and elderly benefits.

Downloading the Costs

When Upper and Lower Canada were joined by the 1867 Act of Confederation, jurisdiction over social welfare was given to the provinces, but the power to raise revenue was assigned to the federal government. Traditionally, this structural imbalance between the responsibility to provide social welfare and the ability to pay for it has been mediated by federal–provincial cost-sharing agreements, the transfer of some tax revenue to the provinces, and equalization payments that redistribute income to the poorer provinces. Given that the federal government cannot regulate areas of provincial jurisdiction, this "spending power" represents the single, but very powerful, instrument available to Ottawa to influence the scope and quality of Canada's social programs.

A hallmark of Canadian social legislation, the Canada Assistance Plan (CAP), which was in place from 1966 to 1995, exemplified the use of the federal spending power to promote national standards and encourage the expansion of provincial social assistance programs and social services. Through CAP, the federal government matched, dollar for dollar, all provincial spending on social assistance and specified services, such as child care, counseling, child welfare, rehabilitative services, and homemaker services. In order to take advantage of this financial incentive, provinces were required to meet only three conditions. First, eligibility had to be determined solely with reference to need. This provision prohibited provinces from categorically excluding particular recipients (e.g., single persons able to work) and was generally interpreted to ban workfare as a condition of social assistance. Second, no residence requirements could be imposed as a condition of benefit. Finally, provinces were required to provide appeal mechanisms in their social assistance procedures.

The federal presence in social programs began to diminish in 1990, when the Mulroney government announced the first major alteration to CAP since its inception. The "cap on CAP" limited annual increases to no more than 5 percent in the three wealthiest provinces (Alberta, British Columbia, and Ontario) and was intended to curtail what was viewed as the increasingly troublesome, open-ended nature of the federal spending obligation. Ontario, the largest province, was badly hit because social assistance costs were rapidly rising, partly in response to a recession. In 1992–1993, instead of receiving 50 percent of the costs, the federal share amounted to only 28 cents of every dollar spent on social assistance and needs-based social services in Ontario.[8]

In contrast to CAP, a very different mechanism was used to fund the federal contribution toward the costs of health care and post-secondary education. In 1977, the Liberal government of Pierre Trudeau introduced the Established Programs Financing Act (EPF) and replaced cost-sharing with an unconditional annual "block" grant that was determined in relation to gross national product (GNP) and population. There was no requirement that the funds be spent on health and post-secondary education, although financial sanctions could be invoked if a province failed to meet the five conditions of the Canada Health Act, which forms the foundation for Canada's universal health care system.[9] In 1990, the Mulroney government froze EPF payments, and the federal contribution to health and post-secondary institutions began to decline (Maslove, 1996).

The Mulroney government's cutbacks to CAP and EPF downloaded the costs of social programs to the provinces and weakened the influence of the federal government. With the introduction of the 1995 Canada Health and Social Transfer (CHST), the Liberals abandoned the principles of CAP and retreated even further from federal responsibility for social programs. The CHST combines all federal contributions to health, post-secondary education, social assistance, and needs-based social services into one giant annual "mega" transfer to the provinces. The CHST was opposed by virtually all advocacy groups, and was called "the worst social policy move in a generation" (Battle and Torjman, 1996, p. 57). In a measure that was designed primarily to reduce federal social spending, there was little apparent consideration paid to its serious implications for social programs.[10]

The CHST has eliminated the fiscal carrots of the 50:50 CAP cost-sharing provisions that had helped to underwrite the expansion and maintenance of need-based benefits and services. Through the mechanism of the CHST, the federal government has abdicated a powerful and important role and has sharply reduced its contribution to social programs. In the last year of CAP (1995), spending decreased by 1 percent from the previous year; the introduction of the CHST was accompanied by a 23 percent decline in transfers, followed by further decreases (Maslove, 1996). Taking into account the effects of population growth and inflation, the overall per capita federal transfer for social programs decreased by 40 percent between 1993 and 1997, with the deepest cuts occurring under the CHST (National Anti-Poverty Organization [NAPO], 1998). Even with the increases announced in the 1999 budget, the value of the cash transfers remained below pre-1995 levels (Battle, Torjman, and Mendelson, 1999).[11]

The implementation of the CHST represents a significant retreat from a general federal responsibility for social programs. While Medicare receives some protection from the Canada Health Act, there is no longer a meaningful mechanism for a strong federal influence in articulating, promoting, and upholding national standards in social programs. The CHST has been called a "foundational pillar in the construction of the New Social Union—

a redefinition of the rights, roles, and responsibilities between Canadian citizens and their governments, among governments of the federation, and between markets and society" (Bach and Phillips, 1997, p. 241).

In February 1999, after three years of consultations that were initiated in the wake of the unilateral change from CAP to the CHST, federal and provincial governments (with the exception of Quebec) agreed to an operational framework that is intended to improve cooperation on social policy. The "Social Union" agreement effectively rewrites some of the ground rules of federal–provincial relations and places constraints on federal spending power. It requires all levels of government to give advance notice and provide for prior consultation before implementing any major changes in social policy, and the federal government must provide one year's notice of any significant change in funding and agrees not to introduce new initiatives without the agreement of a majority of the provinces. The agreement is pragmatic, rather than philosophical, the constraints on new federal initiatives are controversial, and advocacy groups were disappointed by the failure to articulate common standards for social programs and to establish an enforceable right to adequate social assistance.[12]

Retrenching Social Programs

Spending restraints have led to a variety of cost-cutting measures that limit public responsibility and increase the reliance on the private sector and families (i.e., women). This section addresses recent changes in two social policy arenas that shift the balance of responsibility among states, markets, and families: health care and child care.

There has certainly been a rebalancing in the responsibility for health care. In 1984, the federal share of health care costs amounted to 33 percent; by 1995, it had decreased to 21 percent, and it shrank further under the CHST (Maslove, 1996). As the federal contribution to the costs of health care has declined, the private share increased from 25 percent in 1991 to over 30 percent in 1996 (NAPO, 1998). Armstrong and Armstrong (1996) document the variety of forms that privatization has taken. Provinces "delist" some previously insured services; these can include children's dental programs and eye examinations, as well as health coverage for those traveling outside Canada. User fees are also on the increase, and patients may be expected to pay for a variety of services such as sickness certificates required by employers, medical examinations for insurance purposes, and telephone prescriptions. Prescription drug coverage for social assistance recipients has eroded with the introduction of co-payments and deductibles. Similar measures are also evident in the four provinces that have universal drug plans, which are particularly important to the working poor (NAPO, 1998).

Advances in medical technologies allow for earlier discharges, and across the OECD countries, there is a general trend toward fewer hospital beds and shorter hospital stays (OECD, 1997b, pp. 48–49). However, there are concerns about the scope, speed, and impact of a hospital restructuring process that is primarily fiscally driven. From the mid-1980s to the 1990s, one-third of the staffed hospital beds across Canada disappeared. In Ontario, a recent study recommended a slowdown to restructuring and documented the deterioration in patient care that included less nursing time and supervision per patient, high levels of employee stress, and problematic delays in recording patient data (NAPO, 1998).

Cutbacks in hospital beds and nursing care increase the reliance on relatives and friends (i.e., women) to "pick up the slack" by providing care in the home that can include giving injections and inserting catheters and taking on more tasks such as feeding, in relation to inpatient care. In contrast to hospital services, home-care programs expanded during the 1990s. In 1996, some home-care services in Toronto were delivered, for the first time, on a 24-hour basis to cope with discharged patients who were too ill to look after themselves (Neysmith, 1998). Home-care services are the fastest growing component of health spending, but they continue to represent a very small proportion (4 percent) of public expenditures, despite an increasing number of elderly people and a decreasing number of hospital beds (Canada, 1999). The downloading of health costs—from federal to provincial governments, from doctor to nurse, from nurse to family—has the greatest impact on women because they form "the majority of those employed in health care, of those receiving services, and of those providing care in the home" (Armstrong, 1996b, p. 27).

While the federal government can continue to impose penalties on the provinces that violate the provisions of the Canada Health Act (CHA), this leverage diminishes as its share of the cost declines. There are growing concerns about "two-tiered" health care in which access to service divides "payers" from "non-payers." Alberta presents the clearest challenge to the principles of the CHA. This province has established private clinics that are currently permitted to provide only a limited range of services (such as cataract removal), but legislation tabled in March 2000 allows for a much broader range in services. The premier of Ontario has indicated his government's interest in user fees. As cuts in health care spending erode services, and the waiting lists for surgical procedures grow, a two-tiered system becomes more attractive to many Canadians. A 1998 survey found that 26 percent of Canadians thought that the health system was in need of fundamental change, in comparison to 5 percent a decade earlier (Coutts, 1998). A recent poll discovered that health care is identified by a majority of Canadians (55 percent) as the top political priority, dwarfing all other issues (Gee, 2000).

The political fallout from the cuts to health care has been serious, and recent federal and provincial budgets reflect the importance of reassuring

Canadians about the state of Medicare. In April 1999, the Ontario Progressive Conservatives tabled a budget a day before announcing a June election. The budget increased health spending by 20 percent over five years and included funds to hire 10,000 new nurses, the number of nurses who had been let go during the previous 10 years of downsizing. The 1999 federal budget announced a CHST increase of $8 billion over five years, specifically targeted to health care spending and an immediate CHST health care supplement of $3.5 billion.[13] Although a significant increase, it does not restore funding to previous levels, nor has it been indexed to inflation or economic growth (Battle, Torjman, and Mendelson, 1999). Additional funding may alleviate, but does not fundamentally alter, the direction in Canadian health care to an increased reliance on markets and families. This is a shift that affects the most vulnerable: those with the greatest reliance on health care and those who can least afford to substitute and/or supplement services by purchasing through the private sector.

Child-care provision is an area of social spending with particular implications for women. Although proposals for child-care reform have been on the federal political agenda for over a decade, there has been no movement toward a national program of affordable and accessible child care. Across the provinces, child care has remained a patchwork of underfunded services and variable regulations. Nonetheless, there were a number of improvements during the 1980s. Most provinces began to provide direct funding to regulated child-care services, helping to increase the supply and their financial stability.[14] From 1984 to 1990, annual increases in the number of regulated child-care spaces ranged between 10 and 23 percent (Friendly and Oloman, 1996). As Evelyn Ferguson (1998, p. 203) comments about the late 1980s, "the highly public and political nature of the child-care dilemma, with its attendant task force reports and studies, prominence in party leaders' debates . . . was seen as an important development because it moved the caring debate into the political arena."

The optimism of the 1980s, however, faded in the 1990s. Despite a 1993 Liberal election promise to expand the number of regulated child-care spaces by 41 percent over three years, the reality was a 34 percent shrinkage in the federal contribution to child care between 1993 and 1998 (Bach and Phillips, 1997).[15] The number of regulated child-care spaces did not increase by more than 4 percent between 1991 and 1995, and in some provinces, the number actually declined (calculated from Doherty, Friendly, and Oloman, 1998, p. 26). In addition, most provinces froze, reduced, or eliminated direct operating grants to child-care centers, some provinces devolved regulatory responsibility to municipalities, and resources dedicated to monitoring operating standards were reduced.

Child-care subsidies were increasingly targeted in the 1990s. In the 1980s, child-care settings reflected a range of socioeconomic backgrounds, and the simple criteria used for assessing income meant that subsidies did not carry a "welfare" stigma.[16] However, reflecting a combination of cutbacks and a new emphasis on workfare, subsidies are increasingly used to ensure that single mothers on social assistance can enter the workforce, and the subsidy assessment has become more complicated and intrusive. As a result, there is concern in the child-care community that the restricted use of child-care subsidies may change the socioeconomic mix that currently characterizes center-based care (Doherty, Friendly, and Oloman, 1998).

The increasing labor force rates of Canadian women, particularly those with young children, suggest that the unregulated child-care sector is increasing, although it already provides 80–90 percent of the care of all children (Ferguson, 1998). In metropolitan Toronto, there are 22,600 children in subsidized spaces, with another 16,000 children on the waiting list (Metro Task Force on Services to Young Children and Families, 1997). While unregulated care can be very good, regulated care is generally considered to provide greater continuity and more effectively meet the developmental needs of children (Doherty, Friendly, and Oloman, 1998). It is also the sector that provides better wages and working conditions.

Although a national child-care program is not on the agenda, the 2000 federal budget extended the combined maternity and parental leave from six months to one year. However, the parental leave program is administered under unemployment insurance and, as a later section examines, eligibility for these benefits has been severely restricted.

It is difficult to locate systematic material on the impact of retrenchment on general social services. However, a survey of community-based agencies in metropolitan Toronto found that more than four times as many agencies closed in 1996, compared to 1992 and 1994 (33 versus 7). There were other indications of sector stress: the majority of agencies experienced decreases in funding at the same time that service demand increased. More than a third of the agencies had reduced their full-time staff, and over a quarter reported reductions to part-time staff. The authors of the report note: "These cuts have been pervasive and affect the ability of the remaining staff to sustain service delivery and meet client need" (Social Planning Council, 1997, p. 24). Based on the information collected, future cutbacks were expected to fall most heavily on the overlapping categories of services directed to women, immigrants and refugees, and low-income families.

Squeezing Social Assistance

Perhaps the clearest and most problematic impact of the fading federal presence occurs in the area of provincial social assistance. Not only does the CHST drastically reduce the federal contribution to social assistance, but also there is no longer any requirement for provinces to spend it on social assistance; whether they spend a lot or a little, the amount of the federal transfer remains the same. The CHST gives provinces every political incentive to minimize their spending on the historically unpopular welfare program and divert as much funding as possible to the programs that receive more voter support, such as health care (or to underwrite the even more popular tax cuts). The CHST also reduces national standards in provincial welfare: the single condition that provinces must now meet to receive funds, without penalty, is to uphold the federal ban on residence requirements. Provinces are no longer required to provide assistance on the basis of need alone and can, theoretically at least, cut certain "undeserving" categories of recipients off the rolls, such as single employables. While this has occurred in some U.S. states, such an action would have been impossible in Canada before the abolition of CAP. There is no evidence that provinces are completely abandoning their appeal structures, but the National Council of Welfare (NCW) (1997a), a citizen advisory body, reports limitations in the kinds of decisions that can be appealed and an increase in the rigidity of provincial appeal processes.

The deterioration of the safety net was particularly evident in the 1990s. In what is called a "devastating effect" of federal cuts, all provinces, struggling with their own deficits, froze benefit rates at some point during the 1990s. But in addition to the freeze, the majority of recipients in most provinces experienced benefit cuts. Single, employable people were hit hardest. From 1990 to 1996, eight provinces reduced the real value of benefits to single people by amounts that ranged from 11 to 43 percent (NCW, 1997a). Single parents also experienced significant decreases in a majority of provinces, and the hardest hit were those in Ontario, the province with the largest number of recipients. Ontario cut its benefits by 22 percent for all recipients except those with disabilities. But benefit levels were not the only dimension of welfare tightening.

In a province-by-province review, the NCW (1997a) documented other changes that had taken place in social assistance during the 1990s. The report identified several disturbing trends. First, the availability of "special assistance" to meet those needs not covered by basic benefits had been considerably restricted as provinces cut these budgets, eliminating eligible items and tightening the eligibility rules. In addition, some previous categories of recipients were deemed ineligible, such as single parents attending universities and 16- and 17-year-olds in family circumstances that made it impossible for them to live at home. Finally, the level of administrative scrutiny of welfare recipients has increased dramatically, and campaigns to curb "welfare abuse" have gained a new prominence and visibility. The announcement of additional resources dedicated to new welfare "fraud squads" followed by claims of large savings that are regularly disputed by independent studies (NCW, 1997a). In Ontario, mandatory random home visits and a toll-free "snitch line" have been introduced (Morrison, 1997). Recent legislation also subjects single mothers to workfare requirements, curtails the right to appeal, and opens up the future possibility of privately administered welfare (Torjman, 1997).

Workfare programs and the tightening of job-search verification have also increased across the country, although this trend was evident before the arrival of the CHST. Prior to its elimination, the interpretation of CAP was changing, and workfare-type programs were in operation with little apparent constraint (Evans, 1995). Nonetheless, while there has always been considerable variation in the benefits and regulations that accompanied welfare receipt across the provinces, the CHST has eliminated any meaningful federal participation in, and responsibility for, the entire arena of social assistance.

Retracting (Un)Employment Insurance

Unlike social assistance, unemployment insurance is a federal responsibility, and it has been subject to cutbacks over a number of years. As early as 1984, the Mulroney government identified the need to cut back on provisions that were seen as too generous, but it was not until 1989 that major changes were announced. First, approximately $2 billion of federal funding was eliminated from the program, leaving it entirely funded by employer and employee contributions. In cutting its contribution, the federal government further distanced itself from the financial consequences of policies criticized for increasing unemployment, such as free trade and high interest rates.[17] Second, a number of changes were made that reduced the amount of benefits, increased the number of weeks of employment required to qualify, decreased the maximum weeks of receipt, and disqualified those who were judged to have left their employment voluntarily.

A shift from the Mulroney Conservatives to the Chrétien Liberals in 1993 did not alter the direction of unemployment insurance policy. Although the Liberals made cuts early in their term, the major overhaul occurred in 1996, when the Chrétien government unveiled the latest in a series of changes to a program that presented an obvious target in a climate concerned about both reducing the deficit and improving "labor market flexibility." Following the language used in the influential *OECD Jobs Study* (1994) that emphasized the need for "active" rather than "passive" labor market programs, the "Un" was dropped, and the program was retitled Employment Insurance (EI). A number of changes resulted in a 10 percent decrease in program spending. The major change was to shift from determining entitlement by the number of hours to the number of weeks worked. As a result, EI now includes some part-time workers who had been excluded because they worked less than 15 hours a week, and it removes the incentive for employers to restrict employment to under 15 hours per week. However, the number of hours now required for eligibility has more than doubled, and it has tripled for new labor market entrants.[18] The result has been an 18 percent decline in claims since the 1996 changes were introduced. Although these changes were supposed to improve the position of the "non-standard" worker, young people and women were particularly hard hit (Canada Employment Insurance Commission, 1998).[19]

EI also severs the traditional link between contributions and benefits in social insurance. For the first time, some users at the high end of the income scale will have their benefits completely taxed back. At the same time, the benefit level for low earners with dependents was raised and increased further to 80 percent of previous earnings by 2000 (Stoyko, 1997). The revamped EI also includes cost-cutting measures: further reductions in the maximum period of benefits, a decrease in the level of insurable earnings, an increase in the penalties for "frequent" users, and a lower income threshold for taxing-back benefits.

The cumulative impact of changes made in the 1990s has been nothing short of draconian. The proportion of the unemployed who received benefits declined from 83 percent in 1990 to 36 percent in 1998 (NAPO, 1998). The declining number of unemployed who can claim benefits shifts the responsibility for income support for the unemployed to families and to the provincial welfare caseloads and increases the poverty rates. It is hard to argue that the hardship that these cuts have imposed is necessary when the level of the surplus in the EI account now clearly exceeds the amount that can be justified as savings to call upon in case of a recession (Greenspon, 1998).

From Universality to Targeting: Child and Elderly Benefits

At the time that the Conservative government of Brian Mulroney took office in 1983, Canada had two demogrants that were directed to those at polar ends of the age spectrum. A small monthly Family Allowance (FA) was paid with respect to each child under the age of 18, and a much larger, monthly Old Age Security (OAS) benefit was available to all those 65 years and older, without regard to income or previous work record.[20] The universal nature of both of these benefits had eroded during the 1980s through a series of incremental steps, and by the time FA was eliminated, Canadians seemed not to notice.

In 1989, the Mulroney government introduced a "clawback" to FA and OAS that taxed back benefits to recipients whose income exceeded designated levels. The clawback effectively ended an important dimension of universality because some individuals and families had the entire value of their benefits recouped through the tax system, although they continued to receive their checks. The explicit and formal abolition of FA as a universal program occurred in 1993, when it was amalgamated with related income supplements and tax credits to form a single income-tested monthly benefit called the Child Tax Credit (CTC). In line with an emphasis on work incentives, the CTC increased the level of benefits to working poor, but not to welfare families. Consistent with an emphasis on targeted, rather than universal, programs, it reduced benefits to middle-income families and removed them altogether from high-income families (Battle and Mendelson, 1997). Although no longer universal, the policy direction in Canadian child benefits follows the Australian example by providing a broadly based, income-tested benefit that reaches more than 80 percent of Canadian families with children (Finance Canada, 1999).

A further restructuring of child benefits took effect in July 1998, and the direction of the changes suggests that a continuing objective was to increase work incentives. The new national child benefit, the Canada Child Tax Credit (CCTC), increases the amount of the transfer and begins to remove children from provincial social assistance caseloads.[21] Provinces reduce the welfare check by the amount of the increased child benefit so the income of families relying on social assistance does not change. In addition, provinces must direct the money saved to programs for working-poor families with children. The CCTC, along with health care, received a boost in the 1999 Liberal budget, which provided for an improvement in the level of benefits for both low-income and middle-income families, while the 2000 budget further improved benefits but targeted these to middle-income families only. The National Council of Welfare (1997b), while supporting the general thrust of the CCTC, has been critical of the level of benefits, the fact that the increases do not fully extend to children whose families are on welfare, and the government's failure to fully index child benefits. More recently, the Council has advocated spending available funds on child-care programs rather than the CCTC.

The formal appearance of universality lingered longer in seniors' benefits than it did in child benefits. Until 1996, benefits were mailed out to high-income seniors who, each year, paid back the value of the benefit through the tax system. In a policy direction very similar to the Mulroney government's introduction of the 1993 Child Tax Benefit, the Chrétien government had hoped to further increase targeting in benefits for the elderly. The proposed Seniors Benefit was to bundle OAS with other related income and tax benefits to provide a fully indexed and non-taxable benefit that would have excluded a larger proportion of higher-income households than is the case with OAS. In addition, the proposed Seniors Benefit was to shift income eligibility from an individual to a family basis, a shift that was criticized for its impact on married women (Townson, 1996). Those married women who spent most of their lives as homemakers would no longer have received a benefit in their own right, while some married women in paid work would have been ineligible for benefits on account of their husbands' incomes. However, others suggested that the claims of class should take priority over gender and estimated that for every affluent wife who failed to qualify, 50 lower-income women would be better off (Battle, 1997).

Although the new benefit was announced in 1996, it was not scheduled to take effect until 2001, with a promise that seniors receiving benefits at the time of implementation would not be adversely affected. Cutbacks that occur in the future postpone program savings but also offer important political advantages, such as deflecting opposition from the seniors' lobby. As retrenchment is an exercise in "blame avoidance," and as those who lose tend to be concentrated and therefore more likely to mobilize, such a strategy, Pierson (1994) suggests, can be critical to success. However, it does not guarantee success, and the commitment to the Seniors Benefit, which generated increasing criticism, was ultimately abandoned in the summer of 1998.

This section has reviewed changes that have lessened the visibility and the responsibility of the federal government for Canadian social programs. With the exception of child and elderly benefits, the restructured welfare state, in its pursuit of labor market flexibility and a resulting downward pressure on health care, child care, social assistance, and unemployment insurance benefits, has ensured that Canada's most vulnerable citizens bear the brunt of its downloading.

CONCLUSION

Liberal welfare states have responded to global competition and changing economies by efforts to increase labor market and wage flexibility. In the area of income security, this translates into approaches that increase selectivity, erode benefits and coverage, and emphasize workfare (Esping-Andersen, 1996). In the 1980s, Canadian "social policy by stealth" was much in evidence, and the Conservatives left the Liberals, who came to power in 1993, with a "legacy of precedents" (Prince, 1997). These included benefit clawbacks and de-indexation of child and elderly benefits, the more visible changes to the less popular unemployment insurance program, and the beginning of a change in the fiscal "rules" of funding social programs.

The Liberal government of Jean Chrétien, however, altered the stealthy erosion of social policy and embarked on a course that radically transformed the funding arrangements for means-tested income benefits and social services. The CHST eliminated a federal presence in social assistance and, through sharp reductions in the amount of the new mega-block transfer, saved federal funds while shifting the costs to the provinces. Despite coming into power on a platform that proclaimed job creation and economic growth as its major plank, this has been more or less abandoned, while reduction of the deficit was pursued with great vigor (Maslove and Moore, 1997). In the aftermath of deficit elimination in 1998, the Chrétien government has increased funding to health care and child benefits.

Two principal goals were identified in the 1994 discussion paper that launched the Liberals' major review of social security: the removal of work disincentives and reduction in child poverty (Canada, 1994, p. 74). The first objective has been pursued assiduously, but with more attention to the stick than the carrot. Changes in unemployment insurance, coupled with the lengthening spells of unemployment, have cut by half the proportion of unemployed workers who receive benefits. Provinces struggling with the federal downloading of social assistance costs are freezing or cutting benefits and implementing workfare programs; those with neoliberal governments pursue these policies with particular energy.[22] The efforts to ensure that people prefer work over welfare have special impacts on single mothers, who are much more likely than other groups to have to rely upon income from social assistance.

Despite the Liberals' commitment to maintain child benefits, child poverty has increased and in 1997 stood at 20 percent. This stands in sharp contrast to 1989, the year when the House of Commons passed an all-party resolution to eliminate child poverty by the year 2000; at that time 15 percent of Canada's children were poor (Battle, 1999). The Canada Child Tax Credit helps working-poor families with children but has not improved the position of two-thirds of poor children in Canada, those whose parents depend upon social assistance (NAPO, 1998). Parents who are employed or are looking for paid work, however, have not been helped by the fading commitment to child care that this chapter has documented.

By the time that the Chrétien government was elected in 1993, universality had ended in child and elderly benefits, although the well-off elderly continued to receive checks until 1996. Does the death of universality in Canadian income-transfer programs represent a serious retrenchment in a welfare state that has traditionally viewed its universal programs as a feature that distinguishes Canada from the United States? Keith Banting (1997, p. 269) refers to a "Canadian mythology" regarding universality. He compares spending on universal and selective programs in Canada and the United States and finds that in 1960 both countries were spending a high and almost identical portion (79 and 80 percent, respectively) of their income security dollars on universal programs. Over the years, however, Canadian dollars shifted to selective programs, while the U.S. proportion remained stable and then declined. By 1992, the majority of Canadian spending (52 percent) was directed toward selective programs; by comparison, the U.S. share had declined from 20 to 18 percent (Banting, 1997, p. 291). In part, this emphasis on selective or targeted transfers makes Canada's income security system more effective in reducing inequalities than has been the case in the United States.

If the political will is present, income-tested benefits can be structured to reach a significant proportion of a population. In 1995, nearly 4 of every 10 elderly individuals received a full or partial income-tested supplement in addition to their basic OAS (National Council of Welfare, 1996). Although this proportion is not so high as in earlier times, it is considerably larger than the 7 percent of elderly Americans who received Supplementary Security Income in 1993, and it helps to account for a poverty rate among the elderly in Canada that is one-third the U.S. rate (Myles, 1996; Banting, 1997). The Canada Child Tax Credit provides income-tested benefits to approximately 80 percent of Canadian families with children. These simply administered and non-stigmatized benefits maintain a number of the best features of universality, without the attendant costs. For these reasons, criticisms from influential parts of the progressive social policy lobby have been much more frequently directed to low levels of benefits, tax-back rates, and the level of income cutoffs than to the failure to maintain a universal component (see, e.g., National Council of Welfare, 1996, 1997b; Battle and Mendelson, 1997).

The ending of universal benefits for Canada's children and elderly has nonetheless eliminated social citizenship claims to income. No longer does Canada recognize a commitment to all its young and aged citizens. As Myles and Quadagno (1997, p. 255) note, "A readily available moral framework for adjusting to 'hard times' is the principle of need." Keith Banting (1997, p. 297) suggests that the exclusive use of a need-based model of income claims "is heightening a basic schizophrenia at the heart of the Canadian welfare state." The "wealthy banker's" wife or child generated little sympathy as their benefits were dismantled, and it remains to be seen whether a similar principle of need will be extended to health care. This chapter has identified the cuts that have taken place within health care, and arguments for a two-tiered system have gained credence within the ranks of the Canadian Medical Association. While such proposals so far have failed to win the support of a majority of doctors, they fail by an increasingly narrow margin. In the absence of adequate services, the "logic" and "morality" of allowing those with the resources to "top-up" their health care may well alter Canadians' expectations of their last remaining universal program.

In addition to the spending cuts and programmatic restructuring that accompany retrenchment efforts, Pierson (1994, p. 15) identifies systemic retrenchment, which he defines as "policy changes that alter the broader political economy and consequently alter welfare state politics." In the Canadian case, the CHST should not be regarded as a simple policy change but rather as a major shift in direction that has allowed a federal retreat from social programs that could not have occurred in its absence. The CHST has effectively "de-funded" social assistance, the least popular of all social programs, leaving it unprotected in the competitive arena of provincial priorities in an era of declining resources. One long-term effect is the continuing downward pressure on benefits and eligibility conditions and an increasing balkanization and disparity in the provision of welfare across the provinces. While it may be difficult to argue that the "harmonizing down" in social assistance and unemployment insurance is a simple and direct result of free trade, the changes certainly reflect the general competitive pressures on the Canadian economy, most of which emanate from the United States.

The broad-based coverage and simple and non-intrusive administration of child and elderly benefits do not suggest, at the present time, that the death of universality has meant the end of national income programs. But perhaps the most damaging aspect of retrenchment is the apparent success in changing the expectations that Canadians hold of their governments. Although Canadians are concerned about social programs, there is little to suggest that a broad and alternative vision is gaining ground. The politics of resistance are apparent in stands taken by unions and by protests organized nationally and provincially. Protests are more evident at the provincial level, where direct responsibility for programs lie. The Ontario Days of Action, for example, united organized labor and a broad spectrum of social justice groups in a series of one-day strikes across the province's major cities to protest the policies of its neoconservative provincial government. Social progressives across the country were disappointed when Ontario voters in June 1999 gave this government a second mandate. Despite their actual record on social programs, the federal Liberals have not attracted such organized opposition.

Myles (1996, p. 128) argues that "Canada and the United States represent two alternative responses to the economic restructuring and macroeconomic environment of the 1980s." It remains to be seen how distinctive the Canadian welfare state will look in the early years of the twenty-first century.

NOTES

1. In 1993–1994 spending on health, social services, and education amounted to 43 percent of federal spending; by 1997–1998, social spending amounted to 33 percent of total spending. During the same years, total government spending decreased by 4.3 percent. (Information from Statistics Canada's on-line database, CANSIM, matrices 3315 and 3776.)

2. The separatists lost by a few thousand votes. In addition to language, there are regional divisions—central Canada comprises the industry-based provinces of Quebec and Ontario, and the economy of the western provinces is rooted in agriculture and natural resources, while the eastern region is poor and struggling from the effects of the collapse of the fishing stocks.

3. Lipset (1990) suggests that the roots of these differences began in the individualistic and achievement-oriented revolutionary spirit of the United States, which contrasts very sharply with English Canadian counter-revolutionary "Loyalists" or the views of the very influential Quebec clergy toward the French Revolution.

4. In 1992, the unemployment rate was 11.3 percent, and 58.4 percent of Canadians were employed. In 1999, only 60.6 percent of the population was em-

ployed, even though unemployment had fallen to 7.6 percent (Information from Statistics Canada's on-line database, CANSIM, matrix 3472.).

5. Between 1996 and 1997, employment in the private sector grew by 0.8 percent and increased by 6.1 percent among the self-employed, while public sector employment fell by 1.2 percent (Smith, 1997).

6. Part of the difference is also thought to reflect a difference in the political culture of the unions. Canadian unions, more like their European counterparts, have emphasized a form of social unionism that extends well beyond the bargaining table to broader concerns and efforts at coalition-building (Banting, 1997).

7. The year 1996 witnessed the highest level of inequality experienced since the recession years of the early 1980s; there was a very slight decline in inequality between 1996 and 1997 (Statistics Canada, 1999).

8. British Columbia received approximately 36 cents on its social assistance dollar, and Alberta responded by making cuts to its welfare program (Rice, 1995). In the end, the cap on CAP cost Ontario a whopping $8.4 billion, an amount that represents one-third of the total value of the federal CHST in 1997–1998 (National Council of Welfare, 1997a).

9. Provinces must abide by the five principles of Medicare: universality, comprehensiveness, portability, accessibility, and public administration.

10. A major discussion paper on Social Security released four months earlier did not include an option of this kind in its proposals. The CHST proposal was developed within the Department of Finance, with little apparent consultation with the health and social welfare ministries (Maslove, 1996).

11. The increases announced in the 2000 budget bring the absolute value of the transfers slightly above the pre-1995 levels, but this does not take into account population growth or inflation.

12. For debate about the federal spending power, see various articles in *Policy Options* (November 1998). For a view from the ranks of advocacy groups, see National Association of Women and the Law and the Charter Committee on Poverty Issues (1999).

13. The 2000 budget announced an additional $2.5 billion in CHST transfers, not specifically targeted to health. Provincial premiers pointed out that it was less than one-third of the amount that was needed, and the leader of Canada's New Democratic Party pointed out that for every dollar that the budget gave away in tax cuts, two cents was provided for health care.

14. Regulated care refers to care provided in a child-care or family setting that operates under provincial regulation and is independently monitored.

15. This does not include funding directed to aboriginal child-care services, which, although only a small portion of the total child care budget, has grown exponentially. When spending on aboriginal child care is included, the overall decline in the federal contribution is 19 percent (Bach and Phillips, 1997, p. 246).

16. Child-care centers cater primarily to children from low-income or high-income families; the high cost of center-based care combined with the nature of subsidies means that it is relatively less accessible to middle-income families (Doherty, Friendly, and Oloman, 1998).

17. Only $800 million of the $2 billion saved was redirected to training, although there was no increase in the overall training budget (Campbell, 1992).

18. According to the regional unemployment rate, individuals had to work the

equivalent of between 180 and 300 hours to qualify for benefits—this is now increased to between 420 and 700 hours. The number of hours that new entrants must work has tripled, from 300 to 910 hours.

19. Young people's claims declined by 27 percent, and women's claims by 20 percent. In contrast, the fall in men's claims was lower (16 percent) despite the fact that their unemployment increased proportionately less than women's.

20. Family Allowance was worth approximately $35.00 per month per child when it was eliminated. Old Age Security currently pays out $410 monthly, available to each individual 65 and older who meets residency requirements, but without regard to income or previous work record.

21. In July 1999, the CCTC provided a maximum annual benefit of $1,805 for the first child and an additional $1,605 for other children. Eligibility for the maximum benefit ends at a net family income of $27,250, and benefits disappear entirely at $70,390 for families with two children. Income is net of deductions for child care, union dues, pension contributions, and registered retirement savings plans (Battle, Torjman, and Mendelson, 1999).

22. For analyses of workfare in several Canadian provinces, see Shragge (1997); see also Evans et al. (1995).

REFERENCES

Albo, G., and J. Jenson. (1997). "Remapping Canada: The state in the era of globalization." In W. Clement, ed., *Understanding Canada: Building on the New Canadian Political Economy.* Montreal: McGill-Queen's University Press, pp. 215–239.

Armstrong, P. (1996a). "The feminization of the labour force: Harmonizing down in a global economy." In I. Bakker, ed., *Rethinking Restructuring: Gender and Change in Canada.* Toronto: University of Toronto Press, pp. 29–54.

———. (1996b). "Privatizing care." In P. Armstrong, H. Armstrong, J. Choiniere, E. Mykhalovskiy, and J. White, *Medical Alert: New Work Organizations in Health Care.* Toronto: Garamond Press, pp. 11–27.

Armstrong, P., and H. Armstrong. (1996). *Wasting Away: The Undermining of Canadian Health Care.* Toronto: Oxford University Press.

Bach, S., and S. Phillips (1997). "Constructing a new social union: Child care beyond infancy?" In G. Swimmer, ed., *How Ottawa Spends, 1997–98: Seeing Red: A Liberal Report Card.* Ottawa: Carleton University Press, pp. 235–258.

Banting, K. (1997). "The social policy divide: The welfare state in Canada and the United States." In K. Banting, G. Hoberg, and R. Simeon, eds., *Degrees of Freedom: Canada and the United States in a Changing World.* Montreal: McGill-Queen's University Press, pp. 267–309.

Banting, K., and R. Simeon. (1997). "Changing economies, changing societies." In K. Banting, G. Hoberg, and R. Simeon, eds., *Degrees of Freedom: Canada and the United States in a Changing World.* Montreal: McGill-Queen's University Press, pp. 23–70.

Battle K. (aka G. Gray). (1990). "Social Policy by Stealth." *Policy Options* 11(2): 17–29.

————. (1997). "A new old age pension." In K. Banting and R. Boadway, eds., *Reform of Retirement Income Policy: International and Canadian Perspectives*. Kingston: School of Policy Studies, Queen's University, pp. 135–190.

————. (1999). *Poverty Eases Slightly*. Ottawa: Caledon Institute of Social Policy, April.

Battle, K., and M. Mendelson. (1997). *Child Benefit Reform in Canada: An Evaluative Framework and Future Directions*. Ottawa: Caledon Institute of Social Policy, November.

Battle, K., and S. Torjman. (1996). "Desperately seeking substance: A commentary on the Social Security review." In J. Pulkingham and G. Ternowetsky, eds., *Remaking Canadian Social Policy: Social Security in the Late 1990s*. Halifax: Fernwood, pp. 52–66.

Battle, K., S. Torjman, and M. Mendelson. (1999). *The Social Fundamentals*. Ottawa: Caledon Institute of Social Policy, February.

Betcherman, G. (1996). "Globalization, labour markets and public policy." In R. Boyer and D. Drache, eds., *States against Markets: The Limits of Globalization*. New York: Routledge, pp. 250–269.

Blank, R., and M. Hanratty. (1993). "Responding to need: A comparison of social safety nets in Canada and the United States." In D. Card and R. Freeman, eds., *Small Differences That Matter: Labor Markets and Income Maintenance in Canada and the United States*. Chicago: University of Chicago Press, pp. 191–231.

Brodie, J. (1996)."New state forms, new political spaces." In R. Boyer and D. Drache, eds., *States against Markets: The Limits of Globalization*. New York: Routledge, pp. 383–398.

Campbell, R. (1992). "Jobs . . . Job . . . Jo . . . J . . . : The conservatives and the unemployed." In F. Abele, ed., *How Ottawa Spends: The Politics of Competitiveness, 1992–93*. Ottawa: Carleton University Press, pp. 23–55.

Canada. (1994). *Improving Social Security in Canada: A Discussion Paper*. Ottawa: HRDC, October.

————. (1999). *Strengthening Health Care for Canadians*. Ottawa: Finance, February 17.

Canada Employment Insurance Commission. (1998). *Employment Insurance, Monitoring and Assessment Report, Canada*. Ottawa: Human Resources Development Canada.

Canadian Labour Congress. (2000). *CLC Analysis of the 2000–2001 Budget*. Available on the Internet at its Web site http://www.clc-ctc.ca.

Cohen, M. (1997). "From the welfare state to vampire capitalism." In P. Evans and G. Wekerle, eds., *Women and the Canadian Welfare State: Challenges and Change*. Toronto: University of Toronto Press, pp. 28–67.

Coutts, J. (1998). "Canada losing image as Shangri-la of medical care." *Toronto Globe and Mail*, October 27, p. A13.

Doherty, G., M. Friendly, and M. Oloman. (1998). *Women's Support, Women's Work: Child Care in an Era of Deficit Reduction, Devolution, Downsizing, and Deregulation*. Ottawa: Status of Women Canada.

Esping-Andersen, G. (1990). *Three Worlds of Welfare Capitalism*. Princeton, NJ: Princeton University Press.

————. (1996). "After the Golden Age? Welfare state dilemmas in a global economy." In G. Esping-Andersen, ed., *Welfare States in Transition: National Adaptations in Global Economies*. London: Sage, pp. 1–31.

Evans, P. (1994). "Eroding Canadian social welfare: The Mulroney legacy, 1984–1993." *Social Policy and Administration* 28(2) (June): 107–119.

———. (1995). "Linking jobs to welfare: Workfare, Canadian style." In P. Evans, L. Jacobs, A. Noël, and E. Reynolds, *Workfare: Does It Work? Is It Fair?* Montreal: Institute for Research on Public Policy, pp. 75–104.

———. (1997). "Gender, income security and the welfare state." In P. Evans and G. Wekerle, eds., *Women and the Canadian Welfare State: Challenges and Change*. Toronto: University of Toronto Press, pp. 91–116.

Evans, P., L. Jacobs, A. Noël, and E. Reynolds. (1995). *Workfare: Does It Work? Is It Fair?* Montreal: Institute for Research on Public Policy.

Ferguson, E. (1998). "The child care debate: Fading hopes and shifting sands." In C. Baines, P. Evans, and S. Neysmith, eds., *Women's Caring: Feminist Perspectives on Social Welfare*, 2nd ed. Toronto: Oxford University Press, pp. 191–217.

Finance Canada. (1999). *Canada Child Tax Benefit: Update (Budget 1999)*. Ottawa: Author, February 17.

Friendly, M., and M. Oloman. (1996). "Child care at the centre: Child care on the social, economic and political agenda in the 1990s." In J. Pulkingham and G. Ternowetsky, eds., *Remaking Canadian Social Policy: Social Security in the Late 1990s*. Halifax: Fernwood, pp. 273–285.

Gee, M. (2000). "Health care is no.1 concern: Poll." *Toronto Globe and Mail*, February 7, p. A5.

Glenday, D. (1997). "Lost horizons, leisure shock: Good jobs, bad jobs, uncertain future." In A. Duffy, D. Glenday, and N. Pupo, eds., *Good Jobs, Bad Jobs, No Jobs: The Transformation of Work in the 21st Century*. Toronto: Harcourt, Brace, pp. 8–34.

Greenspon, E. (1998). "Martin in bind over UI surplus." *Toronto Globe and Mail*, May 27, pp. A1, A6.

Jessop, B. (1993). "Towards a Schumpeterian workfare state? Preliminary remarks on post-Fordist political economy." *Studies in Political Economy* 40: 7–39.

LeClerc, P. (1991). "Gender equality in the U.S. and Canada: Why the difference?" In K. Banting, M. Hawes, R. Simeon, and E. Willis, eds., *Policy Choices: Political Agendas in Canada and the United States*. Kingston: School of Policy Studies, Queen's University, pp. 99–122.

Lightman, E., and A. Irving. (1991). "Restructuring Canada's Welfare State." *Journal of Social Policy* 20(1): 65–86.

Lipset, S. M. (1990). *Continental Divide: The Values and Institutions of the United States and Canada*. New York: Routledge.

Little, B. (1998). "Why so many jobless don't get UI." *Toronto Globe and Mail*, October 26, p. A2.

Lochhead, C., and V. Shalla. (1996). "Delivering the goods: Income distribution and the precarious middle class." *Perception* 20(1). Available on the Internet at: www.ccsd.ca/per_20–1.html.

Luxton, M., and E. Reiter. (1997). "Double, double, toil and trouble . . . Women's experience of work and family in Canada 1980–1995." In P. Evans and G.

Wekerle, eds., *Women and the Canadian Welfare State: Challenges and Change*. Toronto: University of Toronto Press, 197–221.

Marshall, T. H. (1964). *Class, Citizenship, and Social Development*. Chicago: University of Chicago Press.

Maslove, A. (1996). "The Canada health and social transfer: Forcing issues." In G. Swimmer, ed., *How Ottawa Spends, 1996–97: Life under the Knife*. Ottawa: Carleton University Press, pp. 283–301.

Maslove, A., and K. Moore. (1997). "From red books to blue books: Repairing Ottawa's fiscal house." In G. Swimmer, ed., *How Ottawa Spends, 1997–98: Seeing Red: A Liberal Report Card*. Ottawa: Carleton University Press, pp. 23–49.

Metro Task Force on Services to Young Children and Families (1997). *The First Duty: Report of the Metro Task Force on Services to Young People and Their Families*. Toronto: Municipality of Metropolitan Toronto.

Mishra, R. (1990). *Welfare State in Capitalist Society: Policies of Retrenchment and Maintenance in Europe, North America and Australia*. Toronto: University of Toronto Press.

Morisette, R., J. Myles, and G. Picot. (1995). "Earnings polarization in Canada, 1969–1991." In K. Banting and C. Beach, eds., *Labour Market Polarization and Social Policy Reform*. Kingston: School of Policy Studies, Queen's University, pp. 25–50.

Morrison, I. (1997). "Rights and the right: Ending social citizenship in Tory Ontario." In D. Ralph, A. Régimbald, and N. St-Amand, eds., *Open for Business, Closed to People: Mike Harris's Ontario*. Halifax: Fernwood, pp. 68–79.

Myles, J. (1996). "When markets fail: Social welfare in Canada and the United States." In G. Esping-Andersen, ed., *Welfare States in Transition: National Adaptations in Global Economies*. London: Sage, pp. 116–140.

Myles, J., and J. Quadagno. (1997). "Recent trends in public pension reform: A comparative view." In K. Banting and R. Boadway, eds., *Reform of Retirement Income Policy: International and Canadian Perspectives*. Kingston: School of Policy Studies, Queen's University, pp. 247–271.

National Anti-Poverty Organization (NAPO). (1998). *A Human Rights Meltdown in Canada*. Submission to the UN Committee on Economic, Social and Cultural Rights. Ottawa: NAPO, November 16.

National Association of Women and the Law and the Charter Committee on Poverty Issues. (1999). "Social union framework heartless say social justice groups." Press release, February 4.

National Council of Welfare. (1996). *A Pension Primer*. Ottawa: Author, Summer.

———. (1997a). *Another Look at Welfare Reform*. Ottawa: Author, Autumn.

———. (1997b). *Child Benefits: A Small Step Forward*. Ottawa: Author, Autumn.

———. (1998). *Poverty Profile: 1996*. Ottawa: Author, Spring.

Neysmith, S. (1998). "From home care to social care: The value of a vision." In C. Baines, P. Evans, and S. Neysmith, eds., *Women's Caring: Feminist Perspectives on Social Welfare*, 2nd ed. Toronto: Oxford University Press, pp. 233–249.

O'Connor, J. S., A. S. Orloff, and S. Shaver. (1999). *States, Markets, Families: Gender, Liberalism, and Social Policy in Australia, Canada, Great Britain, and the United States*. Cambridge: Cambridge University Press.

Organisation for Econmic Co-operation and Development. (1994). *The OECD Jobs Study: Facts, Analysis, Strategies*. Paris: Author.

———. (1997a). *Family, Market and Community: Equity and Efficiency in Social Policy*. Paris: Author.

———. (1997b). *OECD in Figures: Statistics on the Member Countries*, published as a supplement to *The OECD Observer*, no. 206, June/July, 1997.

Pierson, P. (1994). *Dismantling the Welfare State? Reagan, Thatcher, and the Politics of Retrenchment*. Cambridge: Cambridge University Press.

Prince, M. (1997). "Lowering the boom on the boomers: Replacing old age security with the new seniors benefit and reforming the Canada pension plan." In G. Swimmer, ed., *How Ottawa Spends, 1997–98: Seeing Red: A Liberal Report Card*. Ottawa: Carleton University Press, pp. 211–234.

Rice, J. (1995). "Redesigning welfare: The abandonment of a national commitment." In S. Phillips, ed., *How Ottawa Spends, 1995–96: Mid-Life Crises*. Ottawa: Carleton University Press, pp. 185–207.

Scott, K., and C. Lochhead. (1997). *Are Women Catching Up in the Earnings Race?* Ottawa: Canadian Council on Social Development.

Shragge, E., ed. (1997). *Workfare: Ideology for a New Under-Class*. Toronto: Garamond Press.

Simeon, R., and E. Willis. (1997). "Democracy and performance: Governance in Canada and the United States." In K. Banting, G. Hoberg, and R. Simeon, eds., *Degrees of Freedom: Canada and the United States in a Changing World*. Montreal: McGill-Queen's University Press, pp. 150–186.

Smith, J. (1997). "The labour market: Mid-year review." *Perspectives on Labour and Income* 9(3) (Autumn): 7–20.

Social Planning Council of Metropolitan Toronto. (1997). *Profile of a Changing World: 1996 Community Agency Survey*. Toronto: City of Toronto and Social Plannning Council of Metropolitan Toronto.

———. (1998). *Income after Tax, Distributions by Size, Canada*, cat. 13-210-XPB. Ottawa: Minister for Industry, June.

———. (1999). *Income Distributions by Size*, cat. 13-207-XPB. Ottawa: Minister for Industry.

Stoyko, P. (1997). "Creating opportunity or creative opportunism? Liberal labour market policy." In G. Swimmer, ed., *How Ottawa Spends, 1997–98: Seeing Red: A Liberal Report Card*. Ottawa: Carleton University Press, pp. 85–110.

Swift, J. (1997). "From cars to casinos, from work to workfare: The brave new world of Canadian employment." In A. Duffy, D. Glenday, and N. Pupo, eds., *Good Jobs, Bad Jobs, No Jobs: The Transformation of Work in the 21st Century*. Toronto: Harcourt, Brace, pp. 35–52.

Torjman, S. (1997). *Welfare Warfare*. Ottawa: Caledon Institute of Social Policy, November.

Townson, M. (1996). *Our Aging Society: Preserving Retirement Incomes into the 21st Century*. Ottawa: Canadian Centre for Policy Alternatives, January.

Wiseman, J. (1996). "National social policy in an age of global power: Lessons from Canada and Australia." In J. Pulkingham and G. Ternowetsky, eds., *Remaking Canadian Social Policy: Social Security in the Late 1990s*. Halifax: Fernwood, pp. 114–129.

Chapter 4

Sweden: Temporary Detour or New Directions?

Helen Lachs Ginsburg and
Marguerite G. Rosenthal

POLITICAL, ECONOMIC, AND SOCIAL DEVELOPMENT

Swimming against the tide on a continent plagued with high unemployment, Sweden had a jobless rate of less than 2 percent and a seemingly secure welfare state as recently as 1990. Since then, Sweden has experienced mass unemployment (although it has recently abated), along with extensive social welfare cutbacks. Why? Had its welfare state simply become unsustainable, especially in a globalized economy, as some have argued? Have Swedes rejected the welfare state and what has been dubbed "The Swedish Model"?

In this chapter, against the backdrop of Swedish capital's growing internationalization and Sweden's entry into the European Union (EU) in 1994, we explore these and related questions: What factors nurtured the rise of the Swedish welfare state and then its weakening? Why did Sweden abandon its commitment to full employment? How has unemployment affected the welfare state? How have budget cuts affected income support and social services for those in need of them? Who are the winners and losers as Sweden's welfare state shifts gears? Finally, is this drift toward diminishing welfare inevitable?

Background

With only 8.8 million people, Sweden is an industrialized nation highly dependent on international trade. Exports equaled 40 percent of gross domestic product (GDP) (Swedish Institute [hereafter SI], 1997a) in 1996. About 3 percent of workers are in agriculture, and just under 1 in 5 are in manufacturing (U.S. Bureau of Labor Statistics, 2000, table 7). Its large public sector employs about 3 out of 10 workers (SI, 1997a).

Poverty once drove Swedes to other lands, especially the United States. But after World War II, Sweden emerged as an egalitarian, slum-free, affluent nation with work for all. The poster child of advanced welfare states and the *bête noire* of its opponents, it also gained renown for its labor–management cooperation; comprehensive, universal, and generous income and family support; and high-quality public services for the elderly, children, and the disabled. It was also known for its high taxes, high union density, and high degree of gender equality.

Perhaps Sweden's most notable accomplishment was its transformation into a full employment welfare state with a strong commitment to equality. Throughout the post-war period, until the early 1990s, unemployment averaged 2 percent (Ginsburg, 1983, p. 113; U.S. Bureau of Labor Statistics, 2000, table 2). This was no accident. Its seeds were systematically planted and developed by working-class movements, the Social Democratic Party (SAP) and its close ally, the Swedish Trade Union Confederation (LO). (LO was initially composed of unions representing blue-collar workers but was joined later by others, including lower-level public sector workers, primarily women.) For many decades, capital allowed full employment to take root.

Before World War II

Sweden has been governed by the SAP, either alone or heading a coalition, for most years since 1932. With support that cut across party lines, the government had maintained full employment and crafted an immensely popular welfare state, income differences fell dramatically, and poverty was nearly eliminated. During the Depression, when the SAP began its long reign, it broke with the dogma that demanded wage cuts to reduce unemployment. Public expenditures were expanded and, ending the poor law practice, jobs were provided for the unemployed at normal wages in order to increase demand for goods (Korpi, 1978). Other traditional ideas, like using austerity to fight the Depression, were replaced as the government budget became an instrument of economic stabilization.

The historic Saltsjöbaden Agreement, signed in 1938 by the Swedish Employers' Confederation (SAF) and LO, was of great importance. To avert government intervention, after decades of intense industrial strife, SAF and LO agreed to self-regulate key issues. The agreement was part of a larger capital–labor compromise to achieve rapid economic growth. Business would benefit, as would labor. Capital would allow unemployment to decline, and growth would provide the means for improved living standards and social welfare. Political sociologist Walter Korpi (1978) attributes this compromise to a widespread belief that the SAP would be in power for a long time and that neither capital nor labor could expect surrender of the other.

The SAP remained in power long enough to implement its goals of full employment, equality, and the welfare state, articulated in the 1930s as "the people's home," where all Swedes should be treated as members of a family (Meidner, 1993, p. 121). While Sweden came out of the Depression sooner than most countries, full employment had to await World War II, in which Sweden remained formally neutral.

After the War: Full Employment Goal Reinforced

The Post-War Program of the Swedish labor movement, issued jointly in 1944 by the SAP and LO, gave absolute priority to full employment. The monetary system, public finance, price and wage policy, and private and public enterprises were all to be geared toward its attainment (Therborn, 1986, p. 102). After the war, labor shortages and inflationary pressures, not unemployment, typified Sweden's high-growth, full employment economy. But inflation fighting was not to check full employment (Lindbeck, 1968, p. 19).

The Rehn-Meidner Model: Modified Keynesianism and Active Labor Market Policy

To overcome the inflation–full employment dilemma, Rudolf Meidner and Gösta Rehn, LO economists, developed a non-inflationary, modified Keynesian approach, which was adopted as government policy in the late 1950s. Traditional Keynesianism was felt to rely too much on general economic expansion and might cause inflationary bottlenecks without eliminating the most stubborn unemployment. The Rehn-Meidner approach, by contrast, combined a less expansive macroeconomic policy with more expansive selective measures tailored to overcome specific labor market problems (Meidner, 1993). It was designed to achieve full employment while reducing boom-induced inflationary pressures through active public labor market policies such as job placement, job creation, labor market training, and mobility grants. Sweden continued to favor active labor market policy over reliance on unemployment benefits (Ginsburg, 1983, ch. 6; Johannesson, 1991).

Wage Solidarity Policy: LO's Egalitarianism in Action

Full employment and active labor market policy were essential to LO's egalitarian, solidarity wages—equal pay for equal work regardless of the firm's profitability. This policy, started in 1956 (and eventually used by other unions and their employers), was dependent on centralized wage bargaining between LO and SAF to subdue interunion wage rivalry and hence curb inflationary pressures. Unions of higher-wage workers also used their strength in bargaining to help low-wage earners gain more. Firms unable to pay these wages had to become more productive or go under. These policies were essential to ensure that workers who lost jobs found others in more profitable firms and sectors (DeGeer, 1992; Erixon, 1995; Meidner, 1997b). Solidarity wages led to dramatically reduced wage differentials from the early 1960s until the early 1980s (Meidner, 1978, pp. 29–34; Ministry of Finance, 1995c, pp. 61–62, 273–274).

Shaping the Welfare State

Pension Reform

Other important features of Sweden's welfare state were also shaped during the post-war period. In the late 1940s and 1950s, voluntary health insurance was transformed into a compulsory, universal, state-financed system, and a universal system of allowances for families with children was developed. Another crucial development was pension reform.

Sweden already had a universal flat-rate pension for the elderly and disabled, dating from 1913. However, even with subsequent changes, it had eliminated only the most severe poverty. Pressure for a national system of mandatory, employer-financed, earnings-related pensions came from LO, whose members lacked the supplementary earnings-related pensions that salaried workers usually had. Sweden's national supplementary earnings-related pension, the ATP, which is now being phased out, became the most controversial postwar social reform. Viewing it as an equality issue, the SAP fought for the ATP despite accusations that they wanted to "socialize" Sweden. It passed in 1959, despite considerable political upheaval, by one vote (Hadenius 1985, pp. 87–95; Olsson, 1990, pp. 163, 218–221).

The ATP strengthened the principle (already the rule in sickness insurance) that social insurance would apply to the whole workforce and would maintain not just a minimum standard but most people's living standards. The ATP and the universal health system strengthened the welfare state by giving most Swedes—not just the poor and the working class—a big stake in it.

A Changing Labor Force

Immigrants. Sweden received many World War II European refugees and since 1954 has been part of a Scandinavian common labor market. In the 1960s, to ease labor shortages, foreigners—mostly from Finland, Southern Europe, and Turkey—were recruited and were allowed to bring their families and become citizens. EU nationals have been able to enter Sweden without a labor permit since the mid-1990s, but except for them and Nordic nationals, only relatives of immigrants and refugees can be admitted without a labor permit. Many refugees, especially from Latin America, the

Middle East, and in the 1990s large numbers from the former Yugoslavia, have sought asylum in Sweden. By the mid-1990s, more than 10 percent of Sweden's inhabitants were foreign-born, and nearly one in five was born abroad or had at least one foreign-born parent. Sweden, once homogeneous, is now a multiethnic society (Jederlund, 1998; SI, 1999a).

Immigration policy aims to achieve social and economic equality. Many immigrants from the 1960s and 1970s have done well, but recent immigrant refugees and non-Nordics live in increasingly segregated outer-ring suburbs. Immigrants, especially non-Europeans, have very high rates of unemployment and poverty (discussed below), and their disproportionate reliance on social assistance provokes xenophobia and racism, which the government has attempted to counter. But in the 1990s, mass unemployment, as discussed elsewhere in this chapter, became a major obstacle working against immigrants, one that threatens core welfare state values.

Women. Work and family roles in Sweden had been very traditional until the mid-twentieth century (Rosenthal, 1990; Hirdman, 1994). Large numbers of women entered the workforce beginning in Sweden's expansive 1960s. From 1965 to 1981, women made up nearly all of the increase in the labor force (AMS, 1984, p. 3). The most dramatic change was among mothers of children under seven years old; these women's labor force participation rate doubled, from 37 to 79 percent (Gustafsson and Jacobsson, 1985, p. 259). Women, as low-wage workers, gained enormously from solidarity wages (Cook, 1980, p. 57). Between 1963 and 1981, hourly wages of women in manufacturing climbed from 72 to 90 percent of men's (Gustafsson and Jacobsson, 1985, p. S261).

Prodded by Liberal and SAP women, equality in work, home, and society became official societal goals (Hirdman, 1994; Furst, 1999). Many supportive policies were implemented in the 1970s, including a shift from joint to individual taxation of earned income, which made it more advantageous for wives to work; government parental insurance to replace most of the wages of parents who care for a newborn and similar benefits for parents absent from work to care for a sick child; the legal right of parents of young children to reduce their working hours with a proportional reduction in pay; a major expansion of highly subsidized, quality, public child care, then in very short supply; greatly expanded efforts directed toward women by the National Labor Market Board; and the first anti-discrimination legislation, effective in 1980 (Ginsburg,1983; Sundström, 1990; Furst, 1999). These policies are grounded in women's right to employment and the assumption that most of them are in the labor market.[1]

Women's labor market participation rate nearly equals men's, and until the economic crisis, it was the highest in the Organisation for Economic Co-operation and Development (OECD) (OECD, 1995, table 2.8, 1998, pp. 8–9). The high labor force participation of women, parental leave, and equality policies generally set Sweden and the rest of Scandinavia apart from other European countries (Sundström, 1995; Esping-Andersen, 1999).

Sweden is second only to Norway on the United Nations (1999) gender-empowerment index, and women make up about 44 percent of Parliament (Furst, 1999, p. 13). Even so, gender discrimination persists, and women work predominantly in gender-segregated, comparatively low-wage occupations (Xu, 1997). Part-time employment has enabled many mothers to maintain their labor force attachment (Sundström, 1987). However, much part-time work is involuntary and it is widespread, especially in the public sector. Nearly 2 out of 5 gainfully employed women but fewer than 1 in 10 men work part-time. The gender–pay gap—like the overall wage spread—although much smaller than in many countries, has widened since the 1980s, partly because of the breakdown of centralized bargaining (Xu, 1997).

The Public Sector

The heart and soul of the Swedish welfare state is its large public sector. Sweden has earned international accolades for its innovative and humane care of the young, the old, the ill, and the disabled, nearly all of it provided by local governments and carried out by women. From 1963 to 1990, public sector employment rose by 900,000, providing paid jobs for women, often for work previously done in the home without pay. This relieved women of the whole burden of caring for family members (Edin and Andersson, 1995, pp. 10–11) and enabled more of them to enter the labor market. In the mid-1990s, nearly half of women employees worked for local governments, and they made up some 80 percent of that workforce (Statistics Sweden, 1995, p. 48). During the 1960s and 1970s especially, Sweden was transformed into a *woman-friendly, full employment social-service welfare state*. In the early 1990s, 78 percent of adult Swedish women were in the workforce, compared to 61 percent in the EU as a whole, and the entire difference was due to women working in the public sector (Edin and Andersson, 1995, p. 11).

Sweden's large public sector has long been attacked by conservatives and neoliberals inside (Lindbeck, 1994) and outside Sweden (Rosen, 1996). But, contrary to a common belief, the increase in public sector employment did not lead to a decrease in private sector employment. Relative to the working-age population, "Sweden in 1990 had more private sector employment than any other country in Western Europe" (Edin and Andersson, 1995, p. 11).

The proportion of public employees in the workforce actually declined in the years preceding the economic crisis that began in the early 1990s, and transfer payments as a portion of GDP grew by only one percentage point in the 1980s (Edin and Andersson, 1995, pp. 1, 11). But when Sweden's economy plunged, critics were quick to blame the public sector and the welfare state as unsustainable. In a familiar reprise, heard in Sweden and abroad, the *Wall Street Journal* claimed that the government (then a Conservative-led coalition) slashed expenditures "because the exorbitant cost of the welfare system sent budget deficits soaring" (quoted in Ginsburg, 1996, p. 21). They failed to note that shortly before the crisis, Sweden had full employment, a strong welfare state, and a hefty budget surplus.

The Real Culprits in the Economic Crisis

What did cause the economic crisis that sent unemployment skyrocketing, led to drastic budget cuts, and sent the vaunted social welfare system into reverse? The answer lies in such factors as the power of business, globalization, political and ideological changes, neoliberal economic policies, and, above all, the abandonment of Sweden's historic commitment to full employment.

Sweden, a small, open economy highly dependent on foreign trade and without domestic petroleum, is quite vulnerable to economic shocks such as the Organization of Petroleum Exporting Countries (OPEC) oil crisis of the 1970s. Like other industrial nations, growth slowed sharply after 1973, while inflation escalated (Rivlin, 1987, p. 4). But, though unemployment typically jumped elsewhere, at least through 1980, in Sweden it remained in the 2 percent range,[2] due mainly to government economic and active labor market policies that gave first priority to full employment.

Changing Capital–Labor Relations

By the mid-1970s, about 8 out of 10 Swedish employees were unionized, including most of the burgeoning female clerical and public sector workforce (Chang and Sorrentino, 1991, p. 48; OECD, 1991, ch. 4). Wildcat strikes over working conditions in the late 1960s and early 1970s led to legislation covering job security, health and safety, employee participation in decision making, the status of trade union representatives, vacations, and educational leaves of absence (Ginsburg, 1983, p.197; Olsen, 1991).

Despite labor's gains, capital had become more concentrated, international, and powerful than ever. By the mid-1970s, the export sector displaced the home market as the dominant part of Swedish capital, and power within SAF shifted to arch conservatives from global-oriented firms that rejected the Swedish model and its capital–labor compromise (Olsen, 1991). Though solidarity wages sharply reduced wage differences, they also accelerated economic concentration. To achieve egalitarian wages, workers in the most profitable firms did not push for the highest wages that their employers—many of them large and powerful multinationals—could pay, since no other firms could pay such high wages. So the most profitable firms reaped additional profits (Olsen, 1991, 1996; Hermele, 1993).

After trying unsuccessfully to tax these excess profits, in 1976 LO proposed wage-earner funds, also called "the Meidner plan," to counteract the concentration of wealth and to extend economic democracy. Part of a company's post-tax profits were to fund shares in the company, collectively owned by workers and managed by their representatives (Meidner, 1980). Vehemently opposed by capital, the plan was hotly contested, but LO and the SAP were divided. According to Meidner (Silverman, 1998, p. 79), the idea of wage-earner funds was not really accepted inside the government or the SAP, despite reluctant passage of a watered-down version in 1983. This was abolished by the Conservative-led coalition in the early 1990s.

Political and Ideological Changes and Deregulation

After 44 years in power, the SAP lost the 1976 election by a small margin.[3] Though non-socialist governments—four in six years—were politically unstable, the welfare state remained basically intact, and some programs—for example, parenthood leave—were expanded. Initially, strong efforts to achieve full employment were continued even with an international recession, a weakening of Swedish competitiveness, oil price hikes, and the threat of new, low-cost producers in South Korea, Hong Kong, and Brazil in shipbuilding, steel, and mining (Hadenius, 1985, pp. 147–149). These non-socialist governments also bailed out many crisis-ridden industries and, ironically, nationalized more industries than the SAP had done in nearly half a century (Hadenius, 1985, p. 148).

Eventually, the non-socialist parties became more neoliberal. Influenced by a worsened economic climate and a more militant SAF, in sync with the interests of multinational giants, they questioned solidarity wages, the public sector, and progressive taxes and considered lowering inflation a higher priority than stabilization (Erixon, 1985, pp. 30–38). A deficit-reduction austerity program contributed to a rise in unemployment (Martin, 1996, p. 3).

What was then considered very high unemployment—around 3 percent—helped bring the SAP back in 1982. So did an unpopular, SAF-inspired decision to change sick pay. Bitterly opposed by LO, it was not implemented by the incoming SAP (Erixon, 1985, pp. 61–62; Hadenius, 1985, pp. 155–158; Palme and Wennemo, 1998, p. 12).

The SAP under Prime Minister Olof Palme faced a dismal economy: 3.5 percent unemployment by early 1983, a burgeoning deficit, a stagnating export sector, a worldwide economic slump, high oil prices, and inflation. The SAP's recovery plan was dubbed the "Third Way," in contrast to the traditional Keynesian reflationary approach as practiced in France under François Mitterrand and the deflationary neoliberal approach of the British Conservatives under Margaret Thatcher. The new slogan was "first growth, then redistribution," with growth assumed to require major increases in corporate profits, that is, a major distribution of income from labor to capital (Pontusson, 1992, p. 315). The plan's centerpiece, a devaluation of

16 percent in 1982 (after a smaller one in 1981),[4] helped turn around the Swedish economy, as did an upturn in the international economy and falling oil prices. By the late 1980s, unemployment was less than 2 percent, the welfare state was secure, and the large budget deficit had turned into a surplus.

A profit-driven recovery and deregulation were favored by capital and were also pushed by a powerful clique of neoliberal economists in the SAP. These policies helped pave the way for growing inequalities and for the crisis of the 1990s. Financial institutions were freed from domestic credit controls, and by the end of the decade virtually all restrictions on the movement of foreign exchange had been lifted (Ministry of Finance, 1995c, pp. 143–149). The assassin's bullet that killed Olof Palme in 1986 seemed to symbolize Sweden's growing resemblance to other countries as it was drawn deeper into the neoliberal system that increasingly dominated the global economy.

Financial deregulation set off a wildly speculative real estate boom. Enormous profits in the 1980s weakened companies' motivation to rationalize and innovate (Erixon, 1995, p. 43). Rather, a large portion was invested abroad, often to acquire foreign firms, especially in Europe. Removal of exchange controls accelerated this process (Pontusson, 1992; Canova, 1994; Ministry of Finance, 1995c, pp. 114–115). With exchange controls gone, capital outflow rose to as much as 60 percent of domestic investment in 1989 and 1990, about 35 percent of it used for speculation, largely in foreign real estate (Hermele, 1993, p. 10). When the bubble burst, it sparked a nearly catastrophic bank crisis. The government had to bail out some of Sweden's largest banks, draining the treasury of a sum equal to 4 percent of GDP in 1992 and 1993 (Ginsburg, 1996).

Abandonment of the Full Employment Priority: The Influence of the EU

The drive toward European integration led to official abandonment of the full employment priority—a major turning point for the Swedish welfare state. SAF supported Sweden's entrance into the EU (De Geer, 1992, p. 169), but most rank-and-file SAP members were stunned when, in 1990, Prime Minister Ingvar Carlson, who had replaced Palme, abruptly reversed the SAP's long-standing policy and announced that Sweden would apply for membership (Burke, 1994, p. 2). In a closely related move, the government then said price stability had replaced full employment as its main economic priority (Ministry of Finance, 1991, p. 167).

The EU had firm rules against inflation but none against unemployment, which it had learned to live with. This heightened the government's determination to fight inflation in Sweden's booming economy. After dropping steadily, inflation rose in the late 1980s as unemployment fell below 2 percent and as labor shortages developed. Previously, Sweden had developed ways to curb inflation without increasing unemployment. One technique was centralized bargaining, which had broken down in the 1980s at the insistence of the employers (Martin, 1991). Another was restricting credit to an overheated part of the economy such as housing (Canova, 1994), an option eliminated by deregulation. This time, however, the government jacked up interest rates across the board, sending the economy into a tailspin and unemployment up to 3.5 percent—a major factor in the SAP's electoral defeat in 1991. Its stance on the EU, its failure to fulfill electoral promises to extend parental leave and child care, and a tax reform modeled on the 1986 Reagan-era changes in the United States also counted with the voters. The tax reform, among other things, sharply reduced the top marginal income tax bracket for the well-to-do from 73 to 51 percent. Billed as self-financed, it was not (Pontusson, 1992, p. 318) and contributed to subsequent budget deficits.

Unlike 1976, when the SAP lost by a small margin, the party's decline in 1991 was steep. Shortly afterward, a SAP board member commented: "The party's problems didn't become acute until it decided to lower income taxes. . . . The party had an implicit contract with Sweden's voters, who were prepared to pay high taxes in return for extensive services, and too many voters felt this contract had been broken" (Rexed, 1991, p. 5). Cleavages also developed between the LO and the party. Many trade union locals withdrew their support (Rexed, 1991, pp. 4–5). As the SAP veered toward the right, perhaps hoping for new support that was not forthcoming, it lost its traditional base. The pattern was to repeat itself in the 1998 election.

The Conservative-Led Era

The non-socialists were back in the driver's seat from 1991 to 1994; the damage done to the Swedish economy during this period brought mass unemployment and further attacks on the welfare state. The new coalition, headed by the Moderates (formerly Conservatives), the most right-wing of the four parties, was far more conservative than previous non-socialist governments.

The government was obsessed with fighting inflation, by then non-existent. It was even more dogmatic about defending Sweden's overvalued krona, then under speculative attack. Lacking currency controls, the government allowed interest rates to soar to stem the outflow of funds (Canova, 1994). The political establishment, including the most influential economists, was determined to fight to the bitter end (Edin and Andersson, 1995, p. 18). The head of Sweden's Central Bank declared that the sky would be the limit, and so it was. The authorities briefly raised the overnight interest rate to *500 percent*. In late 1991 the krona was finally allowed to depreciate, lowering the cost of Swedish exports.

Is the Welfare State to Blame?

The financial fiasco and its aftermath converted a recession into a depression that coincided with an international recession. The slump, deepest since the 1930s depression (Ministry of Finance, 1995c, p. 46), was marked by three years of declining output, the loss of one-tenth of Sweden's jobs, and record unemployment. Between 1990 and 1993, the official unemployment rate, often referred to in Sweden as "open" unemployment, rose nearly fivefold—from 1.7 percent to 8.2 percent—and a budget surplus of 4 percent of GDP became a deficit of 13 percent. This jump was not caused by Sweden's welfare state but rather by the banking bailout, by the loss of revenues from tax reform, and, above all, by mass unemployment, which both cut tax revenues and sharply increased expenditures on the newly jobless (Ginsburg, 1996). Nevertheless, the welfare state was treated as the culprit, requiring budget cuts. These were implemented by both the non-socialists and, after they won the 1994 election, by the Social Democrats. The pursuit of full employment, the welfare state, and equality gave way to deficit reduction, cutbacks, and, after joining the EU in 1995, convergence with EU economic requirements.

The 1992 Crisis Agreements

Raising interest rates to 500 percent, intended to cool financial markets, led instead to further speculation. So, in late September 1992, two crisis agreements to cut the deficit and calm the markets were put together by the ruling Conservative-led coalition and the SAP opposition. Welfare state retrenchment had finally arrived. The package included drastic changes in sick pay and work injury insurance, de-indexing pensions for a year, and a reversal of a recent decision by Parliament to raise benefits for families with children. Though SAP managed to get funds for expansion of adult education and labor market measures, LO criticized the deal vehemently (Carroll, 1993, pp. 33–36).

The dominance of powerful corporate interests—especially the 20 or so Swedish multinationals responsible for much of the currency outflow—is visible in the government's hasty emergency response to a financial crisis (Carroll, 1993, p. 36). When the market regarded the first package as insufficient, the government and SAP agreed to another a week later. At that time, Sweden and Greece had OECD's lowest corporate taxes (Ministry of Finance, 1995c, p. 309). The "austerity" agreement, however, was not austere for employers. It decreased their social insurance contributions by increasing taxes on food and taking away two vacation days from employees. Union members were outraged (Carroll, 1993), and at LO's and some white-collar unions' urging, 200,000 people demonstrated throughout Sweden in early October 1992 (LO, 1992).

The EU Campaign

While an export boom followed the depreciation of the krona, which lowered the cost of Swedish goods abroad, deflationary monetary and fiscal policies worsened slack domestic demand. Pursuing deficit reduction through cuts affecting a wide swath of social programs only made the deficit rise as unemployment grew. Taxes increased for workers and pensioners but decreased for owners of capital (Social Democratic Party, 1994, pp. 16–19, 50–54, 77–79). In the 1930s much of Swedish capital had a big stake in boosting home markets. That important motive for the capital–labor accord no longer holds. Sweden now has the world's most internationalized businesses; most of its largest firms are export-oriented transnationals with the bulk of their sales, assets, and workforce abroad. As a Swedish business magazine said when it reported high corporate earnings in 1993 because of the export boom, "the country's big companies are no longer particularly dependent on Sweden, Swedish markets, or Swedish politicians for that matter" (*Manadens Affärer*, 1994, p. 8).

Swedish firms were heavily invested in the EU, lured there by its huge market. The November 1994 EU referendum passed by a slim margin, with big business lavishly financing the pro-EU campaign. For decades SAF had invested heavily in promoting business interests and ideology. It set up its own publishing house and targeted journalists, among others; got its propaganda into schools by providing free educational materials; and even took thousands of teachers on junkets to Brussels as part of its pro-EU campaign (SAF, 1994, p. 63). SAF also adopted the left's technique in 1983 and mobilized 75,000 to demonstrate in Stockholm against wage-earner funds. In 1990, SAF came to regard opinion building as its most important task (De Geer, 1992, pp. 111–113, 170–175). The pro-EU campaign outspent opponents by at least 10 to 1. All the non-socialist parties, nearly all the press, and even some union leaders endorsed the EU, as did the deeply divided SAP. Its leaders refused to debate the issue until after the 1994 election (which brought the SAP back), held only two months before the referendum. The main opposition was waged by some dissident Social Democrats, the Left Party (formerly the Communist Party) and the Green Party, with the latter two gaining votes. Pleas from Social Democratic leaders to "trust us" helped tip the scale. So did threats from companies that they would abandon Sweden, that only EU membership could save the welfare state while promising that membership would usher in a "Golden Age" of growth and jobs. Finance Minister Göran Persson, who became prime minister in 1996, warned that a "no" vote would mean deeper social benefit cuts (Burke, 1994; Ginsburg, 1996).

Return of the SAP

The EU and the SAP's Austerity Policy

In the 1994 election year, open unemployment was 8 percent, nearly as high as its 1993 peak. The SAP recovered from its poor showing in 1991 and captured 45.3 percent of the vote (SI, 1999b). Although financial markets already exerted the same sorts of pressures, entrance into the EU was a watershed that cemented the new government's fixation on deficit reduction and continuing cuts. The incoming SAP adhered to neoliberal policies as relentlessly as it had once worked for full employment. A sea change distinguishes the SAP's January 1994 proposals for "bolder," more expansionary monetary and fiscal policies to "raise demand in the domestic economy" (Social Democratic Party, 1994, p. 44) from the restrictive ones implemented after taking office in September 1994.

Admission to the Economic and Monetary Union (EMU) at its 1999 inaugural required that a member meet strict "convergence criteria" by the end of 1997 and maintain them thereafter: low inflation, exchange rate stability, low interest rates, low public deficits and debts. There was no requirement for low unemployment. While Sweden had joined the EU, no decision had been made about the EMU. Membership would bring continuous pressure to cut social programs and preclude any independent monetary or exchange rate policy geared toward low unemployment. Some believe that the Maastricht Treaty already commits Sweden to the EMU. Nevertheless, the SAP's economic policy was predicated on meeting the norms whether or not Sweden participated in the EMU (Ministry of Finance, 1995b). For example, to reduce the deficit to no more than 3 percent of GDP by 1997, an EMU requirement, extensive budget "reinforcements"—spending cuts and tax increases equivalent to 7.5 percent of GDP[5]—were adopted in late 1994 and early 1995 (Ministry of Finance, 1995b, pp. 13–14). The government averred that "this will be one of the most comprehensive consolidation programmes to be implemented in any industrial country after the War" (Ministry of Finance, 1995b, p. 14), and deep cuts affecting nearly every aspect of the welfare state followed.

These largely regressive measures and the losses suffered by low and average income households[6] were justified because "everyone will have to share the burden" (Ministry of Finance, 1995b, p. 53), even the unemployed, and by their optimistic view that the program would reduce joblessness (Ministry of Finance, 1995d, p. 72). That approach reflects downplaying the role of fiscal policy as a stimulus of aggregate demand in job creation, a view that had come to dominate Swedish policy circles (Ginsburg, 1998). Economic policies, including the deep austerity program, pushed domestic demand down, led to more rather than less unemployment, and broke the modest export-driven recovery that was already under way. The annual unemployment rate, which had declined slightly in 1995, rose again in 1996 and stagnated until 1998. By 1997, however, Sweden's deficit had dropped even lower than the EMU's 3 percent requirement. The government's shift in priorities was a major retreat from Sweden's national ethos that everyone—even the weakest person—has the right to a job and a meaningful social role.

Mass Unemployment

After a half century of full or nearly full employment, the rapid resurgence of mass unemployment most vividly symbolizes changes in Sweden's welfare state. By 1993, open unemployment had risen sharply to 8.3 percent, and it still averaged 8 percent in 1997, before declining (to 5.6 percent in 1999 and 4.7 percent in 2000),[7] and the labor market participation rate fell considerably for both men and women. If one adds persons in labor market programs (excluding those for the disabled) to the number of openly unemployed, as Swedes sometimes do,[8] *total* unemployment during those years (1993 through 1997) averaged about 12 to 13 percent. But even as the economy boomed (discussed later), it was still 8.5 percent in 1999 and 7 percent in 2000 compared to just over 3 percent in 1990 (LO, 2000, 2001). Further, for many years in the 1990s, an average of more than 1 million persons—about three times the number of openly unemployed— were either openly unemployed, were in labor market programs, or were involuntary part-time (overwhelmingly women) or discouraged workers. By 1999 that figure had declined to just over 800,000, 2.4 times its 1989 level, and by 2000 to 700,000, still double that level.[9]

Immigrants and youth were especially hard hit. For example, between 1989 and 1993, open unemployment among non-Nordic foreign nationals[10] shot up from 4.5 to 33 percent and in 1999 was still more than 20 percent. Among 16- to 24-year-olds, it jumped from 3 to more than 18 percent; with an expansion of programs targeted to youths, the rate dropped to 10 percent by 1999, still triple the 1989 rate. Temporary jobs, disproportionately held by women and young workers, became more common, affecting nearly 1 in 6 employees[11] in 1999, but only about 1 in 10 a decade earlier. In the public sector, permanent workers have sometimes been laid off and later rehired as temporaries (Gonäs, 1994, p. 155).

Sweden lost more than half a million jobs in the first half of the 1990s. Despite a strong economic upturn and job growth later in the decade, employment in 1999 was about the same as in 1973 and was nearly 9 percent less than in 1990. Further, the public sector had changed from an engine of employment to one of unemployment—not just under the Conservative-led coalition but also under the SAP. From 1990 to 1997, nearly one in eight public sector jobs—some 180,000—disappeared before a slight upturn in the late 1990s (LO, 2000). Women were particularly hard hit, and services deteriorated (discussed further, below).

Active labor market policy programs, a linchpin of Sweden's post-war approach to full employment, were also used in the 1990s, though many were narrower and cheaper than previous ones (Olsen, 1999, pp. 250–251). For various reasons, they did not bring Sweden even close to full employment. Unlike in other downturns, the non-socialist government allowed unemployment to rise steeply. Programs were expanded, but with a lag; and despite an increased number of participants, relatively fewer of the unemployed were in these programs. Finally, Rudolf Meidner (1997b, pp. 93–96) notes that active labor market policy can help alleviate long-term unemployment but was not designed to overcome mass unemployment. It cannot do that job, he states, without other supportive economic policies that are based on a fundamental change in political priorities—from price stability to full employment.

In recent years, labor market policy has been scaled down and resources reoriented toward funding adult and tertiary education (Olsen, 1999, p. 251). Though a far better alternative than unemployment, education cannot by itself create jobs, though it may help prepare some of the unemployed for employment in an expanding economy (discussed further below).

Political Reactions

Initially, the incoming SAP worked with the Left Party in order to pass the tax increase. But after the Left refused to agree to some benefit cuts, the SAP collaborated with the non-socialist Center Party (Palme and Wennemo, 1998, p. 21).

Many Swedes felt they had been manipulated into voting for the EU, which grew immensely unpopular. Strong public opposition stalled participation in the EMU, which was supported by the right-wing Moderates, Liberals, and corporate leaders, as well as by Göran Persson, who became the SAP prime minister in 1996, when Ingvar Carlsson retired. Resisting calls for a referendum, the government proposed and Parliament agreed that Sweden would not participate in the EMU in 1999, but the door was left open to later membership (SI, 1998a).

Much dissatisfaction was expressed within LO, between LO and the SAP, and within the SAP, and by attrition from the SAP. Within the SAP, an already deep chasm widened between "traditionalists," wedded to egalitarian values, and neoliberal "renewers," who held power. The latter accept the agenda of business and a shrinking of the welfare state, but they may make some concessions when forced by political necessity. Many members and supporters felt they no longer recognized the SAP, and opinion polls confirmed a significant erosion of their support, especially among women. The biggest winner was the Left Party, which, with a feminist bent and, headed by a woman, seemed ideologically close to what the SAP once was (Ginsburg, 1996).

In other ways, Sweden remained remarkably subdued. Unions did not lead protests as they had done in 1992, at the time of the Crisis Agreements. Though over 80 percent of workers are organized, only a small (12 percent) and declining proportion of them are active members (Vogel, 1997, p. 644). White-collar unions have grown, but LO, with the most militant history, remains the largest labor confederation. However, despite sometimes icy relations, LO's close ties to the SAP helped to curb overt protest after the SAP returned to power in 1994. LO leaders evidently preferred to wield power with the government directly, without stirring up rank-and-file activism. While they forced the government to hike unemployment benefits (back to 80 percent of wages) and to shelve plans to loosen labor legislation, they did not succeed in changing the general direction of economic policy.

A short-lived grassroots movement erupted in late 1996, launched by an unemployed mother of four from a small town. Helped by her union local (but not LO), it brought the issues of unemployment and benefit cuts temporarily into the streets. Its leader received extensive media coverage, as did demonstrations, held in Stockholm and other cities, which led the worried prime minister to postpone implementing new, restrictive rules for unemployment benefits (Ginsburg, 1996).

Politically, the government could not ignore unemployment, and in mid-1996 it unveiled a plan to halve open unemployment to 4 percent by 2000 (Prime Minister's Office, 1996). One component was a large and innovative expansion of adult education with stipends for both unemployed and employed participants with low educational levels and an expansion of higher education. But the plan (discussed later), with no new funds and financed partly by shifting funds from other programs, could not act as a fiscal stimulus to get the economy going, though it could (and did) convert some of the unemployed into students.

In 1997, however, with the election only a year away and polls showing support for the SAP the lowest in decades, the 1998 budget was more expansionary than the government had earlier proposed (Olsen, 1999, p. 262). Government demand, which had been declining, began to increase somewhat and probably triggered the economic upswing that began in the late 1990s (Berglund, 2000). Economic growth rose to nearly 4 percent by 1999, almost twice the EU average (Economist Intelligence Unit, 2000, p. 12). This led to less unemployment and more employment growth. During this expansion, strong domestic demand replaced export markets as the main engine of growth. As in the United States, the expansion was also partly fueled by a speculative stock market boom (Berglund, 2000), which has since abated. However, rising domestic employment has boosted consumer demand, and buoyant growth—though of uncertain duration—in Sweden's main export markets has also helped to sustain the boom.

The economic upturn did not save the SAP in the September 1998 election. While still the largest party, with only 36.4 percent of the votes, it was the SAP's worst showing since the 1920s. Total unemployment (including persons in labor market programs) was 10 percent prior to the election, but the SAP leadership claimed that it had "solved the economic crisis" (Von Otter, 1998, p. 3). Schools, health, and child care emerged as major issues, and, with widespread media coverage of scandalous conditions in some old-age institutions earlier in the year, so was elder care.

Although LO's leadership supported the SAP, only little over half of the rank and file voted for it (Von Otter, 1998). Symptomatic of a widening cleavage between them, this portends less political clout for LO in the future and a dwindling ability of the leadership to deliver votes. Many disaffected SAP supporters moved to the Left Party or stayed at home. Voter turnout, especially among Social Democrats, fell sharply, to 81 percent. Remarkably high by U.S. standards, it was Sweden's lowest turnout for a domestic parliamentary election in half a century (Von Otter, 1998). (Elections to the EU Parliament have had only half that turnout.)

Some (e.g., Burke, 1998) interpret the results of the 1998 election as pro-welfare state, since parties on the left and right that emphasized social welfare gained. The Left Party, doubling its support to 12 percent since 1994, was a clear winner and emerged as the third largest party, after the Moderates. Together, however, the SAP and Left did not do as well as they had in 1994 (dropping from 51.3 to 48.4 percent of the vote). The smaller non-socialist parties lost, but the Christian Democrats, a conservative party with a traditional view of women, campaigned on social welfare issues, especially elder care. It scored sharp gains, garnering nearly as many votes as the Left Party (Von Otter, 1998; SI, 1999b).

Despite deep losses, the SAP remained head of a minority government, dependent on support from both the Left and the small Green Party (which received 4.5 percent of the votes) for a parliamentary majority. As a result, the government has relented somewhat on the welfare state and employment goals (see below). Some Left Party members, however, believe that its leadership does not push the SAP as hard as possible because of a desire for a formal coalition that would make them part of the government, with cabinet positions (Romson, 2000).

A further complication is EMU membership, opposed by the SAP's working political partners. However, Prime Minister Persson said in late 1999 that it is only a matter of when, not whether, Sweden will join (Economist Intelligence Unit, 2000, pp. 14–15). In March 2000, a SAP Congress endorsed participation in EMU, although its membership is deeply divided on the issue. This has heightened tensions within the party and increased resentment among many that leadership elites are once more ignoring the grass roots (Burke, 2000). Barring democratizing and restructuring of the EMU and the EU and reorienting their goals to include full employment and reduction of inequalities, joining the EMU would make it more difficult for Sweden to attain these goals. Such a change was proposed by European Economists for an Alternative Economic Policy (1998) and others (Arestis, McCauley, and Sawyer, 2001), but would require considerable political energy and social movements to put it on the European agenda.

Unemployment at the end of the 1990s, as we have seen, remained far above the pre-crisis level despite its decline in the economic expansion. The government has sent conflicting messages, setting a new goal to increase substantially the proportion of the population in regular employment by 2004 (Ministry of Finance, 1999) *and* continuing fiscal conservatism. Three-year expenditure caps are in place that cannot be exceeded, even though Sweden has had a budget surplus since 1998; these caps take precedence over spending more on unmet social needs. Further, a new goal has been imposed: a 2 percent of GDP surplus over the business cycle. This exceeds even the EMU rule of a 3 percent deficit limit, again threatening budget cuts and even more unemployment in case of a recession, which normally increases the deficit.

Narrow Debate on Economic Issues

Korpi (1996) has shown that the economists who shaped the economic debate in the 1980s ignored critical analysis of what became the conventional wisdom. The official debate on basic economic issues in Sweden still takes place within extremely narrow confines. Price stability and a balanced budget—and now a budget surplus—take priority over increased employment and increased expenditures on social programs. Embracing neoliberal ideology, elites assume that the budget should always be balanced or in surplus, and they forget the lessons of the 1930s Stockholm School economists, who successfully argued for using the national budget as an economic stabilizer and against the orthodox idea of a balanced budget per se (Seligman, 1962, pp. 584–587; Meidner, 1998, p. 9). Also virtually ignored are the 1990s dissenting Swedish economists (e.g., Berglund, 1996; Meidner, 1998) and distinguished American ones (Vickrey, 1993; Eisner, 1995), as well as a critique of EU economic policy by seven Nobel laureates (Modigliani et al., 1998).

The Swedish economic and political establishment is wedded to the idea of a "natural" rate of unemployment, the so-called NAIRU, below which inflation is said to inevitably rise. Questions about its validity (Spånt, 1996; Meidner, 1998) are non-issues, as is the role of corporate Sweden in reshaping the nation to its own needs in the global economy. Even LO (1997, p. 5) has abandoned the primacy of the full employment goal, stating that, due to changes in the world economy, the conflict between full employment and stable prices has worsened gravely and that "we are forced to rank the goal of low inflation before that of full employment."

The government expects to meet its 4 percent unemployment goal early in the new millennium. Thus far, no goal to further reduce unemployment has been set. Even 4 percent, though a substantial improvement over the 1990s, is not full employment. It is high compared to most of Sweden's own post-war record and aspirations—when unemployment averaged 2 percent—and a government could fall if it allowed joblessness to hover around 3 percent. Inflation is virtually nonexistent in Sweden—it has been less than 1 percent since 1996 and is considerably lower than in the United States. Sweden's now autonomous Central Bank, with price stability as its sole responsibility, has a 2 percent inflation target. Fear of inflation could lead to a preemptory strike to prevent unemployment from getting "too low," or it could deflect from focusing on regaining full employment.

A discussion of possible full employment policies is beyond the scope of this chapter,[12] but a necessary requisite would be a strong political will to get there. It takes a high degree of social solidarity to reduce and sustain unemployment well below 4 percent. Whether Swedes, having tasted mass unemployment, will now settle for something less than what they once considered full employment, with the weakest left behind, is not known at present. This is a political and ideological, not an economic, issue. Budget cutting was justified in the 1990s by the oft-repeated official message, widely accepted and disseminated in the mass media, "We can't afford it," even as policies were being pursued that resulted in costly high unemployment. These led to additional expenditures on those made jobless and to a loss of tax revenues, as well as to an enormous loss of potential national output, which made the welfare state more difficult to finance! Full employment was always seen as one of the main economic pillars supporting the welfare state, and the welfare state, with generous income transfers and quality services, has enjoyed strong cross-class support. The status of a few of these many programs and of support for them is discussed later.

THE CURRENT SITUATION: THE DECLINE OF THE WELFARE STATE?

The Swedish Welfare State in Flux

The social solidarity of full employment policies promoted by the SAP in its heyday was reflected, also, in its social policies. Long regarded as the most advanced welfare state in the world, Sweden provided comprehensive services literally from cradle to grave. It did not have a system of privately run institutions. Universal use of readily available public programs, designed to facilitate personal development and societal well-being, encouraged their high quality (Bergmark, 1997; Palme and Wennemo, 1998) as well as support for the welfare state. Social and medical services are integral to the welfare state and account for about 40 percent of social welfare expenditures (Szebehely, 1998, p. 2).

Since the election of the conservative-led government in 1991, the previous pattern of welfare state expansion in Sweden has been reversed. Nearly every benefit program has been changed, some several times. In 1993, Parliament made extensive cuts in public expenditures. Although the SAP was returned to power in 1994, the reductions continued, and additional ones were made. With the recent economic recovery and political backlash from the 1998 pro-welfare state vote, some, but not all, of the cuts are being restored, though not always to their prior levels. There have even been increases in some programs (e.g., parenthood leave). Continuous changes have, however, eroded confidence in programs (Meidner, 1997a).

Over the past decade, several trends have emerged in Sweden's social welfare policies. These include reduced wage replacement rates and stricter eligibility rules for some benefits; decentralized and reduced standardization of services; staff reductions and program changes affecting the quality of social and health services; targeting (rationing) of services that were formerly more readily available; increased reliance on income-tested welfare programs; increases in user fees and the imposition of new ones; and a movement toward privatization of some service delivery. Most dramatic have been changes in the pension system that appear to weaken the economic security of future retirees and privatize a portion of contributions. Despite growing needs, transfer payments have declined as a percentage of GDP from a high of about 20.5 percent in 1992 to about 17 percent in 1997, the same level as in the early 1980s (National Social Insurance Board [NSIB], 1998, p. 12).

Welfare state programs and services are mainly financed by comparatively high taxes, and, since full employment provides their economic base, when employment levels drop, as they did during the 1990s, tax revenues also decline. The perception that Swedish tax levels are in great excess over those elsewhere is somewhat misleading. Many public services that Swedes receive at little or no cost are paid for privately in some countries, and for their taxes Swedes receive many benefits. For example, according to Esping-Andersen (1999, pp. 175–177), when the costs for an average family's health care, education, pensions, and child care—mainly covered by taxes and transfers in Sweden but through taxes, insurance payments, and out-of-pocket expenditures in the United States—are compared, the differences in costs to individuals are minuscule, around 1.5 percentage points. Swedes also get far better coverage in a broad array of benefits, while no one is left without health care, as in the United States.

Income Distribution, Wages, Demographic Trends, and Poverty

Swedes have had high living standards (Vogel, 1991) as well a very egalitarian system of income distribution. Of 15 OECD countries, Sweden had the smallest income gap between rich and poor in 1987 (OECD, 1995). But income inequality, which dropped sharply in the 1970s, has since been rising (Nelander and Lindgren, 1997). Between 1989, just before the onset of the crisis era, and 1997 the real disposable income of the poorest 10 percent of families fell by 29 percent, while the richest 10 percent gained nearly 15 percent, much of it from capital gains. Swedish families' median real disposable income dropped by nearly 4 percent; real disposable income of single-parent families fell by nearly 11 percent, and that of young people aged 18 to 29 and living with their parents (treated as singles with their own income) by nearly 43 percent (Statistics Sweden, 1999, tables 5, 6, 7). Median real earnings of 20- to 64-year-old full-time, full-year workers dropped from their 1990 peak and then stagnated until 1997, when they were about 3 percent higher than in 1990. But this masks a 2 percent drop in earnings for the bottom decile and an 8 percent increase for the top decile. Although the earnings spread has widened, it is still relatively modest. In 1990, the highest-earning decile of workers earned twice as much as the lowest, whereas in 1997, they earned 2.2 times as much (calculated from Statistics Sweden, 1999, table 8).

Sweden also had very low rates of poverty, especially in cross-national comparison, but rates have been rising since the mid-1980s. When the Luxembourg Income Study (LIS) comparative poverty standard of less than 50 percent of median income after taxes and transfers is used, 8.7 percent of households were poor in 1995—the comparable rate for the United States in 1994 was 17.9 percent—but this was up from 7.3 percent in 1992 and 5.6 percent in 1981 (LIS, 1998). Transfers play a major role in poverty reduction, particularly because the pension system has been geared to ensure a basic minimum for the elderly (Bradshaw and Terum, 1997).[13] The child allowances supplement the incomes of families with children; and a rather generous social assistance system assures a basic minimum income (Rosenthal, 1994).

Some of the pressure on the welfare state is attributable to demography. Sweden has a higher proportion of persons 65 and over (17.3 percent) than any OECD nation (OECD, 1998, p. 7) and growing numbers of the "old old." There has been a dramatic decline in poverty among the elderly, but some just scrape by. This is especially so for women over 75 living alone, although the proportion of them with incomes below Sweden's poverty line in 1994 had dropped sharply from 1987 as a result of a previous pension reform (National Board of Health and Welfare [NBHW], 1998a, p. 94). (It is important to note that the Swedish poverty line is based on a different concept and yields much higher poverty rates than the LIS standard.)[14] In contrast to old-age pensioners, persons with disability pensions (called early retirement pensions) experienced a rise in poverty in the 1990s (Vogel, 1997).

Fourteen percent of children live with a single parent (SI, 1998b), most of them mothers, and during the 1990s they became increasingly vulnerable to poverty, though the extent varies with the measure used (NBHW, 1999a, ch. 2; Jansson, 2001).[15] These families have been particularly affected by unemployment (Szebehely, 1998, p. 12); other factors predisposing these families to economic hardship include part-time and contingency work and reductions in social benefits. One telling measure of the inadequacy of their reserves is that 44 percent of single mothers ran completely out of cash at least once during 1994, compared to 25 percent of married or cohabiting women with children, and they were forced to borrow from family or friends or seek public assistance to pay for food or housing (NBHW, 1998a, p. 85).

Young people, especially those from blue-collar backgrounds, have experienced great difficulty establishing a career and have high long-term unemployment rates, partly because of the decline in industrial jobs. They have high poverty rates and utilize social assistance disproportionately compared to other age groups, as discussed further below.

Finally, immigrants, especially recent immigrants and refugees from non-European countries, have had persistent difficulties in gaining regular employment, and they have very high poverty rates compared to others.[16] The financial situation of young, working-age immigrants has been particularly difficult but may improve. With unemployment dropping in early 2000, the government said that immigrants are needed in the labor market and that special initiatives would be taken to help them.

Changes in Selected Programs

The 1990s witnessed repeated changes in income transfers, services, and other programs. A few of these are reviewed below.

Old Age Pensions. Sweden is a world leader in providing economic security for its elderly. This is largely because of its current pension system. But it is now being gradually phased out and replaced by a far more complicated and market-oriented one with an underlying ideology of individualism and some other features seemingly at odds with the economic and political values of its welfare state.

The old system is two-tiered. Its first tier is a universal, flat-rate pension paid in full *as a right* to residents at age 65 and providing basic income security.[17] The second tier, the ATP, is a supplementary earnings-related pension for which the SAP successfully struggled in the late 1950s. Meant to compensate for lost income and to maintain pre-retirement living standards, it is a defined benefit, related by a formula to prior earnings and years of employment. A full ATP, payable at age 65, requires 30 years of pensionable earnings and is calculated from an average of a worker's 15 best earning years. It and the basic pension together replace 65 percent of pre-retirement income (up to a limit), and most workers also receive about 10 percent from an employer-sponsored, negotiated pension (Ståhlberg, 1995). Both the basic pension and the ATP are indexed for inflation, though with budget cutting, full indexing was not always provided in the

1990s (Palme and Wennemo, 1998, p. 24; Olsen, 1999, p. 255). Both can be drawn starting at age 60 (with reductions), and the ATP can be postponed (with increases) until the age of 70. Those with little or no ATP, a diminishing group, also receive a pension supplement.

The basic pension is pay-as-you-go financed, mainly from an employer payroll tax with some contribution from general revenues. The ATP is mainly pay-as-you go, financed by an employer payroll tax with partial funding. Substantial buffer funds, akin to the Social Security Trust Fund in the United States, allow adjustments for demographic changes. They are invested mostly in government and housing bonds (Sundén, 1998).

The new system is entirely different. The ATP is replaced by another primary pension, the basic pension is abolished, and in its stead is a new "guarantee" pension. Unlike the old ATP, a defined benefit, the main component of the new pension is a more actuarially oriented defined contribution, with "no guarantee of a certain pension relative to pre-retirement income" (Ståhlberg, 1995, p. 272). This may create worker (as well as retiree) insecurity, regardless of the size of the eventual benefit, which will be virtually impossible to determine in advance. This may serve as an impetus for further private investing by those who can afford to do so and could weaken their commitment to the pension system itself.

Instead of the 15/30 formulation, the new pension is based on lifetime earnings and favors those with long, steady, full-time work lives. Though some credit is given for years of study or child care (but not elder care), the new system is especially problematic for those with considerable part-time, temporary, and other contingent work. This is part of the system's design, for as a leading proponent says, "it aims to eliminate intra- and intergenerational redistribution" (Ståhlberg, 1995, p. 271), and some are concerned that it will have a negative impact on women (Schönström and Lindkvist, 1998). Benefits at retirement will also be affected by general earnings growth in the economy during a person's work life. Age at retirement (retiring later will result in a higher pension, and vice versa) and remaining years of life expectancy for the cohort will also affect benefits; thus, if life expectancy increases, the pension will be lower, and vice versa. After retirement, annual benefit adjustments are indexed to wage growth rather than to prices and vary according to general earnings growth in the economy. Very slow or no growth automatically impacts negatively on benefits, without having to resort to a political process (Palme and Wennemo, 1998, p. 24). Another significant change is that the system is financed by a payroll tax paid half by the employer and, for the first time, half directly by the employee.

In addition, workers now have private, funded accounts, financed by a 2.5 percent payroll tax (part of the overall 18.5 percent payroll tax). Thus, Social Democratic Sweden has accomplished what a conservative U.S. Congress thus far has been unable to do, but what the new Bush administration may accomplish: partially privatize its old age pension system. These accounts provide "no guarantee" (Ministry of Health and Social Affairs, 1998, p. 15) for the worker, who will bear the financial risk. They can be invested with any authorized private or public pension fund or investment vehicle, domestic or foreign. Insurance companies had been trying for years to accomplish privatization by spreading the message of impending doom for the current system (Hagberg, 1999). Employers were dissatisfied with the ATP, and, according to Kangas and Palme (1996, p. 230), SAF advocated for a pension system that would be compulsory and employer-financed but invested in individual insurance premiums. A Conservative member of the group that worked on the "reform" admitted that private accounts were designed to gradually lure Swedes "away from socialism with the taste of the market" (quoted in Olsen, 1999, p. 256).

The other component of the new system also represents a sharp ideological retreat. The "guarantee pension" does provide a minimum income and is indexed to price changes, but it is *not a universal right*. It is paid only as an income-tested supplement to those 65 and older with little or no pension income. This backsliding from solidarity has political implications. Everyone has had a personal stake in the basic pension, but many, especially higher-income persons, have none in the guarantee pension; its smaller (and narrower) constituency makes it more politically vulnerable (Olsen, 1999), especially since it is financed separately and entirely from general revenues.

There is no longer a specific pensionable age: pension rights continue to grow as long as a person works, and pensions can be drawn anytime from age 61, except for the guarantee, which cannot be granted until age 65. Though not publicly stated, many pensions at age 65 are likely to be less adequate than in the past. The government has already announced that mandatory retirement will be banned until the age of 67; while a positive step in itself, its timing suggests that although some may wish to work to an older age, others will be forced to do so, and this could be especially hard on those who are exhausted from difficult work. This is likely to occur because of rule changes in the 1990s that made it harder for older workers to qualify for disability pensions. Under pension reform, disability pensions, formerly administered and financed through the old age system, are a separate class of insurance (NBHW, 1998a, pp. 55–56; Palme and Wennemo, 1998, pp. 25–27).

Enacted in 1998, the reform was forged by a group comprised of representatives of the major political parties that began working in 1991. All four non-socialist parties and the SAP agreed to the final version. The reform has caused turmoil at SAP party congresses, but the leadership resisted altering its decision to go forward with its support (Palme and Wennemo, 1998, p. 23), and it has been accused of stifling discussion (Hagberg, 1998). The reform was presented to the public as a necessity, with claims that the old system would be unsustainable for the baby boomers. However, two of Sweden's leading actuaries (Hagberg, 1998, 1999; Wohlner, 1999), both Social Democrats, contend that the ATP system is in good shape and that any change, if needed, could be accomplished with minor alterations. The issues, they feel, are political and ideological and demanded a full-fledged debate; instead, the plan was presented as a technical issue and received little public discussion. They predict a worsening of old age security for many Swedes, and an OECD report (1996) suggests that the new pension system may result in increasing numbers of the elderly having to rely on social assistance because those who have not had regular, full-time employment over their working lives will have insufficient pension income. This is, of course, more likely to occur in the absence of full employment, especially if the trend toward contingent work persists.

Insurance for Sickness, Occupational Injury, and Unemployment. Employment-connected benefits have been under attack for some time. SAF has pressured for reductions in benefits, particularly sickness benefits, since the mid-1970s. This insurance has been undergoing constant rule changes affecting eligibility requirements, replacement rates, and duration (Palme and Wennemo, 1998, pp. 31–36).

During the boom economy of the late 1980s, absenteeism rose to levels much higher than in other countries (Edin and Andersson, 1995, p. 6). This resulted in a successful drive to make access to sickness benefits more difficult. However, according to an analysis by Joachim Vogel of Statistics Sweden (1995), a very small group of workers with chronic illnesses and handicaps accounted for a large proportion of compensated sick leave days, and their absences can be seen as part of the "price of full employment" since such an economy employs people who are likely to be out of the labor force elsewhere.

Rule changes have reduced the use of sickness and occupational injury insurance. Since 1993, the first day of sick leave has not been compensated, and the wage replacement rate has been lowered—from 90 percent of earnings in the late 1980s, to 75 percent in the mid-1990s, and then up to 80 percent at the beginning of 1998 (NSIB, 1996; SI, 1997b; Palme and Wennemo, 1998, pp. 27–28). Further, since 1992, employers rather than the insurance fund have administered and paid for the first 14 days of sick pay (NSIB, 1996, p. 38). This is one factor that has resulted in lower use, because employees feel intimidated by this new form of employer authority (Meidner, 1997a).

A dramatic instance of belt-tightening, which has been sharply criticized, can be found in occupational injury insurance. Beginning in 1993, much more restrictive qualification rules and benefit reductions have reduced reported cases by 86 percent from 1991 to 1996; at the same time, the acceptance rate declined from 80 percent to 56 percent (NSIB, 1998, p. 42). (Occupational injuries were formerly compensated at 100 percent of past earnings. Now, unless the injury is permanent, the worker instead receives sickness benefits, which replace only 80 percent of wages [Palme and Wennemo, 1998, p. 17].)

Although some believe that generous unemployment benefits are a disincentive to work, Sweden's benefits were most generous when unemployment was lowest and participation in the labor force highest. Unemployment insurance, which has a five-day waiting period, replaced 90 percent of former wages in the late 1980s but only 75 percent in 1997; in 1998, the replacement rate was raised to 80 percent, but eligibility was made much more restrictive (Salonen and Johansson, 1999a). Eligibility requires a work history and membership in a union-affiliated fund and is time-limited, and the claimant must accept a suitable job offer or retraining (SI, 1997b). Although Sweden has tried to avoid long-term unemployment through labor-market policies, a large problem when there is chronic high unemployment is that benefits are formally limited to little over a year (longer for those 57 and over). In practice, however, many of the long-term unemployed have requalified for benefits after participating in labor-market programs. Some of the unemployed not covered by the main unemployment insurance system may qualify for different, but meager, benefits.

Support for Families with Children. Family policy combines universal child allowances, generous parental leave policies for working parents with newborn or sick children, child support advances to single parents where the absent parent is delinquent in paying child support, publicly supported child care, and income-tested housing grants and social assistance. Together, these policies were highly successful in reducing poverty for families with children and enabling mothers of young children to participate in the paid workforce (Rosenthal, 1990, 1994; Gustafsson, 1995; Sundström, 1999). While these policies continue, they have been modified to reduce costs, and they are less effective than formerly. Families with children—especially those with single parents or numerous children or those with small children headed by young parents—were hit hard by the increase in poverty in the 1990s (Nelander and Lindgren, 1997; Vogel, 1997, p. 632).

The child allowance grew incrementally until 1996, when it was cut 15 percent, and the additional benefit to large families was eliminated (NSIB, 1998, p. 25; Palme and Wennemo, 1998, p. 29). Backlash to these cuts led to the 1998 restoration of the large family allowance (SI, 1998b), and the basic child allowance is going up (Ministry of Finance, 1999).

Parental leave for birth or adoption replaces wages for 360 days, if each parent takes at least 30 days' leave. It declined from 90 percent of former wages in the late 1980s to 75 percent by the mid-1990s, though it has been raised to 80 percent recently. An additional 90 days is compensated at a very low flat rate (SI, 1997b). Parents can also take up to 60 days of leave per year for the care of a sick child under the age of 12, now compensated at 80 percent of wages. Mothers are the primary users of these benefits. In an effort to increase usage by fathers, parental leave will be extended by one month beginning in 2002, with two months reserved for the mother and two months reserved for the father (Ministry of Finance, 2000).

Housing Policies. Homelessness is rare, and its slight increase is primarily related to deinstitutionalization of psychiatric patients whom local authorities have been unable to reach or treat, as required (Burke, 2000). Substandard housing is virtually unknown in Sweden, due in no small part to the "million program" in the 1960s, which resulted in massive housing construction, a housing modernization program in the 1980s, and affordable housing. Affordable housing has been assured through public ownership and financing of large portions of the housing stock and income-tested housing benefits for families and the elderly. Slightly more than half the population live in rented apartments (SI, 1998b), and about 50 percent of them are owned by non-profit municipal housing authorities. Rents are set—both in public and private complexes—by negotiations between owners and tenant organizations (SI, 1996b, p. 2). The trend is to relax rent-setting regulations, and homeownership, including apartment purchasing, is encouraged. Some Conservative-dominated local governments have sold off public housing and adopted other privatizing measures.

Housing benefits are important for low-income households but have been cut. Housing allowances for families with children and the housing supplements for the elderly are different programs and separately administered. In 1993, one-third of families with children received housing allowances, and currently 22 percent of all households, mostly elderly pensioners, receive housing supplements (SI, 1996b, 1998b). A new system for testing income was established in 1996 for housing allowances. Housing benefits for working-age households without children where at least one person is 29 years old or more were eliminated, and the income of each adult, rather than the combined family income, is now examined. The result was a 33 percent drop in housing allowance expenditures between 1995 and 1997 (NSIB, 1998, pp. 29–30). A housing allowance can add somewhat more than 10 percent to the annual income of low-income families, and for low-income pensioners, housing supplements can cover as much as 85 percent of their rent (SI, 1998b, p. 3).

Social Services, Decentralization, and Austerity

Local governments—both municipal and county—have a prominent role in providing social services, but the central government mandates standards or sets guidelines for some services (Gould, 1996; Bergmark, 1997). More than two-thirds of public services—including child care, care of persons with disabilities, substance abuse programs, family and child welfare, social assistance, and care of the elderly and the mentally ill—are provided and financed locally, with some national contributions (Salonen and Johansson,

1999b). Municipalities are also responsible for primary and secondary schools (also formerly a county responsibility) as well as some post-secondary adult education (but not universities) and job training. In the last decade, several county functions have been shifted to municipalities to cut costs and, theoretically, to make social programs more responsive to local needs.

Municipal expenditures amounted to 25 percent of Sweden's GDP in 1995 (SI, 1996a, p. 3). Since communities raise their own taxes and have different tax bases, they have varying amounts of funds to expend, and quality disparities are developing (Szebehely, 1998). (Some funds, however, are transferred from richer to poorer jurisdictions.) National funding of mandated services decreased in the 1990s; in addition, municipal and county coffers were lowered because high unemployment resulted in reduced tax revenues while assistance demands increased. Between 1992 and 1995, municipalities' income decreased by 11 percent (Bergmark, 1997, p. 75). They responded by targeting and lowering benefits and by increasing work demands on employees. Since municipalities have considerable autonomy, the percentage of residents receiving services varies widely from community to community (Thorslund et al., 1997). Starting in 2001, local authorities are required to achieve balanced budgets and many of them have been obliged to cut spending as a result.

Child Care. In Sweden's famous child-care system, which is highly subsidized, the number of children rose by about 60 percent between the mid-1980s and the mid-1990s; by then, 86 percent of preschool children with two working (or studying) parents and 91 percent of children in corresponding single-parent households were in publicly supported child care (Szebehely, 1998, pp. 6, 10)—but expenditures on the system remained virtually unchanged (Bergmark, 1997, p. 77). In addition to raising fees, this was achieved by increasing the average number of children per child-care worker from 4 to 6 in day-care centers and from 8 to 11 in after-school programs (NBHW, 1997, p. 33). The educational requirements for child-care workers have been increased, on the theory that better-trained personnel can handle larger numbers of children (J. Korpi, 1997; Winberg, 1997), but there is a widespread perception that the quality of care has declined (Baude, 1997; NBHW, 1997, pp. 32–34). National funding, formerly earmarked for specific child-care services, is now part of general grants for all municipal activities, resulting in growing variation in service quality and fees, which vary widely among municipalities. Rationing of services has also taken place. Although child care is supposed to be universally available, some children with an unemployed parent have been excluded, even though these children—many of them from immigrant families—are arguably those most in need of care and exposure to the Swedish language (NBHW, 1997, p. 29). Responding to these problems, the government (Ministry of Finance, 2000) announced that children of the unemployed will soon have the right to child care and that fees, which are modest but had been rising and became a cause of major concern, will be limited. Municipalities will be compensated for the cost of these reforms, which are voluntary. In 2003, four- and five-year-olds will have the right to three hours of free, universal preschool daily.

Another significant change is that municipalities have begun to subsidize private child-care centers, primarily parent cooperatives utilized principally by higher-income parents. In 1995, 12 percent of preschoolers were in private facilities (NBHW, 1997, pp. 28–29).

Elder Care. After World War II, Sweden pioneered in publicly provided programs to enable the elderly, including the frail, to live in their own homes as long as possible. These include generous funding of apartment renovation, transportation, shopping services, and day centers. The number of places in large custodial institutions declined. "Service houses," where people live in their own apartments but can get services as needed, were developed (Korpi, 1995; Szebehely, 1998). Rapid expansion of home help was crucial in allowing the elderly to live at home while freeing their family members (mostly adult daughters) for employment (Szebehely, 1998). Care of the elderly—what Korpi (1995, p. 255) has called "one of the main areas for public policy" in Sweden—has changed significantly in the last 15 years. Like child care, responsibility for elder care shifted from the counties to municipalities in 1992, but while child care has expanded, elder care has significantly retracted.

Between the late 1970s and 1995, the number of people receiving home help declined by 100,000, even though the population over 80 years grew by 170,000. In 1980, 36 percent of persons 80 and over received home help, but only 21 percent did so in 1995, and the proportion receiving any kind of help (including institutional care or living in service houses) dropped from 62 to 45 percent (Szebehely, 1998, p. 15). Public expenditures for home help have actually increased since 1980. However, home help formerly was directed at *all* elderly persons who had difficulty managing household chores, not only the poorest or sickest or those without relatives living nearby, on whom this help is now concentrated (Szebehely, 1998). Other cost-reduction strategies include decreasing the amount of care given, cutting personnel, raising fees significantly, and increasing the care burden for family members, particularly women (Szebehely, 1998; SI, 1999c). The trend is for municipalities to deny help to elderly people who need assistance only with cleaning and chores, once considered legitimate home-help functions. Many of the elderly are hiring private helpers, although they prefer public services (Szebehely, 1998).

Similar targeting has characterized nursing home care, also a municipal responsibility since 1992. It is available only for those with severe medical problems, often combined with dementia (Korpi, 1995, p. 267). Elderly persons with other serious impairments must now rely on home help or informal care. In 1991, about 11 percent of nursing home beds were privately operated, some of them with public subsidies (Korpi, 1995, p. 268). Unlike in child care, most non-public old age care is provided by large, profit-making companies, some of them foreign (Szebehely, 1998), and privatization, much of it coming under public fire because of poor conditions, is increasing.

These changes erode the principle of universalism and represent a departure from the solidarity principles underlying the welfare state. Targeting leads to the purchasing of care by those who are not considered eligible for public services but who can afford it. Access to care thus increasingly becomes tied to income (Daatland, 1997). According to Sune Sunesson, when home help expanded significantly in the 1960s and 1970s, it won considerable support for the welfare state because elder care was no longer associated with poor relief (cited by Szebehely, 1998, p. 15). Although support for public services still remains high (Svallfors, 1997), rising fees and the declining availability of home help may erode support for the welfare state. It also threatens women's advances in paid employment since more of them must provide unpaid family care, and indeed, it is now the expectation that family members—especially elderly spouses and adult daughters—have the primary responsibility for caring for their relatives.

Health Care. Health care is universally available and highly subsidized or free. Sweden scores high on international health indicators. Its infant mortality, half that of the United States, is among the world's lowest (OECD, 1998, p. 52), while life expectancy is among the highest, 76.5 years for men and 81.5 years for women. But there are marked and growing disparities in health status across socioeconomic groups (NBHW, 1998b, pp. 31–39; SI, 1999c, p. 1).

Health care is primarily provided through local health clinics and county and regional hospitals. In the 1990s, a declining tax base led to cuts in expenditures, which dropped by 10 percent in real terms (Szebehely, 1998; SI, 1999c, p. 3). Hospitals have greatly reduced the number of beds, the length of stays, and the number of medical personnel. The nursing staff has been sharply cut: primary nurses numbered 85,000 in 1994 but only 70,000 in 1997, and nurse aides experienced even steeper drops, and there are now nursing shortages (SI, 1997c, p. 2, 1999c, p. 3). As in the case of child care, qualifications have increased: nurses are preferred to nurse aides but are expected to perform considerably more work (Baude, 1997; SI, 1999c). Efforts to allow more choice of primary care physicians and to reduce bureaucratic rigidities and waiting times in the county-based health care system have had some success (SI, 1999c). Private medical care has grown, and in some cases, county councils are encouraging competition between public and private sector providers. Hospital fees, set centrally, are uniform and very low, but fees for physicians and ancillary medical services are established at the county level; they vary and recently have risen considerably. Since counties raise their own taxes, wealthier districts can raise more revenues and rely less on fees, which may be lower than in poorer districts. There are, however, ceilings established nationally. The total of annual fees that an adult may pay for health care is approximately $125, and there are no fees for anyone under the age of 20. There is a separate ceiling for pharmaceuticals, and more of their costs are now borne by patients. Dental care is free for those under 20, but costs for adults, who may incur considerable expenses, have been rising (NSIB, 1995, 1996, 1998; SI, 1999c). There is evidence that those with lower incomes and the long-term unemployed seeking social assistance may avoid seeking medical attention and dental care because of the costs (NBHW, 1998b, pp. 33–34, 286–287).

Social Assistance and New Training Programs for Disadvantaged Youth. Social assistance, a residual, means-tested program akin to public assistance in the United States (but far more generous), has survived as a successor of the poor law and is a local responsibility, except for refugees, whom the national government aids for an initial three-year period. Once little discussed, social assistance has become a major ideological and financial concern. Adequacy, equity, and equality as well as the need to connect recipients to training and job opportunities are significant issues. Though Sweden has not invoked time limits for social assistance, recent legislative changes have profoundly affected recipients' rights.

Total outlays for social assistance rose dramatically between 1991 and 1997 as a result of mass unemployment and cutbacks in social benefits (Salonen and Johansson, 1999b, pp. 12–13), a more than doubling of non-refugee immigrant households, and a 32 percent rise in refugee households receiving assistance between 1990 and 1995 (NBHW, 1997, table 17, p. 107). Expenditures declined 8 percent in 1998 and again in 1999, a result of the improved economy and a significant drop in the number of new immigrants, especially refugees, into Sweden. Still, about 10 percent of the working-age households received assistance, and almost half the outlays went to immigrant and refugee households (Statistics Sweden, 2000).

Social assistance is the backup program for individuals and families who have insufficient income from work and/or other transfer programs, including unemployment insurance, child allowances, and housing allowances. Many who qualify for assistance (close to 10 percent of the population) do not apply (NBHW, 1998a, p. 760). Social assistance accounts for only a small proportion of recipients' income in most cases, since they receive other benefits and may have income from earnings. Those totally dependent on social assistance are single adults with no work history or persons who have exhausted their unemployment insurance. Increased utilization of social assistance results from unemployment and cutbacks in other transfers. For instance, an estimated 79 percent of the increase in social assistance in 1996 resulted from these cuts, especially the housing allowance, the child allowance, and education benefits instituted that year (Salonen, 1997).

Childless single adults with inadequate or sporadic income from work are the most frequent recipients, joined in the 1990s by more single-parent and immigrant families. In 1995, at the near peak of unemployment, 40 percent of working-age recipients were aged 18 to 29 (NBHW, 1997, p. 70); this proportion persisted, and in 1998, almost 20 percent of 20- to 24-year-olds received social assistance (NBHW, 2000). Immigrant and second-generation youth are especially hard hit: their rate of dependency is much higher than that of native Swedes, regardless of level of education (NBHW, 1998a, p. 104). One-third of single-parent families receive assistance during the course of a year (NBHW, 1998a, p. 96).

Most recipients receive help for only a short time. The average length of receipt of social assistance for all household types increased slightly from 4.6 months in 1993 to 5.6 months in 1997 and 1998 (longer for immigrant households); 20 percent of the total are long-term recipients (NBHW, 1997, p. 70, 2000). The term "marginalization"—referring to those out of the workforce, dependent on social assistance, living in poor neighborhoods, and suffering disproportionately from personal difficulties such as social isolation, poor health, and exposure to violence—is beginning to surface in the Swedish literature (NBHW, 1998a).

Bradshaw and Terum (1997) have characterized the Nordic model of social assistance as generous but highly discretionary (resulting in inequities) and also rehabilitative and social control–oriented. That is, it enforces behavioral norms, particularly work. In Sweden, social assistance is carefully means-tested by the municipal social assistance offices. The Social Services Law of 1982, the blueprint for all social services administered by the municipalities, made social assistance a right and set a national norm for social assistance, thus guaranteeing a minimally decent living standard. The worsening economy of the 1990s hit municipalities hard, and as the financial burden of providing for the unemployed increased, they cut back on their aid. According to a 1992 study, about 75 percent of municipalities were paying benefits at below the minimum standard (cited by Salonen, 1993, p. 186). The 1982 law also provided for court appeals if applicants or recipients felt that they were being improperly denied assistance or were entitled to more help. This clause was widely invoked, and complainants usually won.

In 1998, changes relieved the municipalities of some financial burden through national contributions to the municipal programs, ensuring better support to recipients. The changes reiterated the requirement that municipalities provide sufficient assistance for a "reasonable standard of living," including access to a telephone, television, and a daily newspaper. But it eliminated the right of legal appeal for allowance increases and special expenditures, thus increasing the discretionary powers of social assistance workers. For example, one social assistance administrator reported that the workload had increased dramatically because municipal authorities were cutting staff and the assistance budget, assistance was becoming much more punitive, and staff were "muzzled" (an illegal practice) from commenting about these trends (Tilander, 1997).

Social assistance regulations have always required unemployed recipients to participate in job training or municipal work relief. With mass unemployment, this requirement was difficult to implement, particularly for the large numbers of never-employed young adults. A new Development Guarantee Program, combining features of Sweden's labor market (re)training practices and poor relief traditions, sets up a voluntary relationship between municipal governments and the nationally run labor market boards (employment centers) (Salonen and Johansson, 1999a). It requires that all unemployed social assistance recipients between the ages of 20 and 24 engage in education, training, or publicly supported temporary work. Public funds subsidize wages of these young workers who find private jobs; however, in most cases, young people are employed directly by municipalities in arrangements that resemble workfare. These are not supposed to be regular jobs, but often they are. Depending on their prior work histories and eligibility, young trainees are paid unemployment benefits, training grants through the Labor Market Board, or social assistance allowances. Thus, trainees may do the same tasks but receive differing compensation, a departure from Swedish solidarity principles.

Another approach to upgrading the skills of the unemployed or poorly educated workers, the Adult Education Initiative, began in July 1997, and 190,000 were involved within a year (Salonen and Johansson, 1999b, p. 10). In addition, adult education at universities and vocational training schools has expanded greatly in recent years to prepare young workers for the high-technology economy and to occupy them constructively while they are unemployed. There was a 48 percent increase in the number of university students between 1990 and 1996 (Salonen and Johansson, 1999a, p. 3), and further expansion of higher education is planned (Ministry of Finance, 1999).

It is not yet known whether these programs have integrated the young unemployed into the labor market, and much of their success or failure will depend on the status of the economy when they enter the labor market. Salonen and Johansson (1999b, p. 10) attribute much of the decline of young adult unemployment to enrollment in the Adult Education Initiative—in other words, a shift from open unemployment to educational activities. In the Development Guarantee program, the goal of keeping young people busy may have displaced that of meaningful job preparation, where the trainee has an active role in choosing his or her training (Salonen and Johansson, 1999a). Nonetheless, these efforts compare favorably to the limited action of many other Western European countries and the United States.

CONCLUSION

To us as Americans, Sweden still looks like a welfare state leader, with an impressive array of social programs and social benefits that seem generous, though less so than in the past. But the welfare state has been under siege, and while mass unemployment has abated and the economy is booming, there is still no commitment to full employment, the bedrock on which the welfare state was built. There are, therefore, reasons to fear that social and economic equality, which has eroded, may continue to do so; that those with no or unstable work may be marginalized; and that although there is broad support for gender equality, Sweden may partly reverse its 30-year effort to achieve it through shrinking the public sector and increasing the unpaid care burden of women. Currently, young blue-collar workers, single mothers, and immigrants are particularly vulnerable to increasing poverty because the changing economy has excluded more of them from stable employment, and social policies are increasingly geared toward rewarding those with long-term, steady work.

How much retrenchment has taken place in the Swedish welfare state? Paul Pierson (1996) has developed three criteria for evaluating retrenchment, discussed in the introduction to this book. They are (1) a significant increase in reliance on means-tested programs (as opposed to universal) benefits; (2) a major shift in responsibility from the public to the private sector; and (3) dramatic changes in eligibility rules that indicate a qualitative change in the nature of a particular program.

Applying these criteria, we find an increased reliance on means-tested programs and changes in many social welfare programs over the past decade. Of particular concern is the pension system, which may, we think, leave more of the elderly poor in the future. Added to this is the significant decline in elder services that both guaranteed a dignified old age and freed daughters from a triple burden. Powerful business interests have and still are pushing for privatization, which has already made an inroad in the new pension system. While it has also made an inroad in the public services sector, it does not yet play a major role there, but that role is steadily increasing. In this regard, most Swedes, including the large and pivotal middle class, prefer public to privately provided social services, and their preference increased during the retrenchment period, with the exception of the elites (Svallfors, 1997), who dominate the seats of administrative and political power. Increasing local governments' responsibilities for providing services has resulted in fewer services, in disparities in their provision, and, in some cases, a decline in quality. Thus, on many fronts, social and economic solidarity has lessened. Sweden's welfare state has certainly not been dismantled, but it has been diminished. Even here, the pattern is uneven. For instance, the proportion of children served by public child care has expanded, while the proportion of the elderly served by public home care has contracted (Szebehely, 1998). Furthermore, the universal old age basic pension is being replaced by an income-tested pension.

Changes in Sweden (and in other welfare states) have been attributed to the inevitable impact of globalization (or Europeanization). That is an over-simplification, however. It masks a shift of power away from labor to capital and implies that nothing can be done about it. While Swedish capital is engaged in an economic, political, and ideological offensive, Swedish labor, albeit weakened by unemployment, has failed to mobilize its rank and file to resist changed conditions and policies. In addition, the SAP leadership accepts many of the premises of the right in its efforts to unravel aspects of the Swedish welfare state. Though global capital sorely needs international regulation and international movements to challenge it, national governments still have power (Ginsburg et al., 1997; Bakker, 1999; Navarro, 1999). Despite constraints, the Swedish government is not as powerless as it has often claimed to be. Ironically, as it cedes power to supranational organizations, it thrusts more responsibility and costs onto local governments. Many of the limits to policy, such as meeting EU convergence criteria or maintaining a budgetary surplus, were self-imposed. Increasingly, significant issues such as financial deregulation, tax reform, and now pension reform and the EMU are presented as technical problems rather than political issues, with solutions to be made by the experts. One result is political apathy.

There is reason to believe, however, that domestic policy making responsive to the electorate survives, as the results of the 1998 election show. Domestic issues—schools, health and elder care—dominated the election, and, with the SAP dependent on support from the Left and Greens, some, but not all, benefits are being restored or even expanded. However, the government's commitment to maintaining a budget surplus and other neoliberal goals may undermine these efforts to make some restorations, and there is no indication that the public sector will be returned to its former level.

Politics still matter in Sweden, and since social welfare policies have been largely universal and generous, support for them is widespread (Korpi and Palme, 1998). Whether the increased reliance on means testing or lower benefit levels and the declining availability and quality of some essential services will undermine this commitment remains to be seen. It also remains to be seen whether a strong political movement to keep pressure on for maintaining the welfare state can be developed and sustained. Finally, it remains to be seen whether commitment to full employment will be reborn in Sweden, and, if not, whether the welfare state can flourish in its absence.

NOTES

The authors thank Al Burke, editor of the Nordic News Network, for helpful comments on an earlier draft of this chapter, and June Zaccone for insightful editorial suggestions. We owe an intellectual debt of gratitude to Rudolf Meidner, and we thank him as well as the more than 100 persons from government, unions, business, political parties, academia, and other organizations who generously shared their time, expertise, and ideas. The staffs of the Swedish Institute in Stockholm, the Swedish Information Service in New York, and the Swedish Embassy in Washington, DC, also provided invaluable assistance.

Two of Helen Lachs Ginsburg's three research trips to Sweden in the 1990s were supported by a grant from the Professional Staff Conference/Research Foundation of the City University of New York, and Marguerite Rosenthal's research trip was part of an academic sabbatical from Salem State College. Helen Lachs Ginsburg also benefitted from discussions with participants at the Columbia University Seminar on Full Employment and at a conference of the unemployed in Hofors, Sweden, as did Marguerite Rosenthal at a conference on Social Exclusion at Lund University and as a member of the Citizenship and Social Policy Seminar at the Minda de Gunzburg Center for European Studies at Harvard University.

1. Equality between men and women in Sweden has been written about extensively. Policies have aimed at both assisting women to work and encouraging men to take a more active role at home. Current assessments are that, although there is not perfect equality either at work or at home, there has been movement toward greater equality. See Furst (1999).

2. Inflation in Sweden and the rest of OECD Europe averaged 4.9 percent from 1960 to 1973, while Sweden's unemployment, which averaged 1.8 percent, was less than Europe's 3.0 percent. From 1974 to 1982, Sweden and Europe had virtually the same average inflation rate, 10.4 and 10.3 percent, but Sweden's unemployment hardly budged, averaging 2.1 percent, while Europe's had doubled to 6.3 percent. From 1983 to 1986, growth increased more in Sweden than in Europe; unemployment rose slightly to 3.0 percent in Sweden and considerably, to 10.7 percent, in Europe; inflation fell to an average of 7.1 percent in Europe and 7.3 percent in Sweden (data from Rivlin, 1987, p. 4).

3. The main issue, nuclear energy, had been championed by the SAP and opposed by the Center (former Agrarian) Party, head of the new government, but supported by their Liberal and Conservative partners (Hadenius, 1985, pp. 143–145). A popular anti-nuclear protest movement resulted in a 1979 referendum recommending an eventual phase-out of nuclear power plants, a process that began in 2000.

4. For their other policies, see Pontusson (1992, pp. 314–315).

5. The figure is 7 percent, if measures adopted by the previous non-socialist regime are excluded.

6. Except for the very highest-income households, who were most affected by tax increases, including those on capital gains, the combined impact of benefit cuts and tax increases was regressive, and the poorest households saw the steepest proportionate decline in disposable income (Ministry of Finance, 1995d, p. 72).

7. All labor force figures are from the annual labor force surveys of Statistics

Sweden, AKU (Arbetskraftsundersökningen) (kindly provided by Olle Wessberg) for various years, and cover employment, unemployment, labor force participation rates, temporary employment, and so on; some are republished in their original (unadjusted) form by the U.S. Department of Labor, Bureau of Labor Statistics (2000). Since these are the figures that are used in public discourse in Sweden, we use them here unless otherwise specified. It should be noted that Swedish unemployment figures rise when adjusted for comparability to U.S. figures by the U.S. Bureau of Labor Statistics (BLS), mainly because students seeking work are counted as unemployed in the U.S. labor force survey, but not in the Swedish one. The gap between Sweden's official rate and the BLS-adjusted one was negligible when unemployment was low. In 1990, when the official rate was 1.7 percent, the adjusted one was 1.8 percent. Rising unemployment widened the gap. By 1997, the official rate was 8.0 percent and the adjusted one was 10.1 percent. The gap narrowed as unemployment fell. In 1999, the official rate was 5.6 percent and the BLS adjusted one was 7.1 percent (U.S. Bureau of Labor Statistics, 2000).

8. Olsen (1999, p. 248) points out that Gösta Rehn always disputed the idea that labor market programs should be equated with open unemployment and "unproductive idleness."

9. Calculations based on data from LO (2000) and Statistics Sweden labor force surveys (AKU).

10. This is a subgroup of immigrants who are not Swedish citizens. Among them, unemployment in 1999 varied from about 14 percent for Chileans to 37 percent for Iranians. Labor force participation among foreign nationals is also much lower for non-Nordics, as is the employment-to-population ratio, which in 1999 was 73 percent for the whole working-age population of Sweden compared to nearly 46 percent for non-Nordic and 66 percent for Nordic nationals.

11. Excludes employers and persons working in family businesses.

12. One multifaceted approach to full employment that eschews deregulation of the labor market has been proposed by Rudolf Meidner (1998). It includes, among many other policies, measures to selectively stimulate domestic demand by restoring purchasing power of low-income groups—a policy that has modestly begun—and an active, government-led industrial and regional policy to help fill the investment gap.

13. Income-tested housing supplements have also played a role.

14. In 1987, about 40 percent of women 75 and over and living alone were below Sweden's poverty line (used in the NBHW Report, 1998a), compared to just under 20 percent in 1994. This poverty line is based on the income needed for a decent standard of living that allows a relatively high rent. This standard influences the poverty rate for some people, especially elderly widows still living in the apartments that they previously occupied with their husbands and children. Using another poverty line—one that uses the average rent for a decent-sized apartment—between 1987 and 1994 the poverty rate for elderly women 75 and over and living alone dropped from 18.2 to 7.6 percent. Both of these methods yield considerably higher poverty rates than one based on a standard of less than 50 percent of median income (Jansson, 2001). For a discussion of definitions and various measurements of poverty, see NBHW (1998a, ch. 2).

15. Between 1994 and 1998, the percentage of single parents and their children living in households with income below the Swedish poverty line that allows *av-*

erage rent for a decent-sized apartment (see note 14) rose from 18.7 to 23.5 percent; the rise is far less dramatic—from 5.1 to 5.7 percent—measuring the proportion living in households with less than 50 percent of median income for all persons (Jansson, 2001).

16. In 1993/1994, 17.4 percent of households with at least one adult born abroad were at or below the Swedish poverty line that allows a relatively high rent (see note 14), compared to 11.2 percent where all adults were born in Sweden (NBHW, 1998a, table 7, p. 99).

17. It is reduced for those who have not lived in Sweden for 40 years; if they have lived in Sweden for less than 40 years but have worked in Sweden for 30 years, it is not reduced.

REFERENCES

AMS [National Labor Market Board]. (1984). *Jämställdhet po arbetsmarknaden statistik* (Equality in the Labor Market, Statistics). Solna, Sweden: AMS.

Arestis, P., K. McCauley, and M. Sawyer. (2001). *The Future of the Euro: Is There An Alternative to the Stability and Growth Pact?* Levy Institute Public Policy Brief No. 63. Annandale-on-Hudson, NY: The Jerome Levy Economics Institute at Bard College. Available on the Internet at www.levy.org.

Bakker, I. (1999). "Globalization and human development in the rich countries: Lessons from labour markets and welfare states." In *Globalization with a Human Face*, Background Papers, Vol. #2, Human Development Report 1999. New York: United Nations Development Programme, pp. 29–80.

Baude, A. (1997). Personal interview with Marguerite Rosenthal, May 14.

Bergmark, A. (1997). "From reforms to rationing? Current allocative trends in social services in Sweden." *Scandinavian Journal of Social Welfare* 6: 74–81.

Berglund, P. G. (1996). *Konsten att avskaffa arbetslösheten*. Stockholm: Ordfronts forlag.

———. (2000). Personal interview with Helen Ginsburg, April 28.

Blomberg, H. (1999). "Do cutbacks pay off? Perceived changes in the standard of municipal services and attitudes towards services among citizens and municipal decision makers in Finland." *International Journal of Social Welfare* 8: 206–220.

Bradshaw, J., and L. I. Terum. (1997). "How Nordic is the Nordic model? Social assistance in a comparative perspective." *Scandinavian Journal of Social Welfare* 6: 247–256.

Burke, A. (1994). "Great European expectations." *The Swedish Example: An International Newsletter* 1(2): 1–6. Lidingö, Sweden: Nordic News Network.

———. (1998). "A different angle on the news from Sweden." Supplement to *Nordic News Network Guide to the 1998 Swedish National Election*. Lidingö: Nordic News Network, p. 4.

———. (2000). Telephone interview with Helen Ginsburg, May 8.

Canova, T. (1994). "The Swedish model betrayed." *Challenge* (May/June): 36–40.

Carroll, E. (1993). "Swedish austerity: Benefits at risk." *Multinational Monitor* (January/February): 33–36.

Chang, C., and C. Sorrentino. (1991). "Union membership statistics in 12 countries." *Monthly Labor Review* (December): 46–53.

Cook, A. H. (1980). "Collective bargaining as a strategy for achieving equal opportunity and equal pay: Sweden and West Germany." In R. Steinberg Ratner, ed., *Equal Employment Policy for Women*. Philadelphia: Temple University Press, pp. 199–226.

Daatland, S. O. (1997). "Welfare policies for older people in transition? Emerging trends and comparative perspectives." *Scandinavian Journal of Social Welfare* 6: 153–161.

De Geer, H. (1992). *The Rise and Fall of the Swedish Model: The Swedish Employers' Confederation and Industrial Relations over Ten Decades*. Chichester, UK: Carden.

Economist Intelligence Unit. (1999). *Sweden: 2nd Quarter 1999*. (Country Report). London: Author.

———. (2000). *Sweden. 1st Quarter 2000*. (Country Report). London: Author.

Edin, P. O., and D. Andersson. (1995). *Seven Myths about Sweden's Economic Crisis*. Stockholm: LO.

Eisner, R. (1995). "Why the deficit isn't all bad: Balancing our deficit thinking." *The Nation* (December 11): 743–745.

Erixon, L. (1985). "What's wrong with the Swedish model? An analysis of its effects and changed conditions 1974–1985," 2nd version. Stockholm: Stockholm University Institute for Social Research.

———. (1995). *A Swedish Economic Policy: A Revindication of the Rehn-Meidner Model*, 2nd rev. version. Working Paper Series 22. Stockholm: Swedish Institute for Work Life Research.

Esping-Andersen, G. (1990). *Three Worlds of Welfare Capitalism*. Princeton, NJ: Princeton University Press.

———. (1996). "After the golden age? Welfare state dilemmas in a global economy." In G. Esping-Andersen, ed., *Welfare States in Transition: National Adaptations in Global Economies*. Thousand Oaks, CA: Sage Publications, pp 1–31.

———. (1999). *The Political Economy of the Welfare State in Developed Capitalist Countries*. Oxford: Oxford University Press.

European Economists for an Alternative Economic Policy. (1998). *Full Employment, Solidarity and Sustainability in Europe*. Available on the Internet at: http://www.barkhof.uni-bremen.de/kua/memo/europe/euromemo/pub/list/htm.

Forsebäck, L. (1976). *Industrial Relations and Employment in Sweden*. Stockholm: Swedish Institute.

Furst, G. (1999). *Sweden: The Equal Way*. Stockholm: Swedish Institute.

Ginsburg, H. L. (1983). *Full Employment and Public Policy: The United States and Sweden*. Lexington, MA: Lexington Books.

———. (1996). "Sweden: Fall from grace." *In These Times* (December 23): 21–23, 36.

———. (1998). "Why Sweden reminds me of home." *Ordfront Magasin* 5. Stockholm.

Ginsburg, H. L., J. Zaconne, G. S. Goldberg, S. D. Collins, and S. M. Rosen.

(1997). "The challenge of full employment in the global economy." *Economic and Industrial Democracy: An International Journal* 18(1): 5–34.

Gonäs, L. (1994). "Transformation of the welfare state and its labour markets." In T. Kauppinen and V. Koykka, eds., *Transformation of the Nordic Industrial Relations in the European Context*, Plenary 1, IIRA, 4th European Regional Conference. Helsinki: Finish Labour Relations Association, pp. 142–174.

Gould, A. (1996). "Sweden: The last bastion of social democracy." In V. George and P. Taylor-Gooby, eds., *European Welfare Policy*. New York: St. Martin's Press, pp. 72–94.

Gustafsson, S. (1995). "Single mothers in Sweden: Why is poverty less severe?" In K. McFate, R. Lawson, and W. J. Wilson, eds., *Poverty, Inequality and the Future of Social Policy: Western States in the New World Order*. New York: Russell Sage Foundation, pp. 291–326.

Gustafsson, S., and R. Jacobsson. (1985). "Trends in female labor force participation in Sweden." *Journal of Labor Economics* 3(1), pt. 2: S258–S274.

Hadenius, S. (1985). *Swedish Politics during the 20th Century*. Stockholm: Swedish Institute.

Hagberg, J. (1998). "De intellektuella har tystnat I partiet." *Malmö Arbetet Nyheterna* (January 10): 3.

———. (1999). Telephone interview with Helen Ginsburg, June 1.

Hermele, K. (1993). "The end of the middle road: What happened to the Swedish model?" *Monthly Review* (March): 14–24.

Hirdman, Y. (1994). *Women: From Possibility to Problem? Gender Conflict in the Swedish Welfare State: The Swedish Model*. Research Report no. 3. Stockholm: Swedish Center for Working Life.

Jansson, Kjell. (2001). Personal communication to Helen Lachs Ginsburg and Marguerite Rosenthal with unpublished Statistics Sweden data, March 22.

Jederlund, L. (1998). "From immigration policy to integration policy." *Current Sweden*. Stockholm: Swedish Institute, March.

Johannesson, J. (1991). *On the Outcome of Swedish Labor Market Policy*. Stockholm: EFA, The Expert Group for Labor Market Policy Evaluation Studies, Ministry of Labor.

Kangas, O., and J. Palme. (1996). "The development of occupational pensions in Finland and Sweden: Class politics and institutional feedbacks." In M. Shalev, ed., *The Privatization of Social Policy? Occupational Welfare and the Welfare State in America, Scandinavia and Japan*. New York: St. Martin's Press, pp. 211–240.

Korpi, J. (1997). Personal interview with Marguerite Rosenthal, May 10.

Korpi, W. (1978). *The Working Class in Welfare Capitalism: Work, Unions and Politics in Sweden*. London: Routledge and Kegan Paul.

———. (1995). "The position of the elderly in the welfare state: Comparative perspectives on old-age care in Sweden." *Social Service Review* 37(2): 242–273.

———. (1996). "Eurosclerosis and the sclerosis of objectivity: On the role of values among economic policy experts." *The Economic Journal* 106 (November): 1727–1746.

———. (1997). Personal interview with Marguerite Rosenthal, May 12.

Korpi, W., and J. Palme. (1998). "The paradox of redistribution and strategies of equality: Welfare state institutions, inequality, and poverty in the Western countries." *American Sociological Review* 63: 661–687.

Lindbeck, A. (1968). "Theories and problems in Swedish economic policy in the post-war period." *American Economic Review,* pt. 2, *Supplement, Surveys of National Economic Policy Issues and Policy Research,* June.

Lindbeck, A., et al. (1994). *Turning Sweden Around.* Cambridge, MA: MIT Press.

LO. (1992). "200,000 demonstrated for justice." *News from the Swedish Trade Union Confederation* 3 (November): 37–39.

———. (1997). *The Solidarity Way: A Modern Wage Formation for Full Employment. Starting-Points and Guidelines.* Stockholm: Swedish Trade Union Confederation, March.

———. (2000). Unpublished data on open unemployment, total unemployment, and public sector employment.

———. (2001). Unpublished data for 2000.

Luxembourg Income Study [LIS]. (1998). *LIS Low Income Measures.* Available on the Internet at http://lissy.ceps.lu/lim.htm. Updated August 25.

Manadens Affärer. (1994). (n.a.) "The crisis is over." *Sveriges 500 Storsta Foretag,* Section 2, p. 8.

Martin, A. (1991). Wage Bargaining and Swedish Politics: The Political Implications of the End of Central Negotiations. Working Paper no. 36. Cambridge, MA: Harvard Center for European Studies.

———. (1996). "Macroeconomic policy, politics and the demise of central wage negotiations in Sweden." Prepared for the Peder Sather Symposium, Center for Western European Studies, University of California, Berkeley. Cambridge, MA: Harvard Center for European Studies, February.

Meidner, R. (1978). *Employee Investment Funds: An Approach to Collective Capital Formation.* London: George Allen & Unwin.

———. (1980). "Our concept of the third way: Some remarks on the socio-political tenets of the Swedish labour movement." *Economic and Industrial Democracy* 1(3): 343–369.

———. (1993). "Why did the Swedish model fail?" In R. Miliband and L. Panitch, eds., *Real Problems, False Solutions: Socialist Register 1993.* London: Merlin Press, pp. 211–227.

———. (1997a). Personal interview with Marguerite Rosenthal, May 14.

———. (1997b). "The Swedish model in an era of mass unemployment." *Economic and Industrial Democracy* 18(1) (February): 87–98.

———. (1998). "An alternative design of macroeconomic policies aiming and restoring full employment." Working Group II, Working Paper 11/9, Targeted Socio-Economic Research (TBER Project: SOE 2-CT97–3025). Thematic Network: Full Employment in Europe. Available on the Internet at www.barkhof.uni.bremen-de/kua/memo/europe/tser/.

Ministry of Finance. (1991). *The Swedish Budget 1991/92: A Summary.* Stockholm: Author.

———. (1995a). *Convergence Programme for Sweden.* Stockholm: Author.

———. (1995b). *Extract of Supplementary Budget Bill 1995/96, Revised Budget Statement.* Stockholm: Author.

———. (1995c). *Medium Term Survey of the Swedish Economy.* Stockholm: Author.

————. (1995d). *The Swedish Budget 1995/96: Budget Statement and Summary, July 1995–December 1996*. Stockholm: Author.

————. (1999). "Speech outline for Swedish embassies on the spring budget bill." Stockholm: Author, April.

————. (2000). "A spring fiscal policy bill for work, development and equality." Press Release. Stockholm: Author, April.

Ministry of Health and Social Affairs. (1998). "The pension reform in Sweden: Final report." Stockholm: Author, April.

Modigliani, F., J. P. Fitoussi, D. Moro, D. Snower, R. Solow, A. Steinherr, and P. S. Lavini. (1998). "An economist's manifesto on unemployment in the European Union." *Banca Nazionale del Lavoro Quarterly Review* 201 (September): 327–361.

National Board of Health and Welfare [NBHW]. (1997). *Social and Caring Services in Sweden, 1996*. Linköpings: Linköpings Tryckeri AB.

————. (1998a). *Social Report 1997: National Report on Social Conditions in Sweden*. Stockholm: Author.

————. (1998b). *Sweden's Public Health Report 1997*. Stockholm: Author.

————. (2000). *Summary: Social Assistance 1998*. Stockholm. Available on the Internet at: www.sos.se, keyword "statistics."

National Social Insurance Board [NSIB]. (1995). *Social Insurance Statistics: Facts 1994*. Stockholm: Author.

————. (1996). *Social Insurance Facts 1996*. Stockholm: Author.

————. (1998). *Social Insurance Facts 1998*. Stockholm: Author.

Navarro, V. (1999). "The political economy of the welfare state in developed capitalist economies." *International Journal of Health Services* 29(1): 1–50.

Nelander, S., and V. Lindgren. (1997). *Inkomst Fördelning och Inkomst Utveckling—Vinnare och Förlorare*. Stockholm: LO, August.

Nordic News Network. (1999). Available on the Internet at http://www.nnn.se (January).

OECD. (1991). *Employment Outlook*. Paris: Author, July.

————. (1995). *Historical Statistics*. Paris: Author.

————. (1996). *Social Assistance: A Comparative Review*. Paris: Author.

————. (1998). *OECD in Figures: Statistics on the Member Countries*. Paris: Author.

Olsen, G. M. (1991). "Labour mobilization and the strength of capital: The rise and stall of economic democracy in Sweden." *Studies in Political Economy* 34 (Spring): 109–145.

————. (1996). "Re-modeling Sweden: The rise and demise of the compromise in a global economy." *Social Problems* 43(1): 1–20.

————. (1999). "Half empty or half full? The Swedish welfare state in transition." *Canadian Review of Sociology and Anthropology* 36(2): 241–267.

Olsson, S. E. (1990). *Social Policy and the Welfare State*. Lund Studies in Social Welfare. Lund, Sweden: Arkiv.

Palme, J., and I. Wennemo. (1998). *Swedish Social Security in the 1990s: Reform and Retrenchment*. Stockholm: Printing Works of the Cabinet Office and Ministries.

Pierson, P. (1996). "The new politics of the welfare state." *World Politics* 48 (January): 143–179.

Pontusson, J. (1992). "At the end of the third road: Swedish social democracy in crisis." *Politics and Society* 20(3): 305–332.

Prime Minister's Office. (1996). *Programme for Halving Open Unemployment by 2000*. Stockholm: Prime Minister's Office.

Rexed, K. (1991). Swedish Labor during the 1990s. Paper presented at the Graduate Faculty Seminar, "Where Is Sweden heading?", The New School for Social Research, New York (November 15–16).

Rivlin, A. M. (1987). "Overview." In B. P. Bosworth and A. M. Rivlin, eds., *The Swedish Economy*. Washington, DC: The Brookings Institution, pp. 1–21.

Romson, J. E. (2000). Personal communication with Helen Lachs Ginsburg, March 23.

Rosen, S. (1996). "Public employment and the welfare state in Sweden." *Journal of Economic Literature* 36: 729–740.

Rosenthal, M. G. (1990). "Sweden: Promise and paradox: A study of Swedish social and economic policy for women." In G. S. Goldberg and E. Kremen, eds., *The Feminization of Poverty: Only in America?* New York: Praeger, pp. 139–155.

———. (1994). "Single mothers in Sweden: Work and welfare in the welfare state." *Social Work* 39(3): 270–278.

SAF. (1994). "SAF campaign for EU membership." *The SAF Year 1993*. English Summary. Stockholm: SAF (The Swedish Employers' Confederation), p. 63.

Salonen, T. (1993). *Margins of Welfare: A Study of Modern Functions of Social Assistance*. Torna Hallestad, Sweden: Hallestad Press.

———. (1997). *Gaps, Barriers and Leakages: Trends in the Swedish Welfare State in the 1990s*. Paper presented at the Conference on Integration and Differentiation, Lund University, Lund, Sweden, May 5.

———. (2000). Telephone interview with Marguerite Rosenthal, June 8.

Salonen, T., and H. Johansson. (1999a). "The Development Guarantee Programme: A case study of youth unemployment policies in Sweden." Work in Progress. Lund University, School of Social Work, Lund, Sweden (Xeroxed).

———. (1999b). "Social inclusion policies in Sweden in the 1990s." Lund University, School of Social Work Lund, Sweden (Xeroxed).

Salonen, T., and S. Sunesson. (1997). Personal joint interview with Marguerite Rosenthal, May 7.

Schönström, A., and P. Lindkvist. (1998). "Pensionssystemet fallgrop för kvinnorna." *Malmö Arbetet Nyheterna* (February 23): p. 3.

Seligman, B. B. (1962). *Main Currents in Modern Economics*. Glencoe, IL: Free Press.

Silverman, B. (1998). "The rise and fall of the Swedish model: Interview with Rudolf Meidner." *Challenge* 41(1): 69–90.

Social Democratic Party. (1994). *A Future for Sweden: The Social Democractic Economic Policy for Employment, Justice and Building the Future*. Stockholm: Author, January.

Spånt, R. (1996). *Den ekonomiska politikens möjligheter*. Stockholm: TCO (Tjanstemannens Centralorganisation).

Ståhlberg, A-C. (1995). *Pension Reform in Sweden*. Reprint 465. Stockholm: Swedish Institute for Social Research.

Statistics Sweden. (various years). *AKU* (Arbetskraftsundersökningen) [Labor Force Survey]. Stockholm: Author.

———. (1995). *Women and Men in Sweden: Facts and Figures 1995.* Stockholm: Author.

———. (1999). *Income Distribution Survey in 1997.* Orebro, Sweden: Author.

Stephens, J. D. (1996). "The Scandinavian welfare states: Achievements, crisis, and prospects." In G. Esping-Andersen, ed., *Welfare States in Transition: National Adaptations in Global Economies.* London: Sage Publications, pp. 32–65.

Sundén, A. (1998). "The Swedish pension reform." Federal Reserve Board (Xeroxed).

Sundström, E. (1999). "Should mothers work? Age and attitudes in Germany, Italy and Sweden." *Journal of International Social Welfare* 8(3): 193–205.

Sundström, M. (1987). *The Growth in Part-Time Work in Sweden.* Stockholm: Swedish Center for Working Life.

———. (1990). "Parenting policies for young families in Sweden." Stockholm: Swedish Center for Working Life, March 23.

———. (1995). *Swedish Parental Leave in the Perspective of European Integration.* Stockholm Research Reports in Demography, no. 94. Stockholm: Stockholm University Demography Unit.

Svallfors, Stefan. (1997). *The Middle Class and Welfare State Retrenchment: Attitudes to Swedish Welfare Policies.* Paper presented at the Third Conference of the European Sociological Association, University of Essex, August.

Swedish Institute [SI]. (1995). *Fact Sheets on Sweden: Social Insurance in Sweden,* November.

———. (1996a). *Fact Sheets on Sweden: Local Government in Sweden,* February.

———. (1996b). *Fact Sheets on Sweden: Housing and Housing Policy in Sweden,* April.

———. (1997a). *Fact Sheets on Sweden: The Swedish Economy,* May.

———. (1997b). *Fact Sheets on Sweden: Social Insurance in Sweden,* August.

———. (1997c). *Fact Sheets on Sweden: The Health Care System in Sweden,* November.

———. (1998a). *Fact Sheets on Sweden: Sweden in the European Union,* March.

———. (1998b). *Fact Sheets on Sweden: The Financial Circumstances of Swedish Households,* August.

———. (1999a). *Fact Sheets on Sweden: Immigrants in Sweden,* April.

———. (1999b). *Fact Sheets on Sweden: The Swedish Political Parties,* April.

———. (1999c). *Fact Sheets on Sweden: The Health Care System in Sweden,* May.

Swenson, P. (1989). *Fair Shares: Union Pay and Politics in Sweden and West Germany.* Ithaca, NY: Cornell University Press.

Szebehely, M. (1998). "Changing division of carework: Caring for children and frail elderly people in Sweden." In J. Lewis, ed., *Gender, Social Care and Welfare State Restructuring in Europe.* Aldershot: Ashgate, pp. 1–29.

Therborn, G. (1986). *Why Some Peoples Are More Unemployed than Others.* London: Verso.

Thorslund, M., A. Bergmark, and M. G. Parker. (1997). "Difficult decisions on care and services for elderly people: The dilemma of setting priorities in the welfare state." *Scandinavian Journal of Social Welfare* 6: 197–206.

Tilander, K. (1997). Telephone interview with Marguerite Rosenthal, May 15.

United Nations Development Program. (1999). *Human Development Report 1999.* New York: Oxford University Press.

U.S. Bureau of Labor Statistics. (2000). *Comparative Civilian Labor Force Statstics, Ten Countries: 1959–1999.* Washington, DC: Bureau of Labor Statistics, Office of Productivity and Technology.

Vickrey, W. (1993). "Today's task for economists." *American Economic Review* 83 (March): 1–10.

Vogel, J. (1991). *Social Report for the Nordic Countries: Living Conditions and Inequality in the Late 1980's.* Copenhagen: Nordisk statistisk skriftserie.

———. (1995). "Working conditions, health and work absenteeism: Recent Swedish experience" (English summary). In D. Jaufmann, E. Mezger, and M. Pfaff, eds., *Verallt die arbeitsmoral?* Frankfurt: Campus, pp. 145–165.

———. (1997). "Living Conditions and Inequality, 1975–1995." English summary of *Välfärd och ojämlikhet I 20- åsperspektiv: 1975–1995.* Report 91. Stockholm: Statistics Sweden, pp. 627–651.

Von Otter, B. (1998). "New Swedish government needs two crutches." *Current Sweden* (October). Stockholm: Swedish Institute.

Winberg, Y. (1997). Personal interview with Marguerite Rosenthal, May 13.

Wohlner, E. (1999). "Pensionsreformen har redan havererat." *Malmö Arbetet Nyheterna* (April 28): 3.

Xu, J. (1997). *Sex Discrimination in the Swedish Labor Market: Present Situation and Legal Practices.* Swedish Institute for Social Research, Working Paper no. 5. Stockholm: Stockholm University.

Chapter 5

Diminishing Welfare: The Case of the United Kingdom

Jane Millar

Over the past 20 years the distribution of income and wealth in the United Kingdom has become increasingly unequal, and poverty has increased. The rich have become richer, and the poor have become poorer. For the millions of men, women, and children living on inadequate incomes, in run-down neighborhoods, and with poor quality services, welfare has certainly diminished. During the 1980s and 1990s the capacity of the British welfare state to protect its most vulnerable members seems to have declined. Is this because the welfare state has been overwhelmed by the sheer extent of social and economic change? Or is it because the welfare state itself has changed and withdrawn from providing adequate support, leaving people more vulnerable to these changes?

This chapter examines the welfare record of the United Kingdom during the two decades of Conservative governments, between 1979 and 1997. Under Margaret Thatcher in particular (prime minister between 1979 and 1990), these were powerful, ideologically driven, right-wing governments in which it was strongly believed that economic inequality is both necessary and acceptable since individuals should be rewarded for their own efforts; that the private market is superior to collective state provision; that poverty is largely caused by people's failing to take responsibility for themselves; and that public expenditure is a drain on the economy, representing a cost and not a benefit, stifling economic growth, and so pulling everyone down. "Rolling back the state" was necessary to free the market, and one of the first actions of the 1979 government was the publication of the Public Expenditure White Paper (HM Treasury, 1979) which began with the words: "Public expenditure is at the heart of Britain's economic difficulties."

Spending on welfare benefits and services—education, health, housing, income maintenance, social care—would therefore have to be reduced and reduced substantially if this goal of reducing public expenditure was to be achieved. The Thatcher government, particularly following the 1987 election, was determined to do this. It had the electoral support, the political will, and a centralized political system to help it. Nevertheless, as most commentators now agree, what the Thatcher government achieved was not a dismantling of the British welfare state but rather a certain degree of restructuring (Glennerster, Power, and Travers, 1991; Pierson, 1994; Clarke, 1996; Oppenheim and Lister, 1996; Alcock, 1997). Public expenditure did not fall in total, but the distribution of spending did change, with more spending in the areas of health and social security and less in housing and education (Hills, 1998). Privatization was encouraged and supported, but the public/private mix across provision, finance, and control remained overall much the same (Burchardt, 1997). There was, it seems, a significant gap between the rhetoric of intentions and the reality of implementation. Nevertheless, even if the Conservatives did not succeed in substantially changing the overall welfare landscape, their policies did have a significant impact on the lives of British people during the 1980s and 1990s and may have left an enduring legacy for the future. This chapter explores these issues, focusing in particular on those policy areas that most directly affect incomes and living standards: social security, tax, employment protection, housing. The first section of the chapter reviews the evidence on rising poverty in Britain in the 1980s and 1990s; the second describes the key labor market trends that contributed to this; and the third looks at the role that Conservative government social policy played.[1] The final section discusses the extent to which these policies did or did not add up to a major restructuring of the British welfare state and considers how far and in what sorts of ways the legacy of these years seems to have affected the policies of the Labour government elected in May 1997.

POVERTY AND INEQUALITY IN THE UNITED KINGDOM

The United Kingdom is a small, densely populated and relatively rich country—rather, countries, since the four constituent parts (England, Wales, Scotland, and Northern Ireland) each retains some separate cultural, linguistic, and legislative identity.[2] In 1996, the total population of the United Kingdom was 58.4 million people. Of these about 12.1 million are children under age 16, about 10.6 million are pensioners (over age 60 for women, 65 for men), and the remaining 35.7 million are men and women of working age (ONS, 1997a). Around 6 percent of the UK population is from ethnic minority groups, most commonly of Indian subcontinent or Caribbean origin. However, the majority of members of ethnic minority groups—especially among young people—are British-born (Modood et al.,

1997). In the 1960s and 1970s emigration from the United Kingdom was greater than immigration into Britain, but since the mid-1980s there has been a small net inward migration, at a level of about 20,000–26,000 people per annum. This has included a rise in immigration from Europe and, in particular, from those seeking asylum, who made up a growing number of those accepted for settlement in the mid-1990s (ONS, 1998).[3] The wealth of the country—as measured by the gross domestic product (GDP)—has risen at an average rate of about 2.4 percent per annum throughout the post-war period, with three significant downturns in this otherwise upward growth in the mid-1970s, the early 1980s, and the early 1990s (ONS, 1997a). Each of these recessions took unemployment to a higher level, and, even after economic recovery, unemployment did not fall back to previous levels.

Compared with other European Union (EU) member states, GDP per head in the United Kingdom is about average. This represents a significant relative decline. In 1960, the United Kingdom was the second most successful world economy, after the United States, as measured by GDP per head. By the early 1990s, the United Kingdom was placed 18 out of 24 among Organisation for Economic Co-operation and Development (OECD) countries for GDP per head (Coates, 1995, p. 8). Levels of social spending in the United Kingdom are also relatively low, with the proportion of GDP going to health, education, and social security standing at just about 27 percent in 1993. In the EU only Portugal, Ireland, and Greece devote a lower share of GDP to social expenditure (Hills, 1997). Although the United Kingdom is a member of the European Union, it had, until the recent change of government, "opted out" of the Social Chapter agreed under the Maastricht Treaty of 1989. This meant that the United Kingdom was not party to, nor bound by, decisions taken on social policy issues (Leibfried and Pierson, 1995). Political attitudes in the United Kingdom toward the EU tend to be polarized, both within and across political parties, and internal party disputes over Europe and the European monetary union were part of the reason that the Conservatives lost the 1997 election.

Poverty in the United Kingdom

The United Kingdom has no official poverty line, and British governments have long been reluctant to commit themselves to any such measure. During the 1980s, the question of how poverty should be defined and measured was increasingly politicized. At the time of the mid-1980s social security review, it was argued by the government that "there is now no universally agreed standard of poverty" (DHSS, 1985, para. 4.7) and that it therefore made no sense to try to judge policy according to anti-poverty criteria. However, that did not stop a government minister in the Department of Social Security from arguing, just a few years later, that the United

Diminishing Welfare

Table 5.1
Number of Individuals in Households with Net Incomes below Half Average
Income, 1979–1994/1995

	Before Housing Costs		After Housing Costs	
	Millions	Percent	Millions	Percent
1979	4.4	8	5.0	9
1981	4.7	9	6.2	11
1987	8.7	16	10.5	19
1988/1989	10.4	19	12.0	22
1991/1992	11.7	21	13.9	25
1992/1993	11.4	20	14.1	25
1993/1994	10.7	19	13.7	24
1994/1995	10.3	18	13.4	23

Sources: Oppenheim and Harker (1996) and DSS (1997a), based on *Households below Average Income* series.

Kingdom had "reached the end of the line for poverty." Absolute poverty, he maintained, had been abolished, and relative poverty was nothing more than inequality under another name (Moore, 1989). The word "poverty" disappeared from official publications and government pronouncements and was replaced by the more innocuous-sounding "low income" or the even more neutral "below average income." According to the official view, poverty simply did not exist, and this position was consistently maintained. In 1997, for example, the Conservative government rejected a proposal from the United Nations Social Summit that governments should set out a national strategy to deal with poverty, on the grounds that this was not necessary for the United Kingdom.

Despite this, however, all the empirical evidence—including the official statistics produced by the government—pointed to rising rates of poverty throughout the 1980s. Table 5.1 is drawn from the "households below average income series" compiled and published by the Department of Social Security (DSS, 1997a). These statistics measure household income from all sources, taking into account household size and composition (number of adults, age and number of children). Income is measured net of tax and other deductions and includes income from state benefits (i.e., it is a measure of post-transfer rather than pre-transfer income). Two sets of figures are produced, one before and one after housing costs, the latter giving the better measure of living standards. The most commonly used "poverty line" is drawn at incomes under 50 percent of the average, and the information is usually presented by counting the number of individuals living in households with incomes below this level.[4] As Table 5.1 shows, the number of people living in poor households rose from between 4 and 5 million in 1979 to between 11 and 14 million in 1993/1994, depending on the income measure used. There was a small reduction in 1994/1995,[5] but this is still equivalent to between one-fifth and one-quarter of the population living in income poverty. This increase in household income poverty was very much a phenomenon of the 1980s. According to Goodman, Johnson, and Webb, (1997, p. 236), the before-housing costs poverty rate fluctuated at around 8–12 percent between 1961 to 1974 and, as the table shows, was at about 9 percent in 1979.[6] Ten years later this poverty rate had more than doubled.

A number of points should be noted about these figures. First they are based on household data and thus tend to exclude the very poorest, for example, people who are homeless or living in institutions. The increasing visibility of homeless people in the major cities of the United Kingdom was a notable feature of life in the 1980s; and the number of the "hidden" homeless (people sharing unsuitable accommodations or those living apart because they cannot find suitable accommodations) has risen substantially, as has the number of those living in "temporary" housing (including squatting and short-term housing). Estimates based on the 1991 census suggest a total of almost half a million homeless households in England, including about 22,000 families with children living in temporary accommodations (Holmans, 1995). Second, because the unit of measurement is the household, these statistics cannot capture the extent to which individuals may be poor, even though they do not live in poor households. This applies particularly to women, who still have much lower individual incomes than men (Millar, 1996). Third, the poverty line is not generous. For example, for a single person the equivalent money value of half the average in 1992/1993 was about £86 per week before housing costs and £68 per week after housing costs (DSS, 1996).[7] Jonathan Bradshaw (1994) estimates that, in 1992, it would have cost a single person about £150 per week to live at a "modest but adequate standard," before housing costs.

Of the just above 13 million people estimated to live in poor households in 1994/1995 (taking the after-housing cost figures), almost 3 million are pensioners, of whom about half live alone; almost 3.5 million are people of working age without children; and about 7 million are parents and their children. Just over 4 million children are estimated to live in poor households compared with just over 1 million in 1979. The risk of poverty has increased for all family types, but Table 5.2 highlights the particularly high risk of poverty for lone parents (60 percent) and single pensioners (32 percent). What unites these groups is that they are both predominantly women—most single pensioners are widows, and most lone parents are mothers. Women are still much more at risk of poverty than men, and, as

Diminishing Welfare

Table 5.2
Risk of Poverty* by Family Type, 1979 and 1994/1995

Family Type	1979	1994/1995
Pensioner couple	21%	24%
Single pensioner	12%	32%
Couple with dependent children	8%	22%
Couple without dependent children	5%	10%
Single person with dependent children	19%	60%
Single person	7%	22%
All family types	9%	23%
Number (millions)	5.0	13.4

*Proportion of each family type in households with incomes after housing costs of below half
the average.

Source: DSS (1997a).

domestic managers in most households, women also bear the brunt of poverty.

An alternative approach to defining and measuring poverty was adopted in two *Breadline Britain* surveys, carried out in 1983 (Mack and Lansley, 1985) and 1990 (Gordon and Pantazia, 1997). These defined poverty as the "enforced lack of socially perceived necessities," based on public opinion surveys about what is and is not "essential" and counting as poor those who lack three or more essential items. The type of items considered essential include, for example, heating, carpets and domestic goods for the home, warm and weatherproof clothing, adequate diets, and toys for children. The figures are not exactly comparable over time because the list of essential items changed somewhat between the two surveys. However, according to this definition, about 7.5 million people lived in poor households in 1983, and about 11 million in 1990. Of that 11 million (equivalent to about 20 percent of the population), about 3.5 million were estimated to be in severe poverty (lacking seven or more essential items).

As noted above, families with children are at increasing risk of poverty. In their recent study of expenditure on children, Middleton, Ashworth, and Braithwaite (1997) followed a similar approach to the *Breadline Britain* studies and defined poverty according to whether children had to go without at least three "essential" items, as identified by parents. They found that 1 in 10 children goes without three or more such items because their parents cannot afford them. Three percent of children go without five or more such items. Children would suffer even more from poverty, except that their parents tend to try to protect them as much as possible. One in

20 mothers goes without food in order to be able to meet her children's needs. The United Kingdom has one of the worst records on child poverty in Europe. According to EU figures (based on the European Community Household Panel), 32 percent of British children lived in poor households in 1993, compared with, for example, 12 percent of French children and less than 5 percent of Danish children (Ditch et al., 1998).

There is also accumulating evidence about the persistence of poverty over time among certain groups. Jarvis and Jenkins (1996) show that although there is quite a significant degree of income mobility each year, most people who move out of poverty usually do not move very far, and there is much "churning" at the bottom, movements from unemployment to low-paid work and back to unemployment again, for example. Those most likely to stay poor over time are again women: lone mothers and elderly women. The likelihood of escaping poverty decreases with the length of time spent in poverty, so there are increasing numbers of people for whom poverty has become a long-term experience. Many of these people are long-term benefit recipients. In 1996, of the 5.5 million households in receipt of income support (the national means-tested social assistance benefit), 3.3 million had been on the rolls in receipt of benefits for at least two years (DSS, 1997b).

The research reported so far has focused on estimating the extent of income poverty. But a number of more qualitative studies have also attempted to describe and understand the experience of poverty and to document its effects on physical and mental well-being. Kempson (1996) brought a number of such studies together to draw a picture of "life on a low income" in Britain in the 1980s and early 1990s:

People living on low incomes show great resilience and resourcefulness as they try to make ends meet. . . . Making ends meet means going without. It generally means having no social life. . . . It leads to poor diets, with choices between eating healthy foods or having sufficient to eat, and to economies in the use of heating and water. These, in turn, contribute to health problems, as does inadequate housing. . . . Money worries are common. (pp. xi–xii)

The Joseph Rowntree Foundation, reporting the results of its *Inquiry into Income and Wealth* (1995, p. 8), concluded:

Policy makers should be concerned with the way in which the living standards of a substantial minority have lagged behind since the late 1970s. Not only is this a problem for those directly affected, it also damages the social fabric and so affects us all. . . . One of our particular concerns is with the living standards and life opportunities of the poorest. In many areas of the UK these are simply unacceptable in a society as rich as ours.

Table 5.3
Employment Status by Sex, United Kingdom, Spring 1997

	Women		Men		Total	
	Number	%	Number	%	Number	%
Full-time employees[1]	6.0m	35	11.0m	59	17.0m	48
Part-time employees	4.5m	26	0.9m	5	5.4m	15
Self-employed	0.7m	4	2.4m	13	3.1m	9
Others in employment	0.2m	1	0.2m	1	0.4m	1
Unemployed[2]	0.7m	4	1.3m	7	2.0m	6
Economically inactive[3]	4.9m	29	2.9m	16	7.8m	22
Total	17.0m	100*	18.7m	100*	35.7m	100*

*Percentages do not total 100 due to rounding.
1. At least 30 hours per week.
2. Those aged 16 and over who are without a job, available to start work in the next two weeks, who have been seeking a job in the past four weeks or are waiting to start a job already obtained.
3. Those who are neither part of the labor force in employment nor unemployed, as defined above, for example, those looking after a home or retired, students, or those permanently unable to work.

Source: ONS (1998).

The Causes of Rising Poverty

Although household and family changes—in particular, the rising levels of lone parenthood and of single-person households—have contributed to economic vulnerability, changes in the labor market have been the underlying cause of these rising poverty rates. Put simply, there has been a significant increase in the number of people who are unable to achieve an adequate and secure income from employment. Table 5.3 shows the labor market position of men and women of working age in the spring of 1997. Of the 35.7 million people of working age, about 25.8 million were employed or self-employed (70 percent of the working-age population, 44 percent of the total population). Only just over half of the working-age population was in full-time work (including full-time self-employment). Women make up about 45 percent of the economically active, but they are much more likely than men to be working in part-time jobs and much less likely to be self-employed.

Labor Market Trends

Unemployment, defined to include people available for and seeking work, stood at about 2.0 million (a rate of about 6.6 percent) in the spring of 1997, although registered unemployment (i.e., the number of people unemployed and receiving benefits) was slightly lower at about 1.6 million.[8] Of those who registered as unemployed, about 40 percent had been out of work for over one year. However, perhaps even more striking is the extent of male economic inactivity—almost 3 million men of working age were defined as inactive. This growth of "worklessness" (unemployment plus inactivity) means that there are an increasing number of households without any workers at all. The percentage of households without an adult in paid work more than doubled between the late 1970s and the mid-1990s, from about 8 to about 19 percent (ONS, 1997a). This polarization between "work-rich" households (with two or more earners) and "work-poor"' households (with no earners) has further increased overall income inequality (Hills, 1996).

Alongside this divide between those individuals and households with paid employment and those without, there are also increasing divisions within the employed population. Employment has become more fragmented, and wages have become increasingly unequal. Since the late 1970s, male full-time employment has fallen by almost 3 million, while female part-time employment has risen by just over 1 million (Cox, 1997). The vast majority of these women are married women with children, the only group for whom there has been any significant employment growth in recent years. Not only have part-time and self-employment increased, but so, too, has flexible or precarious working. In the spring of 1995, about 5.3 million workers worked some form of flextime or had annualized working hours (i.e., a set number of hours worked over a year), about 0.7 million people worked mainly at home, and there were about 1.5 million temporary workers, two-fifths of whom could not find a permanent job (ONS, 1997a). New entrants to the labor market and unemployed people are particularly unlikely to move into full-time, permanent jobs. Only half of those placed by the Employment Service in 1994/1995 went into full-time permanent jobs. A fifth went into part-time jobs, and another fifth into temporary jobs (Cox, 1997). Coates (1995, p. 7) summarized the key trends in full-time/part-time working:

Since the Conservatives came to power in 1979 the number of full-time jobs in civilian employment in the UK economy has been reduced by some three million— 1.8 million of which have gone since 1989. . . . of the part-time jobs created . . . at least 70 percent involve people working for less than 16 hours per week. . . . the 1984 figures for hours worked per week in the UK economy stood at 850 million. It is now some 780 million.

There has been a striking decline in manufacturing in the United Kingdom, both in terms of employment levels and in terms of output and contribution to GDP. Manufacturing employment was at its peak in the United

Kingdom over 35 years ago, in 1966, when 8.5 million people were employed in that sector. In the mid-1990s there were less than half that number—around 4 million—working in manufacturing (Coates, 1995). Almost 2 million jobs were lost in manufacturing in the first five years of the 1980s (Williams, Williams, and Haslam, 1990). By the mid-1990s less than a fifth of the employed population in the United Kingdom worked in manufacturing, and three-quarters worked in service industries (ONS, 1998). Nor did manufacturing output rise as employment fell; indeed, "the U.K. is unique amongst them [the major industrialized countries] in experiencing almost stagnant manufacturing output in the past two decades" (Lee, 1997, p. 168). Between 1979 and 1985 manufacturing output grew, on average, by only 0.8 percent per annum, and the proportion of GDP accounted for by manufacturing fell from about 32 percent in the early 1980s to about 20 percent by the mid-1990s (ibid.). In 1983 the United Kingdom became a net importer of manufactured goods for the first time (outside war years) since the Industrial Revolution (Coates, 1995). Not all sectors were affected in the same way. The decline has been particularly felt in motor vehicles, machinery, and textiles, while aerospace, pharmaceuticals, food products, chemicals, and mechanical engineering remain relatively competitive. Government support for defense-related production in the 1980s also ensured that manufacturing in this sector remained relatively strong (e.g., the United Kingdom was the world's fourth largest arms exporter of conventional weapons by the late 1980s) (Lee, 1997).

Williams, Williams, and Haslam (1990) have argued that the 1980s saw a "hollowing-out" of British manufacturing by UK-based transnational companies. They examined the records of 25 large UK manufacturing companies and found that these companies reduced domestic employment substantially during the recession of the early 1980s. When economic conditions improved, they increased their employment overseas again but did not do so in the United Kingdom. Thus, "between 1979 and 1989, overseas employment [among these companies] increased by some 200,000, or 28.3 percent, while domestic employment declined by 330,000, or 29.1 percent" (Williams, Williams, and Haslam, p. 467). Overseas employment increased from 38 percent of the total workforce of these companies in 1979 to 53 percent in 1989. Inward investment—which is at relatively high levels in the United Kingdom—offset some, but not all, of the impact of this hollowing out (Lee, 1997). About 24 percent of UK manufacturing output is accounted for by foreign companies, which employ about 18 percent of the UK workforce. Of these foreign enterprises about a quarter are European-owned, and the number of Japanese-owned companies increased rapidly from the mid-1980s to the mid-1990s, while U.S. ownership fell (Sawyer, 1996). The United Kingdom thus has a combination of high levels both of UK companies investing overseas and of foreign companies investing in the United Kingdom—a combination that may be particularly vulnerable to global, or non-national, economic and financial policies and trends.

Wages have become increasingly unequal, and this has been a major factor contributing to the overall rise in income inequality in the United Kingdom since the late 1970s (Hills, 1996). Between 1978 and 1992 median male wages rose by about 35 percent in real terms, but, while wages in the top decile rose by 50 percent, those in the lowest decile were stagnant or falling. Defining low pay as less than two-thirds of median hourly earnings, Millar, Webb, and Kemp (1997) estimated that there were about 4.6 million low-paid employees in 1994, 22 percent of all employees (32 percent of female employees and 13 percent of male employees). Not all those who are low-paid live in poor households, but an increasing proportion do. In the late 1970s, about 3 to 4 percent of low-paid workers were living in poor households. By the early 1990s, this had risen to about 12 to 13 percent. Unemployed people face lower wages on return to work than those received by the currently employed population (Gregg and Wadsworth, 1996).

As Hutton (1995, p. 19) puts it, the United Kingdom has had "European levels of unemployment and American levels of working poor." Of course, these trends—high levels of worklessness, long-term unemployment, decline in full-time employment, decline in manufacturing, falling real wages at the lower end, rising risk of low pay—have affected different groups in different ways. Women make up the vast majority of part-time and low-paid workers. Men in unskilled and low-paid jobs are most vulnerable to unemployment. Young people cannot get a secure hold in the labor market and instead move between unemployment, low-paid work, and training schemes. Older workers cannot get back into work if they lose their jobs, especially if they live in those areas that have seen the most decline in traditional manufacturing employment (Scotland, Wales, Northern Ireland, the north of England). Those from ethnic minorities, especially Pakistani and Bangladeshi people, are more vulnerable on all counts: more likely to be unemployed, low-paid, in insecure jobs, and discriminated against. Berthoud (1997) found that as many as four-fifths of Pakistani and Bangladeshi households are living in poverty and that all minority groups (with the exception of the Chinese) were more likely to be poor than the white population. Class, gender, race, age, and geographical location interact to sustain disadvantage for some groups and advantage for others.

As a consequence, for many people, reliance on employment as the major source of income has become much more problematic, especially for those with children or other dependents. Such a reliance was, however, the backbone of the Beveridge scheme of national insurance, introduced in the postwar period. Full employment, wages adequate to support a family, and stable marriages with men at work and women at home—these assumptions were the key to the post-war British welfare state. Welfare provisions, pensions, and unemployment benefits, in particular, were designed to fit those conditions, not conditions of high unemployment and family instability. The gap between the old assumptions and the new realities started to appear in the mid-1970s, particularly after the 1973 oil crisis and the rise in unemployment that followed. In the United Kingdom, the Labour government of the time started the process of trying to reduce public expenditure, but only after the election of the Conservatives in 1979 did this become a goal at the very heart of government policy.

THE IMPACT OF CONSERVATIVE POLICY ON LIVING STANDARDS: 1979 TO 1997

The causes of the United Kingdom's long-term relative industrial decline have been sought for many years and in many quarters, and possible culprits have included the cost of the post-war welfare state, the character of British culture, the nature of the major financial institutions, the adversarial party political system, and the operation of the civil service (Coates and Hillard, 1995; Cox, Lee, and Sanderson, 1997). For Thatcherites, of course, too much government ownership and intervention were seen as the chief problems and causes of industrial decline and, indeed, of moral decline. Privatization of publicly owned companies, reducing and removing state subsidies to private firms, and promoting inward investment by foreign manufacturers—these policies would, it was argued, open up these rather stagnant and inefficient sectors of the economy to the bracing effects of competition in a free market. Alongside this, reductions in welfare spending would not only free up resources from these "unproductive" areas of the economy but reverse the "dependency" culture that was perceived to be emerging among certain sectors of the population. Reductions in welfare spending would, it was proposed, be achieved in a number of ways: efficiency savings, reductions in levels of services and benefits, and privatization of provision so that individuals and families would do more to support one another.

Despite some of the rhetoric over the years, redistribution of income from rich to poor has never been central to UK social policy, even under Labour governments (Powell, 1995). The Beveridge proposals, which set the shape of the post-war welfare state, were not aimed at achieving equality. Rather, the goal was to establish a universal social security system that would pay flat-rate subsistence level benefits. The objective was to ensure minimum standards of welfare for all, rather than to promote economic equality. However, the impact of Conservative policies in the 1980s and 1990s was to put the maintenance of a minimum standard of living for all under threat. The government did not act to protect and sustain the incomes and living standards of the poorest people during this time of rapid economic and social change—quite the contrary, since the key idea driving labor market and social security policy was that the market should be freed in order to create more wealth, which would then "trickle down" to those at the bottom. But, far from this happening, many of the policies introduced added to the numbers of poor people and worsened their situation. This can be seen through an examination of policies of labor market deregulation and privatization and in respect of social security provisions.

LABOR MARKET DEREGULATION

Labor market deregulation, in pursuit of a "free" labor market, was a key policy goal of the Conservatives throughout their terms of office. This deregulation involved reductions in both trade union and individual rights. Legislation to reform trade unions came in the Employment Acts passed between 1980 and 1990, in the Trade Union Act of 1984, and in the Trade Union Reform and Employment Rights Act of 1993. These acts abolished the closed shop, limited rights to industrial action and picketing, increased the liability of trade unions to meet the costs of industrial action, allowed the dismissal of strikers, and introduced secret balloting and union elections (Bowers, Brown, and Gibbons, 1993). Although trade union membership steadily declined (from about 13 million in 1979 to about 8 million in 1994 [Sweeney, 1996]), Farnham (1990) queries how far these policies actually restricted trade union rights in the 1980s. The trade unions were not unsuccessful at protecting the incomes of their members, particularly in the private sector, and unionization remained strong in some areas of employment. But non-unionized, especially public sector, workers were hard hit by deregulation, which led to pay cuts and reductions in individual employment rights. The Employment Acts of 1980 and 1989 and the Trade Union Reform and Employment Rights Act of 1993 restricted rights in respect to unfair dismissal, in access to industrial tribunals, and in conditions of transfers and redundancies. The qualifying period for entitlement to employment rights was increased from six months to two years.

The Wages Councils, which set minimum rates of pay for about 2.5 million workers, mainly in industries such as hotel and catering, retail, hairdressing, and clothing manufacture, also came under scrutiny. The scope of the Wages Councils was first reduced in 1985, when workers under age 21 were removed from their area of responsibility. In 1993, the remaining Wages Councils were abolished, leaving no minimum wage protection at all. The weakening of the Wages Councils during the 1980s contributed significantly to the growing wage dispersion over that period (Machin and Manning, 1994). The Low Pay Network (1996) found that two years after the abolition of the Wages Councils, about 15 percent of jobs formed under jurisdiction of the Wages Councils were paying less in cash terms than the old Wages Councils rate, and about half were paying less in real terms. According to the OECD (1994), by the early 1990s, Britain had one of the most unregulated labor markets in the industrialized world. The weakening of the trade union movement also reduced a potential source of opposition to Conservative policies in other policy areas, and there was little or no collective action in support of the welfare state.

PRIVATIZATION

Privatization can take many forms and apply in different ways across different areas of policy. Burchardt (1997) estimates that in 1979/1980, about 52 percent of welfare activity was purely public (public provision, financed by public money and under public control), and about 24 percent was purely private (private provision, financed by private money and under private control). The remaining 24 percent combined public and private provision, finances, and control in various different ways. By 1995/1996, toward the end of the Conservative years, this balance had shifted slightly but not dramatically, with about 49 percent of welfare activity purely public, about 29 percent purely private, and 22 percent somewhere in between. However, privatization had taken particular hold in certain areas, notably, employment, housing, and pensions.

Privatization of Public Sector Employment

Employment in the public sector fell throughout the 1980s and 1990s. In 1979, total public sector employment (central and local government, public corporations) totaled about 7.5 million. This fell to under 7 million by 1983, to under 6 million by 1991, and by 1995 was down to 5.2 million (ONS, 1997b). Again government policy, in particular, the privatization of public sector employment, played a major role. "Compulsory competitive tendering" (CCT) was first introduced in 1980 and extended in 1988 and 1991. It requires local authorities to put out to contract an increased proportion of their work in areas such as building repair, cleaning, refuse collection, catering, grounds maintenance, vehicle maintenance, and sports and leisure. From 1990 this also applied to community care services. The total value of contract work in the mid-1990s was about £2.2 billion per annum (excluding Northern Ireland), having risen from less than £100 million in 1989 (Escott and Whitfield, 1995). The impact on employment has been dramatic:

The introduction of CCT and community care, in conjunction with restructuring, budget constraints and technological changes, has resulted in major job losses in local government. Full-time and part-time jobs have been affected although . . . the impact has been greater for part-time work. There has also been a substantial increase in the employment of temporary and casual labour. . . . The hours worked by part-time employees have declined in many cases leading to lower take-home earnings. . . . rates of pay, for already low-paid workers, have declined. Overtime and bonus payments have also been reduced. (Escott and Whitfield, 1995, p. 196; see also Equal Opportunities Commission Northern Ireland [EOC-NI], 1996)

The legality of these policies has now been successfully challenged. Under a 1977 European Directive, the employment, pay, and conditions of these workers should have been protected as they were transferred from the public to the private sphere. The Transport and General Workers Union (and other trade unions affected) pursued a number of cases through the courts. These were fought by the Conservative government, but, in November 1997, the newly elected Labour government accepted that the law had been broken and that compensation should be paid to up to 1,500 local authority workers. More cases may follow. The public sector unions have also argued that quality of service has suffered as a consequence of these policies.

Privatization of Housing

The "right to buy" policy introduced in 1981 gave tenants in social housing (i.e., housing provided, financed, and controlled within the public sector) opportunities and incentives to buy their own homes. This took almost 2 million dwellings out of the public sector and into the hands of private individuals. Kemp (1999, p. 127) argues that "in no other area of social policy has privatisation extended so far or with such popular support" but also points out that the impact has been to increase inequality and polarization. Many people benefited financially from this policy and improved the quality of their living standards. But those who could not afford to buy (even at the discounts offered) and who lived in poorer-quality housing found their situations getting worse. The better-off were able to leave, and those who remained tended to be poorer, often unemployed or lone parents. Social housing became much more residual, catering only to those unable to get access to other housing tenures and often with multiple problems and needs. The government also sought to transfer the remaining public housing stock from the control of local authorities into the voluntary and private sectors. By 1996, only 19 percent of UK housing was in the public sector compared with 30 percent in 1981, and within the rented sector, private and voluntary sectors have increased at the expense of the public sector (Kemp, 1999).

Privatization of Pensions

The social security review established by the secretary of state, Norman Fowler, led to a 1985 Green Paper, *The Reform of Social Security*, in which great stress was laid upon individual responsibility and on targeting resources to those in greatest need. Much of the analysis and the rhetoric in the Green Paper was based on a "mixed-economy-of-welfare" model, where state provision is just one of several possible means of support. Thus, it was argued that social security provision should be on the basis of a "partnership" between the individual and the state, which would mean a greater role for private provision and individual saving. This "privatization" model was applied particularly to pensions policy. The government initially proposed to abolish the State Earnings Related Pension (SERPS), which forms the second tier of the UK state pension scheme. SERPS was introduced in the mid-1970s, with a pension entitlement based on the best 20 years' earnings. From 1978 (when the scheme started), all full-time employees had to contribute either to SERPS or to a "contracted-out" employer-provided scheme, which was required to provide benefits at least as good as those provided by SERPS. The Green Paper focused on the future costs of SERPS and argued that these were unsustainable. However, the proposal to abolish SERPS met with little support. Employers were concerned that extra employment and administrative costs would fall upon them. The trade unions and anti-poverty pressure groups were concerned that the poorest workers would not be able to achieve adequate pensions without the protection of SERPS and that women, in particular, with their discontinuous employment histories, would lose out. Therefore, the government decided instead to modify SERPS—to base entitlement on lifetime earnings rather than on the 20 best years and to introduce substantial incentives to opt out of SERPS and occupational schemes and into private pensions.

These changes are estimated to have halved the future costs of SERPS (Johnson, Disney, and Stears, 1996), but the encouragement to private pensions has proved costly in the short term. Up to 1993, about 4 million people opted out of SERPS and took up private pensions. This cost the government about £9.3 billion in incentive payments and lost revenue, with a saving of £3.4 billion on future SERPS payments that would not have to be made—leaving a net cost to the government of £5.9 billion (Nesbitt, 1995). By 1994/1995 this net cost had risen to £7.4 billion (Johnson, Disney, and Stears, 1996). The regulation of the private pension market also became an important political issue, with evidence that some people were being sold pension schemes that were costly and inappropriate and with some highly visible scandals, in particular, the £400 million removed from the Mirror Group pensions under Robert Maxwell, involving the government in additional costs in compensation and hardship payments. Estimates from the House of Commons Public Accounts Committee put the cost of compensation for the selling of inappropriate private pensions at as much as £10 billion. The "mixed economy" proved to be more expensive to the public purse than had been anticipated.

SOCIAL SECURITY BENEFITS: LESS SUPPORT AND MORE MEANS-TESTING

Changes in social security have included reductions in benefits (in respect to both levels and coverage) and a substantial shift from national insurance to means-tested benefits. The 1980 and 1986 Social Security Acts were key pieces of legislation in these respects. The 1980 act changed the basis for calculating increases in state pensions and other long-term insurance benefits. During the 1970s, these benefits had been increased annually in line with either average earnings or prices, whichever was greater. Indexing in this way meant that pensioners were protected against inflation and that their income levels broadly kept pace with earnings.

After 1980, these benefits were indexed to prices only. Pensioners are thus protected against inflation, but—as wages have been rising faster than prices—the incomes of those receiving pensions and long-term benefits have fallen steadily behind the incomes of the working population. In the late 1970s, the basic pension for a single person was equivalent to about 20 percent of average male earnings. By the early 1990s, this had fallen to 15 percent and is estimated to fall to 10 percent by 2020, adding further fuel to the concerns about the long-term future of the basic state pension (Johnson, Disney, and Stears, 1996).

This change in the method of indexing these benefits not only saved the government a significant sum of money (about half of the total savings in social security made between 1979 and 1987) but also meant that, for the first time in the post-war period, long-term benefit recipients were to be excluded from a share in rising national prosperity. The impact of this falls particularly upon those pensioners solely reliant upon state provision, mainly older pensioners and women. Elderly people with private or occupational pensions—mainly younger pensioners and men—have become somewhat less prone to poverty since the 1970s (Goodman, Johnson, and Webb, 1997). Thus, income inequality among the elderly population has increased substantially.

The Green Paper also argued for a range of different types of provision *within* the state sector, with a place for contributory, universal, and means-tested benefits to meet different contingencies and to offer the most appropriate type of support (DHSS, 1985, p. 19). However, given that a central aim of the reforms was to ensure that benefits were targeted to "genuine need," in practice this was likely to mean that means-tested benefits would come to play an increasingly important role. The Beveridge system of social security had been based on social insurance benefits as the main plank of social protection and means-tested benefits as the backup, acting as a safety net but not as the first line of defense. The 1986 Social Security Act was a crucial step in a process that has increasingly reversed that order of priority and put means-tested benefits more at the forefront of UK social security policy, especially for people of working age.

One of the central reforms of the 1986 Social Security Act was the replacement of the "supplementary benefit" with "income support." The supplementary benefit (introduced 20 years earlier to replace national assistance) was the national scheme of social assistance, providing, on the basis of a means test and, for some claimants, a work test, financial support to those with insufficient incomes to support themselves. Income support plays the same role but is intended to provide more targeted support to those in most need. Families with children, sick and disabled people, and the very elderly gained slightly from these reforms, while young people and unemployed claimants lost out, an outcome described by Martin Evans and his colleagues (1994) as "churning" rather than "targeting." Young people aged 16 to 18 lost their entitlements to income support in 1988 and are now aided on a discretionary basis.

One of the key issues driving the 1986 measures and, indeed, policy throughout the 1980s and into the 1990s was a concern with the perceived problem of low work incentives. Unemployment was characterized by the government as predominantly a problem of labor supply and not as a problem of low demand for labor; unemployed people were seen as lacking sufficient incentive to work because claiming benefits was too easy and the level of benefits too high relative to earnings. Sticks and carrots were both needed: the sticks taking the form of reduced levels of out-of-work benefits and tighter eligibility conditions for these, and the carrots taking the form of additional means-tested support for low-paid workers. Unemployment-related benefits had already been reduced in the early 1980s by the abolition of the earnings-related supplement, the taxation of the benefit, and the shift to price, rather than wage, indexing. Atkinson and Micklewright (1989) calculated that unemployed people lost on average about £3 per week as a result of benefits reductions and restrictions made between 1979 and 1988, equivalent to a reduction of about £500 million in annual expenditure on unemployment.

The conditions required to get access to unemployment-related benefits also became increasingly more restrictive (Oppenheim and Harker, 1996). The introduction of compulsory "restart" interviews for unemployed claimants in 1986 was intended to ensure that claimants were genuinely seeking work. An even stricter "availability for work" test was introduced in 1989, and, from 1992, a benefit could immediately be withdrawn from anyone who failed this test. Compulsory short training courses for long-term unemployed people were introduced in 1990. The introduction of the Jobseekers Allowance (JSA) in 1996 was a logical progression from these policies. JSA replaces both the unemployment benefit and income support, but the non-means-tested element is payable for only 6 (instead of 12) months, job-seeking activities are actively monitored and reviewed, and there are powers to withdraw benefits and compel participation in training and work schemes. The introduction of JSA led to an immediate fall in successful benefit claims. A similar approach was adopted in relation to disabled people of working age, and the new Incapacity Benefit (introduced in 1995) includes a stringent "all-work" test, which has also significantly reduced the number of successful claims (Millar, 1997).

Means testing has also been extended to benefits for the working population. Post-war social security in the United Kingdom was focused almost entirely on non-working people and the support needed to assist people through periods of interrupted earnings. There was some support available to working families—child tax allowances and the family allowance—but these were primarily intended to meet extra costs. However, in-work benefits—first introduced in the 1970s—go further than this and are specifically intended to improve work incentives for low-wage workers. "Family credit" (which replaced the similar, but less generous, family income supplement in 1988) provides a weekly cash benefit to low-wage families with children, the amount depending on family size and earnings. Alan Marsh and Stephen McKay (1993) found that lone parents receiving the family credit gained about £30 per week, and couples about £18, not insignificant amounts for these poor families. Family credit was considered by the Conservative government to be a clear success, and the family credit approach was extended to other groups, including disabled people and, on a trial basis, childless couples and single people. In addition, the number of working families receiving the housing benefit (means-tested help with rent) and council tax benefits (means-tested help with local taxes) has risen steadily. Taking family credit and housing benefits together, up to 1 million working people in Britain now receive benefits alongside their wages. This growth in the receipt of means-tested benefits for workers has been one of the most significant trends of recent years, as more people receive a combination of earnings and benefits. For some—lone parents and low-paid, one-earner couples—these "in-work" benefits are increasingly an essential part of income (Millar, Webb, and Kemp, 1997).

The number of people in receipt of means-tested benefits has thus risen sharply in recent years. In 1979, there were 4.4 million people, claimants and their families, dependent on income support. By 1996, this had reached 9.6 million or about 17 percent of the total population. Expenditure on means-tested benefits rose from 17 percent of the total social security bill in 1978/1979 to 30 percent in 1995/1996 (Piachaud, 1997).

A commitment to reducing taxation was also a central part of Conservative government policy, and indeed taxation has become a key political issue in Britain. By the time of the 1997 election both main political parties were pledged to reduce taxation, and there was general acceptance of the view that no party could be elected without promising to cut taxes. During the 1980s, the Conservative governments cut both the basic rate and top rates of income tax but increased national insurance contributions and in-direct taxation (Pile and O'Donnell, 1997). Tax relief on mortgages to help people buy their homes rose significantly in the 1980s, reaching about £7.3 billion in 1989/1990—much higher than the expenditure on public hous-ing—before being cut back quite sharply (Kvist and Sinfield, 1997). As discussed above, tax relief for private pensions was increased in order to support and encourage people to make their own provision, although these too have been reduced somewhat in recent years. The overall impact is difficult to establish, but most commentators conclude that the tax changes of the 1980s tended to raise the tax burden on those with low and middle incomes and reduce it for those with high incomes (Giles and Johnson, 1994; Redmond and Sutherland, 1995).

ASSESSING THE CONSERVATIVE RECORD

To sum up, the 1980s and 1990s in Britain were a period of rising in-equality and poverty, mainly driven by labor market trends that were lead-ing to increased economic divisions. There was a growing divide between the unemployed and those with jobs and also between those households where no one worked and those households with two or more earners. Even among those in employment, there was a widening gap between wages at the top and those at the bottom of the labor market. Poverty increased significantly, especially for women (in particular, lone parents) and children (with child poverty rates rising to among the highest in Eu-rope).

This account of British welfare policy over the past two decades has focused on labor market and social security policy and so gives only a partial picture of changes in the British welfare state. Nevertheless, these policy areas provide an important test of the capacity and willingness of state provision to offer security and protection from market risks. The Con-servative polices clearly failed to provide that protection. They failed to protect the poorest and most vulnerable and, in some respects, acted to reinforce inequality and poverty. There were reductions in benefit levels; more restricted access to benefits through greater use of means testing and through tighter conditions of eligibility; and privatization policies that re-duced welfare services and placed more emphasis on family, as well as market, support.

The effects of these policies were felt in somewhat different ways by men and by women. Many of the benefit cuts discussed above—the freezing of the child benefit throughout most of the 1980s, the linking of the basic pension to prices rather than to earnings, the cutbacks to the state earnings-related pension scheme, the replacement of the supplementary benefit with the income support—disproportionately affected women. The abolition of the Wages Councils also particularly affected women, who make up the bulk of low-paid workers, as did the privatization of public services. Women have been less able than men to take up private welfare opportunities (e.g., private pensions and health care) because they are less likely to be able to afford these. Men, on the other hand, have seen a number of their rights and benefits reduced or removed, especially in respect to national insurance benefits. Sickness and unemployment benefits, along with pensions, were at the center of the Beveridge welfare state, paid to all those entitled on the basis of their contributions, not means-tested and not discretionary. Although this excluded many married women, most men were covered by these rights-based benefits. This is no longer the case, and men, as well as women, are increasingly to be found within the means-tested net.

Paul Pierson's (1994) three indicators of welfare retrenchment are privatization, significant increases in means testing, and tightening conditions of eligibility. He also argues that welfare cuts tend to fall mainly on those least able to protect themselves against them, the politically weak and unorganized groups in society. In the UK case, there was some privatization in the provision of social security benefits, but this generally reinforced the existing "mixed economy of welfare" rather than reflecting a radical break with the past. Thus, for example, the private sectors in pensions and in health care have continued to grow and form an integral part of provision in these areas. Privatization has also played an increasingly significant role in respect of service delivery. "Contracting out" has given private sector companies a major role in the provision of social care and has led to reductions in services and conditions of employment. But, in respect of social security provisions, the growth in means testing and the restrictions on benefit eligibility are at the center of the Conservative legacy. In addition, the cuts in welfare in the United Kingdom did indeed fall disproportionately upon the poorest and most disadvantaged groups in society. David Piachaud (1997, p. 82), for example, concludes:

The period since 1979 has seen a major extension in means testing. There has not, however, been a clear, consistent and comprehensive shift. . . . If there had been a consistent policy . . . with all social security benefits income tested, rather than picking on the unemployed and low paid—then the impact of means-testing would have been more broadly shared. It is hard to avoid the conclusion that the more politically vulnerable and expendable have been more harshly treated in order to curb public expenditure and limit any potential political damage.

Conservative policies exacerbated economic inequality and led to deeper poverty, and it is important to recognize these distributional consequences of welfare restructuring.

The focus of this chapter has been on issues of unemployment and social security benefits and not on other policy areas. But the general points do apply more widely. For example, public expenditure on health care increased in real terms, but, if National Health Service specific costs (mainly on pay) and increased demand (e.g., due to the aging of the population) are taken into account, then spending fell relative to needs (Hills, 1997). Full-scale privatization was rejected, but there was an increased emphasis on bringing the market into this sector. The "internal market," which separated purchasers and providers, was central to the Conservative policy, alongside other measures such as the "private finance initiative" (under which new hospital building would be financed by the private sector) and the "patient's charter" to increase consumer power (Paton, 1999). In education, too, schools were able to "opt out" from local authority control and to control their own budgets, and parents were given more opportunities to choose and manage schools for their children. This has also led to increased inequality in provision. The reduction in student grants and the introduction of fees for higher education have transferred more of these costs onto individuals and families.

The Conservative governments between 1979 to 1997 did not succeed in reducing public expenditure and did not dismantle the welfare state. The latter has proved rather more robust than many thought 20 years ago, not just in the United Kingdom but also in other industrialized countries (Klein, 1999). However, the Conservatives did create a more residual, less rights-based welfare system. It may not be possible for governments to entirely opt out of welfare funding and provision, but it is possible for governments to make choices about the type and extent of welfare services that will be supported. The Conservatives did make such choices and put them into effect, reducing support for the poorest and making them subject to more onerous requirements before offering any help and assistance. Their policies were popular enough for a record-breaking series of election victories. But there seem to have been limits to the popularity of privatization, not just among the population in general but also among private sector providers. Employers and private pension companies, for example, provided an important part of the opposition to the abolition of SERPS. In general, public opinion has remained broadly in favor of welfare spending, especially in respect of health and education. The landslide victory of the Labour Party in May 1997 showed that the electorate was ready for a different approach. But how different has the Labour government turned out to be?

THE NEW LABOUR FUTURE?

After about three years in power, it is possible to identify and chart some key continuities and discontinuities between Labour and Conservative policies. The Labour government has been very active over the past three years, with many policy reviews across a wide range of areas and with new legislation coming forward in many areas. Martin Powell's (1999) edited collection provides a review of these, but here there is space to concentrate on only some policy areas, with the aim of trying to assess which, if any, aspects of Conservative policy have persisted into the Labour era. The relevant areas to consider here are policies toward public expenditure and toward poverty and inequality.

Public Expenditure

Hills (1998) examines the public expenditure issue in some detail and points to both continuities and discontinuities in the early days of the Labour government. On the one hand, the targets for public expenditure that were set by the Conservative government just before the election were used as the basis for spending plans by the new government for the first two years. This reduced options and meant that any additional expenditure on one group or area of provision had to be financed by reducing expenditure on another. This was said to be one of the reasons that a cut in benefits to lone parents—planned by the previous government—was put into effect (discussed further below). It also meant that spending plans for social security were based on a continuation of the price-link rather than a return to the wages-link, and so there was no move to restore the benefit losses of the Conservative years. In fact, welfare spending fell by 0.8 percent of GDP between 1996/1997 and 1997/1998 (Hills, 1998). However, there have been spending increases in both the 1999 and 2000 budgets, particularly for health and education. The spending plans for 2001 to 2004 include an increase of 2.5 percent in a year in real terms (HM Treasury, 2000). Thus, Labour is not seeking to reduce overall spending levels in the way that Conservatives sought to do, and it is redistributing spending into certain areas where, the government argues, it is for future investment in skills and communities.

Combating Poverty and "Social Exclusion"

We argued above that Conservative policies increased inequality and poverty and also that this was justified in terms of economic growth and efficiency. The Labour government is also looking for economic growth and efficiency but takes a very different view on poverty. This is apparent both in the rhetoric and in various policy developments. Tony Blair, the prime minister, has made a number of very clear commitments about the importance of reducing poverty. In 1996, he said that "if the Labour government has not raised the living standards of the poorest by the end of its term in office, it will have failed," and he has also promised, in a speech to commemorate 50 years of the post-Beveridge welfare state, to eliminate child poverty in 20 years. There have been a number of specific initiatives—including the setting up of the "Social Exclusion Unit" and a range of area-based policies for local economic and social regeneration—aimed at combating poverty. The Treasury has published various papers analyzing the nature and causes of inequality in the United Kingdom (e.g., HM Treasury, 1999a, 1999b, and two annual poverty audits have been published (DSS, 1999, 2000). There has been a special focus on children, with the commitment to end child poverty being pursued by a range of measures, including benefit increases, more money going into education and child care, and a particular focus on the need for "early years" support for the most disadvantaged young children. All this is a very significant change from the Thatcher years in particular, where the very existence of poverty was questioned.

However, the means by which this poverty reduction is to be achieved are at the heart of the debates about the future direction of Labour policy and the differences between "new" and "old" Labour. The term "new Labour" refers to ideological and policy differences between the "old" Labour Party and the "modernizers" of the "new Labour" Party (Brivati and Bale, 1997; Deacon and Mann, 1997; Ellison, 1997). The "old" Labour approach is associated with social and economic planning, government ownership of key industries, and welfare collectivism. The "new" Labour approach accepts a greater role for the market and a mixed economy of welfare and wants to reform social security and welfare to create a more "active" system of support (Labour Party, 1996, 1997). General increases in benefit levels are, therefore, low on the priority list.[9] This is clearly expressed in the words of Gordon Brown, chancellor of the Exchequer for new Labour: "For far too long we have used the tax and benefit system to compensate people for their poverty rather than doing something more fundamental—tackling the root causes of poverty and inequality . . . the road to equality of opportunity starts not with tax rates but with jobs, education" (Brown, 1996, cited in Powell, 1999, p. 17).

The main thrust of government social security policy for working-age people has thus been the "welfare-to-work" programs (funded from a windfall tax and so outside the spending constraints noted above), coupled with tax and benefit changes intended to "make work pay" (discussed below). This conflict between extra spending on benefits against extra spending on support for employment came up in a politically dramatic way during Labour's first year in office, in relation to lone parents.

Lone parents are one of the poorest groups in society and are very often dependent upon social security policy. Under the system that had developed in the 1970s and 1980s, lone parents were entitled to receive two small additional benefits in support of their extra costs. The one-parent benefit was paid as an addition to the universal child benefit and was mainly received by employed lone parents. The lone-parent premium was paid as an addition to income support for lone parents and thus went mainly to the non-employed. The cash amounts were small, but these are very poor families. The Conservative government had planned to abolish both of these benefits, and Labour decided to go ahead with these cuts. But doing so caused immediate controversy for the government, with widespread opposition, including from some Labour Members of Parliament (MPs). Concern was expressed that other vulnerable groups—disabled people, for example—might also find their benefits reduced and restricted. Although there was no danger that the measure might fail to get through Parliament, it did cause considerable adverse publicity at the time. The savings were relatively small, but the move was important in that it clearly signaled that the new government would not give priority to improving benefit levels for those not at work. It is benefits for those in work or to help non-workers move into work where the main thrust of policy lies.

THE ACTIVE WELFARE STATE

Welfare reform has taken center stage under new Labour, and policy has focused on getting people into work and supporting them while in work. According to the Green Paper *New Ambitions for Our Country: A New Contract for Welfare* (DSS, 1998b), "Work is the best form of welfare," and the first principle for welfare reform states, "The welfare state should help and encourage people of working age to work where they are capable of doing so." The key policies being implemented are:

- Compulsory "New Deal" programs for long-term unemployed and young unemployed persons, offering training or employment in subsidized and non-subsidized jobs;
- Voluntary "New Deal" schemes for lone parents and disabled people, offering advice and support to move into work;
- The National Child Care strategy, promising affordable care for all children aged 0–14;
- National Minimum Wage (£3.60 per hour);
- Reductions in National Insurance contributions for low-paid workers;
- Tax Credits—for working families, child care, disabled people;
- Increases in child benefit for the oldest child and in Income Support rates for children;
- From 2001 a merger of the existing Employment Service and Benefits Agency in order to create a new "working age agency" dealing with both income support and employment and training and placement services;
- Area-based programs, such as the "new deal for communities" and "employment zones," to target resources on disadvantaged areas.

There is much here that is new. For example, there has never been a national minimum wage before in the United Kingdom, and this is also the first time that a UK government has accepted broad responsibility for ensuring child care for all children (not just children "in need"). The pledge to end child poverty has been important in redirecting resources to children, and the number of children estimated to be living in poor households has fallen by about 1.2 million (Millar, 2001). The labor market and social security reforms have clear resonance with policy developments in other countries such as the United States and Australia, and the election promise to cut youth unemployment by 250,000 has been met. Pensions reform (DSS, 1998a) has introduced a "minimum pensions guarantee" that provides a means-tested minimum income for pensioners without adequate National Insurance pensions. There have also been additional payments for poor pensioners toward fuel and other costs. However, the link with earnings has not been restored. A new "stakeholder" pension will be introduced as a second tier to the basic pension. This is for low earners without occupational or private pensions, for persons with disabilities limiting their employment, and for carers (who will receive credits toward these pensions).

But there are also some continuities with the Conservatives. Targeting support on the poorest through means testing is still important, although the means tests are increasingly operated through the tax rather than the benefit system. Making benefits subject to strict conditions is also central to New Labour. Long-term unemployed people and young people are required to take part in the New Deal schemes and must take up either employment or training or lose their benefit. New Deal interviews are also to be made compulsory for lone parents with children of school age. This focus on the responsibilities and obligations of claimants is very strong under Labour and has clear continuities with Conservative policy.

The government itself has tried in various ways to map out exactly where and how these policies and the underlying values that they reflect are different from both "old" Labour and the Conservative "new Right." They are pursuing, they say, a "third way," different from both. This appears in the welfare reform Green Paper (DSS, 1998b) as a contrast among three futures: a "privatized" future with a residual safety net for the poor (implicitly, the Conservative approach); the "status quo" but with higher benefits (implicitly old Labour); and the "third way" (new Labour), "promoting opportunity rather than dependence." But, as Hills (1998) and Powell (1999) both point out, it is not yet clear what exactly the third way is and whether or not it is, or can be, different from past approaches. The idea of an "active welfare state" is both a reaction to, and a consequence of, the experience of the past 20 years, and so contains a mixture of old and new policy objectives and programs. The measures introduced so far have started to have an impact on child poverty in particular, but it remains to be seen how much and how soon the Labour government will be able to reduce the high rates of poverty and inequality bequeathed by the Thatcherite era.

NOTES

1. These sections extend and update a previous work, "The Continuing Trend in Rising Poverty" (Millar, 1993), presented at the annual meeting of the British Association for the Advancement of Science. Thanks to Tess Ridge for research assistance.

2. The establishment of a Scottish Parliament (with policy and revenue-raising powers) and a Welsh Assembly (with policy but no revenue-raising powers) in 1999 will probably widen these differences in the future (Parry, 1998; Sullivan, 1998).

3. In 1996 the Conservative government introduced legislation to restrict the rights of asylum seekers to social security support. This caused substantial hardship to those arriving in the United Kingdom seeking asylum and led to a significant decline in the number of asylum applications (Bloch, 1998). The Labour government has also restricted the rights of asylum seekers to financial support from the social security system.

4. It is also possible to look at other measures, such as incomes below 60 or 40 percent of the average (DSS, 1997a).

5. The data on which these figures are based are drawn from a variety of sources, including some figures that are pooled over two years in order to make more robust estimates. This is also true for some of the other statistics quoted in this chapter.

6. There is a gap in the figures for the years between 1981 and 1987 because no figures were published for that period.

7. Throughout this chapter the British pound is valued at a rate of £0.65 = $1.00. This is broadly the value in Purchasing Power Parities (as calculated by the OECD) in the latter part of the 1990s.

8. Unemployment fell rapidly in the latter part of 1997. The figures for the autumn quarter show the Labour Force Survey count at 1.85 million and the claimant count at 1.4 million (Convery, 1998). Like counting poverty, counting unemployment became a controversial issue in the 1980s. Over 30 changes to the official definition made the unemployment levels look lower than they would have been and led to a highly critical report from the Royal Statistical Society (1995). The production and publication of official statistics are currently under review (CM 3882, 1998).

9. However, benefits for children, including Income Support rates, have been increased substantially (Millar, 2001).

REFERENCES

Alcock, P. (1997). "Consolidation or stagnation? Social policy under the Major governments." In M. May, E. Brunsdon, and G. Craig, eds., *Social Policy Review*, vol. 9. London: Guildhall University Social Policy Association, pp. 17–33.

Atkinson, A. B., and J. Micklewright. (1989). "Turning the screw: Benefits for the unemployed, 1979–1988." In A. B. Atkinson, ed., *Poverty and Social Security*, Hemel Hempstead: Harvester Wheatsheaf, pp. 155–157.

Berthoud, R. (1997). "Income and standards of living." In T. Modood, R. Berthoud, J. Lakey, J. Nazroo, P. Smith, S. Virdee, and S. Beishon, *Ethnic Minorities in Britain*. London: Policy Studies Institute, 150–183.

Bloch, A. (1998). "Ethnic inequality and social security policy." In A. Walker and C. Walker, eds., *Britain Divided: The Growth of Social Exclusion in the 1980s and 1990s.* London: Child Poverty Action Group, 111–122.

Bowers, J., D. Brown, and S. Gibbons. (1993). *Trade Union Reform and Employment Rights Act 1993: A Practical Guide.* London: Longman.

Bradshaw, J. (1994). *Household Budgets and Living Standards.* York: Joseph Rowntree Foundation.

Brivati, B., and T. Bale, eds. (1997). *New Labour in Power: Precedent and Prospects.* London: Routledge.

Brown, W. (1991). "Industrial relations." In M. Artis and D. Cobham, eds., *Labour's Economic Policies, 1974–1979.* Manchester: Manchester University Press, pp. 213–228.

Burchardt, T. (1997). *Boundaries between Public and Private Welfare: A Typology and Map of Services.* CASE Paper no 2. London: London School of Economics, Centre for the Analysis of Social Exclusion.

Clarke, J. (1996). "The problem of the state after the welfare state." In M. May, E. Brunsdon, and G. Craig, eds., *Social Policy Review,* vol. 8. London: Guildhall University Social Policy Association, pp. 13–39.

CM 3882. (1998). *Statistics: A Matter of Trust. A Consultation Document.* London: Stationery Office.

Coates, D. (1995). "UK underperformance: Claim and reality." In D. Coates and J. Hillard, eds., *UK Economic Decline: Key Texts.* Hemel Hempstead: Harvester Wheatsheaf.

Coates, D., and J. Hillard, eds. (1995). *UK Economic Decline: Key Texts.* Hemel Hempstead: Harvester Wheatsheaf.

Convery, P. (1998). "Strong employment growth is patchy." *Working Brief* 91: 23–24.

Cox, G. (1997). "Low pay." Annex, in the Council of Churches, *Unemployment and the Future of Work.* London: Council of Churches of Britain and Ireland.

Cox, A., S. Lee, and J. Sanderson, eds. (1997). *The Political Economy of Modern Britain.* Cheltenham: Edward Elgar.

Deacon, A., and K. Mann. (1997). "Moralism and modernity: The paradox of New Labour thinking on welfare." *Benefits* 20: 2–6.

Department of Education and Employment. (1998). *Childcare: A Framework and Consultation Document.* London: Author.

Department of Health and Social Security (DHSS). (1985). *The Reform of Social Security.* London: HMSO.

Department of Social Security (DSS). (1996). *Households below Average Income, a Statistical Analysis, 1979–1993/4.* London: Stationery Office.

———. (1997a). *Households below Average Income, a Statistical Analysis, 1979–1994/5.* London: Stationery Office.

———. (1997b). *Social Security Statistics 1997.* London: Stationery Office.

———. (1998a). *A New Contract for Welfare: Partnership in Pensions.* London: Stationery Office.

———. (1998b). *New Ambitions for Our Country: A New Contract for Welfare.* London: Stationery Office.

———. (1999). *Opportunity for All: Tackling Poverty and Social Exclusion.* London: Stationery Office.

———. (2000). *Opportunity for All—One Year On: Making a Difference.* London: Stationery Office.

Ditch, J., H. Barnes, J. Bradshaw, and M. Kilkey. (1998). *European Observatory on National Family Policies: A Synthesis of Family Policies in 1996.* Brussels: European Commission.

Donnelly, C. (1998). "JSA regulations changed to make way for the New Deal." *Working Brief* 91: 6–7.

Ellison, N. (1997). "From welfare state to post-welfare society? Labour's social policy in historical and contemporary perspective." In B. Brivati and T. Bale, eds., *New Labour in Power: Precedent and Prospects.* London: Routledge, pp. 34–61.

Equal Opportunities Commission Northern Ireland (EOC-NI). (1996). *Report on the Formal Investigation into Competitive Tendering in the Health and Education Services in Northern Ireland.* Belfast: Author.

Escott, K., and D. Whitfield. (1995). *The Gender Impact of CCT in Local Government.* Manchester: Equal Opportunities Unit.

Evans, D., D. Piachaud, and H. Sutherland. (1994). *Designed for the Poor—Poorer by Design? The Effects of the 1986 Social Security Act.* London: Suntory-Toyota International Centre for Economics and Related Disciplines.

Falkingham, J., and J. Hills. (1995). *The Dynamic of Welfare: The Welfare State and the Life Cycle.* Hemel Hempstead: Harvester Wheatsheaf.

Farnham, D. (1990). "Trade union policy 1979–89: Restriction or reform?" In S. Savage and L. Robins, eds., *Public Policy under Thatcher.* London: Macmillan.

Field, F. (1997). *Reforming Welfare.* London: Social Market Foundation.

Ford, R., and J. Millar. (1998). *Private Lives and Public Responses: Lone Parenthood and Future Policy.* London: Policy Studies Institute.

Giles, C., and P. Johnson. (1994). "Tax reform in the UK and changes in the progressivity of the tax system, 1985–95." *Fiscal Studies* 15(3): 64–86.

Glennerster, H., A. Power, and T. Travers. (1991). "A new era for social policy: A new Enlightenment or a new Leviathan?" *Journal of Social Policy* 20(3): 389–414.

Goodman, A., P. Johnson, and S. Webb. (1997). *Inequality in the UK.* Oxford: Oxford University Press.

Gordon, D., and C. Pantazia, eds. (1997). *Breadline Britain in the 1990s.* Aldershot: Ashgate.

Gregg, P., and J. Wadsworth. (1996). "More work in fewer households." In J. Hills, ed., *New Inequalities: The Changing Distribution of Income and Wealth.* Cambridge: Cambridge University Press, pp. 181–207.

Hills, J. (1990). *The State of Welfare.* Oxford: Oxford University Press.

———, ed. (1996). *New Inequalities: The Changing Distribution of Income and Wealth in the United Kingdom.* Cambridge: Cambridge University Press.

———. (1997). *The Future of Welfare: A Guide to the Debate,* rev. ed. with K. Gardiner and the LSE Welfare State Programme. York: Joseph Rowntree Foundation.

———. (1998). *Thatcherism, New Labour and the Welfare State.* CASE Paper No.

13. London: London School of Economics, Centre for the Analysis of Social Exclusion.

HM Treasury. (1979). *The Government's Expenditure Plans, 1980–81.* Cmnd 7746. London: Stationery Office.

———. (1998). *Modern Public Services for Britain: Investing in Reform.* CM 3901. London: Stationery Office.

———. (1999a). *The Modernisation of Britain's Tax and Benefit System: Tackling Poverty and Extending Opportunity.* London: Author.

———. (1999b). Supporting Children through the Tax and Benefit System. London: Stationery Office.

———. (2000). *Prudent for a Purpose: Building Opportunity and Security for All. 2000 Spending Review: New Public Spending Plans 2001–2004.* London: Stationery Office.

Holmans, A. (1995). *Housing Demand and Need in England.* York: Joseph Rowntree Foundation.

Hutton, W. (1995). *The State We're In.* London: Jonathan Cape.

Jarvis, S., and S. Jenkins. (1996). *Do the Poor Stay Poor? New Evidence about Income Dynamics from the British Household Panel Survey.* Colchester: ESRC Research Centre on Micro-Social Change, University of Essex.

Johnson, P., R. Disney, and G. Stears. (1996). *Pensions 2000 and Beyond.* London: Institute for Fiscal Studies.

Joseph Rowntree Foundation. (1995). *Inquiry into Income and Wealth.* York: Publishing Services for Joseph Rowntree Foundation.

Kemp, P. (1999). "Housing policy under New Labour." In M. Powell, ed., *New Labour, New Welfare State?* Bristol: Policy Press, pp. 123–147.

Kempson, E. (1996). *Life on a Low Income.* York: Publishing Services for Joseph Rowntree Foundation.

Klein, R. (1999). "The crises of the welfare states." In R. J. Cooter and J. V. Pickstone, eds., *Medicine in the Twentieth Century.* Amsterdam: Harwood Academic Publications, pp. 155–170.

Knijn, T., and M. Kremer. (1998). "Gender and the caring dimension of welfare states: Towards inclusive citizenship." *Social Politics* 4(3): 328–361.

Kvist, J., and A. Sinfield. (1997). "Comparing tax welfare states." In M. May, E. Brunsdon, and G. Craig, eds., *Social Policy Review,* vol. 9. London: Guildhall University Social Policy Association, pp. 249–257.

Labour Party. (1996). *Getting Welfare to Work: A New Vision for Social Security.* London: Author.

———. (1997). *New Labour—Because Britain Deserves Better.* London: Author.

Lee, S. (1997). "Manufacturing British decline." In A. Cox, S. Lee, and J. Sanderson, eds., *The Political Economy of Modern Britain.* Cheltenham: Edward Elgar, pp. 166–205.

Leibfried, S., and P. Pierson. (1995). *European Social Policy: Between Fragmentation and Integration.* Washington, DC: Brookings Institution.

Low Pay Network. (1996). *Priced into Poverty: An Analysis of Pay Rates in Former Wages Council Industries.* London: Author.

Machin, S., and A. Manning. (1994). "The effects of minimum wages on wage dispersion and employment—evidence from the UK Wages Councils." *Industrial and Labor Relations Review* 47(2): 319–329.

Mack, J., and S. Lansley. (1985). *Poor Britain.* London: Allen and Unwin.

Marsh, A., and S. McKay. (1993). *Families, Work, and Benefits.* London: Policy Studies Institute.

McCarthy, M. (1986). *Campaigning for the Poor: CPAG and the Politics of Welfare.* London: Croom Helm.

McCormack, J., and C. Oppenheim. (1998). *Welfare in Working Order.* London: Institute for Public Policy Research.

Middleton, S., K. Ashworth, and I. Braithwaite. (1997). *Small Fortunes: Spending on Children, Childhood Poverty, and Parental Sacrifice.* York: Joseph Rowntree Foundation.

Millar, J. (1993). "The continuing trend in rising poverty." In A. Sinfield, ed., *Poverty, Justice, and Inequality.* New Waverly Papers Social Policy Series No. 6, pp. 11–18. Edinburgh: University of Edinburgh.

———. (1996). "Women, poverty and Social Security." In C. Hallett, ed., *Women and Social Policy: An Introduction.* Hemel Hempstead: Harvester Wheatsheaf.

———. (1997). "Gender." In A. Walker and C. Walker., eds., *Britain Divided: The Growth of Social Exclusion in the 1980s and 1990s.* London: Child Poverty Action Group.

———. (2001). "Benefits for children: The United Kingdom." In K. Battle and M. Mendelson, eds., *Benefits for Children: A Four Country Study.* Ottawa: The Caledon Institute, pp. 197–256.

Millar, J., S. Webb, and M. Kemp. (1997). *Combining Work and Welfare.* York: Publishing Services for Joseph Rowntree Foundation.

Modood, T., R. Berthoud, J. Lakey, J. Nazroo, P. Smith, S. Virdee, and S. Beishon. (1997). *Ethnic Minorities in Britain.* London: Policy Studies Institute.

Moore, J. (1989). *The End of the Line for Poverty.* London: Conservative Central Office.

Nesbitt, S. (1995). *British Pensions Policy Making in the 1980s.* Aldershot: Avebury.

Office for National Statistics (ONS). (1997a). *Social Trends.* London: Stationery Office.

———. (1997b). *Economic Trends.* London: Stationery Office.

———. (1998). *Social Trends.* London: Stationery Office.

Oppenheim, C., and L. Harker. (1996). *Poverty—the Facts,* 3rd ed. London: Child Poverty Action Group.

Oppenheim, C., and R. Lister. (1996). "Ten years after the 1986 Social Security Act." In M. May, E. Brunsdon, and G. Craig, eds., *Social Policy Review,* vol. 8. London: Guildhall University Social Policy Association, pp. 84–105.

Organisation for Economic Co-operation and Development (OECD). (1994). *Employment Outlook.* Paris: Author.

Parry, R. (1998). "The view from Scotland." In H. Jones and S. McGregor, eds., *Social Issues and Party Politics.* London: Routledge, pp. 194–213.

Pascall, G. (1997). *Social Policy: A New Feminist Analysis.* London: Routledge.

Paton, C. (1999). "New Labour's health policy: The new healthcare state." In M. Powell, ed., *New Labour, New Welfare State?* Bristol: Policy Press, pp. 51–75.

Piachaud, D. (1997). "The growth of means testing." In A. Walker and C. Walker, eds., *Britain Divided: The Growth of Social Exclusion in the 1980s and 1990s*. London: Child Poverty Action Group, pp. 75–83.

Pierson, P. (1994). *Dismantling the Welfare State? Reagan, Thatcher, and the Politics of Retrenchment*. Cambridge: Cambridge University Press.

Pile, H., and C. O'Donnell. (1997). "Earnings, taxation, and wealth." In A. Walker and C. Walker, eds., *Britain Divided: The Growth of Social Exclusion in the 1980s and 1990s*. London: Child Poverty Action Group, pp. 32–47.

Powell, M. (1995). "The strategy of equality revisited." *Journal of Social Policy* 24(2): 163–186.

———, ed. (1999). *New Labour, New Welfare State?* Bristol: Policy Press.

Redmond, G., and H. Sutherland. (1995). *How Has Tax and Social Security Policy Changed since 1978? A Distributional Analysis*. Cambridge: Cambridge University Press.

Royal Statistical Society. (1995). *Report of the Working Party on the Measurement of Unemployment in the U.K.* London: Author.

Sawyer, M. (1996). "Industry, its structures and policies towards it." In M. J. Arts, ed., *The UK Economy*, 14th ed. Oxford: Oxford University Press, pp. 225–260.

Sefton, T. (1997). *The Changing Distribution of the Social Wage*. York: Joseph Rowntree Foundation.

Sullivan, M. (1998). "The view from Wales." In H. Jones and S. McGregor, eds., *Social Issues and Party Politics*. London: Routledge, pp. 223–242.

Sweeney, K. (1996). "Membership of trade unions in 1994: An analysis based on information from the Certification Officer." *Labour Market Trends* 104(2): 49–53.

Whiteley, P., and S. Winyard. (1987). *Pressure for the Poor*. London: Methuen.

Williams, K., J. Williams, and C. Haslam. (1990). "The hollowing-out of British manufacturing and its implications for policy." *Economy and Society* 19(4): 456–490.

Chapter 6

The Triple Exceptionalism
of the French Welfare State

Mark Kesselman

There is a burgeoning literature on the character and crisis of contemporary welfare states. France is one of the most interesting and significant cases—whether viewed from the perspective of its theoretical underpinnings, political importance, or extent of social protection (among the greatest in the world). Yet it is also one of the least studied and understood by American scholars.

This chapter seeks to explore three puzzles. First, why does France have one of the most extensive systems of social provision in the world, despite the absence of what is conventionally thought to explain strong welfare state growth, that is, a strong Christian Democratic Party, as in Germany or Italy, or, alternatively, a hegemonic Social Democratic Party linked to a unified, centralized labor movement, as in Scandinavia? I suggest that the welfare state reflects a strong consensus among a wide range of otherwise divergent political forces in France, including the Communist and Socialist Parties on the Left and Christian Democratic, Gaullist, and centrist forces across the political divide. The welfare state constitutes a kind of common meeting ground or lowest common denominator that symbolizes republican unity and a collective commitment to providing a strong safety net, values to which the Left has historically assigned priority; state responsibility for promoting the common good, a value that the Left and Gaullism championed; and Christian solidarity. At the same time, ideological and political forces typically hostile to social provision, those that typically defend the importance of individual entrepreneurship and responsibility, are weakly represented in France. (Although "laissez-faire" is a French term, it has few champions in France!)

Second, why is the French welfare state different? France fits poorly within the two most influential welfare state typologies, the Bismarckian and the Beveridgean. The former is a status-preserving welfare regime, and the latter is universalistic. France contains important elements of both but is not predominantly one or the other.

According to Esping-Andersen's typology (1990), there are three broadly different "worlds of welfare capitalism": (1) social democratic welfare states that emphasize equality of treatment (universalism); (2) Christian Democratic and conservative corporatist states that provide benefits based on one's relation to the labor market rather than as a citizen right (entitlement) and thereby support income maintenance to stabilize existing stratification; and (3) liberal welfare states that target poverty alleviation for those at the bottom, confining welfare provision to those in greatest need, while emphasizing that, given equality of opportunity within labor markets and society, people sort themselves out in unequal ways on the basis of differences in merit. The last two regimes provide cash benefits primarily, while the social democratic model emphasizes both income maintenance and social services distributed on a universal basis (Esping-Andersen, 1990; for a thorough and superb recasting of his approach to contemporary political economy, see Esping-Andersen, 1999).

In important respects, France does not fit comfortably within the social democratic category, that is, regimes dominated by a hegemonic Social Democratic Party closely linked to a strong labor movement, in which centralized and unified trade unions organize the bulk of the labor force. On the political level, too, France has little in common with the social democratic model. During most of the post-war period, when Social Democratic Parties were hegemonic in Northern Europe, France was ruled by centrist and center-right coalitions. In 1981, a socialist government, headed by François Mitterrand, was elected and promptly increased social spending. But the Mitterrand administration soon abandoned its reformist commitments. Moreover, a hallmark of social democracy during its heyday in the 1950s through 1970s was a close, cooperative relationship between the ruling Social Democratic Party and a powerful, unified labor movement. Yet this is far from what characterizes France, both before and after the socialists' election in 1981.

The French labor movement is intensely divided, with three or four competing central confederations (depending on whether one counts the managers' confederation). Each one is relatively decentralized, and the labor movement's cumulative "reach" or density is exceptionally low. Along with the United States, France ranks at the bottom of the league table of industrialized democracies in terms of union density: less than 10 percent of the French labor force belongs to a union, and the percentage is significantly lower in the private sector. Nor has the labor movement ever entertained close ties with the French Socialist Party. Especially noteworthy is how tense were the relations between the Mitterrand government and French unions (see Chapman, Kesselman, and Schain, 1998). Indeed, in an analysis of the Mitterrand government during its early years, I characterized the situation as "socialism without the workers" (Kesselman, 1983).

At the same time, France is quite unlike the conservative corporatist and Christian Democratic regimes of Southern Europe. For one thing, since the Gaullist tidal wave of 1958, it has lacked a major Christian Democratic Party. Moreover, although the Catholic Church is quite powerful, ideologically and in other ways, its influence is limited to a particular subculture. Moreover, France's secular, republican tradition is hostile to the church. Finally, France is not typically corporatist. Rather than socioeconomic regulation occurring through institutionalized class compromise and coordination, it occurs in quite chaotic fashion, through grassroots protest eliciting employer concessions and state intervention. For example, Pitruzzello (1997) describes France as a case of "discordant corporatism"—an awkward phrase that captures the reality of the beast.

In brief, as Levy (1998, p. 4) cogently argues, "France's welfare state defies easy classification." Levy suggests that the French welfare state "combines elements of Bismarck and Beveridge, of categorical privilege and the universal rights of citizenship. Esping-Andersen places France in the conservative corporatist or Christian Democratic welfare world, but it is an awkward fit at best" (Levy, 1998, p. 4).

The French welfare state is a hodge-podge of different elements that developed according to divergent logics under the aegis of ruling coalitions with different social, ideological, and partisan orientations. "Perhaps the best way to conceptualize the French welfare state is as a sedimentation of different welfare agendas, with successive layers imposed and blended in response to shifts in the political context" (Levy, 1988, p. 4).

Most social programs in France other than medical care are earnings- or income-based, rather than the universal, flat-rate type, and the proportion of social services relative to cash transfers is low. The ratio of social services to cash transfers is .12 in France, compared to .06 in Italy and .16 in Germany but .33 in Denmark and .29 in Sweden (Esping-Andersen, 1996b, p. 85, n. 2). On the other hand, France has important universal programs, including family allowances and basic health care.

France resembles the Scandinavian countries in not imposing a "marriage tax" on earnings, the effect of which is to discourage female employment. In recent decades, social spending has encouraged women, especially mothers, to work outside the home, and the proportion of French women in the paid labor force has increased. The labor force participation rate of French women (59.9 percent in 1996) exceeded the European Union (EU) average of 57.0 percent (Organisation for Economic Co-operation and Development [OECD], 1997). Moreover, the proportion of working women in France with young children is exceptionally high, and working women, compared to those elsewhere in Continental Europe, are relatively more likely to hold full-time jobs. As two specialists observe:

While in West Germany family policy confirms and strengthens the antagonism between maternity and employment, in France the model of the "working mother" . . . is fully integrated into the family policy. . . . State policies in France are crucial in supporting high rates of participation in full-time employment by diverse groups of women. (Monk and Garcia-Ramon, 1996, pp. 16, 20)

To illustrate: whereas 40.5 percent of economically active German women 25–44 years old with one or two children work full-time, this compares with 74.3 percent of the comparable group of French women. During the years before the first child enters primary school, 64 percent of German mothers but only 41 percent of French women stop working. Moreover, 18 percent of German working mothers but 47 percent of the comparable group of French women work full-time (Fagnani, 1996, p. 131). These policies place France "at the forefront of developments in employment policy designed to make child-bearing compatible with employment" (Fagnani, 1996, p. 133). Esping-Andersen classifies France as among a handful of countries that pursue what he calls de-familialization, that is, "policies that lessen individuals' reliance on the family; that maximize individuals' command of economic resources independently of familial or conjugal reciprocities" (Esping-Andersen, 1999, p. 45). The reason is that France provides subsidized and publicly regulated (as well as high-quality) day care, enabling women to work outside the home (Esping-Andersen, 1999, pp. 65, 66). According to Esping-Andersen's data, France has the lowest net, post-transfer cost of child care for the average family among the eight countries included in his sample (including Denmark and Sweden) (Esping-Andersen, 1999, p. 66, table 4.4; the data are for the mid-1990s).

Women have recently achieved another significant advance which, because of the linkage between social provision and political representation, could influence the course of the French welfare state. In 2000, landmark legislation was passed promoting gender equality in political representation. The parity law, as it is called, requires all political parties to nominate an equal number of men and women for elected bodies. Public campaign subsidies are significantly reduced for any party that fails to comply. The 2001 municipal elections were the first held since the reform was adopted. (The 2002 legislative elections will also be governed by the parity law, which means that the number of female candidates running for the National Assembly will soar.) The 2001 municipal elections produced a dramatic increase in women's representation. Nearly without exception, election slates in towns throughout France had as many women as men. (The law applies to all villages and towns with populations over 3,500.) From one election to the next, the number of women on France's town councils increased from about 7,000 to 39,000, which represents close to half of the 83,000 municipal councilors in these municipalities. Within several years, women should achieve close to equal representation within all of France's representative institutions. Women, having a greater stake in the welfare state, are more likely to support it as public officials. More women in government should thus mean more support for the welfare state.

The French case is useful in reminding us that typologies merely identify tendencies; they should not be mistaken for accurate road maps. France fits the usual typologies so poorly because it is a political hybrid. The fact that diverse socioeconomic forces have supported the welfare state for quite different reasons—as well as the fact that such support may be expressed by extensive grassroots mobilization to oppose attempts at retrenchment—helps explain why France continues to have an exceptionally robust welfare state in the current era.

Third, why hasn't France retrenched more in the current era? Indeed, why has it bucked the dominant trend in industrialized capitalist nations and substantially expanded social spending in the 1980s and 1990s? Pierson (1994, 1996) and others stress that there is generally far less welfare state retrenchment than meets the eye; however, he underestimates the extent of retrenchment. One reason is that Pierson measures the extent of retrenchment in terms of long- and short-term spending levels. However, one should measure retrenchment not in absolute expenditures but relative to social need. In an era of greatly increased social stress and dislocation—a situation prevailing for decades in the countries that he analyzes—it is plausible to suggest that the absence of dramatic increases in social expenditures constitutes retrenchment.

Whatever the criteria used to measure retrenchment, France is an outlier during the period of welfare state crisis and stagnation: in recent decades, social spending has increased significantly, relative both to past social expenditures in France as well as to other OECD countries. An important reason is the reformist bent of the socialist government elected in 1981. Whereas France ranked sixth among OECD countries in terms of social expenditures when the socialist government assumed office, it ranked third by the late 1990s (Olivennes, 1998). These quantitative changes partly reflect an expansion of social coverage: within the past decade, a host of new programs was added to France's already extensive welfare state. The puzzle, then, is why French practice runs counter to the dominant trend in the recent period.

This chapter attempts to describe and explain France's "triple exceptionalism" in the realm of social welfare. The first part describes the broad contours of the French welfare state—the extent and character of social provision. The next part describes the historical trajectory of the French welfare state: the establishment of the welfare state following the end of

World War II through the creation of the Fifth Republic in 1958; the expansion of the welfare state after the election of François Mitterrand in 1981, followed by fiscal austerity from 1983, culminating in the attempted fundamental overhaul of welfare in 1995; the resultant massive strikes in 1995; and the possible new turn symbolized by Socialist Party leader Lionel Jospin's election in 1997.

THE CHARACTER AND HISTORICAL TRAJECTORY OF THE WELFARE STATE

France was 40 years behind Germany and Britain in establishing general and mandatory social insurance. Borrel (1996) suggests that French social policy should be defined as an aggregate of social benefits, the minimum wage, and the length of the working day. I focus here, as do most accounts of the welfare state, on social benefits, although I also note the Jospin reform of reducing working hours below. Only in 1930 did a conservative French government sponsor means-tested health, maternity, disability, death, and old age insurance for workers. Its motives were electoral, as were those of post-war conservative governments that expanded welfare: to deprive the Communist and Socialist Parties of credit for passing reforms. In addition, enlightened business interests supported reforms in order to promote economic efficiency, and Catholic reformers defended social assistance on moral grounds. The reason for the lag in France was mainly the persistence of an extensive and powerful sector of small capital fiercely opposed to social reform. As a result, whereas only 15 percent of the French labor force was covered by public pension insurance in 1930, the comparable figure was 64 percent in Germany and 90 percent in Britain (Ambler, 1993, Introduction).[1]

The 1930 reform was made possible only because of a change in the class structure, with a growth of large business firms replacing small business and the consequent swelling of the ranks of the industrial working class. For example, between 1906 and 1930, the proportion of the industrial labor force employed in single-person firms dropped from 27 to 14 percent, while workers employed in firms with 100 employees increased from 25 to 37 percent (Ambler, 1993, Introduction).

As Ambler (1993) points out, the French welfare state was, in many respects, a conservative creation, at least in its modern guise. Although the welfare state expanded significantly in two short bursts during which the Left participated in government—in the Popular Front and Liberation—it grew most in the long period of conservative rule in the first two decades of the Fifth Republic. Between 1960 and 1980, French social spending as a proportion of all government spending soared from 38.2 percent to 58.1 percent. By contrast, in social democratic Sweden, known for its generous welfare state, social spending declined significantly, from 58.1 percent to

51.9 percent over this period. When Mitterrand took office, France devoted 29.5 percent of the gross domestic product (GDP) to social expenditures, including health, education, retirement, family benefits, and public housing, the sixth highest of the 19 OECD countries. Moreover, in 1980, France ranked first among the OECD countries in terms of social spending as a proportion of all government spending. This brief review suggests, in Cameron's apt phrase, that "more than is the case in almost any other nation, the French state is a 'welfare state' " (Cameron, 1993, p. 63).

From the beginning, the French welfare state has had a predominantly Bismarckian cast, in that "means testing is rare, most benefits are universal, many (pensions, unemployment compensation, and sickness pay) are linked to former income, and funding comes largely from contributions of employers and employees rather than from a progressive income tax" (Ambler, 1993, p. 12). Until recently, the French system of social security has been largely financed through payroll taxes rather than general tax revenues. In 1989, over 80 percent of social spending derived from payroll taxes, compared to 71 percent for Germany, 46 percent for Britain, and 66.2 percent for the EU as a whole (Ross, 1998, p. 7). There are two conservative consequences. First, payroll taxes are not levied on profits, dividends, and other unearned income. Second, payroll taxes are regressive in that the tax rate is flat, and there is a ceiling on the salary or wages subject to the tax.

The welfare state was given its definitive shape in the social security plan established by ordinance in 1945 following World War II. Initially, the system was to be based on the Beveridge principle of universal benefits distributed in a uniform way without regard to income (not means-tested), unified—that is, one contribution would cover all risks (health, old age, family, and disability) and would be centralized. The system was intended to generalize a program designed in the late 1920s for low-wage workers that, in turn, had been added to the system of health care and retirement for separate occupational categories, for example, miners, merchant marine, railway workers, and civil servants. This was known as the general regime. However, because many well-organized occupational groups that had achieved coverage prior to 1945—industrial workers and miners, railway workers, and civil servants—successfully fought to retain their previous coverage and insurance funds, a uniform and unified system was not achieved. This was the origin of the division between the general regime, which covers most of the population, and special regimes for specific groups. The general regime initially covered all non-agricultural wage workers; it was gradually extended to non-wage workers—students, writers, artisans, and independent shopkeepers—and since the 1970s, to handicapped adults, widows, divorced women, single parents, and other hitherto uncovered categories. By 1985, less than 1 percent of the French population of citizens and legal residents was not covered for health care, primarily the poor (Ambler, 1993). The Jospin government made medical coverage fully universal in 1999.

Unemployment insurance is not financed by the general fund. Business organizations and unions have negotiated sectoral agreements through the years, but a general program was established only in 1958 as a result of a national-level collective bargaining agreement between organized business and labor. Unemployment compensation remains a private program financed by employers' and workers' contributions and jointly administered by business organizations and unions (Merrien, 1998).

In 1996, French social spending totaled roughly 2.3 trillion francs (about $384 billion). The lion's share was devoted to pensions (40 percent) and health (27 percent), with the remainder going for family benefits (9 percent), unemployment compensation (6 percent), disability and occupational injury (5 percent), and active labor market programs (4 percent) and the rest (8 percent) going for low-income housing subsidies, cash payments to the poor, and services for the elderly (calculations made by author from data supplied by the Ministry of Social Affairs, 1999).

Although the various social funds are financed by payroll taxes, general tax revenues cover deficits for benefits for employed workers; youth and the unemployed receive other benefits (Jobert, 1993). This is the origin of a fundamental problem in financing French welfare programs, since the state has traditionally not controlled the administration of social security but has accepted responsibility for financing deficits. That situation changed in the late 1990s as the state tenaciously sought to gain greater control over the sprawling system. The shift has provoked some of France's (and, indeed, Europe's) most severe social conflicts, both because of the opposition of groups that stand to lose power and other resources by the shift—doctors and other health care workers, unions, and pharmaceutical companies—and because of widespread distrust that reforms will involve retrenchment.

Overall, French social provision is extensive and has expanded steadily throughout the post-war period. For example, social benefits as a percentage of household disposable income rose from 19.3 percent in 1960 to nearly double that figure in 1983 (Ambler, 1993, p. 13).

Health Care

Although the French health care system is of high quality, and the system of social insurance assures widespread access at low cost to patients, its organization promotes steadily escalating costs (Wilsford, 1996).[2] There are two segments of the health care system: hospital care and outpatient care. The hospital sector is quite fragmented. A major division is between public hospitals, which account for about two-thirds of all hospital beds and range from small rural hospitals to major regional hospitals associated with medical schools, and hospitals in the non-profit and for-profit sectors, each of which accounts for roughly one-sixth of all beds. Until the early 1980s, patients were fully covered for hospital care. Hospital costs were typically very high, since the system of reimbursing hospitals on a per bed, per day basis created an incentive to maximize hospital stays. Hospital costs soared 16–20 percent annually in the 1960s and 1970s. Since then, governments of diverse ideological persuasion have generally agreed that there is a need to contain burgeoning hospital costs.

In 1984, as part of the socialist government's "right turn" toward fiscal austerity, it sponsored a fundamental overhaul of the system of financing public hospital care. It established a global budget for every hospital, from which hospitals were required to finance operating and capital expenditures, and it imposed a daily co-payment fee. The reform limited the rise in hospital costs to 3.1 percent in 1985. The Chirac government further reduced the rise to 1.9 percent in 1987 (Wilsford, 1996). The process provoked periodic strikes by a variety of health care workers, from nurses and nurses aides, to medical students, to physicians, to professors of medicine. There have also been periodic and massive efforts to rationalize hospital care, most recently by the Jospin government after its election in 1997. For instance, there have been moves to consolidate costly services to avoid duplication. The result of decades of reform efforts has been mixed in a number of senses. The reforms have had somewhat limited impact because of the powerful forces opposing change, including general hospital administrators, health care workers, and citizens. To the extent that change has occurred, there is controversy over whether the predominant effect is to produce an overdue and sensible rationalization of a bloated, needlessly costly system and/or an assault on the health and well-being of French citizens, especially the less affluent, who cannot afford supplementary insurance and private hospitals.

The system of outpatient medical care is even more decentralized and illogical than the inpatient sector and embodies extensive incentives to escalate costs. Prior to reforms passed in the late 1990s, patients could choose to consult as many general practitioners and specialists as they wished and were entitled to reimbursement for all consultations and most prescribed medication. Reimbursement varied from 70 to 99 percent. and those with supplementary insurance from private companies or mutual aid societies— nearly 90 percent of the population—were covered for co-payments. This system created an implicit alliance of patients, physicians, and pharmaceutical companies to maximize consultations, treatment, and consumption of medication. The result was that, until recently, the health insurance funds ran substantial annual deficits. Overall, it should be noted, physicians' salaries are relatively low in France: in 1960, the Gaullist government established ceilings on the fees that physicians could charge in order to be eligible for reimbursement by the sickness fund. As a result, in 1986, the average French physician's income was $42,512, and that of a German physician was $86,704, while the average American physician received $119,500 (Wilsford, 1996, p. 241).

Retirement and Unemployment Compensation

The enormous institutional complexity evident in French social provision is especially prevalent in the field of retirement, with over 100 different plans for various categories of population: the general fund, complementary pensions, pensions for miners, farmers, civil servants, and others. Bruno Jobert (1993, p. 241), a leading French expert on the welfare state, calls it "a baroque system, resistant to any overall policy of regulation."

Pensions are composed of a basic portion financed from the general fund and a supplement financed by separate funds. In 1975, a minimum guaranteed retirement benefit was legislated and melded with the earlier system based on the principle that people finance retirement through membership in mutual aid societies. The private funds originated in the nineteenth century for some categories of workers and were incorporated in the social security system when it was fundamentally overhauled and expanded after World War II. The system was again reorganized, and coverage was expanded under de Gaulle in 1958. The retirement system is a complex mix of public and private elements. Basic pensions, financed through the state pension on a pay-as-you go basis, replace about 55–70 percent of pre-retirement income, and a host of mutual aid societies and special pension funds provide supplements (Ambler, 1993).

In addition, state funds facilitate early retirement in cases of industrial restructuring. For workers in designated industries or firms, state funds provide a transitional pension until the regular pension begins at the specified retirement age. Conversion pensions were initiated under the conservative Giscard presidency in the 1970s, soon after the onset of the post-1973 economic crisis. They were substantially expanded by the socialist government in the 1980s to reduce the opposition of displaced workers to the massive structural transformation of the French economy. They have generally been very effective: despite deindustrialization, most displaced workers have been able to maintain their living standards. But this socially progressive program has been very costly.

Unemployment compensation, like pensions, blends income maintenance and income redistribution, as well as redistributes income between the employed and eligible unemployed. During the boom years of the early 1970s, when unemployment was negligible, organized business and labor negotiated a peak-level bargaining agreement that reorganized the program of unemployment compensation, with benefit levels replacing 90 percent of former income for one year. However, as unemployment began to rise steadily in the late 1970s, the program was scaled back, with eligibility requirements tightened and benefits reduced. Most important, those who have not obtained stable work, especially young people, are excluded from the program.

Family Allowances and Preschool Education

France has afforded high priority to family policy, a terrain on which conservative Catholics, patriotic natalists seeking to increase France's stagnant population, and the Left agreed (Lenoir, 1993). Family allowances were created in 1932 for families with wage earners and two or more children, and the system expanded to provide additional coverage to families with three or more children in 1946.

Family benefits occupied a prominent place within French social policy in the post-war period into the 1960s. The conservative Christian Democratic Party, the pivotal party in Fourth Republic ruling coalitions, provided generous family allowances in order to promote large families and encourage mothers to remain at home. Family allowances, paid to non-working mothers, represented nearly one-third of the entire social security budget (Levy, 1998, p. 5). Indeed, family allowances were initially called the "mother at home" (*la mère au foyer*) payment.

As a result of pressure from the women's movement and the Gaullist government's modernization program, family policy changed dramatically in the 1960s and 1970s. In a complete reversal, the new goal was to enable women to work outside the home. Family programs were created to provide vocational training for women, subsidized child care, preschool instruction, paid maternity leave (16 weeks of leave at 84 percent of earnings), and the right to parental leave for three years following maternity leave. Parental leave is unpaid save for parents with three or more children; parents of three children receive approximately $500 monthly. Although family payments remain extensive, increased spending on other social programs in recent decades, notably health and old age pensions, has meant that family payments declined from close to one-third of social spending after World War II, to 21 percent in 1970 and 15 percent in 1980 (Lenoir, 1993, p. 174). By 1996, they represented only 9 percent of social spending (calculation by author from data provided by the French Ministry of Social Affairs, 1999).

France's day-care programs and parental leave policies have been key factors enabling women to work outside the home. In 1981, 34.8 percent of all two-year-olds and 90 percent of all three-year-olds were in preschool programs (about half the cost of which was central government funded, and the other half was funded by means-tested user fees and local funding); by 1988, the proportions were 36 percent and 97.4 percent (Ministry of Education statistics, cited in Ambler, 1993, p. 25). French preschool facilities are justly famous. They are in attractive settings, and preschool teachers, who must have advanced degrees, are well paid and highly competent.

Family benefits are especially important for poor families. For example, they represent over half the income of those families with four children under age 10 in which one family member is employed in industry. The Mitterrand government substantially increased family benefits, although allowances are still not available, except on a means-tested basis, to the first child or only child in a family. The Left also greatly expanded crèches and preschool facilities.

Benefit programs for families are increasingly targeted toward lower-income groups. Basic family allowances are universal, but other family benefits, including a housing allowance, a complementary family allowance, and loans to young couples, are means-tested. However, this redistributive effect is nullified and even reversed when income tax deductions, worth far more for upper-income families, are calculated. Socialist governments in 1981–1986 significantly increased family allowances and introduced new benefits open to all families without income restriction.

Vocational Training

Employers must allot 1.2 percent of their gross revenues to vocational training, defined quite broadly; and all employees of the firm are eligible for subsidies for training programs. However, managers and technicians are twice as likely as manual or white-collar workers to take advantage of these programs. France and Sweden are the two countries that devote the most resources to this program (Jobert, 1993).

EVALUATING FRENCH SOCIAL WELFARE

The French have devised among the most extensive systems of social protection in the world. Although shot through with illogical, contradictory, and sometimes inequitable features, it does a relatively excellent job of socializing risks. As Ambler's authoritative account concludes:

With the exception of the chronically unemployed, the French safety net provides effective protection against the risks of illness, accident, and old age. If it maintains incomes more than redistributing them, if it is paid for by regressive payroll taxes rather than by a progressive income tax, the reason may be that the leading political parties as well as the population are accustomed to this style of welfare state. It emerged from the era of strong socialist majorities (1981–1986) with a slightly more egalitarian impact, but with its essential character intact: it is a system that lends security to the more affluent as well as the less. (Ambler, 1993, p. 20)

The French welfare state has come under considerable criticism in recent years. First, critics claim that the overly high cost of unskilled labor acts as a drag on economic productivity and job creation. Wage costs are high as a result of France's minimum wage, to which all employees are entitled and which is 40 percent higher than the minimum wage in the United States; in addition, until recently, social spending was financed mostly by payroll taxes, which generated four times as much revenue as income taxes.

Another criticism is that extensive labor market regulation provides benefits for those with stable employment at the expense of flexibility for employers and job creation. As a result, unemployment is extremely high and affects different groups in a highly unequal fashion. Youth are among the hardest hit: whereas in the United States the rate of unemployment among young workers is double that of their elders, it is five times higher for young French persons (Fondation Saint-Simon, 1997, p. 44). Further, unemployed French workers receive more extensive unemployment compensation than unemployed Americans and are likely to remain unemployed far longer: the average American who loses a job is unemployed three months; the average French person, over one year (Fondation Saint-Simon, 1997, p. 44). Higher minimum wage and payroll taxes in France are thought to restrict hiring. However, using OECD data, Vicente Navarro (1998) showed that between 1984 and 1992, France had a gross job gain of 13.9 percent of its labor force (7.2 percent openings and 6.7 percent expansion) and gross job loss of 13.2 percent (7.0 percent closures and 6.3 percent contractions). France created a slightly higher percentage of jobs than the United States and lost nearly 3 percent more. Given this dynamism in the French labor market, it is necessary to seek other reasons for high unemployment, such as restrictive fiscal and monetary policies.

Some critics have charged that, by seeking to reduce unemployment by shrinking the labor force (through early retirement and shortening the workweek), welfare programs are Malthusian: they limit growth and employment and thereby provoke a vicious downward spiral. Thus, the more protection that occurs, the less growth and job creation—which, in turn, spur the call for more protection from market forces. Esping-Andersen (1996a) claims that the Continental approach, which France exemplifies, seeks "to induce labor force exit" rather than boost public employment, as in Scandinavia. The result is to fuel high fixed labor costs, which inhibit employment creation.

In brief, these systems find themselves locked into a self-reinforcing negative spiral and are today particularly ill-suited to address pressures for greater labour market flexibility and women's demand for economic independence. In brief, the continental Western European welfare states are coming into conflict with the emerging needs of a post-industrial economy. (Esping-Andersen, 1996a, p. 6)

A final criticism is that the French system of social provision channels benefits on a quite inequitable basis. It provides generous benefits to those with stable employment (especially civil servants), the elderly (whose average income exceeds that of the active population), and the more affluent, while distributing meager benefits to the long-term unemployed and youth. In these respects France exemplifies the corporatist approach of maintaining status distinctions.

As long as unemployment was low and social spending did not produce large fiscal deficits, criticism was muted. However, in the past two decades, slow population growth, an aging population, rising unemployment, higher costs, and dwindling revenues (a product of high unemployment and a smaller proportion of the population that is economically active) have produced severe stresses on the welfare state, in France as elsewhere. What makes France distinctive is not that deficits fueled attempts to retrench but the response that followed the announcement of these proposals.

Surviving the Crisis: Back to French Exceptionalism

The social security system was created in a long period of rising and secure employment, economic growth, and expanding population. These favorable conditions began to change in the 1970s. Large sectors of the French economy were destabilized, with extensive layoffs, downsizing, and even the elimination of large firms and entire industries. The result was havoc in France's industrial heartland.

Since the 1970s, the typical situation has been high unemployment rates (over 10 percent in the 1990s) and a decline in stable, full-time jobs. Most newly created jobs are part-time or temporary. For example, whereas two decades ago, 80 percent of all jobs were covered by full-time, permanent labor contracts, as opposed to part-time or fixed-term contracts, only 65 percent are presently of this kind (Merrien, 1998).

In France as elsewhere, the welfare state is under particular stress as demographic changes—notably, later entry into the labor force, lower labor force participation rates, and an aging and stagnant population—fuel a scissors movement involving rising social needs and a smaller working population able to finance the greater burdens placed on the welfare state. Thus, whereas there were 2.6 employed workers for 1 retiree in 1970, the ratio was 2.2 to 1 in 1995, and predictions are that it will be 1.6 to 1 in 2020 (Fondation Saint-Simon, 1997, p. 61). The result of rising costs and declining social contributions has been chronic deficits. Consider the financing of pensions: "[T]he standard [average] individual worker pays 15 percent less towards retirement and collects 30 percent more than was the case in the golden 1950s" (Fondation Saint-Simon, 1997, p. 78). (These data are for all of Western Europe.)

This oft-repeated analysis of the crisis of the welfare state, while accurate, is only part of the explanation. It ignores that the way priorities have been shaped is a political process. In brief, the political orientation chosen by advanced capitalist nations in the face of demographic changes and the structural shift from an industrial to post-industrial economy has, on balance, increased rather than mitigated social strains. (One is reminded in this connection of how, in the late 1920s and early 1930s, the fiscally orthodox policies pursued by these same nations intensified the Great Depression.)

Despite immense affluence in the industrialized capitalist nations—and sustained economic growth (albeit at a slower pace than in the "golden years" of the post-war era)—priority has been given not to assuring full employment and decent standards for citizens but to the fiscally conservative goal of eliminating inflation. Low inflation, while praiseworthy in itself, has been pursued at the expense of abandoning the commitment to social equity that was inscribed at the top of political agendas in the post-war era. Of course, there was always a yawning chasm between paying ideological obeisance to social equity and taking necessary measures to achieve it. But it was during the "thirty glorious years" (as a French economist described the post-war period) that the "European model" of fairly extensive social provision was put in place. From this perspective, an ideological and political sea change has occurred since the 1970s. To paraphrase Ronald Reagan's inaugural address, from the welfare state's being viewed as the solution to the problem (of social inequity), it is widely regarded as being the cause of the problem (of fiscal imbalance). According to a view commonly held by the Right but also by many on the Left—New Democrats in the United States, "Third Way" Labour leaders in Britain, the new Swedish Social Democrats, and others—the European model of relatively generous social benefits is alleged to have produced fiscal deficits, high unemployment, and generally mediocre economic performance. Pierson and others remind us that the "politics of retrenchment" have made relatively little progress, but there is no gainsaying the contrast in social policy between the two last quarters of the twentieth century.

In trying to unravel the relationship between economic difficulties and the welfare state, I suggest that the causal arrow may be in the opposite direction than neoliberal doctrine proclaims: that is, to a considerable extent, the crisis of the welfare state is the result, not the cause, of Europe's poor economic record in recent years. If Europe's economic difficulties have contributed to the strains that the welfare state is supposed to alleviate, rather than the reverse, what explains this poor economic record? Although space does not permit developing the argument, I would ascribe great importance to the turn toward neoliberalism among the countries of Western Europe (following the United States' lead). These policies have been enshrined at a supranational level by the EU since the 1980s, culminating in the creation of a single European currency in the late 1990s.

For the past two decades, as the EU moved toward developing the euro to replace national currencies, an apparently implacable economic logic, spelled out many years ago by economist Robert Mundell (1961), has dictated the need to pursue deflationary economic policies. The determination to pursue the holy grail of monetary union—at all costs and full speed ahead—has been an important cause of Europe's poor economic performance and high unemployment. As Gerald Friedman observes,

For 35 years after World War II, European unemployment rates were substantially below the American level and rates of productivity growth far exceeded the American experience. By the 1980s, however, these were changing. European unemployment rates rose to and then surpassed the American rate, and European productivity growth rates have drifted down towards American levels. These are measures of how European political authorities have abandoned the struggle for prosperity for the political goal of establishing a strong European union. Instead of using economic policy to fight unemployment, they have behaved as if their primary responsibility is to protect the value of their currency in international markets. Currency stability has become the goal of economic policy, deepening and lengthening Europe's period of slow growth with huge costs in unemployment and social suffering. (Friedman, 1999, p. 21)

As Pitruzzello succinctly notes, "the fiscal reforms imposed by the Maastricht Treaty were in important ways reforms of national welfare systems" (Pitruzzello, 1997, p. 1625).

What has been the political response to the pursuit of neoliberal measures at the national and EU levels? In most countries, there has been a mixture of anger and apathy, illustrated by the frequent electoral swings that have occurred in the past two decades. In France, however, that anger has taken an exceptional form and has been expressed through grassroots mobilization: a high incidence of strikes and political demonstrations, in some cases explicitly directed against the neoliberal policies designed to conform to EU directives. This exceptional militance has produced an exceptional state response to strains in the welfare state.

Esping-Andersen (1996a) claims that the three clusters of welfare states initially responded to the demographic stresses on the welfare state in divergent and path-dependent fashions. The liberal welfare cases of the United States and Britain responded by promoting low-wage "flexibilization" of labor markets through the route of low-wage, part-time job creation. The Scandinavian welfare states responded by expanding public sector employment, both to absorb labor and to increase social services, often those that induced mothers to enter the labor force. The Continental European states, on the other hand, chose the strategy of labor force reduction via early retirements and crackdowns on alleged abuses by welfare recipients, and they attempted expelling immigrant workers. This description is partially valid for France, where the initial response was the expansion of "passive" labor market programs, which encouraged early retirement and other means of persuading workers to exit from the labor force. The French government also sponsored active labor market programs to promote job retraining and inclusion of the unemployed in the labor force. During the early 1990s, France was second only to Denmark in the proportion of the labor force involved in public training and employment measures: Denmark, 12.8 percent; France, 9.9 percent; Sweden, 6.3 percent; and Germany, 4.9 percent (Esping-Andersen, 1996a, p. 12). It should be noted that since Frances's unemployment rate was about double that of Sweden and Denmark, it is understandable that it would devote a large proportion of its resources to public training and employment programs. The more apt comparison, hence, is with Germany, where unemployment levels were then only slightly lower than those of France.

However, France has proved a notorious exception to path-dependent continuity and change at two key points, in 1981–1983, when the Mitterrand government sponsored an ambitious reform agenda, including a dramatic expansion of the scope and depth of social provision; and in 1995, when nationwide strikes immobilized the country and put a temporary halt to a plan for retrenchment proposed by the conservative government of Alain Juppé.

Socialism in One Country?

The story of the radical-reformist socialist experiment of 1981–1983 has been told often and is merely summarized briefly here. (I have described it more fully elsewhere [Kesselman, 1983, 2001].) Thanks to its sweeping electoral victory of 1981, Mitterrand's governing Socialist Party, allied with the communists, sponsored a range of economic measures to revive the ailing economy, create jobs, and recapture domestic markets. The major reforms included:

- a substantial increase in social benefits, including a 25 percent increase in the minimum wage, 25–50 percent increases in family allowances, a 38 percent increase in minimum old age pensions, 50 percent hikes in rent subsidies, and an increase in state-mandated paid vacations from four to five weeks;
- expansion of public sector employment;
- a vigorous industrial policy, including state assistance to develop high-tech industrial technologies (including biotech, telecommunications, and aerospace);
- a hefty expansion of the nationalized industrial and banking sector.

There were two previous periods when French governments extended public control over the economy, the socialist government of Léon Blum during the Popular Front in 1936 and at the Liberation following World War II. In 1981–1983, the socialist government went further. As a result of the nationalization measures in 1981–1983, public sector firms accounted for

28 percent of gross domestic production (an increase of 7 percent), 23 percent of French exports (compared to the previous level of 11 percent), and 36 percent of investments (from 29 percent) (Ménière, 1993, p. 18). Following the nationalization reforms, 13 of France's 20 largest industrial firms and virtually all banks were in the public sector.

The socialist approach was a radicalized version of the post-war dirigiste approach, supplemented by newly created mechanisms for increasing participation by rank-and-file workers and labor unions in economic decision making. (For example, industrial relations granted labor unions greater rights on the shop floor and at higher levels as well as introduced channels for worker consultation.)

How successful was the socialist program? On the one hand, the reforms provided many French citizens with significant benefits. Moreover, many of the newly nationalized firms, which were in financial difficulties when they were nationalized, were put on a firmer footing thanks to lavish government subsidies. But the socialists' economic and social measures failed in a decisive respect: they did not revive the economic growth needed to create new jobs and generate the financial resources for the added government spending. There were two reasons. First, private business executives in France and international investors were hostile to the government's policy orientation. Rather than investing in French industry, they exported capital to safe havens abroad. Second, an international economic recession in the early 1980s meant that the increased French purchasing power made possible by government spending was often used for imports. Economic stagnation abroad meant that there was little international demand for French products.

Many of the socialist reforms had beneficial long-run consequences. But in the short run, they provoked a severe economic and financial crisis that drove France to the brink of bankruptcy. Budget deficits soared, international investors avoided France like the plague, and France's international currency reserves were rapidly exhausted. Something had to give—and fast.

The crisis cruelly demonstrated how limited the margin of maneuver was for a medium-rank power like France. Given rapidly escalating economic difficulties, Mitterrand's government was forced to choose between reversing its reformist course or, if it preferred to maintain the policies that it adopted after winning office in 1981, adopting strong protectionist measures to shield France from international pressures. The latter strategy involved high risks, because it would provoke international isolation—especially given conservative governments in Washington, Bonn, and London at the time. After intense soul-searching, Mitterrand ordered a complete about-face in the government's economic policies in 1983. The decision to turn back from radical statism was one of the most important made within the Fifth Republic and set France on a conservative course from which it has not fundamentally departed ever since.

Treading Water

Yet even while abandoning audacious progressive reforms, governments from 1983 to 1995, conservative and socialist alike, retained a fundamental commitment to preserving—and even expanding—welfare state programs. The period from 1983 to 1995 presents a mixed picture: along with attempts at incremental retrenchment, there was what might seem a surprising—indeed, sometimes dramatic—expansion of social programs. Grassroots militancy is a key part of the explanation.

In the 1980s and 1990s, the French "discovered" poverty, with new terms appearing in public discourse like the "social fracture," the "socially excluded," and the "new poor."[3] These concepts designate what the French see as a new cleavage separating privileged "insiders" from excluded "outsiders," a tendency that either had not existed before or (more likely) that the French had failed to recognize. Beginning in the 1980s, a host of government commissions identified a disturbing array of specific social problems and groups at risk, while these and other commissions warned of a fiscal crisis of the social security system. For example, Eurostat figures show a relative poverty rate (50 percent of a country's average expenditure adjusted for family size) of 14.9 percent for France in 1989 (as compared to 12.00 percent for Germany, 17 percent for the United Kingdom, 4.2 percent for Denmark, 6.2 percent for the Netherlands, and 6.6 percent for Belgium around the same time (Paugam, 1996). Governments have responded by altering the character of the French welfare state. Reforms have often combined cutbacks in universal social programs with the creation or expansion of programs targeted at specific groups of the population, notably, the poor, long-term unemployed, urban youth, immigrants, women, and the homeless.

The new social programs are often administered in a fashion quite unusual in France. Rather than being run by civil servants, non-profit agencies are often mandated to administer them. As a fine study of the process describes,

> To policy makers, nonprofits seem better equipped than government bureaucracies to reach marginalized populations, to provide culturally sensitive services, to run small-scale and personalized programs, and to offer clients avenues for participation in the management of their care. They often have experience and skills in acting in those domains newly defined as public responsibility, where the state has no prior experience. (Ullman, 1998, p. 140)

Ullman (1998) suggests that the restructuring of the welfare state—involving the expansion of the scope of social provision and delegating responsibility to non-profit agencies for administering new social programs—has contributed to a growing autonomy of civil society in France, a develop-

ment of historic importance. Two programs particularly noteworthy in this
regard are the creation of a minimum income program and youth training
programs.

In 1998, Socialist Prime Minister Michel Rocard gained unanimous parliamentary approval for the creation of a minimum income program, the
Minimum Income of Insertion (RMI). The RMI is a means-tested minimum
income program aimed at unemployed youth and the long-term unemployed. Recipients must work as a condition for receiving assistance, and
it is designed to integrate the previously unemployed into the labor market.
The RMI was initially planned as a relatively small program, but, given the
scope and growth of unemployment, the ranks of the RMI swelled to 1
million by 1998.

Governments in the past two decades have sponsored a variety of active
labor market programs aimed primarily at unskilled, unemployed youth.
The programs typically subsidize youth employment in the public and non-
profit sector (e.g., as social workers, camp counselors, and sports coaches).
From 1984 to 1989, 1.2 million young people were covered by the program. It was changed several times and revived by the socialist government
elected in 1997. (It is presently called employment solidarity contracts, or
CES.)

I do not claim that these programs have been successful—quite the contrary. For example, in July 1999 a government commission, the High Committee for the Housing of the Underprivileged (*défavorisées*) called the
inadequate supply of public housing "completely shocking" (*Humanité*,
1999). The most intensive studies have focused on job training programs,
and the evidence suggests that they are not very effective in providing participants with stable employment. Half or more of those completing training programs later failed to find jobs. Regarding the RMI, one study found
that only 13 percent of those in the program were employed later. Further,
many of the graduates of these programs who find jobs displace those already employed (Merrien, 1998, p. 19). In effect, rather than creating new
jobs, the state subsidizes the replacement of some workers by others, as
well as subsidizes employers who employ low-wage workers. While the
French unemployment rate has declined in recent years, the expanding
economy may have been more responsible than active labor market programs. Moreover, the unemployment rate, especially for youth, remains
alarmingly high. Given these findings, as well as mounting fiscal pressure,
governments in the 1990s increasingly focused their efforts on retrenchment.

Cutbacks?

Since the 1970s, the French social security system ran consistent but
generally small deficits. However, deficits began to rise dramatically in the

1980s, and, by the 1990s, they mushroomed—to 56 billion francs in 1993, 55 billion francs in 1994, and 62 billion francs in 1995. A succession of prime ministers beginning in the 1980s sought to reform social security and reduce deficits, in order to restore fiscal balance. The need to reform became more pressing as a result of the Maastricht Treaty of 1992 and subsequent EU agreements organizing a single European currency. The most severe constraint for France mandated that budget deficits be limited to 3 percent of GDP. Successive governments instituted marginal reforms: raising user charges in health care, reducing pensions and unemployment benefits, and increasing social taxes. However, the high level of payroll taxes limited further attempts to increase revenues to balance the social budget until the Rocard government tapped new revenue in 1988 by sponsoring a 1 percent solidarity tax on all earnings, whether capital, property, or income.

The largest source of deficits in social expenditures, in France as elsewhere, is in the field of health care. France has the highest per capita expenditures on health care in Europe and, after the United States, the second highest in the world. It devotes 9.9 percent of GDP to health care, compared to 14.5 percent in the United States, 9.6 percent in Germany, and 6.9 percent in Britain. Health costs increased an average of 5 percent annually since the 1980s, and the sickness funds registered deficits of 27.3 billion francs in 1993, 31.5 billion francs in 1994, and 40 billion francs in 1995. (The total social budget deficit was 67 billion francs in 1995 and 51 billion francs in 1996 [OECD, 1997].) Health care costs are so hard to contain because a coalition of users (patients), providers (doctors, hospitals), and pharmaceutical companies presents a solid front in favor of increased consumption of medical services. Citizens with co-payment insurance face no financial constraint in obtaining medical treatment: they are free to consult a specialist on their own initiative and can choose to consult as many doctors as they wish. Moreover, the French consume several times the volume of medication compared to citizens of comparable countries.

In 1993, the Balladur government sponsored a modest reform by reducing reimbursement for medical services from 75 percent to 70 percent. But this reduced access by poorer citizens: while more affluent and stably employed citizens have company-provided or other private health insurance to cover co-payments, about 12 percent of the population does not. More generally, France spends about as much per capita on medical care as the United States—the world's leader in this regard—but medical care is unequally distributed (although far less so than in the United States). France ranks only among the middling group of industrialized countries in terms of public health indicators.

The other main source of deficits in the social security system derives from financing pensions. The deficit in this sphere was 39.4 billion francs in 1993, although it was reduced to 12.7 billion francs in 1994 and 13.2

billion francs in 1995. The Balladur government sponsored a major reform
of private-sector pensions by increasing the base on which pension levels
would be calculated from a worker's 10 best years of earnings to 25 years;
even more important, it increased the number of years of work required to
qualify for a full pension from 37.5 to 40. (It remained unchanged at 37.5
years in the public sector.)

In sum, the period from 1983 to 1995 represented two steps forward
and about the same back in the field of welfare reform: some expansion,
some retrenchment, and basic continuity in overall contours. France was
somewhat exceptional in its continued commitment to preserving the welfare state, expanding some programs, and even creating new ones. When
Prime Minister Alain Juppé proposed a sweeping program of retrenchment
in 1995, the popular response made France even more exceptional. The
crisis provoked by the Juppé plan is the second important moment in the
recent period that illustrates the extent of French exceptionalism.

Déja Vu All Over Again

In late 1995, France was both galvanized and immobilized by a series of
strikes and demonstrations that saw no equal elsewhere and rivaled in
scope and depth the May 1968 uprising that nearly toppled President
Charles de Gaulle from power. The strikes resulted from a vast outpouring
of opposition to Juppé's plan for drastic cutbacks in welfare programs (for
a fuller account, see Kesselman, 2000). The origins of the massive strikes
in 1995 may be found in the conjunction of France's severe economic difficulties, the expectations raised by Jacques Chirac's 1995 presidential election campaign advocating a change, and the subsequent disillusionment
provoked by Chirac's reneging on his electoral pledges.

France has been undergoing extensive economic restructuring, which has
produced both modernization for many industries but also devastation for
entire regions and sectors of the population. Since the socialists' "right
turn" in 1983, governments of Left and Right have promoted the intensive
modernization of French industry by a program involving deregulation,
privatization, and high interest rates.

In the 1995 presidential election, the Rassemblement pour la Republique
(RPR) candidate, Jacques Chirac, attempted to differentiate himself from
other conservative candidates, as well as from Socialist Party candidate
Lionel Jospin, by holding out the hope that things could be different. As a
respected journalist commented in a book about Chirac's campaign, "He
was forced to adopt the strategy of an outsider, gambling that victory
would go not to a candidate proposing continuity, but to the candidate
who advocated change" (Jarreau, 1995, p. 9). For the first time since the
Socialist Party's U-turn of 1983, a candidate from one of the "big three"
centrist parties proposed a progressive reformist course. Chirac announced

a plan to create 700,000 new jobs and, in a famous phrase during the campaign, declared, "the pay stub [i.e., a decent wage level] is not the enemy of employment." Following his election, he proclaimed, "Our battle has a name: the struggle against unemployment."

Chirac's strategy was electorally successful but ultimately proved politically costly. Only months after he had escalated expectations that things could be different and that government policy would accord priority to reflation and social ends, he was forced to orchestrate an about-face. The need to comply with the fiscal requirements of Maastricht, especially the requirement that government budget deficits be reduced to 3 percent of GDP by 2000, collided with Chirac's electoral promises, and the promises lost. The first salvo was the announcement in September 1995 by Prime Minister Alain Juppé (Chirac's closest associate) that public sector wages for France's 5 million civil servants would be frozen. This was followed by Chirac's admission, in a television interview in October, that his initial optimism about the possibilities for reflation was mistaken. The situation was more difficult than he had foreseen, and there was no alternative to returning to fiscal orthodoxy. His words were quickly followed by actions.

Immediately after Chirac's interview, Prime Minister Juppé announced a series of major reforms that—both in form and in substance—represented virtually a declaration of war on labor unions, especially those in the public sector. One target of the plan was the public sector retirement system. Without prior consultation with unions, Juppé proposed tightening requirements for civil servants' pensions and ending preferential retirement benefits for particular categories of public sector workers: railway workers, Paris subway workers, electrical and gas workers, and postal workers.

The second major target of Juppé's budget-cutting ax was the health care system. The Juppé plan proposed extending state control over the health insurance system by authorizing Parliament to establish an annual ceiling for health insurance expenditures (for physicians, hospital care, and pharmaceuticals), limiting union representation on the governing board of social security funds, and increasing the state's power to organize agreements (conventions) between doctors' organizations and sickness funds to contain costs. The Juppé plan also generalized elements introduced in specific sectors earlier, for example, an annual budget ceiling for ambulatory care for private nurses and hospitals, as well as a system of performance evaluation within the health insurance system.

As important as policy changes was a paradigm shift in priorities from coverage of health risks to emphasizing cost-cutting in the health system, that is, from social equity to economic efficiency. The shift had begun earlier and produced a decline in the share of public spending for health care costs from 80 to 74 percent between 1980 and 1994, with a corresponding rise in the share of co-payments. A leading specialist on French public health terms this a "silent privatization" of health care (Hassenteufel, 1999, p. 8). But Juppé proposed going much further.

To top it off, Juppé proposed revamping the state-run railway system, including partial privatization, closing unprofitable sectors, and laying off workers. He mandated financial austerity for universities, including cutbacks in hiring of new staff, as well as limiting new construction and maintenance. Finally, government ministers hinted that additional reforms would soon follow, including the partial privatization of France Télécom, the sprawling state telecommunications agency, and increases in income taxes.

Reaction to the proposed reforms was swift (see Bornstein and Tixier [1996] for a good description). True to their tradition of militant action, railway workers were the first to strike. (Although railway workers represent only 1 percent of all French wage earners, they account for one-fifth of all the work time lost due to strikes.) Other transport workers quickly followed their lead: Paris métro workers and bus drivers, public transport workers in other French cities, and air traffic controllers and Air France personnel. France was quickly brought to a halt, as gridlock and miles of traffic jams immobilized Paris and other large cities. Massive demonstrations brought out ever-more participants, climaxing in a 2-million-strong demonstration on December 7. Soon, as other public sector workers stayed home, the postal system ground to a halt, garbage began to accumulate on city streets, schools closed, and power slowdowns occurred.

In the face of this overwhelming and sustained opposition to the proposed reforms, Juppé retreated on some key points. For example, he agreed to put on hold the restructuring of the railway system, shelved plans to curtail pension benefits for public sector employees, and convened a "social summit" with leaders of unions and business organizations to discuss job creation. On the other hand, he did not withdraw his commitment to restructure the health care system.

The strikes and demonstrations reached a peak by mid-December and quickly began to subside. Unions proclaimed victory and called for a return to work on December 19–20, just in time to prevent the strikes from disintegrating.

Although Juppé abandoned the plan to achieve cutbacks in the public retirement system, he rapidly implemented other elements of the reform plan. A constitutional amendment was passed in 1996 authorizing Parliament to set a ceiling on health care expenditures. As a result, the increase in health care expenditures was limited to under 2 percent beginning in 1996 (less than half its previous rate of increase). The increase in hospital expenditures had been even more severe, and newly created regional hospital boards have begun targeting some hospitals for downsizing, mergers, and closure. The government also negotiated an agreement with several doctors' unions in 1997 to limit severely the increase in fees and prescriptions. He created a new tax specifically targeted for reducing the social security deficit. The Juppé government also increased the solidarity tax created by the Rocard government (and increased by the Balladur government) that was designed to finance health care deficits. Juppé believed that a fresh electoral mandate was needed to institute new social cuts. President Chirac dissolved Parliament in 1997, but the gamble resulted in the defeat of the conservative coalitions and the election of a socialist parliamentary majority.

Despite Juppé's defeat, many of the reforms proposed in his 1995 plan have been implemented both by his own government and by the Jospin government that followed it. For example, health care coverage has become universal, the balance has shifted toward financing the social security system from payroll taxes to general tax revenues, and considerable power over the social security system has shifted from business–labor co-management to the government. As one account observes, "What these measures have in common, is that they contribute to change the original Bismarckian nature of the French social security system, and move towards a state-run, tax-financed system, at least in the areas of health care and family benefits" (Palier and Bonoli, 1998). What they also do is enable the government to gain control and potentially impose further spending cuts.

A New Beginning? Or Old Wine in Old Bottles?

Lionel Jospin's socialist coalition was elected because of widespread opposition to the Juppé plan. But Jospin's options were limited. What has been his response? In general, Jospin sought to demonstrate his leftist credentials and commitments by an adroit combination of symbolic gestures, substantive reforms, and redistribution of the costs of social welfare in a more equitable fashion.

Levy (1998) cogently argues that Jospin's major strategy for finding ways to engage in expansive reform has been to "turn vice into virtue," by exploiting the possibilities created by conservative sponsorship of the welfare state. This involves attacking "historic inefficiencies or inequities established by the right ('vices')" and hereby extracting "resources with which to pursue a variety of 'virtuous' objectives" (p. 54). Among these objectives are "redistributing income toward the poor without increasing public spending; improving the functioning of the economy without reducing benefits to the truly needy; facilitating (through side-payments) the negotiation of far-reaching, tripartite 'social pacts' to redesign basic parameters of welfare, labor market, and fiscal policy" (pp. 25–26; I draw on Levy's account of Jospin's strategy). Jospin has sought to extend income testing to exclude the wealthy from universal programs, as well as to favor anti-poverty programs. His reforms have promoted two general changes in the character of the French welfare state: (1) a shift from a Bismarckian system of social insurance to financing social provision from general tax revenues and (2) a targeting of welfare assistance to those most in need. In the short run, this strategy can effect significant savings, on condition that those excluded from benefits are a small proportion of potential recipients and that their opposition can be overcome. The change can provide welcome relief for the great majority of wage earners, who formerly paid high payroll taxes. Yet, over time, the change can erode support for the welfare state and start France down the slippery slope in which welfare programs are regarded as social assistance for the undeserving poor.

Jospin's specific reform proposals have included:

- reducing the income tax deduction for hiring domestic child care (a measure that affects only .25 percent of French families). He also proposed—and then abandoned, in face of strong opposition—the imposition of a means test for distributing family payments.

- more than doubling the solidarity tax to finance the social security deficit and reversing the Balladur government's decision to provide a tax credit for the solidarity tax. This increase has been coupled with a near elimination of low-income workers' contributions for health insurance. The net effect has been to increase workers' purchasing power at the bottom of the income pyramid while increasing taxes for those whose income derives from property or capital.

- stiffening cost control by tightening provisions for regulating physicians' and pharmacists' fees and increasing fines for non-compliance. This policy sought to promote such cost-cutting measures as standardized treatment procedures, increased use of generic medicines, and reduced reliance on specialists. These reforms have been controversial and have triggered a rash of strikes in the health care sector, as well as lawsuits brought in administrative courts (which struck down some aspects of the reforms).

- sponsoring a law against exclusion, voted in July 1998, which included a number of public programs, subsidies, and tax write-offs aimed at facilitating access by the least favored groups in French society (including unskilled youth, long-term unemployed, and the poor) to jobs, housing, medical care, and education.

- reducing the workweek from 39 to 35 hours. Work-sharing is the Jospin government's signature reform to reduce unemployment.

Despite stiff opposition from business, work-sharing was implemented and has produced gains for both employers and businesses. Why should businesses have benefited? The agreements negotiated as a result of the legislative mandate to reduce the work week have usually authorized employers to schedule work in a more flexible fashion, both within the week and seasonally. Work-sharing has made a modest contribution to bringing down France's high unemployment rate in the current period, after decades of a steady climb in unemployment.

Jospin's reign has not been without conflict. For example, in December

1997 unemployed workers launched a widespread protest movement that included occupying unemployment offices in order to demand higher benefits and job creation. Jospin initially negotiated with movements of the unemployed and offered to increase benefits for the long-term unemployed, but he followed this by directing the police to evict those occupying unemployment offices.

Jospin also sought to Europeanize the attempt to reduce unemployment by advocating coordinated social and economic policies designed to favor job creation. He succeeded in inserting into the Amsterdam Treaty of 1997 (negotiated soon after his election as part of the process of launching the euro) language committing member states and the EU to promote "a high level of employment and social protection." The treaty authorized the EU to sponsor measures to promote employment and created a Committee for Employment, a weak counterpart to the EU Monetary Committee, established in connection with the launching of the euro. (Thanks to Jospin, the EU sponsored a ministerial summit conference in Luxembourg in 1997 devoted to employment policy, which set a variety of goals relating to job creation). The process of developing EU social and employment policy culminated in the negotiation of a European Pact for Employment at a June 1999 EU summit meeting in Cologne. (It should be noted that at this point, the stirring language remains just that, in that no concrete measures have yet been taken to achieve these worthy goals, mostly because of the opposition of several member states.)

In brief, although hardly radical in his approach, Jospin and much of the French Left remain wedded to a more traditional social democratic orientation. Symbolizing the contrast with other recently elected social democratic leaders in Europe, Jospin refused to support the joint declaration issued by Tony Blair and Gerhard Schröder in June 1999, "Europe: The Third Way, the New Center." The document calls for a reorientation of social democracy, involving the abandonment of the classic goals of equality, redistribution, and social security—in brief, the underpinnings of the welfare state—in favor of a more market-oriented approach. (Some have dubbed this "Thatcherism with a human face"!)

CONCLUSION

What lessons emerge from this analysis of French social policy? First, it is important to emphasize that no crystal-clear lessons or tendencies emerge. France cannot serve as an ideal type for scholarly analysis or a model for political action since it is such a patchwork quilt—a result of the complex balance of forces that underpinned the development of its welfare state. There is no "French model" that can fit comfortably within the framework developed by Esping-Andersen, nor does its welfare state clearly exemplify the principles underlying either Beveridge or Bismarck, since it combines elements of both in a fashion explicable more by historical analysis than Cartesian logic.

In a similar way, there is no clear-cut principle governing retrenchment in the current era. Alongside great stability, there have been significant reforms—yet these reforms are themselves somewhat contradictory in their impact. For example, restricting unlimited patient choice and over-consumption of medical services and medications might be commended, as could controlling physicians' fees and pharmaceutical companies' prices. However, progressives can hardly applaud the cutbacks in pensions.

One lesson does apparently emerge from our analysis: political struggle pays. France's welfare state was constructed and extended as a result of political struggles. In the recent period, retrenchment would doubtless have proceeded further in the absence of protest, especially the enormous movement of late 1995. Borrel's (1996) fine-grained statistical analysis supports this contention. She observes that "regression results show that strike waves and generalized disputes significantly influenced social benefits, the minimum wage and working hours" (p. 6). She further notes that "strikes in France were a powerful predictor of social benefits" (p. 7). Although protests may be less successful than some observers claim, for dramatic victory may prove short-lived when the streets empty, the character of the French welfare state is heavily influenced by the exceptionally great mobilization that periodically occurs in France. One should beware of idealizing the situation, for the French welfare state is quite imperfect. But, in a situation where retrenchment continues to rank among many governments' highest priorities, one is tempted to proclaim, "Vive la différence!"

NOTES

I am grateful to Graeme Robertson and Salvatore Pitruzzello for help preparing this chapter, and for expert editorial guidance by Gertrude Goldberg and Marguerite Rosenthal.

1. This account draws heavily on John Ambler's excellent introduction in Ambler (1993).

2. The account on changes in health insurance is largely based on Wilsford (1996).

3. This section draws on Levy (1998); Merrien (1998); Hassenteufel (1999).

REFERENCES

Ambler, J. S., ed. (1993). *The French Welfare State: Surviving Social and Ideological Change.* New York: New York University Press.

Bornstein, S., and P. E. Tixier. (1996). *The Strikes of 1995: A Crisis of the French Model?* Working Paper no. 5.46, presented to conference Considerations on the Evolution on the French and American Industrial Societies, Center for

German and European Studies, University of California at Berkeley, February 19–23.

Borrel, M. (1996). *Strikes, the Welfare State, and Union Strategies in the Postwar Period: What Can Be Learned from the French Experience?* Working Paper 5.45, presented to the conference Considerations on the Evolution on the French and American Industrial Societies, Center for German and European Studies, University of California at Berkeley, February 19–23.

Cameron, D. R. (1993). "Continuity and change in French social policy: The welfare state under Gaullism, liberalism, and socialism." In J. S. Ambler, ed., *The French Welfare State: Surviving Social and Ideological Change*. New York: New York University Press, pp. 58–93.

Chapman, H., M. Kesselman, and M. A. Schain, eds. (1998). *A Century of Organized Labor in France: A Union Movement for the Twenty-First Century?* New York: St. Martin's Press.

Esping-Andersen, G. (1990). *The Three Worlds of Welfare Capitalism*. Princeton, NJ: Princeton University Press.

———. (1996a). "After the Golden Age? Welfare state dilemmas in a global economy." In G. Esping-Andersen, ed., *Welfare States in Transition*. N.p.: UN Research Institute for Social Development, pp. 1–31.

———. (1996b) "Welfare states without work: The impasse of labour shedding and familialism in Continental European social policy." In G. Esping-Andersen, ed., *Welfare States in Transition*. N.p.: UN Research Institute for Social Development, pp. 66–87.

———. (1999). *Social Foundations of Post-Industrial Economies*. New York: Oxford University Press.

Fagnani, J. (1996). "Family policies and working mothers: A comparison of France and West Germany." In M. D. Garcia-Ramon and J. Monk, eds., *Women of the European Union: The Politics of Work and Daily Life*. London: Routledge, pp. 126–137.

Fondation Saint-Simon. (1997). *Pour une nouvelle république sociale*. Paris: Calmann-Lévy.

Friedman, G. (1999). "Has European integration failed?" Amherst: Department of Economics, University of Massachusetts at Amherst, unpublished paper.

Garcia-Ramon, M. D., and J. Monk, eds. (1996). *Women of the European Union: The Politics of Work and Daily Life*. London: Routledge.

Hassenteufel, P. (1999). *How Do Health Insurance Systems Change? France and Germany in the 1990s*. Paper presented to the conference Beyond the Health Care State, European University Institute, Florence, February 26–27.

Humanité. (1999). Report of the High Commission, July 21.

Jarreau, P. (1995). *La France de Chirac*. Paris: Flammarion.

Jobert, B. (1993). "Democracy and social policies: The case of France." In J. S. Ambler, ed., *The French Welfare State: Surviving Social and Ideological Change*. New York: New York University Press, pp. 232–258.

Kesselman, M. (1983). "Socialism without the workers: The case of France." *Kapitalistate*, no. 10/1: 11–41.

———. (2000). "France." In M. Kesselman, J. Krieger, and W. Joseph, eds., *An Introduction to Comparative Politics: Political Challenges and Changing Agendas*. Boston: Houghton Mifflin, pp. 79–132.

————. (2001). "France." In M. Kesselman and J. Krieger, eds., *European Politics in Transition*, 4th ed. Boston: Houghton Mifflin.

Lenoir, R. (1993). "Family policy in France since 1938." In J. S. Ambler, ed., *The French Welfare State: Surviving Social and Ideological Change*. New York: New York University Press, pp. 144–186.

Levy, L. (1998). *France in a Globalizing Economy: The Shifting Logic of Welfare Reform*. Paper presented at the workshop The Adjustment of National Employment and Social Policy to Internationalisation, European University Institute, Florence, Italy, October 19–20.

Ménière, L. (1993). *Bilan de la France, 1981–1993*. Paris: Hachette.

Merrien, F. X. (1998). *Reforming the French Welfare State*. Paper presented at conference Nuova Europa, Nuova Welfare, Pavia, Italy, November 27–28.

Monk, J., and M. D. Garcia-Ramon. (1996). "Placing women of the European Union." In M. D. Garcia-Ramon and J. Monk, eds., *Women of the European Union: The Politics of Work and Daily Life*. London: Routledge, pp. 1–30.

Mundell, R. (1961). "A theory of optimum currency areas." *American Economic Review* 51: 657–665.

Navarro, V. (1998). " 'Eurosclerosis' versus U.S. dynamism." *Challenge* 41 (July/August): 66–75.

————. (1998). *National Accounts*, vol. 2. Paris: Author.

Olivennes, D. (1998). "Réformer le modèle social français." *Le Débat*, special issue on "Social: Quelle réforme?" no. 101 (September/October).

Organisation for Economic Co-operation and Development (OECD). (1997). *Labour Force Statistics*. Paris: Author.

Palier, B., in collaboration with G. Bonoli. (1998). *Changing the Politics of Social Programmes: Innovative Changes in British and French Welfare Reforms*. Paper presented to the European Forum project on Recasting the European Welfare State: Options, Constraints, Actors. European University Institute, Florence, Italy, October 28.

Paugam, S. (1996). "Poverty and social disqualification: A comparative analysis of cumulative social disadvantage in Europe." *Journal of European Social Policy* 6(4): 287–304.

Pierson, P. (1994). *Dismantling the Welfare State? Reagan, Thatcher, and the Politics of Retrenchment*. Cambridge: Cambridge University Press.

————. (1996). "The new politics of the welfare state." *World Politics* 48(2) (January): 143–179.

Pitruzzello, S. (1997). "Social policy and the implementation of the Maastricht fiscal convergence criteria: The Italian and French attempts at welfare and pension reforms." *Social Research* 64(4) (Winter): 1589–1642.

Ross, G. (1998). "The Euro, the 'French model of society,' and French politics." *French Politics and Society* 16(4) (Fall): 1–16.

Ullman, C. (1998). *The Welfare State's Other Crisis: Explaining the New Partnership between Nonprofit Organizations and the State in France*. Bloomington: Indiana University Press.

Wilsford, D. (1996). "Reforming French health care policy." In J.T.S. Keeler and M. A. Schain, eds., *Chirac's Challenge: Liberalization, Europeanization, and Malaise in France*. New York: St. Martin's Press, pp. 231–256.

Chapter 7

The Dismantling of Welfare in Germany

Gerhard Bäcker and Ute Klammer

THE END OF BASIC CONSENSUS IN SOCIAL POLICY?

The welfare state in the Federal Republic of Germany (FRG) is suffering from massive pressure. We are no longer talking merely about individual cuts. Increasingly, the principles of the welfare state itself are at stake. A growing chorus of voices in the academic and political world is beginning to demand a fundamental restructuring of the sociopolitical regime that has determined the structure of the Federal Republic as well as other European countries. In the political rhetoric of almost all parties in the FRG, the guiding image of the "social market economy," which has for decades been considered a precondition for the unparalleled economic progress and the high degree of political and democratic stability that shaped post-war Germany, is being challenged. Within a few years, radical market positions demanding a fundamental reshaping of society have moved from the fringe to the center of political discourse (Bäcker, 1996). The dominant thesis is that the "social market economy," though singularly successful in its day, cannot be projected into the future under the changed political and economic conditions of the present decade.

Certain ominous symptoms can be discerned: increasing unemployment, a low rate of economic growth, financing and debt problems affecting public budgets, and the burden of taxes on jobholders. The diagnosis of the problem is that the welfare state has become the real cause of the problems that Germans now face. The charge is that "exorbitant" social standards and "non-wage labor costs" hinder the German economy in international competition. At the same time the welfare state is also accused of excessive generosity and a lack of effective work incentives. The political conclusions drawn from this diagnosis give rise to the demand that the market be freed from restrictive social welfare regulations, that social security be privatized, and that public benefits be reduced significantly in order to improve the competitiveness of the economy, stimulate growth, and decrease unemployment (SVR, 1996).

In Germany, this radical change toward a basic questioning of the welfare state began during the first half of the 1990s. It is not as though the welfare state had been totally unchallenged before that. Those people who had no need of state benefits were among those who furiously fought the idea; the same goes for all manner of enterprises that, following their internal economic logic, have always regarded the welfare state's "decommodification of labor" (Esping-Andersen, 1990) as alien. Nevertheless, the "expansion phase" of the welfare state, which lasted until the mid-1970s, and its subsequent phase of restriction, which extended into the early 1990s, took place without major political conflicts (Schmid, 1988; Alber, 1990).

After the experience of fascism and war, it was obvious that an "unadulterated" market economy could not serve to construct a stable democratic society. A living democracy not only presupposes technical equality before the law but is also based on civic rights and social justice. The Weimar Republic had taught us that there is another side to the blind submission of society and the economy to market forces and the acceptance of mass unemployment, social destabilization, and poverty, a side that is called extremism and violence. In addition, post-war Germany was placed at the boundary of two competing systems, capitalism and socialism. The conflict with the German Democratic Republic (GDR) was meant to prove not only that a capitalist economy was economically efficient and bound to guarantee a high level of income and consumption but that it also could, with the aid of social welfare, provide social security and political stability at the same time.

It is not remarkable that the Social Democratic Party (SPD) and the trade unions of the FRG have traditionally advocated the welfare state. What is remarkable, however, is that the other national party, the conservative Christian Democratic Union (CDU), has also considered itself a guardian of the welfare state. Indeed, the two powerful wings of the CDU, Christian socialist and conservative paternalistic, have thus far prevented neoliberal policies, like those pursued in the United Kingdom under the Conservative regime of Margaret Thatcher, from gaining sway in the CDU.

In the post-war period West Germany adopted a number of important, progressive social policies in the areas of pensions, sickness pay, health, housing, the labor market, asset formation, and, particularly since the mid-1960s, education. The four existing social insurances (accident, health, pension, and unemployment) were continually expanded until the early 1980s with regard to funding, risk coverage, and level of payments. Measures assisting families (child benefits, tax relief, and child-care allowances) were also increased.

A first turning point, in the early 1980s, occurred when the coalition government of socialists and liberals (SPD and FDP [Free Democratic Party]) crumbled and was replaced by a coalition of the Conservative and Liberal Parties under Helmut Kohl. Up until the early 1990s the Kohl government repeatedly made cuts in the system of welfare benefits but until that time always shunned a radical restructuring of the overall social system. Even in the 1990s, a more advanced branch of social insurance, the Care Insurance Law, was passed against stiff resistance of employers and FDP politicians. It remains to be seen whether demands for a total revision of the social system will soon begin to dominate the programs of the big national parties. Despite the discourse of politicians and academics, the social welfare state continues to enjoy a high degree of public acceptance, and opinion polls report scant support for its dismantling (Wagner and Rinne, 1996).

AN OVERVIEW OF THE WELFARE STATE IN GERMANY

Social welfare provision in Germany includes the entire complex of state institutions and regulations that limit and complement the economic market. Apart from the cash and non-cash benefits of social security (the focus of this chapter), there exist a number of important structural elements: legal stipulations regulating the labor market; employment contracts and conditions; the public labor market (a second and third labor market partly financed by unemployment insurance); occupational policies; health care; tax law; workplace labor relations and Labor Management Act; collective bargaining laws; and social institutions and services on the communal level.

Most social welfare regulations are national and thus uniform throughout the country although the federal states have retained their own independent regulations with regard to school and university education. Local governments are responsible for financing local social infrastructure (social services and institutions for children, youth, families, and handicapped and aged people) as well as social assistance and other means-tested welfare benefits. Most free services are made available by independent, non-profit-making providers, that is, the large, nationwide welfare organizations, but are nonetheless financed by taxes.

Regulation of the labor market by the national government, on the one hand, and collective bargaining, on the other, has created conditions in the German labor market that guarantee a high degree of social security and social rights to German employees. German labor law provides protection against dismissal, occupational health and safety regulations, continued remuneration in case of sickness (full gross wages for the first six weeks of an illness), child-care leave (legal entitlement of either father or mother to a leave of up to 36 months after the birth of a child, including a return-to-work guarantee), and paid leave to care for sick children (10 days annually per child and parent).

The establishment of work councils required by the Labor Management Act gives employees a share in policy making in their workplaces. Members of work councils—predominantly, but not necessarily, trade union members—are elected and have the right to co-determination in matters such as distribution of working hours and overtime.

Regulation of the labor market by legislation is complemented by agreements between the employers (and their associations), on the one hand, and the trade unions, on the other. Legal norms merely set minimum standards on which collective agreements can be based. Regulations arising from collective bargaining usually cover employment relations and working conditions (e.g., protection against dismissal; regulations regarding leaves of absence; in-company social benefits; duration, placement, and distribution of working hours; vacations; overtime) as well as remuneration. Among the achievements of the trade unions in collective bargaining are fully paid annual vacations of six weeks, an average workweek of 37 hours (35 hours in certain lines of business), special agreements for employees of advanced age, sick pay exceeding the statutory limits, special vacation pay, and Christmas bonuses. Industrial disputes are rare, but the more important agreements (such as the 35-hour workweek in the metal industry) were achieved only after extensive industrial conflicts.

The national government does not involve itself at all in wage settlements; for the vast majority of employees these are determined by collective bargaining agreements. Characteristically, collective wage settlements are valid for entire branches of business or large geographical areas. Settlement clauses become effective at once and are absolutely binding; the parties to these clauses can deviate from them only in favor of the employees.

Public labor market policy, practiced by the federal government and the Federal Labor Agency under the Employment Promotion Act, can also be said to reduce unemployment and undesired inequalities of the labor market. Among the instruments of labor market policy are the public employment service and vocational guidance, job creation measures and occupational projects, payment of wage and recruitment subsidies in occupational rehabilitation of the long-term unemployed, financing and implementation of training and retraining measures, and occupational and educational aid for young people.

BASIC STRUCTURES OF SOCIAL INSURANCE AND TAX-FINANCED TRANSFERS

The German system of social security began with Bismarck's social legislation at the end of the nineteenth century, a body of law that has had a decisive influence on several other European countries as well. The characteristic feature of Bismarck-type social policy is that contributory social insurances protect certain groups of employees and professionals whose benefit payments are related to their contributions.

Excluding the workplace rights that we have already described, the present German welfare state consists of social insurance for income loss resulting from unemployment, occupational accidents, sickness, disability, old age, and death of the family provider; payment of health care; and, quite recently, payment for nursing care in the private home or in public institutions. For tradesmen, certain groups of self-employed workers, civil servants, freelance workers, artists, writers, and farmers, other insurance arrangements exist, so that only some groups of self-employed persons are not covered by compulsory insurance. Social insurances cover not only the insured worker but also his or her dependents and survivors. In many cases optional insurance coverage is also possible.

The amount of benefits from insurance varies from 53 percent of previous net income (for means-tested unemployment assistance) to about 80 percent of previous net income (for sickness benefits and maximum pension claims). Pensions are based on the relation between one's own earned income and the average earned income as well as the duration of one's contributions to the pension fund. All benefits are indexed according to average (nationwide) net earnings and are revised regularly. By and large, the individual branches of the social security system are based on the idea of an equivalence of contributions and benefits, but there is some redistribution in favor of women and lower-wage earners.

Compulsory health insurance covers the cost of health care for workers and salaried employees (up to certain income limits), recipients of unemployment and welfare benefits, and their family members. People with higher incomes, civil servants, and most of the self-employed have to join private insurance plans. Only about 0.1 percent of the population has no health coverage whatsoever. Since 1995, Care Insurance covers nursing care for practically the entire population.

Social insurance, which constitutes more than two-thirds of social expenditures in Germany, is regulated by federal law. As para-state institutions, providers of the five types of social insurance enjoy a certain degree of autonomy; they are in charge of their own budgets. Their budgets are largely financed by contributions earmarked for specific purposes. These contributions are related to the gross income of earners and are shared equally by the insured person and his or her employer. There are no additional charges payable either for special risks or for the joint insurance of children and marriage partners. In the case of Pension and Unemployment Insurances, the federal government increases the income from contributions by tax-financed subsidies. The national social insurances are based on pay-as-you-go financing.

The supervisory bodies of social security agencies are formed in equal numbers by representatives of the trade unions and the employers' associations. This arrangement, referred to as "self-government," is one reason that the employers' associations have so far supported and shaped the German social security system.

Transfer payments financed from general tax revenues complement earned incomes and social insurance benefits. Tax-financed benefits are related to special requirements that are not taken into account either in wages or in social insurance. They mainly comprise items such as child benefits and parental, housing, and education allowances for pupils and students, subsidized housing, and special tax relief. With the exception of the child benefits, these are income-tested and, in contrast to social insurance, raised only by discretion and at irregular intervals.

Pension Insurance

The Statutory Pension Scheme (Gesetzliche Rentenversicherung or GRV), with its more than 44 million compulsory members, is the biggest branch of social security in Germany. Except for civil servants, all those employed with wages above a certain threshold (at present 630 DM per month, $1 U.S. = 1.9 DM), as well as trainees and the unemployed who are eligible for unemployment insurance benefits, are compulsorily insured. GRV covers retirement, disability, and survivors' pensions as well as rehabilitation payments. The level of pensions is based on remuneration points, which are primarily calculated on the basis of the length of covered employment and lifetime earnings. To a certain extent periods of child care, education and training, illness, and unemployment contribute to remuneration points and pension entitlements. The benefits are supposed to secure living standards after retirement similar to those attained during working life. A survivor's pension amounts to 60 percent of the pension of the deceased partner. These benefits are derived from contributions (combined employer and employee contributions equaled 19.5 percent in 1999) as well as federal grants (at present 21 percent of overall expenses).

In 1998, the average monthly GRV pension in the Old Federal States (former FRG) amounted to DM 1,873 ($986) for male pensioners and DM 833 ($438) for women. In the New Federal States (former GDR) men on average received DM 1,988 ($1,046), and women, DM 1,158 ($609) (VDR, 1999; figures relate to independent pensions only).

Allowances granted by the "first pillar," the state old age pension system, can be supplemented by a second pillar, the (voluntary) company pension schemes. This second pillar extends to over 50 percent of the dependent (wage and salaried) labor force, though numbers are declining.

Health Insurance

The Statutory Health Insurance Scheme (Gesetzliche Krankenversicherung) is by far the most important safeguard against the expenses of illness; in the more than 100 years since its inception, the system constantly increased its membership; at present almost 90 percent of the entire population is covered. Today, people in wage employment and below a certain maximum income are compulsorily insured against illness, as are pensioners, students, farmers, artists, and the unemployed. Family members do not have to pay contributions if their personal incomes do not surpass certain limits. Approximately 11 percent of the population is not covered by Compulsory Sickness Insurance, but they are completely covered, predominantly through private insurance.

Presently, about 1,000 sickness insurance agencies of different sizes provide health coverage on regional, occupational, or trade-specific bases, being part of the Statutory Health Insurance Scheme. The range of benefits that they offer is uniformly organized: apart from medical, dental, in- and outpatient therapeutic treatment, it also comprises measures relating to prophylaxis and early diagnosis of illnesses, as well as to rehabilitation. Services offered by the agencies are the same for all insured people; it is the aim of the health agencies to ensure all "medically essential" treatment. No direct rationing takes place. The insured are entitled to a free choice of doctors and dentists, nearly all of whom are practicing under the Health Insurance Scheme.

Providers deal directly with medical practitioners, hospitals, and pharmacies on a contractual basis, concluding agreements that entail the obligation to treat insured persons on behalf of the health insurance agencies. These contractual negotiations determine amounts of hospital care and the level of fees. Tighter controls of drug costs have been repeatedly blocked by the pharmaceutical industry.

Services in the public health sector are rendered according to the principle of solidarity. Although contributions can vary slightly from one agency to the next, persons who are publicly insured, in contrast to the privately insured, do not have to pay additional contributions based on age, gender, or risk.

Unemployment Insurance

Social safeguards against unemployment have been provided to all workers and salaried employees since passage of the Unemployment Insurance Act in 1927. After one year of contributions, the insured are entitled to unemployment benefits, provided they register with the employment office as fit for work and "at the disposal" of the labor market. Unemployed persons have to accept all "reasonable" work; if they turn down the job offered, the receipt of benefits is suspended, and, on repeated refusal, eligibility for benefits lapses. In evaluating the reasonableness of work offered, a certain regard for qualifications, income, and status does exist. After a six-month unemployment period, however, any work is considered reasonable, as long as it is not paid below the rate of the unemployment benefits to which the worker was entitled.

Payments are divided into unemployment benefits and unemployment assistance. The unemployment benefit is an insurance benefit and not subject to means testing. It amounts to 60 percent of the previous net income (67 percent for unemployed workers with children). The period of receiving unemployment benefits is restricted: beyond a minimum period of six months it is related to the period of prior contributions and also to the age of the person concerned; it can be paid for up to 32 months. After an unemployment benefit has run out, it is followed by unemployment assistance, receipt of which is basically unlimited. Unemployment assistance is somewhere between insurance and welfare. On the one hand it is paid only in case of need and is financed from the general revenues of the federal government, while on the other hand certain preconditions do exist, and the level of payment is related to the previous net income (53 percent; 57 percent for unemployed workers with children).

About two-thirds (68 percent) of all unemployed persons receive unemployment benefits or assistance, while the remaining third are either not entitled to them, that entitlement has run out, or their incomes are too high for means-tested assistance. In West Germany, average monthly unemployment benefits are DM 1,375 ($724), and for unemployment assistance, DM 1,008 ($531). As expected, benefits for men and women are significantly different: men receive average monthly unemployment benefits of DM 1,651 ($869) and unemployment assistance of DM 1,105 ($582), while the amounts for women are merely DM 1,028 ($541) and 810 ($426), respectively (Bäcker et al., 2000, pp. 355 ff.).

Care Insurance

Following extended public discussion, compulsory Care Insurance was introduced nationwide in Germany in 1995 as the fifth branch of the social insurance system. It was meant to close a gap that had existed up to that point in the health security system, a deficiency to which both the rapid growth of the aged population and an increasing emphasis on individual over family responsibility have contributed significantly. This development had led to a strong growth of expenditures for social assistance because people in need got their expenditures reimbursed. One of the reasons to introduce the Care Insurance, therefore, was the aim to diminish the financial burden of social assistance. Compulsory insurance to cover care at any age now extends to the entire population. Allowances depend on the degree of care needed and alternatively include cash and non-cash benefits for home care as well as benefits in kind for residents of nursing homes. In the latter case, however, only nursing costs are covered; board and lodging expenses have to be paid privately. To that extent we can talk of only a partial insurance against the risk of institutional care, which continues to entail substantial costs to those who require it or to their relatives.

Social Assistance and Other Public Welfare Benefits

Benefits granted by social insurances do not necessarily guarantee a minimum level of subsistence. Indeed, they reflect market inequalities and may not allow for basic, minimum amounts. A loss of up to 50 percent of an income that is already low rapidly drags people below the subsistence level, especially when there are dependent children.

When people's incomes, regardless of the reasons, fall below the politically established subsistence level, they are entitled to social assistance. The aim is to enable the recipient of such assistance to lead a life in keeping with the principle of human dignity. In this context the cause of indigence is irrelevant. Subsistence aid relates to the community (household or other) in which the needy person lives and is specified according to what is needed in the individual case (principle of individuality). Before receiving any help at all, the recipients of social assistance are required to use any income and assets that they possess.

Persons who are able and fit to work are expected to earn their own livelihoods. Here, all kinds of work or job opportunities can reasonably be expected to be taken up, unless the person concerned is not in a position to carry out the job for physical or intellectual reasons or because he or she at the time is bringing up children. If a recipient of social assistance turns down a job without any cogent reasons, the welfare benefit is first curtailed and ultimately completely withdrawn.

Since July 1999 the average ordinary rate in the West German states amounts to DM 547 ($288) per month for the adult head of the household. The amount of benefit paid to the remaining members of the household is based on a percentage scale that, according to age, ranges between 50 to 90 percent of the basic benefit. This basic allowance is supplemented by demand-oriented lump-sum payments and, as regards certain groups of people (e.g., pregnant women, single parents), by additional allowances. Housing costs are also provided. The drawing of social assistance is not limited in time.

To get this into perspective: a single-person household with medium-sized rent payment achieves a subsistence level of DM 1,068 ($562) per month, and a family with two children is entitled to a payment of a monthly DM 2,573 ($1,354). Households living on social assistance usually reach an income level about 50 percent of the poverty line or slightly above, depending on the number of family members and their claims to additional payments such as housing benefits. Social assistance is financed by the local governments. From the early 1960s, when the entitlement to social assistance was introduced for all citizens, the minimum benefit has been raised periodically, approximately in line with the average increase in wages.

THE QUANTITATIVE DIMENSION OF THE WELFARE STATE

The welfare budget shows that total welfare expenses presently amount to about 34 percent of the German gross domestic product (GDP) (Bundesministerium für Arbeit und Sozialordnung, 1997).[1] More than half of total expenses go to the pension, health, and care insurances. Further important factors are employment promotion (unemployment insurance and active labor market policies), which consumes 11 percent; welfare benefits carried by employers (especially remuneration continued in case of sickness and company pension schemes), which amount to 8.3 percent; and social aids and services (especially welfare benefits, child and youth welfare), which account for 8.9 percent. Since different institutions are often responsible for the same kind of welfare task, it makes sense to subdivide total welfare benefits in terms of "purposes." It then becomes apparent that more than a third of the total expense (38 percent) is used for old age insurance, and almost as much (35 percent) for health insurance.

THE CHALLENGE OF DIMINISHING GROWTH AND INCREASED INTERNATIONAL COMPETITION

The German model of the "social market economy" combines dynamic industrialization, world market orientation, stable currency, high productivity based on technological advance, high wages, and a well-established system of social provision. The market economy resulted in high growth rates and increased incomes and thus created the material basis for the welfare state, which, in turn, markedly contributed to high (labor) productivity and political stability.

Meanwhile, however, the German market economy is beginning to show signs of weakness. The "economic miracle" of the post-war period has been succeeded by a phase of growing unemployment and diminishing economic growth, as well as stiffening international competition in commodity, services, and especially money markets. The GDP growth rate has been decreasing from one trade cycle to the next.

Relatively low growth rates are accompanied by high increases in labor productivity, which in turn have led to a significant reduction in the volume of labor. The fact that the growth of production in Germany does not suffice any longer to absorb the employment losses created by this growth in labor productivity is one of the reasons for the high rate of unemployment.

In addition to this, the labor market is glutted with an increasing supply of labor. Due to high birthrates of cohorts now joining the labor market, immigration (work migrants from other European countries, refugees, and German repatriates from Eastern Europe), and, last but not least, a significant increase in the labor force participation of women, more people than ever are looking for employment.

Whether globalization or the increasing integration of the world economy has contributed to these growth problems cannot definitely be answered here. The public debate on this question is dominated by the view that German manufacturing is too expensive and is thus losing out in global competition. It is true that the FRG has recently faced stiffer competition from the Asian countries and certain Central and East European countries that are producing technologically sophisticated products with cheap labor. Globalization also seems to have achieved a new dimension of internationalization of the money and capital markets, a fact that strongly restricts the free action of German monetary policy. Nevertheless, we cannot necessarily deduce from this that the Federal Republic is losing out in this trade rivalry, for even with high wages and social benefits, unit labor costs in Germany are still relatively low. Indeed, a high level of labor productivity continues in this country. Thus, high wages and high productivity offset each other.

Over the last few years unit labor costs in the FRG have risen significantly less than in its trading partners. The increase of direct wage expenditure as well as the non-wage labor costs can be said to have been "earned" by increased production (Köddermann, 1996, pp. 6ff.). The continuing high export surplus, which achieved a new high in the first half of 1997, supports this statement.

This expansion of productivity, however, resulted in an equally drastic reduction of workplaces. Moreover, the difficult, even endangered situation of individual branches of industry in Germany cannot fail to be noticed; the structural changes in a world economy under pressure from labor market competition become a threat to the people working in that economy and for it, forcing them to accept worsening working and social conditions. Company decisions on investments and jobs serve as levers to exert pressure on the labor force and the trade unions. Such pressure usually results in "stay-behind negotiations" (i.e., attempting to keep company production in the country), for which a price has to be paid in terms of the loss of remuneration (e.g., the dismantling of allowances paid in excess of negotiated scales) or deterioration in the conditions of work such as introduction of Sunday work and increase of working time without wage compensation.

As the most powerful economy in Europe, the FRG is well able to defend and even consolidate its position, though obviously for the price of payrolls that continuously decrease in value and a worsening of the social welfare situation. The European welfare states find themselves in need of "social dumping"; they feel forced to go along with the trend, but none of them can hope for long-term improvements of the social situation (Bäcker, 1997, pp. 12–20). The Federal Republic, however, is the initiator and driving force of this disastrous devaluation race in the field of state welfare, not merely its helpless victim. The position of German trade unions—that a developed welfare state helps to ensure "social peace" and thus itself contributes to a country's economic efficiency—increasingly proves to be a blunt argument, as international development in recent years shows that social peace has become a "bargain," gained without paying for it in social welfare. The predominant European example for this is Great Britain, where the loss of the social punch of the trade unions has been accompanied by severe cuts in social security benefits.

PERSISTENT UNEMPLOYMENT

To our mind, the successful legitimization of cuts in social benefits is essentially a consequence of the present labor market situation and not the result of a German welfare state that has lost its competitiveness. Experience of recent years has shown that all interventions in the labor law (e.g., cuts in the continued payment of wages in case of sickness, relaxing of the Dismissal Protection Law) have been justified as means of securing and creating jobs, without, however, any noticeable expansion of employment.

On the contrary, the job market in Germany has constantly worsened and, in July 1997, achieved a new low with an unemployment rate of 11.4 percent. If one adds the "hidden reserves," jobless persons not counted in the labor market statistics, unemployment rises by one-third. There are significant differences, moreover, in the incidence of unemployment depending on profession, qualifications, gender, and age as well as region. At particularly high risk of becoming and remaining unemployed are workers in traditional industrial areas, unskilled and semiskilled workers, older persons, and/or those with special health problems. Unemployment of young people is still below average, but the indications are that their unemployment rates will rise sharply. The situation of the long-term unemployed, however, is of particular concern (see Figure 7.1). Numbering one-third of all those registered as unemployed, they find it virtually impossible to secure a job.

High unemployment almost inevitably pushes the welfare state into a financial crisis. The influence of the level of employment and the number of unemployed on the financial situation of public treasuries is particularly critical. On the one hand, the level of contributions to unemployment insurance funds shrinks considerably; at the same time, direct and indirect

Figure 7.1
Trends in Unemployment in the Old and New Federal States, 1970–1998

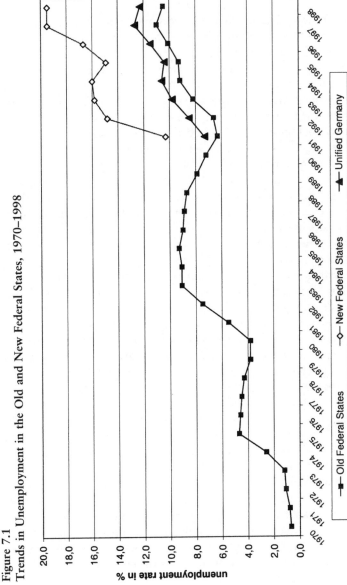

Source: Data supplied by the Federal Labor Agency, ANBA Jahreszahlen.

obligations for unemployment rise sharply (i.e., there is a trend toward earlier retirement, which increases the costs of pension insurance and ultimately public welfare). In 1995, the total cost of unemployment—additional expenses and reduced revenues—amounted to DM 142.5 billion ($75 billion) or just under 5 percent of GDP (Martens, 1997). We also have to take into account that over and above direct money benefits, welfare services and benefits in kind are also affected by unemployment. With growing social problems and distress, the need for social services automatically grows as well. For those working in the fields of child and youth welfare, homelessness, delinquency, and drug addiction, direct links with the employment crisis become apparent. We are, moreover, skeptical of whether political and business leaders are in a position to prioritize a reduction in unemployment. Though the former federal government set an ambitious target of halving the unemployment rate by the year 2000, there are as yet no major signs of improvement. Indeed, unemployment was in the 10 percent range in mid-1999. Germany's favorable position in the export markets cannot offset the lack of domestic demand. Restrictive budget policies of the federal government, the states, and the municipalities, including cuts in social expenditures and reduction of government staff and public investment, stunt growth of the economy and the labor market and increase unemployment.

All this is aggravated by the fact that job creation measures have been significantly reduced over the last few years because the Federal Labor Office has been obliged to spend an increasing share of its budget on unemployment benefits and assistance as well as on compensation for part-time work. For fiscal reasons, the federal government, in its turn, was not prepared to finance active, high-volume labor market policies. As a result, the number of people aided by job creation measures fell from 925,000 in 1993 to less than 500,000 in 1996 (Sitte, 1997, pp. 780–789).

Were it not for one public policy—reduction of average work time—the impact of unemployment would be even worse. Credit for this development must go to the trade unions, because since the mid-1980s they have managed to put reduction of work time at the center of their collective bargaining policy, intending to spread the all-too-sparse volume of work as widely as possible. In the big branches of industry (steel production, metalworking, printing, and retail trade) the 35-hour week has been realized. In addition, part-time work is beginning to spread (though very slowly, with, to date, 16 percent of all employment contracts). Supported by early retirement regulations in the pension and unemployment insurances, businesses offer early retirement at 60 years of age at the latest, thus also alleviating job shortages.

The positive effects of these policies notwithstanding, the process of reducing working hours has almost ground to a halt. The promotion of early retirement has been replaced by measures intended to stabilize the financing of pension insurances by increasing the length of the working life and raising the age of retirement. The reduction in working hours has also come to a halt, as trade unions, weakened by the pressures on the labor market and suffering from loss of members, find it difficult to achieve wage increases that keep pace with inflation. Unions lack the power to achieve agreements that reduce work time without wage loss, and work-time reductions entailing loss of income seem still not acceptable to their members.

GERMAN REUNIFICATION AND THE CRISIS OF PUBLIC FINANCES

The analysis thus far has pertained mainly to conditions in the "old" Federal Republic. A large part of our sociopolitical problems, however, results from German reunification (Bäcker, 1992). Although it is a decade since the unification contract took effect and the five New States were incorporated into the Federal Republic, the economic, social, and political challenges of this unique event have by no means been met. The basic and persisting problem is that the New States are far less efficient economically than the Old States. At present it is an undisputed fact that the currency and economic union between the two parts of Germany has not proved to be the stimulus for a rapid transition of the New States into the Western market economy but, on the contrary has resulted in wasting a large part of the industrial capacity of East Germany.

This dramatic process of economic restructuring or "crisis of transformation" is not finished. The outdated enterprises, producing ineffectively in a competitive world market, have disappeared without, however, being replaced by new workplaces in the trade and (expanding) services sectors. Unemployment in the region, close to 20 percent (registered unemployment only), threatens to undermine the economic, social, and political situation in East Germany.

A key question is whether and when a self-supporting improvement in investments and production will take place that will equalize the productivity and production of East and West Germany. It is not clear what period of time can reasonably be required for this adjustment process. Even under the most favorable conditions, the former GDR would not be able to achieve a standard of living comparable to that of the West earlier than 15 years from now. The longer we have to wait for economic improvement in East Germany and the longer employment remains low, the more social and political compensatory measures will be necessary to prevent social decline.

The 1990 contract for the union of the FRG and the GDR aimed at transferring the complete West German system of social security to East Germany, with the exception of some minor and special institutional regulations. Benefits, however, were based on the East German wage level, which at the time of reunification was just under 50 percent of the West German figure; currently, it is about 85 percent. Whereas initially it was expected that the wage levels of East and West Germany would adjust to each other within a few years, estimates in the meantime have become more pessimistic, with complete adjustment not expected before 2005. As a result, the difference in the level of social benefits will persist. On the other hand, the transformation of East German pensions resulted in a substantial increase in most pensions there so that the majority of pensioners in the former GDR were able to improve their position in relation to jobholders. East German pensioners thus became the real "winners" in reunification.

The problematic development of the New Federal States has had significant effects upon the Old States as well, especially with regard to overburdened public budgets. Indeed, in hindsight, the early predictions of the federal government that reunification would be "free of charge" and would not unduly burden citizens in the West seem quite unfounded. It was claimed that unification could be financed by the increased taxes from economic growth and by limiting new public borrowing, but declining production and employment kept down tax revenues and contributions in the New States, while these same economic problems are causing social security expenditures at all levels of government to rise steeply. Since only part of the expenses of the states, local authorities, and social insurance agencies in the East can be met by their own revenues, a permanent transfer of funds from the West is needed.

This transfer sum amounts to 5 to 6 percent of the West German GDP and, since the beginning of the 1990s, has burdened the treasuries of all regional authorities and also of the social security providers. The result is growing deficits and increased direct and indirect taxes and social insurance contributions. In the years 1992 and 1993 alone, contribution-financed transfers of the Federal Employment Agency and of the pension insurance agencies to the New States amounted to about DM 38.7 billion ($20.4 billion) and DM 39.7 billion ($20.9 billion), which corresponded to 21.7 percent and 18.3 percent of the total income of the East German treasuries (Bundesministerium für Arbeit und Sozialordnung, 1997). The fact that these contributions burden only part of the working population can hardly be considered justifiable and conducive to the growth of national unity in Germany. The enormous size of social expenditure in the New Federal States emerges from a separate analysis of the rate of social security expenditure: in 1997, social spending in the Old Federal States was 31.7 percent of GDP, thus being significantly below the rates of the mid-1970s. In the New States, however, the figures in recent years were at the 60 percent mark (see Figure 7.2). While in the majority of European countries high unemployment was a major contributor to fiscal problems, the burdens of reunification made the German case a very special one.

The budget deficits, which have risen steeply in recent years because of

Figure 7.2
Social Expenditures as a Percentage of GDP

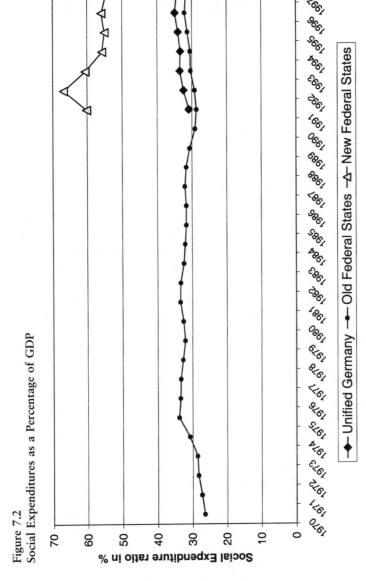

Sources: Bundesministerium für Arbeit und Sozialordnung, 1997; Breier 1998.

Table 7.1

Contributions to Social Insurance as a Percentage of Employees' Wages, 1977–1999*

Year	Pension Insurance	Health Insurance	Unemployment Insurance	Care Insurance	Total
1977	18.0	11.4	3.0	—	32.4
1982	18.0	12.0	4.0	—	34.0
1987	18.7	12.6	4.3	—	35.6
1992	17.7	12.5	6.3	—	36.5
1997	20.3	13.4	6.5	1.7	41.9
1999	19.5	13.5	6.5	1.7	41.2

*Total of employers' and employees' contributions. Until 1996: Old Federal States; since 1997: Unified Germany.

Source: Ministery of Labour, various years.

reunification and labor market problems, are exacerbated by the additional pressures created by the "convergence criteria" for membership in the European Monetary Union (EMU). To carry out a strategy of consolidation in an era of high unemployment and poor economic growth is bound to lead to an unsolvable dilemma: cuts in public expenses, which, in turn, lead to reduced consumer demand, slower economic growth, and increased unemployment. The result is an increase in state expenses and a rise in public debts.

INCREASED EXPENDITURES AND CONTRIBUTIONS

The discussion pertaining to cutbacks and possible dismantling of the welfare state in Germany is dominated by concern over expenses. The central issue of this criticism is the fact that the increasing rate of social benefit payments has brought with it a steady rise in the rate of contributions to social insurance, so at present the total of employers' and employees' contributions amounts to about 41 percent of individual salaries and wages (Table 7.1).

Contribution rates, moreover, rose much more than could have been expected from the rise in social benefits alone. One reason is that a greater share of benefit costs is financed by social security contributions, with a smaller part coming from general revenues. Whereas in 1970, for instance, almost 40 percent of the social budget was financed from general revenues, the share sank to just under 32 percent in 1994 (Bundesministerium für Arbeit und Sozialordnung, 1997). At the same time, however, wages declined as a share of national income. In 1982, gross wages in the FRG were 76.9 percent of total national income; in 1994, they had dropped to 70.1 percent. For the entire FRG the figure was only 69 percent in early 1996 (Schäfer, 1996). Since social benefits are predominantly financed by social security contributions on wages, a rise in the payment of welfare benefits has meant a heavier burden on a wage share that is itself shrinking as a proportion of national income.

An additional factor in this development is the trend toward forms of labor that are not liable to social insurance contributions, such as marginal employment and (sham) self-employment.[2] At the beginning of 1992 an estimated 4.5 million people held marginal employment as either their principal or secondary source of income and thus were not paying social insurance contributions on these earnings (ISG, 1993).

Finally, the Care Insurance introduced in 1995 has raised contribution rates, initially by 1 percent and more recently by another 0.7 percent. Although the Care Insurance partly meant a refinancing of benefits that formerly were paid for by the (tax-financed) public assistance scheme, it has, nevertheless, to be stated that it included an expansion of the range of social welfare benefits in a period when many other benefits were cut.

Rising contributions and direct wage tax are burdens on workers and their families. At present, the average wage earner with two children retains about 70 percent of gross earnings, an unmarried earner without children only 59 percent (Bäcker, 1996, p. 150). At the same time, increases in the average, inflation-adjusted gross income have been slowing. Disposable net income of the average wage earner rose only slightly in the 1980s and has been decreasing continuously since 1993.

It is generally feared that contributions will continue to rise because of demographic changes. The share of the population that is of retirement age will increase from 15.1 percent in 1992 to between 25.7 and 27.7 percent by the year 2040. These demographic changes will lead to further rises in contribution rates, especially in the area of old age security, unless the system is financed differently. According to the Prognos Institute, contributions will have to rise from 17.2 percent in 1992 to between 26.3 percent and 28.7 percent, depending on economic conditions (Eckerle, Schlesinger, and Blaha, 1995). In view of the aging of the population and new, expensive forms of therapy, further rises in contributions for health care are also expected.

GENDER ISSUES

In the old FRG, the model unit for social policy was the single wage-earner family, with the husband as breadwinner and the wife as homemaker. In recent years, West German women have gradually entered the labor market. Consequently, the problem of combining the obligations of job and work in the home has become a focus of public discussion. Between 1970 and 1994 the proportion of women in the labor force had risen from 35.8 to 42.4 percent. On a European scale, however, the (West) German ratio of working women is no more than average.

The increase in gainful employment of women is largely due to the expansion of part-time work. At present in Germany, about a third of working women are employed in part-time positions, as against less than 3 percent of working men, and women profit from the increasing importance of the services sector. Public discourse often still refers to a three-phase model for women—an initial period of full-time work, a subsequent period of family leave, and a third phase of reduced employment as a "supportive earner." All available indications are that West German women are increasingly inclined toward earning an income (DIW, 1996); so far, however, entering the labor market is frequently thwarted by deficits in public child care. In the labor market itself, gender-specific forms of segregation are clearly apparent, even though women have caught up remarkably well in terms of educational attainment. Yet, typical workplaces for women are still defined in terms of low qualifications, working conditions, wages, and levels of advancement.

Although the German constitution calls for equal treatment of men and women, women still remain unequal as far as social security protection is concerned. One reason is that the decision of wives not to work is encouraged in many ways. To begin with, the tax system favors a single wage earner, typically the husband. Financial incentives for non-working, married women to become employed are rather unattractive, given high marginal tax rates. In addition, family members with no or merely minimal incomes are entitled to health insurance on a noncontributory basis, while employed spouses are both subject to the full payment of contributions. Child-rearing periods (up to three years per child) are taken into account in the calculation of pensions, but so far the precondition is that the child-rearing or educating parent—in most cases, the mother—is not working during this period. Finally, the comparatively generous survivor's pensions enable a widow or widower to sustain an accustomed living standard without having worked outside the home or contributed to the system.

With persisting sexism in the family and the labor market, it is not surprising that women's independent claims on social security are, on average, much poorer than those of men. Most elderly women in the former FRG would barely be able to survive on their own old age pensions. At the end of 1998, only 27.4 percent of all female pensioners, compared to 77.2 percent of all male pensioners, in the statutory pension scheme achieved an individual monthly pension of DM 1,200 ($632) or more (VDR, 1999). In retirement, an adequate subsistence level can be achieved, if at all, only by those women who are able to combine their own retirement pensions with widows' pensions to which they are entitled. This derived form of protection, however, has become more fragile as a result of the increase in divorce, separation, and other non-traditional family forms.

The situation in the New Federal States looks somewhat different. Reunification of the two Germanys at the beginning of the 1990s brought together two entirely different conceptions of women's employment. In the late 1980s, the female labor force participation rate in the GDR was more than 80 percent, one of the highest in the world. In contrast to the former FRG, gainful employment of women, even of mothers of small children, was considered a matter of course. Underlying this were a "right to work" or full employment policy as well as a sufficient supply of child-care institutions. Although the GDR also had a gender-segregated job market with "male" and "female" training courses and job specializations, women in the GDR, on average, had a relatively better position in the labor market and were far more frequently employed in leading positions than their counterparts in the FRG.

Particularly in the age group between 20 and 55 years, the labor activity rate (comprising those in employment and all registered unemployed) is still far higher in the former GDR than among West German women. Consequently, the average East German woman has considerably higher pension claims than her counterpart in the West. Nonetheless, as already noted, there are large differences between the average pensions of men and women in the former GDR. Presently, the average independent monthly pension drawn by East German men is about 70 percent greater than that of women.

RESHAPING AND DISMANTLING

The economic, fiscal, and social conditions that we have described have put increased pressures on the German welfare state. As a result, there are serious proposals to restrict social expenses as well as to alter basic elements of the welfare state, including its auspices. Proposals include a restriction of the public welfare system to minimum supply as well as the move toward privatization.

Reshaping and Dismantling Statutory Health Insurance

For some decades now, the cost of the national health system has increased at a higher rate than wages. This has been caused by numerous factors, the most decisive of which are extension of the range of benefits, the costs of medical and technological progress, and changes in both the range of illnesses treated and the age structure of the population. As early as the second half of the 1970s there was talk of a "cost explosion in the health service," and a policy of "cost abatement" was introduced. The professed aim was to restrict the growth of expenses in the health service to the development of contribution payments of the insured, in order to be able to achieve a certain stability of contributions. These efforts, however, achieved little success. Since the end of the 1980s, therefore, stronger measures were taken to curb health expenses, specifically, passage of three reforms entailing considerable benefit cuts in a period of only a few years. The insured now have to contribute more for many services (such as dentures and drugs), while other items (especially some medical drugs) are no longer covered. Significantly, there were no attempts to reduce overcapacities in the ambulatory and inpatient sectors (e.g., an unnecessarily high supply of costly hospital beds in some regions) or to restrict excess quantities and prices of medical supplies, which had got out of control.

Since the first Health Reform Act of 1989 did not succeed in limiting the increase in expenditures as was planned, an additional attempt to control costs was made in 1992. The growth rate of benefits was pegged to the growth of wages. Another innovation was to limit the licensing of medical practitioners, thereby curbing the number of service providers. The number of hospital beds available to insurees was also restricted, while long hospital stays were limited by such measures as encouraging ambulatory operations.

Even this reform did not effect a lasting restriction of rising expenses. A Third Stage of the Health Reform Act, passed in the summer of 1997, centered on market-oriented and competition-boosting elements in the health system. Any increase in contributions by one of the statutory health insurances was tied to a parallel rise in the additional payments by the insured. In an attempt to achieve more efficiency through increased competition, the insured were granted the right to terminate membership with one agency and change to another. In addition, payments for drugs were raised, in some cases by more than 100 percent. Similarly, patients now have to pay more out of their own pockets for dental replacement, massage treatment, and hospitalization. Benefits paid during prolonged sickness as substitutes for earnings have been cut from 80 to 70 percent of prior earnings. Health-promotion measures, introduced in 1989, were short-lived. Cumulatively, these changes show a trend toward reducing the level of governmental health provision to a mere basic provision, with the insured required to pay for the remaining services. By and large, the development moves toward a shifting of financial burdens from employers to employees or the insured and from the well to the sick members of the plans. Thus, the potential for redistribution within the health system is diminished.

The cuts in the health system have also created great financial problems for many providers in the health sector (e.g., sanatoriums and spas, hospitals, medical practices). Many jobs in these facilities are endangered. Ever more doctors are making use of the newly introduced possibility of privately billing their health fund patients. Creeping privatization of the health service is discernible.

Reshaping and Dismantling Statutory Pension Insurance

In 1989, the German Bundestag agreed to a reform of pension insurance, which went into effect at the beginning of 1992 (the 1992 Pension Reform Act). Substantial points of the reform, which was supposed to ensure the long-term viability of pension insurance, included indexing pensions on the basis of net, rather than gross, wages; extending the child-rearing periods that are taken into account for the educating parent's pension from one to three years for children born since 1992; gradually raising the pensionable age, beginning in the year 2001; and significantly reducing education and training periods that count toward pension entitlements. Basic elements of the Statutory Pension Insurance were, however, retained, although some rather radical reform ideas had been discussed, such as a reorientation toward a basic pension system with flat-rate benefits or a change from financing by a pay-as-you-go system to a capital-funded system. As a result of the reform, the increase in pensions was halted. Redistribution within the pension system was reduced, disadvantaging smaller pensions. Whether the official targets of establishing a "fairer" distribution of financial burdens and improving the social protection for non-working mothers were achieved remains debatable. Although this reform was considered to be a long-term solution, it sufficed only for a rather short period. The consequences of German reunification and surging unemployment led to further increases in contribution rates.

In 1996, further cuts in the Pension Law were made at short notice. Once more, for instance, the countable periods of education and training were reduced. Moreover, the process of raising the retirement age for women, unemployed persons, and the long-term insured to 65 years was accelerated; anyone who wants to retire earlier will, in the future, have to accept a reduction of up to 18 percent of his or her pension. Once again changes brought statutory pension insurance closer to private insurance. Hardest hit by these changes are women and others drawing small pensions.

In addition to these cuts, a renewed general pension reform discussion got under way from 1996 onward. Government and opposition commissions presented reform concepts; further demands and contributions to the discussion were submitted by trade unions, employers' organizations, and other social groups. The advocates of a change toward a basic pension system with flat-rate benefits gained in strength but in the last resort were not able to prevail. The new 1998 Pension Reform Law diminishes pension indexation. The burden on pension funds arising from a rising average life expectancy is to be shifted equally onto the pensioners and contributors. This means that in the future, pensions will grow more slowly than net incomes, and in the long run the replacement rate for a retiree with a complete insurance record (45 years) will drop from the present 70 percent of prior earnings to 64 percent. There will be further substantial cuts in the level of disability pensions, which account for about 20 percent of new benefits. The Pension Reform Act passed the Parliament in late 1997; there is no need for the opposition-dominated Bundesrat (Upper House) to agree, as was the case with tax reform.

The Social Democratic Party and the trade unions do not think it necessary to lower pension levels at the present time. They argue that as a result of reductions already adopted, a large number of pensions will sink to the level of social assistance payments. This means that people who have made pension contributions for many years will be no better off in their old age than those who never contributed.

One proposal for reducing financial burdens on the pension system that would not involve benefit cuts is to relieve the system of "extraneous" benefits—that is, obligations connected with reunification, repatriation of former emigrants of German descent, and the financial equalization of family burdens. The total share of these non-contributory benefits amounts to almost a third of entire expenses (Ruland, 1995).

In the long run, a further dismantling of provision for old age security can be foreseen. The problem, often not considered sufficiently, is that the intended cuts in the theoretically achievable level of pensions (after a full working record) will be joined by concrete future losses in pensions due to unemployment and the increase of precarious forms of employment, which are not covered by the social security schemes. The overall level of social security will, in all probability, further be decreased because coverage by the German company pension schemes, the second pillar of old age security, is declining, according to all available empirical evidence. A decade ago, 72 percent of all employees in industry had a claim on a company pension, while the figure has decreased to 65 percent (ptz, 1997). Consequently, many voices call for an expansion of private provision as a fully funded "third pillar" of old age security (e.g., IW, 1997). Such a solution, however, overlooks the fact that income distribution in Germany, as elsewhere, is becoming more unequal, so that a considerable part of the population is not in a position to accumulate additional private savings.

Reshaping and Dismantling Unemployment Insurance

Only well-paid employees with a previous long-term record of regular employment whose unemployment is short-term are likely to be well protected by the Employment Promotion Act. It is the "problem groups" in the labor market that usually fail to be caught by the social security net. Among these are the large numbers of unregistered job seekers, the so-called hidden reserves, who have no claims to benefits. Especially vulnerable are young people after they finish school, apprenticeship, or university education and women joining the labor market after an extended period of child rearing. Similarly unprotected is the large and growing number of employees who are part-timers with low incomes and/or pseudo-self-employed, both of whom are not covered by compulsory unemployment insurance.

Even when they are covered by unemployment insurance, persons who previously worked in lower to medium income brackets may find their benefits insufficient. Families with several children whose sole breadwinner earned an average wage and has become redundant almost invariably fall below subsistence level and are forced to depend on public welfare benefits.

Despite the problems caused by increasing unemployment, expansion of social protection for the unemployed has not been a topic of public discussion in recent years. On the contrary, earnings-replacement benefits went from bad to worse on several occasions in the years since 1982: the terms of entitlement were tightened by expanding the periods of insurance prior to an entitlement to benefits. The payment levels of unemployment benefits and unemployment assistance have been lowered; the so-called bad-weather allowance for outdoor workers has been abolished; it has been made more difficult for the unemployed to refuse work beneath their qualifications; and, last but not least, according to a new regulation, unemployment assistance benefits for long-term unemployment are now lowered annually by 3 percent.

Fiscal considerations or attempts to relieve the strained budgets of the Federal Labor Office and the federal government are among the reasons for these restrictions. So far the restrictions have not led to an appropriate relief of the public budgets, however. Therefore, to a large extent, a redistribution of finances is taking place by means of which the federal government wishes to stabilize its own budget at the cost of the local authorities, who are forced to foot more of the welfare bill. But this is actually only part of the motivation for austerity. The emaciation of social safeguards in unemployment, at the same time, serves as a kind of lever to differentiate the wage system. To the extent that government regards far-reaching deregulation of labor as a precondition for growth and employment, the obvious conclusion seems to be that unemployment must lead to significant cuts in income, even bordering on impoverishment. Social protection is being diminished so that workers will be obliged to accept whatever job is available.

Reshaping and Dismantling Social Assistance

Even the ultimate social safety net has not escaped cuts. Reductions in public welfare include limiting benefit levels and tightening disciplinary measures. The proclaimed intention was to retard the growth of expenses in this area and thus offer financial relief to local authorities that were hard hit by the mounting burden of welfare benefits. It was argued that the cuts had become necessary because of widespread misuse of the benefit system and provision of allowances well above the survival level. It is maintained further that there is no longer a significant difference between incomes of low-wage groups and the level of benefits paid as subsistence aid; that surviving on welfare benefits is easier and more convenient than existing on a working income in the lower segment of the labor market; and that such benefits prevent the unemployed from accepting low-wage work.

Research, however, shows that wages are still more adequate than social assistance (Bäcker and Hanesch, 1998). The present level of social assistance for nearly all family constellations lies significantly below the available income of working people, even when poorly paid groups are considered. Overlapping occurs only when several older children are part of the household or when rent is high and only one member of the household receives a regular income, in short, reasons unrelated to the level of asistance benefits.

In the political as well as scientific discussions, however, these facts are hardly taken into account. Those employees who are relatively safely placed in the labor market are receptive to the idea that unemployment, especially if it is long-term, is the result of personal failure, and consequently cuts in benefits meet with general approval. This pattern of thought is reinforced by the enormous pressure on the labor market to which the opening of Central and East European labor markets and subsequent (legal as well as illegal) entry of newcomers have contributed. Such policy interpretations of unemployment, labor, and wages are of decisive importance for the present discussion of reforming social security programs.

SOME TRENDS AND THEIR EVALUATION

Women as Losers in Employment and Social Provision

Women are losing ground as a result of declining labor market conditions and diminishing social provision. In East Germany, for example, women have suffered much greater unemployment than men in the process of restructuring. In July 1998, the unemployment rate of women in the New States rose above the 20 percent mark (21.8 percent against 13.1 percent for men). Once out of a job, women find that their chances of reemployment are much lower and that their average period of unemployment is almost twice as long as that of men.

Especially women with infants and young children, single mothers, and women beyond 50 years of age have an extremely hard time. In addition, young women are facing greater difficulties in finding company traineeships than their male counterparts. In all branches of the East German economy the share of women in the labor force is declining significantly; in certain branches and areas of activity women are increasingly restricted to the lower rung of work hierarchies or to precarious forms of employment like part-time work. Moreover, there is an obvious tendency to retrain women formerly employed in the professions, trades, technology, or natural sciences for the traditional women's occupations (Engelen-Kefer, 1993).

Many of the changes adopted in recent years suggest that women's position in the labor market and in the social security system will decline still further (Klammer, 1997). Women are especially hard hit by the general trend toward removing from the social security code those regulations that have a redistributive effect and on which women have been particularly dependent.

Income Distribution and Poverty

Income distribution and poverty can be regarded as sure indications of the degree to which a country manages to achieve its targets of social provision. Income distribution in the old FRG had been quite stable over many years (Statistisches Bundesamt, 1994). From the early 1970s to the early 1990s only marginal changes occurred in the relative assets of the individual groups. Transfer payments have, on the whole, provided households in need with appropriate shares in the development of social prosperity in the FRG.

Since the beginning of the 1990s, all calculations support a trend toward increasing inequality in the distribution of net incomes (Hauser and Becker, 1996). This trend becomes particularly apparent in the New Federal States or the former GDR. According to socialist philosophy, it could not be expected otherwise; income distribution at the time of reunification was far more evenly balanced in the GDR than in the FRG. Since then, however, income distribution in the former GDR has rapidly moved closer to that in the FRG.

Regardless of the relative poverty standard chosen (40, 50, or 60 percent of the average net equivalence income), in the former FRG there were a decrease in the rate of poverty during the 1960s and 1970s and a continuous rise since the end of the 1970s that intensified in the 1990s (Table 7.2). In the new Federal States relative poverty rates are lower than in the former FRG: 11.8 percent of the population in the West, compared to 8 percent in the East in 1995 (50 percent standard).

Although relative poverty in the Old Federal States is as high as in the early 1960s, the groups of individuals affected have changed. The population group most vulnerable to poverty 30 years ago, older people, run a below-average risk of being poor today. Neither is the "feminization of poverty" a serious problem in Germany anymore. Although women are indeed overrepresented in several of the groups with a high risk of poverty, men's poverty rates have risen far faster than those of women over the past two decades, so that women's rates are currently only marginally higher than those of men. It is the foreign population, the unemployed, and single parents—who, in fact, in most cases are single mothers—whose risks have risen sharply. The high percentage of children among the poor today has

Table 7.2
Poverty Relative to Income in West and East Germany with Alternating Poverty
Limits (40, 50, and 60 percent of average net equivalent income)*

Year	Former FRG (Old Federal States) Percent			Former GDR (New Federal States) Percent		
	40%	50%	60%	40%	50%	60%
1962/1963	4.1	10.6	20.9			
1969	2.0	7.1	17.1			
1973	1.7	6.5	16.1			
1978	1.8	6.5	16.0			
1983	2.9	7.7	16.9			
1988	3.4	8.8	17.1			
1990	4.2	10.5	18.8	0.8	3.7	10.3
1991	4.2	10.1	19.6	2.3	4.3	10.3
1992	4.1	9.6	20.2	2.2	6.3	10.9
1993	5.3	11.0	21.1	2.8	6.3	10.9
1994	5.0	11.5	22.2	3.4	8.1	13.7
1995	5.6	11.8	21.6	2.6	8.0	13.9
1996	4.4	9.6	18.9	4.0	12.3	22.1
1997	3.6	8.6	17.1	4.5	11.4	19.6

*Impoverished individuals in percentage of the population total. Income standards differ for
the Old and New Federal States. All calculations are based on the old OECD equivalence
scale (1/0; 7/0; 5).

Sources: EVS data bank (until 1988) and SOEP (from 1990)—cf. Hauser (1997).

led to concern over the "infantilization of poverty," with a poverty rate of
14 percent (e.g., Hauser and Hübinger, 1993; Hauser, 1997). Causes of
child poverty are growing instability of marriage and relatively low percentages of working women, which is, in turn, related to the paucity of
child-care facilities. The growing risk of being reduced to poverty through
unemployment has now reached the formerly safe middle class. Especially
within the income segment close to the 60 percent poverty limit—that is,
among those who are rather "precariously well-off"—considerable shifts
can be observed, as current research shows (Hübinger, 1996).

The development of poverty in Germany is reflected by a growing number of welfare recipients. When the public welfare system was introduced
in the early 1960s, it was generally assumed that with the continuing development of prosperity, ever fewer people would have to depend on

Table 7.3
Percent of Populating Receiving Means-Tested Social Assistance[1]

Year	Old Federal States			New Federal States		
	All	Male	Female	All	Male	Female
1963	1.3	0.9	1.7			
1973	2.1	1.0	1.8			
1983	4.0	2.4	3.0			
1991	4.3	4.2	4.5	2.1	2.1	2.1
1997[2]	3.8	3.4	4.1	2.5	2.3	2.6

1. Social assistance, branch subsistence aid, annual total.
2. Data for 1997 are not comparable to those for earlier years. Due to legal changes and changes in the social assistance statistics, asylum seekers are not included in the 1997 data anymore. In addition, data for 1997 relate to the end of the year, not to the average of the whole year.

Source: Federal Office for Statistics, Fachserie 13 Sozialleistungen, Reihe 2 Sozialhilfe, various annual volumes.

means-tested benefits. The opposite was the case, however. Since the beginning of the 1970s, the share of welfare recipients has risen continuously (Table 7.3). In the early 1990s about 5 percent of the population in the former FRG received, if only temporarily, social assistance payments; since then, the official quota has gone down, but due only to legal and statistical changes.[3] Though originally it was mainly women who were dependent on assistance, in the course of time the risks of men and women have become almost equal. In the New Federal States the number of welfare recipients has risen rapidly since reunification. We also have to note that the figures concerning the drawing of welfare benefits only inaccurately reflect the need for social welfare; working on reliable estimates, we can assume that between one-third and one-half of those entitled to welfare benefits never realize their claims, whether deterred by the stigma or from sheer ignorance (Hauser, 1995).

All indigent persons in Germany can, of course, avail themselves of welfare assistance as a minimal security, a safeguard that is generous by international standards. Welfare benefits manage to lift recipients close to the poverty line. However, the steeply rising number of recipients of income-tested social assistance clearly is a result of the dismantling of the different social insurance benefits in Germany. Additionally, it has created difficulties for both the states and the local authorities that carry the main burden for financing the social assistance system. Conceived as an emergency measure for exceptional cases, welfare assistance for a certain part of the population has become a regular line of support.

EUROPEAN INTEGRATION

Despite differences in historical development and the current shape of their social security systems, most European countries at present have to cope with problems similar to those outlined for Germany, that is, high unemployment and changing ways of life, immigration (legal and illegal), and demographic pressures of various sorts. The parallels that can be observed are particularly remarkable when one considers that the European Community agreed to leave social welfare policies, except protection for migrant workers, entirely in the hands of the individual member countries. Although so far no incisive assimilation of national social security systems has been arrived at, we are increasingly able to recognize signs of a de facto approximation. National legislation also has a considerable share in this assimilation (Schulte, 1997).

Thus far, the European Union has exerted upward pressure on Southern European countries with less developed and generous welfare systems and in most cases avoided the danger of "social dumping," in which benefits are harmonized downward. Very strong downward pressures on welfare systems have, however, now been exerted by the "convergence criteria" established for entry into the EMU by the Maastricht Treaty. In order to be eligible to join the EMU, a country must limit its net new borrowing to 3 percent of GDP. The aim to reach this goal has been decisive for recent cuts in social welfare programs in several European countries. Meanwhile, however, many of the responsible players in this game seem to realize that in view of similar problems being faced by all member countries, it is only sensible to search for corresponding solutions in the area of social policies. Some stages of this common endeavor to improve social safeguards on a European level have already been incorporated in the Green Book on the future of social policies (Kommission der Europäischen Gemeinschaften, 1993) and the White Book (Kommission der Europäischen Gemeinschaften, 1994), in passing the medium-term Socio-political Action Programme, the statement of the European Commission on the "Modernization and Improvement of Social Safeguards in the European Union" (Spring 1997), the agreement on minimum standards, and the acceptance of the social protocol into the revised Maastricht (Two) Treaty (Summer 1997). In order to continue this dialogue, international groups of experts have been established recently to deal with certain sociopolitical topics. Nevertheless, while there is ample discussion about a monetary union—and there will be a single currency soon—there is only a weak effort to promote social integration and to come to a sort of "social union," with harmonized rights, or at least minimum rights, in social welfare benefits such as social security, social assistance, and family-related benefits.

NEW GOVERNMENT, NEW HOPE FOR SOCIAL PROTECTION?

During the campaign for the general elections of the autumn of 1998, social policy played a major role. The Social Democratic Party heavily criticized the cuts in social security that had been realized during the period of conservative government and announced its intention to cancel some of the most controversial cuts implemented in 1996. The SDP also promised to stop the Pension Reform Law before its final implementation in 1999. According to public opinion polls, pensions contributed significantly to the final victory of the Social Democrats and the change of government.

After coming to power, the new government of the Social Democratic Party and the Green Party kept their campaign promises by passing a "correction law," increasing sickness pay to its original level and canceling the restrictions in the protection against unlawful dismissal. They also stopped the pension reform before its implementation, mainly the planned cuts in disability pensions and in the general pension level. Within their first year in office they enacted some of their other promises concerning social security reform. For example, an eco-tax was introduced, and its yield is used to lower payroll taxes. The aim is to limit the "additional labor costs" to employers and by that to reduce unemployment. Laws have been passed to extend the coverage of the social security systems to the employees with minor jobs (630 DM/month [$332]) and the so-called dependent self-employed. This attempt to stop employers' endeavors to avoid payroll taxes by splitting jobs and changing their character led to a storm of protest and criticism from both employers as well as employees (who in some cases have to bear a higher tax burden now). The law had to be revised several times but still is a bone of contention. Another proposal that has been criticized heavily by different groups in the society was the secretary of labor's initiative for an obligatory pension agreement in the wage agreements.

Meanwhile, it has become obvious that the change of political power does not mean that welfare state retrenchment will come to an end. The present secretary of the treasury has left no doubt that he will pursue a strict path of budget consolidation to reduce public debt. Savings will have to be realized in all departments, including those responsible for social security.

The ideology of a "third way," as advocated by Chancellor Gerhard Schröder and Britain's Tony Blair, is that the current social security benefits might still be too generous and might produce an inactive attitude on the part of beneficiaries. The view that social welfare expenditures are an obstacle to innovation, growth, and employment has even gained influence among leftist politicians.

In the short term, cuts in social protection are likely to affect the health care and pension systems. At present there are fierce controversies about a comprehensive reform proposal for the health sector presented by the Ministry of Health. The core of the draft bill is a ceiling on the health budget, an attempt to balance revenues and expenditures. The pension system became a political battlefield again when the Ministry of Labor presented central features of a new pension reform proposal, some of which has been enacted and some of which is expected to be enacted after two years of debate. Mainly the government's intention to restrict the indexation of the pensions for two years has been used by the conservative parties, the current opposition, to turn the tables and to take the offensive. Now Conservatives are the ones pointing at cuts in social security and accusing the government of cheating the elderly out of their pension rights.

A LOOK AHEAD

As long as the welfare state is seen as the decisive obstacle to innovation, growth, employment, and strength of the economy, its political and moral foundations will continue to erode. The welfare state needs a considerable volume of money to accomplish the task of reducing social and economic inequality. Therefore, the population at large must be prepared to help carry the burden and to accept the loss in incomes. Those who count themselves among the losers in this game of redistribution will not see any use in taking part in it and will orient themselves increasingly toward private forms of provision that they regard as less costly. Such narrowing of sociopolitical perspectives to short-term, cost-effective calculations threatens the ideal of solidarity or community. Predicting the future of the German welfare state involves an assessment of its overall social and moral advantage to a democratic society. If the welfare state is in crisis, then this is ultimately not an economic and financial crisis but one of political acceptance. The problem that Germans face is serious: the welfare state can administer solidarity but cannot engender it. Solidarity cannot be decreed but must be propagated continuously on the political level if people are to be convinced of its value. In a society pervaded by the need for economy, this proves to be difficult, because in such a society solidarity, which is needed most to overcome division and disintegration, is the first value to be eroded.

NOTES

1. The OECD figures are even lower, but are generally used for reasons of international comparability.

2. In Germany, the term "marginal employment" refers to jobs that yield a maximum monthly payment of DM 630 ($332); sham self-employment is understood to be similar to marginal employment, albeit officially carried out as self-employment and also not subject to social security contributions.

3. For example, asylum seekers were excluded from social assistance.

REFERENCES

Alber, J. (1990). *Der Sozialstaat in der Bundesrepublik*. Frankfurt: Campus.

Bäcker, G. (1992). "The new Germany—a divided society." In P. Welfens, ed., *Economic Aspects of German Unification*. New York: Springer.

———. (1996). "Sozialpolitik zwischen Abbau und Umbau—Reformansätze aus Sicht der Gewerkschaften." In W. L. Schönig and R. Hoest, eds., *Sozialstaat wohin? Umbau, Abbau oder Ausbau der Sozialen Sicherung*. Darmstadt: Wissenschaftliche Buchgesellschaft.

———. (1997). "Der Sozialstaat hat eine Zukunft." *Aus Politik und Zeitgeschichte* 48–49: 12–20.

Bäcker, G., R. Bispinck, K. Hofemann, and G. Naegele. (2000). *Sozialpolitik und soziale Lage in Deutschland*. Wiesbaden: Westdeutscher Verlag.

Bäcker, G., and W. Hanesch. (1998). *Arbeitnehmer und Arbeitnehmerhaushalte mit Niedrigeinkommen*. Landessozialbericht vol. 7. Düsseldorf: Ministerium für Arbeit, Gesundheit und Soziales des Landes Nordrhein-Westfalen.

Breier, B. (1998). "Sozialbudget 1997." *Arbeit und Sozialpolitik* 11–12 (November–December): 44–60.

Bundesministerium für Arbeit und Sozialordnung. (1997) *Übersicht über das Sozialrecht*, 4th ed. Bonn: Author.

DIW (Deutsches Institut für Wirtschaftsforschung). (1996). *DIW-Wochenbericht* 28/1996.

Eckerle, K., M. Schlesinger, and G. Blaha. (1995). *Perspektiven der gesetzlichen Rentenversicherung für Gesamtdeutschland vor dem Hintergrund veränderter politischer und ökonomischer Rahmenbedingungen, Prognos-Gutachten*. Frankfurt a.M.: Verband Deutscher Rentenversicherungsträger.

Engelen-Kefer, U. (1993). "Frauenerwerbstätigkeit im demographischen Wandel." In H-U. Klose, ed., *Altern hat Zukunft*. Opladen: Westdeutscher Verlag.

Esping-Andersen, G. (1990). *The Three Worlds of Welfare Capitalism*. Princeton, NJ: Princeton University Press.

Hauser, R. (1995). "Das empirische Bild der Armut in der Bundesrepublik Deutschland—ein Überblick." *Aus Politik und Zeitgeschichte* (July 28) 31–32: 3–13.

———. (1997). "Armut, Armutsgefährdung und Armutsbekämpfung in der Bundesrepublik Deutschland." *Jahrbücher für Nationalökonomie und Statistik* 216: 524–548. Stuttgart: Lucius & Lucius.

Hauser, R., and I. Becker. (1996). "Zur Entwicklung der personellen Verteilung der Einkommen in West- und Ostdeutschland 1973 bzw. 1990 bis 1994." *Sozialer Fortschritt* 12 (December): 285–293.

Hauser, R., and W. Hübinger. (1993). Arme unter uns: T. I, Ergebnisse und Konsequenzen der Caritas-Armutsuntersuchung. Freiburg: Deutscher Caritas verband.

Hübinger, W. (1996). *Prekärer Wohlstand—Neue Befunde zu Armut und sozialer Ungleichheit*. Freiburg: Lambertus.

Institut für Sozialforschung und Gesellschaftspolitik (ISG). (1993). *Sozialversicherungsfreie Beschäftigung*. Forschungsbericht Nr. 181a des Bundesministeriums für Arbeit und Sozialordnung. Köln/Bonn: Bundesministerium für Arbeit und Sozialordnung.

Institut der Deutschen Wirtschaft (IW). (1997). *Reform des Sozialstaats, Vorschläge, Argumente, Modellrechnungen zur Alterssicherung.* Köln: Institut der Deutschen Wirtschaft.

Klammer, U. (1997). "Wieder einmal auf der Verlierer(innen)seite—Zur arbeitsmarkt- und sozialpolitischen Situation von Frauen im Zeitalter der 'Sparpakete'." *WSI-Mitteilungen* 1 (January): 1–12.

Ködderman, R. (1996). "Sind Löhne und Steuern zu hoch?" *IFO-Schnelldienst* 20 (July): 6–15.

Kommission der Europäischen Gemeinschaften. (1993). *Grünbuch über die europäischen Zozilpolitik Weichenstellung für die Europäische Union* (Green Book). Luxembourg: Author.

———. (1994). *Europäische Sozialpolitik: Ein zukunfsweisender Weg für die Union* (White Book). Luxembourg: Author.

Martens, R. (1997). "Teures Elend. Die fiskalischen Kosten der Arbeitslosigkeit in West- und Ostdeutschland—Ausgaben und Einnahmeausfälle entstehen auf sieben unterschiedlichen Ebenen." *Blätter der Wohlfahrtspflege* 4–5 (April–May): 82–84.

ptz (July 16, 1997). "Betriebsrenten zu unattraktiv." *Frankfurter Rundschau*: 7.

Ruland, F. (1995). "Versicherungsfremde Leistungen in der gesetzlichen Rentenversicherung." *Deutsche Rentenversicherung* 1 (January): 28–38.

Schäfer, C. (1996). "Mit falschen Verteilungs-'Götzen' zu echten Standortproblemen. Zur Entwicklung der Verteilung in 1995 und den Vorjahren." *WSI-Mitteilungen* 10 (October): 597–616.

Schmid, M. (1988). *Sozialpolitik—historische Einführung und internationaler Vergleich.* Opladen: Leske und Budrich.

Schulte, B. (1997). "Europäische Sozialpolitik—Auf dem Weg zur Sozialunion? Die 'soziale Dimension' der Gemeinschaft: Europäischer Sozialstaat oder Koordination nationaler sozialpolitischer Systeme." *Zeitschrift für Sozialreform* 3 (March): 165–186.

Sitte, R. (1997). "Bilanz der Politik für mehr Arbeitsplätze." *WSI-Mitteilungen* 11 (November): 780–789.

Statistisches Bundesamt. (1994). *Verfügbares Einkommen, Zahl der Haushalte und Haushaltsmitgliedernach Haushaltsgruppen—Aktualisierte Ergebnisse der Volkswirtschaftlichen Gesamtrechnungen für die Jahre 1972 bis 1993.* Wiesbaden: Metzler-Poeschel.

———. Series 13, Sozialleistungen, Subseries 2: Sozialhilfe, various annual volumes. Wiesbaden: Metzler-Poeschel.

Sachverständigenrat zur Begutachtung der gesamtwirtschaftlichen Entwicklung (SVR). (1996). Jahresgutachten 1996/97, Bundestagsdrucksache 13/6200. Bonn: Deutscher Bundestag.

Verband Deutscher Rentenversicherungsträger (VDR). (1999). *Statistik Rentenbestand am 31. Dezember 1998.* Frankfurt a.M.: Verband Deutscher Rentenversicherungsträger.

Wagner, G., and K. Rinne. (1996). "Droht ein 'Krieg der Generationen?' Empirische Evidenz zur Zufriedenheit mit der sozialen Sicherung." *Sozialer Fortschritt* 12 (December): 288–295.

Chapter 8

Diminishing Welfare: The Italian Case

Enrica Morlicchio, Enrico Pugliese, and Elena Spinelli

INTRODUCTION: THE ITALIAN WELFARE SYSTEM WITHIN THE MEDITERRANEAN MODEL

The Italian welfare system falls within the Mediterranean model. The countries of Southern Europe—Italy, Greece, Spain, and Portugal—although profoundly different in their levels of economic development, employment structure, and history and traditions, are nevertheless united in some significant social characteristics, particularly the central role of the family in the economy and society and in the welfare system itself. This Mediterranean model of welfare, as Ferrera (1996a) defines it—or what Leibfried (1993) designates as the "Latin rim regime"—is characterized by a high degree of fragmentation, with systems of benefits different for the various sectors of the population and a dualism between "strong" and "weak" beneficiaries, particularly as far as social security is concerned; a traditional predominance of cash subsidies (money transfers) over direct social services; the relatively recent institution of national health services (based on the principle of universal protection and standardization with uniform benefits throughout the country); and, as already mentioned, a central role for the family in compensating for deficiencies of the welfare state or in serving functions assumed by the welfare state in other developed countries. The existence of these attributes has led various authors to see the Italian system as a distinct model rather than an underdeveloped and distorted form of the corporatist-Continental welfare state (Rhodes 1997). In fact, this system and the welfare mix that characterizes it are strictly interwoven with the social and political aspects of the national social context. By paying attention to these aspects, one is better able to understand the retrenchment process as well.

The Italian welfare state system reflects the profound divide between the northern and southern parts of the country, the north characterized by a higher level of economic development and lower level of unemployment, and the South, by a degree of underdevelopment that, even today, is manifested in a rather high level of employment in agriculture, a low level of industrialization, and only a modest presence of women in the labor market.

In the more economically disadvantaged parts of Italy, the social services sector itself is another factor in perpetuating the difference in the quality of life. Indeed, the divide among different regions and territorial areas of Italy is marked not only by the unequal levels of economic development but also by characteristics of the welfare state. This difference in the level of benefits, in the quality of services, and in the quality of life, however, is not the result of diverse welfare systems in the north and the south, since the Italian system has been institutionally whole and largely centralized. The differences between the economic and employment structures in the north and the south correspond to the differences in the social structure of the two areas, to the differing strengths of the working class and its organizations, and, last but not least, to the differing attitudes toward citizenship rights that are apparent in the operation of the welfare system, especially people's access to services.

These same social and economic differences probably make their effects felt in the retrenchment of the welfare state or, in the parlance of official government documents and much of the literature on the subject, "welfare reform." In fact, the reduction of welfare expenditures is also realized through devolution, with an increase in responsibilities and costs for local jurisdictions. Given fewer resources in the south, this has the effect of increasing the internal differences of the country.

Along with the "Mediterranean" characteristics that the Italian welfare system shares with its neighbors are other, specifically national traits. The Italian welfare system has been defined by Massimo Paci (1989), one of the most eminent Italian scholars of the welfare state, as *particolaristico* (particularistic) and *clientelare* (clientelistic). The first attribute corresponds to selectivity in Richard Titmuss' typology of the welfare state,[1] while the second refers to the way in which welfare provision and welfare services are managed in Italy, that is, with informal and arbitrary criteria and the importance of personal relations. Undeniably, a fragmented and selective model has characterized the Italian welfare system since its beginning, while clientelism has always characterized its management.

Another Italian characteristic concerns the social actors in the process of development of the welfare state. According to Ian Gough's (1983) formulation, the welfare state is the vector of two forces: "reforms from above" and "pressures from below." In the most advanced European societies, the industrial working classes were the primary generators of these pressures from below. However, in Italy, particularly during the first 10 years following World War II, farm laborers, that is, the agricultural working class, were among the main social actors, at least as far as social security is concerned (Pugliese, 1983). These chronically unemployed and underemployed workers fought for extensions of social welfare through the improvement of unemployment and sickness benefits, and they pushed for public works programs. This is not to say that the industrial working class had a lesser impact; however, it concentrated on other themes, such as industrial relations, job protection (e.g., against workplace accidents), and the general extension of social policies.

Another social group that has played a large part in the evolution of the Italian welfare system, giving it one of its most problematic characteristics, is the self-employed—small farmers, traders, and artisans. These groups have enjoyed benefits in terms of social security and pensions out of all proportion to their financial contribution. Welfare state expenditures in Italy have substantially favored the self-employed (including some middle-class and upper-middle-class professionals). Wage workers and other employees, particularly from the industrial working class, carry an unequal burden of the total social security bill. This, then, is the perverse redistributive paradox of the Italian welfare state.

As far as the role of the family is concerned, the literature has tended to exaggerate the cultural factors, such as the Italian familist tradition or even "amoral familism," as a characteristic ethos of Italian society, especially of the Mezzogiorno (the south) (Banfield, 1958). Greater attention to structural factors, such as the importance of the agricultural sector and of the rural population in Italian society, would have been more helpful in explaining some attributes of the Italian welfare system. In a country that as late as the 1950s still had a much larger agricultural than industrial workforce (9 million in agriculture compared to 3 million in industry), it would not have been surprising to find a persistent central role for the family in the society and in the economy.

On the other hand, this persistence was also connected to the general underdevelopment and limits of the welfare system that—and this is peculiar to the Italian system—instead of concentrating on providing direct social services provided cash benefits. This, in turn, continues the dependence on the family and the burden on women. As sociologist Chiara Saraceno has recently said, "in our country, to take away the risks of the market and to fulfill a series of needs is still a job for the family, and, when someone is ill, for women in particular" (1998, p. 9).

The Mediterranean character of the Italian welfare system is also more evident in the south, where money transfers for pensions and other cash benefits are relatively more important and where the development of social services has always lagged behind that of the rest of the country. Health care (hospitals and other medical facilities) as well as child-care services and assistance for the aged are still of very poor quality in these regions. In past years pensions and other forms of cash subsidies in southern Italy also compensated for the insufficiency of the social services and for the poverty of market income related to the poor economic and employment conditions in that region. Welfare expenditures for social security and other cash welfare benefits are managed in a rather benevolent way (i.e., in a non-selective way and with relatively little control) to compensate for the failure of economic policies to increase productive employment.

This "benevolent" management of state expenditures in the area of social security is now being seriously criticized, and welfare expenditures are subjected to greater control. Not only are there cuts in pensions and social security benefits, but welfare benefits are also diminishing in other areas, particularly in the health care system. Finally, workers' contributions to their pensions are increasing, while benefits decrease. The Italian welfare state is now being "reformed" or restructured, also, through more effective management, for example, "targeting" benefits to specific groups, some of which were traditionally excluded from coverage.

DEMOGRAPHIC TRENDS AND CHANGES IN THE FAMILY STRUCTURE

In order to understand the process of reform and diminishing welfare in the general framework of Italian society, it is important to give a brief description of recent trends in the demographic and economic structure of the country. The size of the Italian population has changed very modestly in the last two decades. In fact, in the 1980s the population growth of 200,000 persons was one of the lowest in the history of the country. The situation was less static in the 1990s, when the population rose from 56.7 million in 1990 to 57.3 million in 1997, an increase of 900,000. However, these moderate aggregate figures conceal very complex changes in the demographic structure and population flows.

The demographic trends have to be analyzed in terms of natural and social movements of the population, that is, birthrates and death rates as well as migration. While the latter has increased sizably in the last two decades, the natural increase has been very low. In recent years Italy has had one of the lowest birthrates in the world, even experiencing a negative population growth. At present the natural demographic growth is less than zero (−0.4 per 1,000).

The population growth of the 1990s is basically the effect of immigration of foreign citizens or of former Italian emigrants to their native country. In less than 20 years the structure of the Italian population and the factors affecting it have changed dramatically. In the 1970s the country still had high rates of population growth, owing to high birthrates (and low death rates) and very low or negative net immigration. Immigration is quite a recent phenomenon; indeed, it is a well-known fact that up until relatively recently Italy has been a country of emigration. From the second half of the 1970s there has been a modest, but continual, influx of immigrants coming mainly from Third World countries. Among these people there is a modest, but increasing, presence of refugees (or people applying for the status of refugee). Immigrants enter the Italian labor market immediately, but most of them, even if legally resident, have informal or irregular jobs.

Most immigrants are workers. Spouses, minors, and other family members still constitute a rather small proportion of immigrants. Given the composition of this immigration, its consequences for the welfare system are still limited. There are not many welfare beneficiaries among the immigrants, largely because of their demographic characteristics. The situation will change very soon since there are both immigrants and mixed-marriage couples who are having children, but this phenomenon is still at a rather early stage. Foreign nationals with a resident permit (and thus, at least theoretically, with access to the benefits of the welfare state) are still only around 2 percent of the total population, a level much lower than the European average, particularly of that in France and Germany.

Italy, like other Mediterranean countries, exhibits an interesting paradox in the relationship between its demography and its labor force participation. The paradox is the coexistence of a low fertility rate, a low rate of labor force participation on the part of women, and high unemployment rates. Although women have fewer children than they used to, they still do not have a strong presence in the labor market. Even so, a large proportion of those women who are in the labor market are unemployed.

Italy's current very low birthrate contributes to the growing proportion of elderly people in its population. The reduction in the birthrate has occurred rather recently, but its effect on the demographic structure is already clear. Between 1980 and 1992, the percentage of the population over 65 grew from 13.2 percent to 15.5 percent. Italy is the only country in the European Union in which the number of older people (over 65) is larger than the number under 20.

It should be added that these demographic characteristics are not homogeneous throughout the country. The average birthrate of 9.2 per 1,000 is the outcome of the combined rates of the north, which has a rate much lower than the European average, and of the south, which has a relatively high rate.

Another Italian demographic characteristic that has attracted the interest of many scholars is the *famiglia lunga* (long-lasting family). This term refers to the fact that in Italy children live at home with their parents for a much longer period of time than in other industrialized countries. As has been shown from the national census and also from other surveys carried out by the National Statistical Institute (ISTAT) in 1996, 58.5 percent of young people between the ages of 18 and 34 were still living with their families. The percentage increased in the course of the 1990s (in 1990 it was 51.8 percent) and is much above the European average. The phenomenon of this "long-lasting family" is linked to the prevalence of youth unemployment and to the related one of late marriages. However, these two reasons are not sufficient to explain why young people stay so long with their families. Indeed, in the northern regions a large proportion of the young have regular work and yet keep on living with their parents. The high average age of marriage, however, does not mean that young people are obliged to live with their parents—they could easily live alone or in couples as the majority of Europeans do.

An alternative explanation advanced by Bettio and Villa is that "the conflicting requirements that the family should act as the primary welfare unit throughout the process of economic development, while at the same time progressively granting independence to its members, have produced a model of independence within rather than away from the family" (1995, p. 8). In other words, children are staying with their families because the social control exerted upon them by the family has diminished greatly. In the past, social emancipation from family control was achieved only through economic independence: children had to become economically independent in order to leave their families and to be independent in their behavior.

One of the paradoxes of Italian families is that they are becoming both "longer" and "slimmer." Italy, indeed, has one of the lowest fecundity rates in the world. Couples nowadays often defer having children until later in life, and this is an explanation for the high and increasing number of single-child families. In 1988 two children per family was the most common (42.9 percent), although not the majority. Now the modal family (43.2 percent) has only one child. The number of childless couples has also increased in recent years.

For the majority of Italian families the cost of raising children is particularly high. The public services for infants (kindergartens) have developed very slowly, especially in the south. Private kindergartens are expensive and poor in quality (or at least the service is not equal to the cost). Thus, families who do not have the assistance of relatives are constrained to pay someone to look after their children while they are at work.

Obviously, the burdens on employed women grow in the case of single motherhood. In Italy, single-parent families grew from 5.5 percent to 6.4 percent in the 1980s, and, as in other countries, the single parent is almost always a woman (82.4 percent). On the other hand, single parenthood, even though it is becoming more frequent, still lags behind rates in other countries. Furthermore, according to the last ISTAT Multiscope Survey (1996), which took into account the marital status of single mothers, widows represent the largest group among them. In 1991, widows accounted for 68.6 percent of single mothers (72.9 percent in the south). The remainder are largely divorced or separated, with very few never married. Although there are few single mothers in Italy, their rates are gradually rising. Single motherhood, though uncommon, is relevant because of its welfare implications. As a recent study (Zanatta, 1996) based on data from the ISTAT multiscope study has shown, families supported by women are only somewhat more likely to be poor than other types of families with dependent children. In fact, 9.7 percent of single-mother families are poor, compared to 8.5 percent of families with both spouses present and 6.3 percent of single fathers. Zanatta concludes that "it is not therefore the condition of single parenthood per se which increases the risk of poverty but rather that of the single parent woman" (p. 73), indeed, as elsewhere. The condition of single mothers is aggravated by the difficulties that adult women have in reentering the labor market, difficulties which are, in turn, related to their increased family responsibilities and the "patriarchal" character of the Italian labor market.

These demographic characteristics are closely interwoven with the structure of the labor market and the Italian welfare state. The drastic reduction of the fertility rate in the last two decades, that is, in the period following the great process of urbanization of the Italian population, is certainly related not only to the factors already cited but also to the lack of welfare services for mothers and children. This lack of services helps to keep mothers out (or at the margins) of the labor market and to explain their low rate of participation. But this is only a part of the story. In order to understand these and other welfare-related issues better, one needs an overview of the Italian labor market.

EMPLOYMENT, UNEMPLOYMENT, AND POVERTY

One of the characteristics of the Italian economic system has been its incapacity to achieve a sufficient level of employment. In Italy for many decades there have been both a low rate of participation in the labor market and a high rate of unemployment. As a consequence, the percentage of the population actually at work has always been very low, lower than the European average.

In 1998, Italy, with 57 million inhabitants, had 20 million employed people and more than 3 million unemployed. The so-called active population, or people present in the labor market (both employed and unemployed), amounted to 22.7 million (with a participation rate of 40 percent). The "employment rate," the percentage of employed people in the entire population, was 35 percent. Except for Spain, this was the lowest rate in Europe.

The unemployment rate in Italy is only slightly above the European level.

But the average national level of 12 percent is an aggregate measure of two radically opposite situations: the south, where the rates are regularly more than 20 percent, even reaching 25 percent in some urban areas, and the north, where the unemployment rates are much lower than the European average, at times almost reaching full employment. The internal differences within Italy can clearly be seen from the evidence of some labor market indicators. In the north and central regions the "employment rate" stood at 40 percent, whereas in the south it was just below 28 percent.

With regard to differences in gender, the most significant fact is the low participation of women in the labor market, and the situation is particularly grave in the south, where the rates of female unemployment are higher. Among the various forms of discrimination against women in the Italian labor market, two are fundamental: the power of tradition, which pushes them out of the labor market, and, more recently, first appearing in the beginning of the 1980s, the problem of unemployment itself.

The story of the entry of women into the Italian labor market is particularly interesting. In the period of Italy's intense industrialization (which began in the 1950s), the number of housewives rose owing to a very large decline in the number of women working in agriculture. In the early 1970s, this process reached its climax. Afterward the number of employed and unemployed females rose.

At the base of this apparent paradox are social and cultural factors—especially the great advances in female emancipation linked to the policy of mass schooling. Since the second half of the 1970s, young women, after finishing their studies or at least after leaving school, entered the job market and stayed there in spite of serious discouragement. Part of this first wave of women workers found jobs in the new and expanding public service sector; another part, although they failed to find jobs, remained in the labor market but were unemployed. The story of the relationship between women and the Italian job market in the last 50 years is exemplified by a typical family (and there are millions of examples like this): the grandmother was a peasant worker, the mother is a housewife, and the daughter is educated and working or, if she lives in the south, probably in search of a first job (Siebert, 1991).

In the distribution of the active population and of the people employed in different economic sectors, one can find significant differences between the north and the south. The southern part of the country has traditionally been less industrialized. However, the main changes that took place during the last half century in the country as a whole consisted of a continual reduction in the numbers of people employed in the agricultural sector and a concurrent increase in the number employed in the service sector. In industry the period of expansion lasted until the first half of the 1970s, while the period of contraction and downsizing has been occurring since the 1980s.

The number of people employed in industry in Italy in 1980 numbered 7.7 million, compared to 6.5 million in 1995. In this 15-year period more than 1.2 million industrial jobs were lost. These data are even more startling if we consider just the situation of the blue-collar workers. The number of places available to blue-collar workers was reduced from 5.4 million to 3.9 million (in other words, a loss of over 20 percent).

The deindustrialization and downsizing that have taken place in Italy, as in the rest of Europe, have not reduced the industrial output. In fact, in the same period, the reduction of the numbers employed in industry has been concurrent with an increase in the added value of industrial output and in productivity. Productivity increased by 60 percent between 1980 and 1990 at the same time that employment in industry declined by more than 20 percent. Thus, a decreasing number of people are producing a growing quantity of goods and wealth in the industrial sector. This means, among other things, that the number of workers who contribute payments to the social security system is declining. If we consider, then, that the Italian welfare system has always been based on the mechanism of contribution, the implications of this unemployment are grave.

It is understandable in these circumstances that the trade unions have lost strength. As early as the 1960s, the agricultural trade unions had obtained significant improvements for hand laborers and similar categories of workers structurally hit by unemployment, and a benefits system that covered unemployment. With industrialization and the reduced importance of the agricultural sector in the 1950s, the agricultural trade unions lost their relevance, and the industrial unions consolidated their position, a process that reached its apex in the late 1960s and the early 1970s. In these very years some of the most important innovations in the Italian welfare system were realized, particularly the national health system.

The Italian union structure is based on three main organizations: the Confederazione Generale Italiana del Lavoro (CGIL), the Confederazione Italiana Sindacati Lavoratori (CISL), and the Unione Italiana del Lavoro (UIL), each of which is subdivided into specific industrial branches. There are also other unions, but these are the major ones. There has also always been a certain degree of coordination among the major unions. A traditional attribute of the major Italian trade unions was that they represented the interests of both workers and non-workers. In other words, they were not strictly corporatist (Regini, 1980). These characteristics allowed the Italian trade unions to maintain a representative capacity and political strength, even when, from the 1980s onward, their membership was reduced because of the decline in the number of people working in industry. In these years the unions attempted to move from a more strictly militant stance to a new neocorporatist one that involved a trade-off between low wage increases and guaranteed levels of employment and welfare provision. The objective of guaranteeing a level of employment was never reached;

nevertheless, there was a series of union agreements that attempted to reduce mass layoffs.

Notwithstanding the basic principle of solidarity, the system of industrial relations has always had at its core the defense of the positions of workers who were already employed in steady jobs. Layoffs during a period of normal economic activity have always been difficult—and companies are finding it ever more difficult, especially after the introduction of the main laws concerning industrial relations: Statuto dei lavoratori (Workers' Charter) of 1970. This high degree of protection of those who are already employed—also an expression of the patriarchal character of the Italian system of industrial relations—helps to explain the character of Italian unemployment (Mingione, 1991; Pugliese, 1993). The patriarchal character is related to the fact that men predominate in the labor force and are the most protected workers. The unemployed, then, are mainly those who have not entered employment: largely young people (especially in the south) and women (particularly young women). These people are structurally disadvantaged in the job market and have never enjoyed the right to claim unemployment benefits because this type of benefit has historically been limited to those unemployed who have previously been employed at some time. However, in Italy the insider-outsider pattern (Ichino, 1997)—with the existence of two distinct sectors of workers in the labor market, one highly protected and the other very poorly protected—has worked in a particularly dramatic way in the past. The contradiction has recently been reduced only because of a cutback in the protective system for the insiders. In Italy, the outsiders—those people who are more disadvantaged in the job market—not only fail to enjoy a system of economic protection against unemployment, but they also lack other forms of assistance and protection, for instance, a guaranteed minimum wage or a minimum revenue of insertion (RMI) such as in France.[2]

Strictly linked to this situation is another distinctive attribute of the Italian system of industrial relations, namely, high membership in retired worker unions (whose relevance in the labor movement is becoming greater and greater). This sector of the unions, quite understandably, actively resists welfare state reductions.

To conclude this part of the discussion, one can say that in the last few years there has been a substantial reduction in the power of the trade unions as a consequence of the reduction of the number of industrial workers. There have also been a growth in the numbers of pensioners and a reduction in the ranks of industrial workers. Finally, there has been a modification in the unions' strategy in the direction of neocorporatism.

The same dualism observed in the labor market can also be observed in the spatial distribution of poverty. According to the last Commission on Poverty and Social Exclusion Report (Commissione di indagine sulla povertá . . . , 1999), 11 percent of the families (2.5 million) and 13 percent of the total population (7.5 million people) of Italy live below the poverty level (below 50 percent of the median disposable income adjusted for family size). Poverty is concentrated in the south: 33 percent of the Italian families and 65 percent of the poor Italian families live in these regions. The process of spatial concentration of poverty has been increasing in the last decades. In 1980, the percentage of families in poverty was 16 percent in the south and 4.5 percent in the north. In 1998, the figures were, respectively, 24.5 percent and 6.6 percent.

Not only are there many more poor in the south, but they are also comparatively poorer: the average deviation from the poverty line for poor families in the south is 24 percent, while it is only 19 percent for poor families in the north. Finally, the north–south differences concern not only the concentration and the gravity of poverty but also its characteristics and the subjects who are affected by higher risks of poverty. In the north poverty affects mainly people who live in a situation of social isolation and lack of primary social networks or people who experience dramatic events in their lives (imprisonment, mental illness, drug addiction, etc.). These categories are also present in the south, together with aged people living alone and single mothers with little external support, but their incidence is lower. The risks of becoming impoverished in Italy are largely related to labor market problems and, in particular, to unemployment. Large, regular families with many unemployed members (families *with* unemployed members) or with an unemployed family head (families *of* the unemployed) are much more frequent among the families living below the poverty line in the south.

THE DEVELOPMENT OF THE ITALIAN WELFARE STATE: PROTAGONISTS, INTERESTS, BENEFICIARIES

The development of a modern welfare state in Italy has been rather recent. The reasons for delay are both political and economic, including the occupational structure of the country (Pugliese and Rebeggiani, 1997). As noted, in the 1950s agriculture still had a very important role in the Italian economy. Peasants and other agricultural workers were the largest part of the active population, while the size of the industrial working class was still relatively modest.[3] This delay was in part a result of fascism's policy of impeding the process of economic development. The role of fascism in slowing down the development of the Italian welfare state was both direct (reducing social policies) and indirect (conservative economic policies); that is, fascism effected retrenchment in the early process of welfare state development that had started in the previous decades.

After the constitution of the unified Italian state in the second half of the nineteenth century (the creation of a united Italy and the enlargement of the state to cover the entire peninsula), the birth and growth of the first socialist and cooperative movements brought with them the creation of *Società di mutuo soccorso* (mutual aid societies). The state's attitude toward these initiatives was neither benevolent nor particularly repressive, nor was it competitive with them, as in the case of Bismarck's Germany. The state's view was, if anything, distrustful but indifferent toward these organizations, probably because there was no state intervention in social policy. The management of the "social question" and the problems of poverty were wholly given over to private charity and to the church (Bartocci, 1999).

A significant intervention came about in the period immediately preceding World War I, when a series of progressive initiatives in the field of social policy was introduced by the government. In this period of intensive capitalist development (the *Periodo giolittiano*, after the name of the prime minister who was in office for the longest time during these years), the country passed its first significant social legislation (Bartocci, 1999). Also in the same period the push to modernize production methods and expand industrial and agricultural capitalism reached its peak, especially in the north. One of the results of this was the formation of a large industrial and agricultural working class. In this period, too, state intervention was not Bismarckian, as there was no competition between the government and major working-class organizations: the Socialist Party, the union Confederazione Generale del Lavoro (CGDL), the socialist cooperatives, Catholic labor organizations, and cooperatives (the "white leagues"). In fact, the contrary is true: the government tended to acknowledge the demands for the introduction of social legislation, particularly with regard to social security and benefits for injured workers. These early forms of intervention, though of course still embryonic, were won by the workers' aristocracy of the country through their representatives in Parliament and the unions. But remaining outside the powers of this legislation were the large mass of peasants and casual workers, especially from the south.

Italy's embryonic welfare state accelerated rapidly in the period just after World War I, a time of enormous social tension known as the *biennio rosso* (the red two years), but ceased to develop with the advent of fascism. Between 1922 and the end of World War II (when fascism fell, and the Italian Republic was established in 1946), there was a clear retrenchment in social policy initiatives. Indeed, there were not only a cessation of positive initiatives but also a radical change in the welfare system that included the introduction of some elements that became typical of the Italian welfare state: the extreme variety in and fragmentary character of its social interventions and its strong corporatist character, all stemming from fascist ideology. The new organizational structures (*corporazioni*) that replaced the trade unions united employers and employees (capitalists and workers) in the industrial sector. Fascism, after a first phase of pure repression and destruction of mutual aid societies and cooperative organizations (socialist, Catholic, and democratic) assumed direct management of social policy and social security, strengthening some welfare institutions that were born in the previous decades or even encouraging new ones. But these institutions (which became objects of large-scale propaganda and rhetoric) presided over a drastic reduction in the effectiveness of the social policies that had been launched in the preceding period.

Because of all this, Italy, in comparison to many other European countries, was much slower in creating a modern welfare system. The principles that underpin the modern Italian welfare state are in the Republican Constitution of 1946, born out of the defeat of fascism and the victory of the Resistance. The dialectic between universalism and the particularist/meritocratic principles that would accompany the subsequent development of the Italian welfare system was already apparent in the Constitution and in the deliberations of the Assemblea Costituente (the first democratically elected Italian Parliament after the war and the first Parliament elected on the basis of universal suffrage for men and women). The effective shaping and consolidation of the modern Italian welfare system took place between the 1950s and the 1970s. In this period, it became clear that the Italian system had inherited certain characteristics from the past (including the fascist period), namely, its particularism and the fragmentary nature of its interventions, but it had also progressively assumed universalist elements, especially in new areas of state intervention such as health care (Ferrera, 1984).

The Assemblea Costituente experts compared the merits of a universalist approach (which saw the citizens as the base of the welfare system) and the more meritocratic/worker-based approach (which saw the workers and their paid contributions as the base). This second line won, especially regarding matters of social security, because, generally, the workers' movements favored it and threw their weight behind it. In the tradition of the Italian workers' movement, the basic principle was not "welfare for the citizens" but "welfare for the workers." According to this view, the needy citizens, the poor, would have recourse only to social assistance. In Italy, inside the workers' movements and within the parties of the Left, the difference between *previdenza* (social insurance) and *assistenza* (social or public assistance) was also emphasized. Social security benefits were seen as rights of the workers whose contributions pay for them and should come in various forms from invalidity pensions to old age pensions and unemployment benefits. Welfare assistance, on the other hand, was intended— and is today—as a set of measures destined for needy people who are unable to work. The beneficiaries of the Italian welfare state, hence, were not citizens as such but workers. Therefore, the Italian welfare system has been defined as *lavorista* (workerist). Italians received the most important benefits as workers, ex-workers, or unemployed workers. Needy citizens without such status as workers would, instead, receive social assistance. It is not by chance that Article 38 of the 1946 Constitution singled out two distinct areas of intervention, dealing with both citizens and workers. "Citizens unable to work and lacking the necessary means to live" would be guaranteed "the right to maintenance and social assistance." This was different from the rights of workers who, "in case of accident, illness, invalidity, old-age, and involuntary unemployment" must be guaranteed "adequate means to meet their life requirements."[4]

In fact, the two functions *assistenza* and *previdenza* highlighted in the debates in the Constituent Assembly and present in the text of the Constitution have been intertwined ever since. A recurring leitmotif of the Italian trade unions' criticism of the management of the Italian welfare system has been the confusion between these two functions. In other words, the unions have always resented that assistance for the needy citizen has been realized at the expense, in a literal sense, of the workers who have contributed to the social security budget. This criticism is largely correct.

The particularistic *lavorista* ideology of the Italian welfare system tended in principle to exclude from social protection needy citizens who were not (and had not been) part of the labor force (and therefore had not contributed to their social insurance and other welfare benefits). In fact, direct expenditure for social assistance, in particular, for relief, was substantially reduced in relative terms in the period from the end of the war to the beginning of the 1990s. On the other hand, the necessity of giving economic assistance to those who had been excluded from employment and had not been able to contribute to the social security system resulted in inappropriate use of the social security budget. The poor, particularly in the south, did not receive direct social assistance but were instead given it in forms intended for workers, as pensions, invalidity subsidies, and even health care. In other words, they were assisted not as being poor but, in a disguised way, as workers (Boccella, 1982; Pugliese and Saraceno, 1989).

This system of disguised assistance in the form of social insurance and related benefits was made possible by a peculiar balance between contributions and benefits. The paradox of the Italian particularist welfare system in the last decades was that, on the one hand, the benefits were justified on the basis of contributions, but, on the other hand, there was a great disparity in the size of contributions. Some groups, such as the industrial working class and employees in general, have always contributed in a very substantial way, while others (mainly the self-employed artisans, shopkeepers, and peasants) have always contributed minimally.

This difference between the size of contributions and benefits illustrates the privileged position of the self-employed in the Italian welfare system. As Giacinto Militello, a former CGIL union executive and chairman for some years of Istituto Nazionale della Previdenza Sociale (INPS) remembers:

[T]he extension of the right to receive a pension to the self-employed (1957 to the farmers, 1959 to the artisans, and in 1966 to traders) took place under the heading of an objective contradiction. . . . There prevailed a clear line of intervention with low rates of benefits in relation to the very small contributions, almost symbolic. This created a deficit which would later on damage the whole image of the public social security system. (1989, p. 11)

Apart from the image, the increasing welfare expenditures for pensions and other benefits (in particular, health care and subsidies for disabled workers), in no way balanced by corresponding contributions, created serious financial problems for the Italian welfare system.

On the other hand, this system was useful to the ruling political parties, in particular, the Democrazia Cristiana (DC), which used this welfare policy to gain wider support. This also explains why the Christian Democratic Party's hegemony lasted for so long in these particular sectors of the population. The middle classes (small professionals, the medium echelon, and, above all, self-employed people) benefited most from this system and were central in the consensus mechanisms. This biased management of welfare expenditures has been one of the strongest points characterizing the Italian social and political process from the 1950s to the 1970s, as some scholars have very clearly pointed out (Pizzorno, 1974). In the fragmented Italian welfare system, there are, besides the self-employed, some categories of employees who have received better welfare payments, namely, agricultural workers and others who are structurally underemployed and are concentrated in the poorest areas of the country. Here pensions and other social security benefits have compensated for the lack of employment and income.

To summarize the argument so far, one can say that the strategic role of pensions and other kinds of subsidies and the fragmentation of intervention characterized the Italian welfare state in the period of its development and consolidation between the 1950s and the 1970s. An expression of the same phenomenon is the fact that the Italian welfare state has favored cash benefits over social services to such a great extent. Indeed, Italy is among the countries in Europe with the smallest percentage of social expenditures for services (OECD, 1999). Finally, the uncontested priority in social provision has traditionally been given to the elderly for old age pensions, with a consequent neglect of the young, especially youth looking for their first jobs. In 1993, Italy spent 2.7 times as much on transfers to the elderly as it did on benefits for the non-elderly, the highest in Organisation for Economic Co-operation and Development (OECD) European countries.

Employment policies as well as active labor market policies are an interesting area of the Italian welfare state, particularly in view of the low rate of employment of the population. In the first decades after the war the Italian welfare system was structured to provide employment opportunities instead of a system of unemployment benefits. At the beginning—before the years of great economic expansion in the late 1950s and in the 1960s—there was large-scale intervention in the field of public works aimed at reducing unemployment, particularly in the south. This specific employment policy was terminated in the late 1950s, when demographic pressure and the oversupply of labor in the poorest area of the country were reduced by internal migration toward the more developed industrial areas and by emigration abroad.

Unemployment subsidies, along with old age and disability pensions, have been very important in the Italian welfare state. But, as noted, unemployment benefits have never been granted on the basis of universalistic principles. Different categories of workers have benefited from specific unemployment schemes, while those who now constitute the core of the Italian unemployed do not have any form of assistance. Unemployment insurance in Italy, in fact, covers only those workers who have previous work experience and excludes those who are in search of a first job, in short, the majority of the unemployed. Unemployment insurance was developed in the first decade after World War II to cover structural unemployment, a phenomenon affecting mainly agricultural and construction workers, who were, at that time, a very large section of the working class. Other categories of the unemployed received only a symbolic subsidy, which, until the mid-1980s, amounted to 800 lire (60 cents) a day. More recently, after the industrial crisis related to the first oil shock in 1973, other specific schemes for industrial workers in temporary layoff (Cassa Integrazione Guadagani) have been devised.[5] But never in Italy has a general system of unemployment insurance or subsidies existed.

While in the field of active and passive labor policies the degree of fragmentation (and consequently of particularism) has been very high, other areas of the Italian welfare system are characterized by a much higher degree of universalism. Indeed, Maurizio Ferrera (1984), in analyzing the evolution of the Italian welfare state, speaks of a "long march towards universalism." In the development of the Italian welfare state, the social security system and the health system represent two opposite poles, based on different models and different criteria. The former is selective or particularistic, and the latter is based on universal principles.

With the act introducing the general national health system in 1978, medical assistance was extended to all categories of citizens regardless of their occupations and previous forms of benefits. Before then, the Italian health care system was much poorer and fragmented into a series of *mutue* (mutual funds), each one covering specific categories of workers and autonomously managing their funds. In addition, free medical care (to non-insured people) was provided on the basis of residual principles, that is, only to those who were able to prove that they were poor. The reform of the national health system was the most innovative moment in the development of the Italian welfare state. The systems of health care for the various categories of workers were unified, and the coverage was expanded. Not only were the amount and type of health services provided extended, but also the number of recipients increased. Practically all citizens became eligible for medical assistance, and health care became free and available throughout the country. However, the health system has never been able to meet the increasing demand for services. The tardy creation of the Servizio Sanitario Nazionale (National Health Service) accounts for its incomplete implementation. Health care facilities (hospitals, diagnostic centers) are still insufficient, particularly in the south. In fact, the structures and the quality of services offered remain rather poor. The dualism in the Italian economy and in the Italian welfare state between north and south is particularly evident in this area. The universal right to medical care and health assistance—acknowledged in principle—does not correspond to an equal availability of services. This accounts also for the complexity of the restructuring process that the National Health System is undergoing now.

A very problematic area—very little developed within the Italian welfare system—is services such as child care, assistance to the aged, assistance to the mother, and related services. These services did not grow even in the period of welfare state expansion, and this is a clear expression of the burdens that the deficiencies of the welfare system continue to impose on families, particularly women. Now some recent forms of support to needy families with dependent children provide only cash subsidies instead of services and are limited in duration.

The last area of social provision to discuss is the educational system. Since the creation of the Italian state, education has been public, free, and non-religious. The existence of private schools has always been allowed, but the Republican Constitution of 1946 states that "private schools are allowed under the conditions of not implying economic burdens for the state." Although the situation may change because of the trends toward privatization, private schools in the past have always played a very limited role in the Italian educational system. Particularly at the secondary level some exclusive Catholic schools are very well known, but their elite social status does not imply a correspondingly high academic status.

State intervention in the educational system in Italy had a great boost in the 1960s. The school reform of 1961 made education compulsory until the eighth grade (or the age of 14). This reform instituted the *scuola media unificata* (universal junior high school system), which allowed access to the educational system for youngsters living in small villages and in the poorest areas of the country. In this way the class composition of the student population has changed, with a larger proportion of students from working-class backgrounds. Soon after, in the late 1960s, access to the higher level of the secondary school (senior high school) also increased.

This increased access to education represents one of the most important, progressive social changes in Italian society. The process of educational reform was completed in the late 1970s with universal public education at the secondary level and greater access to higher education. No further improvement or reform took place in the 1980s. Finally, in the late 1990s a general reform of the senior high school took place, aimed at giving it a more universal character.

Another important issue on the agenda now is state financing of private schools. It should be mentioned that the pressures to increase funding for private schools—namely, to Catholic schools—are very heavy now and are motivated by equal opportunity principles, while in fact they are also and above all an aspect of the general trend toward privatization of social services. But this leads us to the question of "welfare reform" and retrenchment of the Italian welfare state.

TRENDS IN THE LEVEL AND COMPOSITION OF SOCIAL WELFARE EXPENDITURES

The evolution of the various areas of state intervention can be better understood by analyzing the level and composition of welfare expenditures. The figures that we present are not sufficient to show the complexity of the situation and the most recent trends, but they can give an idea of some characteristics of the Italian welfare system. In addition, figures of this kind are not always comparable because sometimes they are based on different categories of aggregation.[6]

Soon after the 1996 national elections, the new government (Center-Left) nominated a commission to analyze the country's social expenditures and to make a proposal for welfare reform: Commissione per l'analisi delle compatibilità macro-economiche della spesa sociale (Commission for the Analysis of Macroeconomic Compatibilities of Public Expenditures). The work of the commission was not followed by a significant political initiative based on its results. But its proceedings are useful for the analysis of public expenditures. Most of the information available in the final report is based on Eurostat data for the year 1994 and is presented comparatively. According to these data, Italy's social expenditures, both per capita and as a share of gross domestic product (GDP), are at the European average, between those of the developed industrial countries of northern European and the Mediterranean countries. The share of GDP for social expenditures was 25.3 percent, which was slightly below the European Union average of 26.1 percent (Ferrera, 1996b, p 2).

According to Eurostat data, pensions and related benefits in Italy absorbed more than 70 percent of total expenditures (61.5 percent for old age and survivors, 8.7 percent for disability) in 1994. In the same year in Europe these categories absorbed less than 50 percent (42.4 percent for old age and survivors and 8 percent for disability). Health and sickness absorbed only 20.5 percent of Italian social expenditures versus a European average of 26.4 percent.

The amount of total social expenditures dedicated to health care in Italy has always been below the European average. This contrasts with the common view prevailing in Italy that health expenditures are too high. Nonetheless, a recent report issued by ISTAT (1997) points out that in 1980 resources devoted to the "health function" as percentage of the GDP were lower than those devoted to the same function in France, Germany, Holland, and Denmark, and higher only than in Greece and Portugal. In the 1980s, the gap between the Italian position and the European average was narrowed, but in the 1990s the trend reversed itself (p. 139).

Expenditures for social assistance in Italy are much below the European average. This category of expenditures includes not only assistance to the poor but also expenditures for labor market policies, direct benefits to families (mothers and children), and other minor welfare benefits for specific targeted groups. Expenditures for families and children in Italy are only 3.4 percent of the total (versus 7 percent in Europe), while nothing is spent for public housing, compared to a European average of 1.6 percent. In addition, according to Peracchi's (1997) analysis, the percentage of expenditures devoted to unemployment and training or to passive and active labor policies stagnated between 1980 and 1994 (0.7 percent per annum increase), while the percentage devoted to family and maternity had negative growth (−1.3 percent).

It is interesting to see how Italy fits the Mediterranean model with reference to the amount and structure of social expenditures. On the one hand, it differs significantly from the other countries of the "Latin Rim," which have much lower levels of welfare spending. In 1994, Spain's welfare expenditures as percent of GDP (23.6 percent) were further below the European average (26.1 percent) than Italy's, while Greece and Portugal spent even less (16 percent and 19.5 percent, respectively). But there are also similarities in composition of expenditures. In all Latin Rim countries, pensions and related benefits are a larger proportion of total spending than in the rest of Europe. Greece is the only country where the ratio of expenditures on pensions to total welfare outlays (63.4 percent) is greater than Italy's (61 percent), and both are much higher than the European average (42.1 percent). Italy increased its social welfare expenditures in a very significant way between 1980 and 1995, and only recently has this trend been interrupted. The Italian GDP per capita increased 29.5 percent between 1980 and 1995, while per capita welfare expenditures rose more than twice that much (79 percent). But more detailed analysis shows the existence of recent retrenchment. In the period 1990–1995 the average annual growth of social expenditure was 1.6 percent, less than half the European average. If the interval is subdivided into two periods (1990–1993 and 1993–1995), one finds an increase of 2.8 percent in the first but a negative growth (0.2

percent, but −0.1 when adjusted to exclude unemployment benefits) in the second. The component of social expenditures that increased most from 1980 onward—old age pensions—is what was already a greater share at the beginning of this period, and it is under scrutiny now.

THE RETRENCHMENT PROCESS IN THE 1990s

In Italy welfare retrenchment is occurring in an unusual political climate. Unlike Great Britain under Thatcher and the United States under Reagan, Italy did not move to the Right. Welfare reduction is occurring in a political climate that is moderately progressive, with the parties of the Left in power. Only for a very short period (from March 1994 to April 1996) was there a right-wing government, but its attack on welfare did not have a chance of being implemented. Indeed, this cabinet was forced to resign after a general strike called in opposition to its proposal to reduce pensions.

The greater control and reduction of welfare expenditures taking place in Italy have been a slow, long-term, moderate process that has been going on at least a decade and has accelerated in recent years. This is understandable if one considers the fact that the main official objective of the last government was the reduction of the public deficit and a consequent reduction of social expenditures. "Reform of the welfare state" has been another widely publicized objective of these governments. It is aimed at rationalizing and correcting abuses but also at reaching new beneficiaries who had previously been excluded. The aim is to reduce expenditures in some areas through more efficient management, less waste, and reduction of benefits to those considered overprivileged. In other words, there is retrenchment along with an attempt to innovate. It is no accident that in political and official jargon the commonly used terms are "welfare reform" rather than "welfare cuts" or "welfare reductions." It is also noteworthy that progressive intellectuals and scholars in Italy use the designation "welfare reform."

In Italy we see both a modification and a reduction of the welfare system, and the reduction jeopardizes the results of reform. The evolution of the Italian welfare system created a dualism: some groups excluded and others overprotected. With welfare reform, the extension of benefits to those formerly excluded cannot be taken for granted, but the reduction of the privileges of the overprotected is certain. Some groups will lose, particularly in the area of pensions, but it is doubtful that the disadvantaged will be reached. This is because reform is not motivated or promoted by social justice but by budgetary restrictions (Mingione, in press). Therefore, new targeted interventions will be minimally supported.

In Italy, as in other countries, we may observe certain tendencies toward an increasing "residualization," which, according to Diane Sainsbury's definition, "implies enlarging the role of the market in welfare provision and restricting state provision to a minimum safety net in cases of market failure and family breakdowns" (1996, p. 198). One must bear in mind that this is only a tendency, and, certainly, in Italy the state's role is not going to be reduced to a "minimal safety net." In any case, one may certainly observe a greater recourse to the market, that is, to the acquisition of services on the market that the state either never supplied or supplied in an irregular and insufficient way.

There are also some interesting innovations concerning the management of public welfare policies and the relationships between the state and the market. On the one hand there is indeed a tendency toward state withdrawal from direct intervention, but on the other hand the state is financing private organizations or firms that operate in the area of social welfare services. This fits perfectly with the prevailing view of the advantages of "privatization" and of reduction of the role of the state in the economy and in society. But it should be clear that this state withdrawal does not imply a corresponding reduction of cost for the collectivity. In fact, the government is paying or subsidizing private organizations that deliver the services.

Meanwhile, state intervention is gradually extending to particularly disadvantaged sectors. A further important aspect of this process of "residualization" is the growth in the number of means-tested provisions for the poor alone. Finally, "residualization" also manifests itself in a less direct way through the reduction or withdrawal of benefits whenever income exceeds a certain level. So far, this form of intensified targeting has concerned only "benefits on request" (nursery schools, health service coupons, welfare checks for persons over 65, etc.) and not statutory benefits like minimum, integrated social security pensions. Let us look at some examples.

In 1992, so-called tickets were introduced in the public health sector. The English word "ticket" is the term used for the percentage of expense paid by the patient. Only people who received forms of economic assistance from the local communes and were, therefore, officially recognized as poor were excluded. In 1994, two other factors began to be considered for ticket exemption: poor health (chronic diseases) and advanced age. But, in 1995, new limitations were imposed on ticket exemptions.

This combination of often contradictory measures has resulted in financial burdens on individual families. In just one year (between 1993 and 1994) the number of citizens who purchased medicines at full cost grew from 28.8 percent to 32.4 percent. Furthermore, the reduction of public health costs has corresponded to an increase in private ones: in the decade 1985–1996 these costs escalated from 21 to 29 percent (ISTAT, 1997).

In the health sector, then, the reduction of the state's role and the reduction of coverage express themselves in the increase of families' contributions or tickets. For tests and examinations, the required contribution becomes an ever-higher percentage of the total cost for categories of persons who are not exempted. Yet, the continuous effort to identify these categories is itself an expression of the process of residualization.

Another example regards *assegni per il nucleo familiare* (checks for the family unit), which have substituted for *assegni familiari* (family checks) since 1998. This slight terminological difference hardly represents a substantial difference: "[With the new rules] we have passed from a weak benefit given to all workers supporting a family, regardless of their salaries . . . to more generous measures, but ones of a markedly means-tested nature, affecting the families of workers who live in particular economic conditions" (Negri and Saraceno, 1996, p. 37). This appears to be consistent with Sainsbury's observation that "greater targeting to help the worst off has been a principal argument to legitimize a conversion of benefits to means tested programs" (1996, p. 198).

This also appears evident in the case of the "minimum insertion income," a provision advocated by the present progressive government. This was designed to extend the coverage to sectors of the population that were excluded from Italy's "workerist" welfare system. Introduced in June 1998, this provision was applied experimentally until December 31, 2000. The minimum insertion income is intended for those persons at great risk of social exclusion because, for psychological, physical, or social reasons, they are not in a position to maintain either themselves or their children. Beneficiaries must have an income lower than the poverty threshold. The final report of the commission that laid out the guidelines for reforming the social protection system points out that "the minimum insertion income is designed to mitigate the poverty trap" (Commissione per l'analisi . . . , 1997a, p. 19). The reference to the "poverty trap" may not be appropriate, but this provision certainly reaches sectors of the population traditionally disadvantaged by the Italian welfare system but, at the same time, introduces a series of elements of control (e.g., those who do not comply by actively searching for employment lose benefits) that limits its scope.

The process of "targeting," the attention to particularly disadvantaged sectors of the population, and the introduction of means testing are some of the innovations of the Italian welfare system that are both positive and negative. Among these the most important is residualization. The other prong of the process of restructuring and reducing the Italian welfare system consists of the cuts to which we referred earlier. The overall effect is certainly a worsening in the conditions of the population that experiences a reduction in occupational and income stability as a result of the crisis of the fordist model and, at the same time, a reduction in the welfare measures designed to combat job instability. The effects can be detected in the increase of poverty.

The decline in living conditions for a large number of families explains the strong resistance to the reductions of pensions on the part of the working-class trade unions. In the previous section we pointed out the critical importance of pensions in the Italian welfare system and also the "generous" ways in which they were granted in the past. Pensions, as well as other forms of income support for those who are no longer employed, are very important in counterbalancing the precariousness of labor. Given the role of the family in Italian society and its welfare system, pension reductions imply serious risks to economic security, particularly in certain regions.

Generally speaking, southern Italy suffers disproportionately from the process of welfare retrenchment because of its more precarious economic conditions and the incomplete implementation of some welfare plans (such as the national health system). The reduction of pensions will affect most severely those areas in which people are heavily dependent on social welfare. In general, the effects of pension cutbacks will not be felt immediately because these penalize future claimants more than those now collecting benefits.

We conclude by observing that those groups who have been privileged in the Italian welfare system will gradually tend to lose ground. Their losses will not be offset by other forms of opportunity, especially in the labor market. At the same time, welfare provisions for newly targeted groups appear to be unreliable and inconsistent. The generally poor conditions of southern Italians and others who have been disadvantaged in the world of work but relatively advantaged in the welfare system are likely to worsen.

NOTES

1. Richard Titmuss (1974, pp. 30ff) classified the welfare systems not only on the basis of expenditures or numbers of beneficiaries but also on the basis of social solidarity. Hence, his three models are "residual" (welfare policy is to help only the disadvantaged); "industrial achievement—performance" (which selectively confines itself to special categories, mostly notably, the workers), and "institutional redistributive or universalist" (providing universalist services to all citizens). In the Italian literature (and in the international literature concerning the Italian welfare system), the term "particularistic" is used in order to identify the "industrial achievement—performance" model.

2. The RMI is an allowance, a guaranteed income, provided to citizens in order to facilitate their entry in the labor market and society by making the benefit contingent on employment search. See also Chapter 6.

3. According to the 1951 census, people employed in agriculture were still more than 8 million (42 percent of the total active population). Industrial employment was already 32 percent, but most of these "industrial workers" were, in fact, small artisans. People employed in the service sector were then only 26 percent.

4. According to Mattia Persiani, "the idea of social insurance was accepted only in an implicit mode and resulted . . . in an ambiguous formulation of the article" (1982, p. 237).

5. Workers in Cassa Integrazione are temporarily unemployed workers who en-

joy a privileged situation as compared with other Italian unemployed workers. In fact, they maintain the right to their jobs, and although they are unemployed, they are still officially employed for all legal and statistical purposes.

6. Italian literature on the subject, although usually based on Eurostat data, sometimes differs with respect to the amounts spent for various social programs. This is mostly owing to different criteria of aggregation and to different definitions of the components of social expenditures in different countries. For example, while Eurostat provides data subdivided on the basis of 12 areas of need (sickness, maternity, unemployment, etc.), Italian sources classify expenditures on the basis of only four areas.

REFERENCES

Ascoli, U., ed. (1984). *Welfare State all'italiana*. Bari: Laterza.

Banfield, E. C. (1958). *The Moral Basis of a Backward Society*. Glencoe, IL: Free Press.

Bartocci, E. (1999). *Le politiche sociali nell'età liberale (1861–1919)*. Roma: Donzelli.

Bettio, F., and P. Villa. (1995). "A Mediterranean perspective on the break-down of the relationship between participation and fertility." University of Pavia, mimeo, December.

Boccella, N. (1982). *Il Mezzogiorno sussidiato. Reddito prodotto e trasferimenti alle famiglie nei comuni meridionali*. Milano: Angeli.

Castles, F. G., and M. Ferrera. (1996). "Casa e welfare state: Le contraddizioni dei paesi sud-europei." *Stato e Mercato* 48 (December): 409–431.

Commissione di indagine sulla povertà e l'emarginazione. (1996a). *Povertà abitativa in Italia 1989–1993*. Roma: Presidenza del Consiglio dei Ministri.

———. (1996b). *La Povertà in Italia 1980–94*. Roma: Presidenza del Consiglio dei Ministri.

———. (1999). *La Povertà in Italia 1998*. Roma: Presidenza del Consiglio dei Ministri.

Commissione per l'analisi delle compatibilità macroeconomiche della spesa sociale. (1997a). "Relazione finale." Mimeo, February 28. Roma: Author.

———. (1997b). "La spesa per l'assistenza." Mimeo, February 28. Roma: Author.

Esping-Andersen, G. (1995). "Il welfare state senza il lavoro. L'ascesa del familismo nelle politiche sociali dell'Europa continentale." *Stato e Mercato* 45: 347–380.

Ferrera, M. (1984). *Il Welfare State in Italia. Sviluppo e crisi in prospettiva comparata*. Bologna: Il Mulino.

———. (1993). *Modelli di solidarietà. Politica e riforme sociali nelle democrazie*. Bologna: Il Mulino.

———. (1996a). "Il modello sud-europeo di welfare state." *Rivista Italiana di Scienza Politica* 26(1) (April): 67–101.

———. (1996b). *La spesa sociale italiana in prospettiva comparata*. Commissione per l'analisi delle compatibilità macroeconomiche della spesa sociale, Documento di base, no. 1.

Gough, I. (1983). *The Political Economy of the Welfare State*. London: Macmillan.

Harrison, B. (1994). *Lean and Mean: The Changing Landscape of Corporate Power in the Age of Flexibility*. New York: Basic Books.

Ichino, P. (1997). *Il lavoro e il mercato*. Milano: Mondadori.

ISTAT. (1996). *Indagine Multiscopo sulle famiglie. Stili di vita e condizioni di salute. Anni 1993–94, Argomenti 2*, Roma.

———. (1997). *I conti degli italiani*. Bologna: Il Mulino.

Kazepov, Y., and G. Orientale Caputo. (1998). "No organization, no services, no money: The poor and the excluded from welfare in Italy." In R. van Berkel, H. Colnem, and R. Vlek, eds., *Beyond Marginality? Social Movements of Social Security Claimants in the European Union*. London: Ashgate Publishing, pp. 119–155.

Leibfried, S. (1993). "Towards a European welfare state?" In C. Jones, ed., *New Perspectives on the Welfare State in Europe*. London: Routledge.

Militello, G. (1989). "Introduzione." In A. Bondioli, ed., *Cgil e welfare state*. Ires Materiali, no. 6: 2–10.

Mingione, E. (1991). *Fragmented Societies*. Oxford: Basil Blackwell.

———. (in press). "The Southern European welfare model and the fight against poverty and social exclusion." In *Encyclopedia of Life Support Systems*, vol. 14. Paris: UNESCO.

Negri, N., and C. Saraceno. (1996). *Le politiche contro la povertà in Italia*. Bologna: Il Mulino.

OECD. (1999). *OECD Social Expenditure Data Base, 1980–1996*. Paris: Author.

Paci, M. (1989). *Pubblico e privato nei moderni sistemi di welfare*. Napoli: Liguori.

Peracchi, F. (1997). "La spesa per la protezione sociale: un confronto tra i paesi dell'Unione Europea." *Ceis Newsletter* no. 6 (November).

Persiani, M. (1982). Article 38. In G. Branca, ed., *Commentario della Costituzione*, vol. I. Bologna: Zanichelli.

Pizzorno, A. (1974). "I ceti medi nei meccanismi del consenso." In F. L. Cavazza and S. R. Graubard, eds., *Il caso italiano*. Milano: Garzanti.

Pugliese, E. (1983). *I braccianti agriocoli in Italia. Tra mercato del lavoro e assitenza*. Milano: Angeli.

———. (1993). *Sociologia della disoccupazione*. Bologna: Il Mulino.

Pugliese, E., and E. Rebeggiani. (1997). *Occupazione e disoccupazione in Italia (1945–1995)*. Roma: Edizioni Lavoro.

Pugliese, E., and C. Saraceno. (1989). "Reddito di cittadinanza e dintorni." *Politica ed Economia* 6 (June): 49–52.

Regini, M. (1980). *I dilemmi del sindacat*. Bologna: Il Mulino.

Rhodes, M., ed. (1997). *Southern European Welfare States: Between Crisis and Reform*. London: Frank Cass.

Sainsbury, D. (1996). *Gender, Equality and the Welfare State*. Cambridge: Cambridge University Press.

Saraceno, C. (1997). "Riforma di un welfare diseguale: Limiti e prospettive di cambiamenti possibili." *Il Mulino* 3: 158–169.

———. (1998). *Mutamenti della famiglia e politiche sociali in Italia*. Bologna: Il Mulino.

Siebert, R. (1991). *E' femmina, però è bella. Tre generazioni di donne al Sud.* Torino: Rosenberg e Sellier.

Titmuss, R. (1974). *Social Policy: An Introduction.* London: Allen & Unwin.

Zanatta, A. L. (1996). "Famiglie con un solo genitore e rischio di povertà." *Polis* no. 1: 63–79.

Chapter 9

Hungary: Retrenchment amid Radical Restructuring

Phineas Baxandall

INTRODUCTION: THE WELFARE STATE IN THE HUNGARIAN CONTEXT

The inclusion of Hungary in this volume is important because it represents an example of restructuring that has resulted in perhaps the most generous welfare state of a former communist country. It is also important because it helps to illuminate a critical issue in debates over welfare state retrenchment. The increasing use of the term "retrenchment" by welfare state scholars, as opposed to "cutbacks" or "dismantling," is perhaps a recognition that under changing economic conditions it is possible to have both increases in total spending on transfer payments and a diminished commitment to social protection.

It is a matter of debate which "needs" are relevant for appraisals of welfare retrenchment. Clayton and Pontusson (1998, pp. 78–79) argue that a critical function of welfare states is to maintain levels of equality and that a failure to do so constitutes retrenchment. In contrast to previous decades, they show that—when measured against the number of poor, unemployed, and aged—social spending has grown far less than the gross domestic product (GDP) per capita. Challenging Pierson's characterizations of continuity (see Introduction in this volume), they argue that in the West, "to maintain the disposable income distribution that had been achieved by the late 1970s, a significant expansion of redistributive welfare state activities would have had to occur in the 1980s" (p. 76).

This chapter examines whether the Hungarian welfare state has undergone retrenchment since the fall of Communism in 1990. On the one hand, a strong case could be made that social spending in Hungary has become more generous since the fall of Communism. When the Communist Party lost its monopoly on power in 1990, Hungary's social spending was already 25 percent of its GDP, a large portion of the economy compared to that of other countries at a similar level of development, and it approached that of advanced social welfare states.[1] Between 1990 and 1991, in the first years of post-Communism, social spending actually grew from 25 to 30 percent of GDP before falling to 22 percent in 1996. New programs for unemployment, training, and poverty relief were also created. According to some, the years since the fall of Communism should therefore be interpreted as modernization but not retrenchment. The initial growth in social security spending was seen by many as excessive and further evidence of what one prominent economist called a "premature welfare state" that spent beyond its available means of economic development (Kornai, 1992).

But we get a very different picture of Hungary when we view social protection in relation to growing social needs and as part of a changing relationship between social policy and other sources of income. Social payments under Communism functioned as supplements to the very low level of wages. In the post-communist years, wages have fallen sharply, and subsidies for basic consumer goods and services have been largely eliminated. Much restructuring since 1990 has consisted of limiting the degree to which spending can be increased to address rising poverty and inequality. These changes, as well as the alterations in distributive principles for preexisting programs, constitute the Hungarian version of welfare state retrenchment.

Pierson (1996) has developed a format for evaluating welfare state retrenchment that includes the following characteristics: (1) significant increases in means-tested benefits in place of universal benefits; (2) a major shift of responsibility for social provision from the public to the private sector; and (3) dramatic changes in benefit and eligibility rules that indicate a qualitative change in the nature (presumably toward less redistribution) of a particular program. Hungary has made a shift toward means testing and private provision. Further, deep recession and displacement resulting from economic restructuring has increased the demand for social protection; fiscal austerity has dictated the reorganization of programs that would otherwise have increased in response to rising needs. This is a "qualitative change" that also fits under the third form of retrenchment despite the fact that aggregate social expenditures increased over the period.

Significant as these changes are, Hungary's welfare state has retrenched less than most formerly communist countries. Compared to other former Soviet bloc countries, Hungary has been relatively skeptical of neoliberalism (compared to Poland, for instance) and suffered a smaller fall in overall economic activity. Hungary is relatively prosperous and has pursued a more gradualist approach to reform than the radical market prescriptions for "shock therapy" preferred by many Western advisors (e.g., Lipton and Sacks, 1990). After years of criticism from international lending organizations such as the World Bank and the International Monetary Fund (IMF) about its slow pace of reform and purportedly overgenerous social spending, Hungary is now held up as a poster child of post-communist prosperity. Hungary has become part of the North Atlantic Treaty Organization (NATO) and is among the first in line to join the European Union. Investment guides now choose Hungary as the most favorable business climate in East Europe, and it has received the lion's share of the region's foreign direct investment despite its small size and population. Hungary had the benefit that much of the legal and institutional infrastructure for a market economy had already been created by the departing communist government in the late 1980s, and trade was already partially reoriented toward the West before the collapse of the Soviet-led Council for Mutual Economic Assistance (COMECON) trading system. While Hungary's GDP fell by a staggering 30 percent after the demise of Communism, this was actually less than in Poland, the Czech Republic, or most other neighbors. Due to the fiscal burden of a large, inherited national debt, it would be too strong to claim that Hungary represents a "least-likely case" for post-communist retrenchment; nonetheless, the forces of Hungarian retrenchment largely represent those of other East European countries.

HUNGARY AND THE LEGACIES OF STATE SOCIALISM

Hungary is a small country of only 93,000 square kilometers and 10.2 million people. Approximately two-thirds of Hungarians live in cities, and one in every five lives in the capital, Budapest (OECD, 1997). About 30 to 40 percent of employees are estimated to be unionized (OECD, 1997), and income per person was $4,287 at the end of 1995 (OECD, 1997). Ethnically, the population is mostly homogeneous, with a Roma (Gypsy) minority of about 4 percent particularly concentrated in high-unemployment areas such as the northeast (OECD, 1997). Women's participation in the labor force has fallen sharply from extraordinarily high levels to below the European Union (EU) average.

It is important to understand the particular political and economic roles that social benefits played under Communism. Social policy was subordinated to the goals of rapid industrialization and the Communist Party's monopoly of power. When the Party took power after World War II, national planning assigned industrial investment and rapid growth as economic priorities, while individual consumption was viewed as a regrettable diversion of resources. The relationship of social policy to the labor market reflected these priorities in a number of important ways, which are discussed below: "public consumption" was favored over family or individual consumption; wages were systematically depressed; universal employment was encouraged; benefits were almost exclusively employment-based; and economic inequality was low. With full employment, high labor participation rates, and relatively egalitarian wage scales, there was a different role for social policy under state socialism than under capitalism (Milanovic, 1994, p. 188). Social policies were not aimed at absence of labor income; there was only a small population of people who were outside the state employment and pensions system. In general, social policy was a wage subsidy for insufficient wages.

In the effort for rapid industrialization, consumption was regarded as a residual cost, and its levels stagnated in the first years of Communism as resources were channeled into heavy industrial investment. There was also a strong bias for what was termed "social consumption," as opposed to personal consumption. State spending on culture or subsidized transportation, housing, and basic necessities, for instance, was meant to substitute for much individual spending. This was regarded as both more ideologically pure and a more efficient way of satisfying needs. After the 1956 popular uprising that was suppressed by Soviet tanks, the harsh reductions in consumption gave way to a new, implicit social contract in which popular quiescence was exchanged for expectations of rising living standards. Consumption and wage rates still lagged behind GDP growth, but at least they increased, fed partly by growing programs for old age pensions, sick leave, child benefits, public medicine, and maternity benefits (Ferge, 1979).

Social spending played a critical role in supporting consumption levels and wages that were extremely low by international comparison. The state set social supplements at seemingly high levels, but this did not begin to compensate for the anemic wage levels. Compared to other countries with similar levels of income per capita, Hungary had relatively high levels of social spending, but Hungary's private consumption was far lower than its level of development would otherwise predict. In 1989, Hungary's expenditure on social benefits (including income in kind) was 4 to 5 percent greater than in other countries with similar levels of development, but this did not compensate for a share of private consumption that was as much as 18 to 20 percent below that of other countries of comparable income. The share of total income going to consumption fell short of the Organisation for Economic Co-operation and Development (OECD) average by 10 percent; through the 1970s and much of the 1980s, total consumption was even less than other countries' private consumption (Kovács, 1994).

Low wages were the result of government planning, both during and after Communism. One legacy of the communist strategy for rapid industrialization is average wages that provide a smaller portion of an average family's income than in the West. Hungarians, on average, received only 52 percent of their income from wages in 1989 (World Bank, 1995, p. 150). This pattern was well established in the 1980s. Unpublished figures by Hungary's Central Statistical Office for 1984 show that the calculated subsistence minimum of 2,500 forints (3,050 for head of a working household) exceeded the 2,000 forint minimum wage by 20 percent.[2]

During the 1980s, amid a stagnant economy, the political imperative for raising living standards was largely met by increasing the opportunities for earnings outside of standard state employment: overtime, second jobs, and informal economic activity. Hungarians who have a primary job as well as those who were officially out of the labor force often tend to moonlight at secondary jobs, grow and sell vegetables from small plot farming, and trade unpaid labor among colleagues and neighbors. When a 1992 poll asked, "Do you get enough money from your regular job to buy what you really need?" only a quarter of Hungarians said they received even barely enough, compared to almost three times that number in neighboring Austria (Rose and Haerpfer, 1993). Only 22 percent of Hungarians relied solely on activities officially recognized as employment.

Communist social policy was premised on full employment far more than any Western welfare state ever was. The guarantee of a job had been a central pillar of state socialist legitimacy ever since post-war reconstruction, when the Communist Party staked its claim on having put the nation back to work. Full employment provided Hungarians with basic economic security and represented central planning's putative superiority over capitalism. Managers of communist enterprises had many incentives to generate a perpetual labor shortage. Consequently, the communist social safety net was not set up to address involuntary joblessness. Under Communism the assumption had been that all able-bodied citizens would work. Thus, state employment provided the basis for administering most social benefits, including pensions, sickness benefits, maternity leave, child subsidies, child care, state vacation homes, meal and travel subsidies, housing, special loans, and emergency financial aid in case of a birth or death in the family. Pensions in the limited private sector were available only through the payment of a high social security tax. Because most social programs were administered through employment, they were universal only in the sense that employment was universally guaranteed.

Social policy largely succeeded in placing a floor below the level of any citizen's standard of living. Pensions and other employment-based forms of income replacement re-created the earning inequalities between occupations as they do in other insurance-based welfare states. Some amenities, including higher education and, especially, state apartments, were more unequal because their distribution was heavily affected by political connections (Szelenyi, 1978). Despite this, low levels of inequality were an undeniable achievement of state socialism. While income distribution in the final years of Communism became less egalitarian than in Sweden, income was still far more egalitarian than in the United Kingdom and much more so than in the United States.

Qualitatively, the level of social services was worse than aggregate statistics might suggest. Because welfare was centralized and geared toward legitimation after 1956, programs tended to be insensitive to particular needs of individual groups. Gypsies, for instance, were usually excluded from social programs. Social work has been recognized as officially acceptable only since the mid-1980s, and professional social work training was started only in 1990. All forms of social assistance ended in 1950 because poverty was officially declared to have ceased under socialism. Some forms of assistance slowly crept back from 1960 on, first for the elderly and later, from 1974 on, for families with children. But up to 1989, social assistance remained bureaucratic and discretionary and quantitatively inadequate, and it excluded the "undeserving" poor. The shabbiness of Hungarian services was evident in health and education, where state spending consumed a far smaller portion of GDP than in OECD countries (Gács, 1986). The Communist Party touted the fact that Hungary had a relatively high number of doctors and hospital beds per capita and an extensive nursery system for infants. But the relatively low level of resources was reflected in poor equipment and low salaries for health workers.

POST-COMMUNIST ECONOMIC CHANGES

Large-scale economic restructuring included price liberalization, subsidy cutbacks, and the opening of foreign trade with the West. Private sector employment grew from a mere 8 percent of the workforce in 1989 to nearly 30 percent in 1992 (Institute for World Economics, 1995, p. 37). The sectoral distribution of employment also became more Western, shifting from heavy industry and agriculture toward previously underprovided services. In 1989, agriculture and industry accounted for 55.8 percent of the labor force, compared to 44.2 percent in services. As early as 1993, these distributions had reversed, with services making up 54 percent of the labor force (World Bank, 1995). A similar shift took place from gigantic firms of 300 or more employees toward smaller enterprises. In the process of these changes the economy shrank by an average of 4.8 percent annually from 1990 to 1993 (OECD, 1997). Growth had returned to 1.3 percent in 1996 and reached 4 and 5 percent in 1997 and 1998, respectively. As of this writing, economic activity has only barely regained its 1989 levels.

Foreign trade is especially important to Hungary because of the country's small size and dependence on foreign markets. Previously protected state enterprises were exposed to new Western competitors and the threat of bankruptcy. The COMECON trading arrangements that had previously guaranteed markets for Warsaw Pact countries were dismantled overnight, leaving firms scrambling to find new customers and suppliers. Many firms that might have been able to navigate these problems nonetheless failed because of a lack of banking infrastructure to substitute for old sources of state credit (Amsden, Jacek, and Taylor, 1994). Exports have since recovered to become a major engine of the economy. Around 21 percent of exports are "outward processing trade" where semicompleted goods are imported, completed, and re-exported, chiefly to the European Union. Hungarian trade of this sort is concentrated in apparel and clothing accessories, although new plants have also been created for auto parts and electronics. Exports, which grew over 13 percent a year in real terms from 1994 to 1996, have helped buoy an economy otherwise depressed by wage cuts and government cutbacks (OECD, 1997, p. 19). Foreign direct investment and exports allowed the government to pay off some foreign debt before maturity, bringing net foreign debt down from 50 to 22 percent of GDP and allowing Hungary to pay off its loans to the IMF without further extending credit for the first time since 1984 (*VilagGazdaság*, February 5, 1998, p. 15).

For the typical Hungarian wage earner, life has been less sanguine. According to a 1992 New Democracies Barometer poll, 73 percent of Hungarians said their overall household economic situation was worse off than five years earlier, compared to 7 percent who said that they were better off. A majority expected their situation to deteriorate further five years into the future (Rose and Haerpfer, 1993). Sure enough, five years later another poll commissioned by the EU found nearly 75 percent of Hungarians believed that their finances had worsened in the past year, and 53 percent foresaw further deterioration. Barely more than a third said that they supported a market economy (*VilagGazdaság*, April 11, 1997, pp. 1–2).

These dark opinions reflect the overall trends in Hungarian wages and material living standards. After Communism's fall, the abnormally low wage portion of people's incomes did not converge upward toward Western levels. Hourly compensation (including non-wage costs to employers) was a mere $1.93 in Hungary in 1991 (Godfrey, 1994). This was lower than in many Third World nations such as Singapore or Mexico ($4.39 and $1.95 per hour, respectively). According to the Hungarian business weekly *VilagGazdaság*, 1997 wages in Budapest were on a par with those in Bombay and only 1/18th of wages in Zurich (October 2, 1997, pp. 1, 5). From 1990 to 1994, real net wages fell over 20 percent (Institute for World Economics, 1995). After the socialist government took power in 1994, it initiated new austerity measures that created further drops of 3 and 5 percent in 1995 and 1996 (CESTAT, 1997). Wages in 1997 reversed a trend by rising almost 5 percent, a significant gain but nowhere near to making up lost ground or altering the fundamental wage inadequacy that makes supplemental income activity the norm.

Government policies since 1990 have sought to depress wages by indexing them below inflation. Low wages were desired to prevent inflation, to increase competitiveness, and, in the case of government employees, to reduce the budget. Depressing public sector wages has also been a strategy for pushing people into the private sector. Public employees at the end of 1997 made approximately 35 percent less than private employees in similar jobs. In uncharacteristically frank terms, the OECD acknowledges that "the fall in real wages produced a major transfer in the distribution of income from labour to capital" (OECD, 1997, p. 2). The portion of the population living below the minimum standard of living was around 10 percent in the 1980s and 25 percent by 1992 (Ferge, 1993). In 1997 the Central Statistical Office estimated that 25–30 percent of the population's income fell below subsistence levels.

Inequality has grown quickly in recent years, and with it new demands for social relief. A comparison of the richest and poorest households, the ratio of the income of the top decile to the bottom one, was 5.8 in 1988 and rose steadily to almost 7.3 in 1995 (Kolosi and Sági, 1996). These measures underestimate the increase in inequality because the largest income declines have been those in the middle. In 1994, a quarter of the population could be classified as in poverty, with the highest concentrations in small villages (Andorka, 1994, pp. 34–35). Two-thirds of Roma (Gypsies) were in the lowest income quintile. With cutbacks to subsidies of basic consumption goods, bread and cereal consumption fell 18 percent between 1989 and 1994; meat consumption fell 14 percent; and dairy products, over 25 percent (OECD, 1995). A rapid rise in crime and homelessness has been one sign of the growing divide. On the other side, a Price Waterhouse study indicates that top executives' salaries have grown at 50 percent a year, even during years of sharp overall wage decline (_Magyar Hírlap_, November 27, 1997, p. 9).

Those hardest hit have been Hungarians whose living standards benefited most under Communism and epitomized the socialist worker. In the 1960s and 1970s millions of Hungarian peasants came to the cities to take the swelling number of state jobs, especially in industry. It is precisely these kinds of jobs—of the lower middle class—that have been eliminated most frequently and in which wages have fallen most sharply. These typically blue-collar or government workers most depended on the subsidies for transportation, utilities, and rents that have been curtailed. Nor do they have the information technology, personal services, or foreign-language skills that are most in demand. These are also the people who, uprooted from their village life, have the fewest personal networks for supplementary forms of informal income. Having cast their lot in what was to be the way of the future, they have been left out in the cold.

Perhaps the most monumental change since 1990 has been the onset of widespread unemployment. Previously, unemployment had been almost unknown. Small-scale income maintenance and reassignment programs were established as early as 1983 for workers displaced by restructuring. A widescale unemployment insurance system was established in the final years of Communism, but this was done against a general background of labor shortage. It was widely anticipated that the adoption of Western-style markets in Eastern Europe would entail mass unemployment. Joblessness was seen as a prod to accelerate economic restructuring, but few expected the large and sudden rise in unemployment that was fed by the deep fall in overall economic activity and the sudden collapse of the COMECON trading bloc. The rate of unemployment rose from 0.7 percent in 1990 to 3.0 percent in 1991, 9.6 percent in 1992, and then 13.5 percent in 1993 (OECD, 1997), from which it eased back down to 8.8 percent by November 1998. Women's unemployment has been consistently lower than men's, but the main cause is that cutbacks in child care have forced women out of the labor market. Unemployment has been highest in regions where heavy industry was most concentrated. Even firms that survived that deep decline in the economy nonetheless have tended to reduce their staffing levels as a way to cut costs.

At both the firm and sectoral level, post-communist restructuring displaced workers from their jobs. In the massive shift from public to private ownership there has been an ongoing exodus from state enterprises, and privatizing firms likewise trimmed their personnel. Post-communist policies to shift labor from manufacturing and agriculture into services caused at least temporary unemployment for many workers who, under Communism, had been employed in factories and farms. This unemployment would be less of a problem if it were merely transitory, but about half of the unemployed remain jobless for over a year (World Bank, 1995, p. 41). Hiring firms generally choose among workers who are already employed in other jobs rather than from the pool of unemployed. The unemployed more often disappear into local poverty relief programs with minimal benefits or resign themselves to early retirement schemes and disability pensions.

The number of employed persons in Hungary fell a staggering 30 percent from 1989 to 1996 (International Monetary Fund, 1998). This precipitous drop occurred very quickly: in 1990, there were 5.2 million employed Hungarians; by the end of 1996, only 3.6 million (OECD, 1997). Finally, the trend seems to have bottomed out with employment rising minutely in 1997 for the first time in 10 years and then again in 1998. Much of the initial increase in social spending after 1990 was to absorb those workers who had little chance of ever returning to the rapidly shrinking labor market. Of the 1.4 million reduction in employment in the five years following 1990, only 500,000 continued looking for work, while the other 900,000 left the labor market altogether. The dependency ratio leaped from 98 per 100 employees in 1990 to 167 in 1995 (Institute for World Economics, 1995, p. 94).

Exit from the labor force has been facilitated by a number of policies, including parental leave, sick leave, disability, and early retirement benefits. The beneficiaries of these programs constitute 20 percent of the working-age population, "more than three times the unemployed and six times those on unemployment benefits" (OECD, 1997, p. 102). Such programs not only are expensive but also provide inadequate incomes. Eligibility criteria for these programs have actually been made more stringent, but they have, nonetheless, expanded as partial compensation for rising unemployment and falling wages. The use of sick leave, which pays three-quarters of wages, for example, has clearly helped to reduce the active workforce and to facilitate secondary income earnings, as evident in the very high rates of utilization. In 1995, 7.8 percent of Hungarian employees were out sick on any given date. In 1994, the average Hungarian worker lost 26.5 days per year due to health problems, over twice the 1970 rate of 12 per year. By contrast, the 1996 U.S. rate was merely 5.6 days per year. Similarly, 9 percent of Hungarians over 15 years of age collected disability pensions (OECD, 1997).

The fall in employment has also been mitigated, as it was under Communism, by informal markets and public works. The nature of unreported income makes its size difficult to estimate, but the most authoritative studies estimate that it adds an additional 30 percent to GDP (Árvay and Vértes, 1995). Under Communism the informal economy reduced inequality by disproportionately supplementing the income of poorer Hungarians, especially those working in agriculture. Since 1990, informal income has become even more unequal than reported incomes as rising tax rates have driven entrepreneurs largely outside the official economy. It is unclear whether the informal economy has been reduced by recent efforts to increase tax compliance. But the informal economy, once a social leveler, now contributes to inequality. It is not clear that the "true" level of employment is any higher than what is reported because a great many of the officially "self-employed" have little work but use their status to avoid taxes for their limited activity. One form of employment that has clearly been increasing is low-wage public works, mainly by local governments, which also use it as a screening mechanism for those seeking benefits. While only 11,000 persons were engaged in public works in 1991, the number increased to 87,000 in 1995 and 160,000 in 1996 (*Napi Gazdaság*, July 22, 1997, p. 3).

THE POLITICS OF RETRENCHMENT AND THE DEFENSE OF SOCIAL WELFARE

Curtailment of social policy has taken place despite egalitarian values and some resurgence of the Socialist Party. The political dynamics of transition has favored popular sentiments for social protection and even a resurgence of the Left. After the fall of Communism it was uncertain what would be the rules of the game or who would be the major political actors. The task of post-communist restructuring has ironically been to use centralized plans for creating a market economy. Unlike the practice in long-established capitalist economies, the choice of East European alternatives for how to transform economic institutions was far more transparently the choice of economic winners and losers as well (Elster, 1993; Ollman, 1997).

Big wins and big losses were more clearly the result of political decision making rather than long-standing and seemingly neutral rules. Despite the embrace of Western capitalism, the political dynamics of the post-communist transition ironically also reinforced long-established egalitarian values. A majority of Hungarians in 1992 (52 percent) said, for instance, that they strongly favored government intervention to provide jobs for all (Freeman and Branchflower, 1997).[3]

Against this background the Center-Right Hungarian Democratic Forum (MDF) government, elected in 1990, proclaimed that it sought to establish "a social market economy," a phrase that was a clear reference to the German model and a direct contrast to the neighboring Czech prime minister's stated desire for "a market economy free of hyphens." The largely amateur government, however, found itself in the unenviable position of distributing austerity after having promised prosperity and accommodating foreign powers after having positioned themselves as nationalists. The MDF government sought to make minor cuts to satisfy international creditors and then wait for economic growth to help boost living standards. The economic recession was much deeper and more persistent than they anticipated. In elections six years later the modernized and transformed Communist Party—now the Socialist Party—won a majority of Parliament. Ironically, the Socialists were most aggressive in imposing austerity and slashing social programs, an approach that soured their political support and contributed to electoral defeat in 1998 at the hands of a new right-wing populist coalition. At this writing, the new government appears to be more generous than the MDF in providing family subsidies and education but has restrained pensions and institutionally undermined future support for social spending.

The first major humiliation for the MDF government came in 1991, when, after denying the intention to do so, it instituted a sudden gasoline price hike, which was met with nationwide blockades by taxi and truck drivers. Transport was crippled for three days, and the police refused to remove protesters by force. Although the price increases were merely delayed, the experience showed that government actions to reduce living standards came at the peril of the party in power, at least if done without prior consultation. Overall, however, there have been few mass protests. Street demonstrations have generally focused on other issues such as state media policies or agricultural land-ownership laws. The two exceptions were student protests when tuition was introduced for higher education and large demonstrations against cutbacks in family benefits in 1995. While protests are few, it is difficult to gauge their importance in checking radical retrenchment.

One reason for welfare state cutbacks has been the relative weakness of the unions. Although they retain some strength within the Socialist Party, they have offered little organized resistance in defense of social policy. Under Communism unions had been little more than transition belts for carrying party propaganda and recruiting loyal cadre. Union leaders in 1990, finding themselves with little legitimacy, sought to avoid the appearance of being anti-market and concentrated their energies on improving the terms of privatization in individual firms. Unions were also thrown into internal struggles by 1990 legislation requiring them to compete against one another for re-registration of members. At stake in these elections was also the distribution of the substantial assets of the union federations. There has been little labor militancy despite strong formal protection of the right to strike. The OECD (1997) observes that there have been fewer than five strikes per year between 1991 and 1995, and those have generally involved less than 1 percent of all workers and lasted less than two days. Tripartite bargaining institutions ensure official consultation with organized labor, but there are no mechanisms to ensure that the government complies with labor demands. Both left-wing and right-wing governments have disregarded tripartite demands when cutting social welfare.

The Constitutional Court has not been so easy to dismiss. In strictly formal terms Hungary has perhaps the world's most powerful Constitutional Court and a Constitution that is one of the most assertive in the area of social rights. In practice the court has generally avoided direct conflict with the government and has restrained from exercising some of its exceptional powers—such as declaring the need to make certain laws. The court has thwarted certain kinds of pension cutbacks as violations of prior commitments. Portions of the proposed changes to family payments and child allowances in 1995 were also declared unconstitutional. The court's role in protecting social rights may change if the current government's plans to rewrite the Constitution are successful.

No account of social policy making in Hungary would be complete without a discussion of the influence of international lending organizations. Hungary's deep indebtedness makes it particularly dependent on the support of foreign creditors. The government must worry that Western bond-rating agencies will downgrade its credit risk, forcing the state to pay very significant additional sums in higher interest rates to finance its debt. It is unclear whether it is more accurate to say that supplicant Hungarian governments have provided the political cover for the agenda of world lending agencies, or whether a better characterization is that world lending agencies have provided political cover for the unpopular policies of governments. The politics of welfare state retrenchment, as has been noted, is most characterized by the politics of blame avoidance and the displacement of responsibility (Weaver, 1986; Pierson, 1996). Post-communist policymakers intent on emulating the West have been greatly influenced by international agencies providing advice and model legislation. But there are often inconsistent and contradictory recommendations from organizations such as the EU, Council of Europe, World Bank, OECD, and International Labor Organization (ILO) because of changing staff and consultants, as well as internal disagreements within these organizations (Deacon and Michelle, 1997). So long as politicians placate international creditors, they have leeway to pick and choose among which expert advice to use as political justification or cover.

The International Monetary Fund, in particular, has pressed for an American-style residual welfare state and workfare strategies. The World Bank's Structural Adjustment Loans have often been conditional upon certain kinds of social policy legislation. Many welfare state retrenchment measures have been strongly advocated by the bank, such as an increased pension age, private pension programs, more targeting, family allowances differentiated by the number of children, and shorter and reduced unemployment benefits. When the World Bank was displeased with persistent social security deficits, it refused release of a $2 million loan earmarked for transforming social security until changes that it desired were implemented. Another sign of imposed fiscal discipline is that as of 1996, the social security and health funds' administrative boards no longer submit their budgets directly to Parliament; instead, a budget must go first to the Finance Ministry, which amends it and then sends it to Parliament for approval. The fund boards have the option of submitting their original budgets to Parliament and asking it to choose between the two.

Pierson (1996, p. 149) argues against the likelihood of retrenchment on this basis: "Politicians in democratic systems generally worry first and foremost about getting elected. Helping improve the economy may make that easier, but not if it requires hugely unpopular policies, and not if the economic benefits are likely to appear at some point in the distant (that is, post election) future." It is true, on the one hand, that Hungarian politicians are acutely aware of the unpopularity of cutbacks. Hungarian governments of both Left and Right have sought wide coalitions both among parties and within tripartite bargaining to implement austerity programs. Governments have sought to obscure accountability by hiding real benefit cuts behind inadequate indexing against inflation. The timing of Socialist Party cutbacks early in its term, as well as the (failed) attempt to gain previous consensus with unions, moreover, indicate the fear of electoral retribution for cutbacks and a persistent strategy of blame avoidance.

Politicians, however, are not only fixated on the next general election. Hungary faced absolute threats to fiscal insolvency in both 1981 and 1993–1994. If these crises had kept world lending agencies from approving further loans and issuing favorable bond ratings, it would have become impossible to keep the fiscal ship of state afloat. No governmental head wants to face the uncertain consequences of such events. Moreover, the perception of having been a competent economic manager in the eyes of international agencies has allowed many former government officials to go on to prosperous and prestigious careers. The prime minister of the last Communist Party government, Miklós Németh, for instance, moved into the position as vice president at the European Bank for Reconstruction and Development. Similarly, the finance minister responsible for pushing radical cutbacks in 1995, after resigning in the face of popular anger, received a high post at the World Bank.

Another increasingly important international influence has been that of private foreign investors. By 1995, 70 percent of manufacturing exports were from foreign-owned firms, up from 50 percent in 1993 (*Business Central Europe*, April 1996). Foreign investors held 49.3 percent of registered capital in Hungarian banks and owned 54 percent of Hungary's bank by assets; the latter was expected to reach 60 percent after expected privatization in 1997 (*Napi Gazdaság*, July 15, 1997, p. 4). A recent Deloitte Touche Tohmatsu survey of international investors in Central East Europe found that nearly half were offered some tax break as an incentive (Ellingstad, 1997, p. 11). Of the world's 35 largest multinationals, 20 are in Hungary, and they account for 20 percent of its GDP. The government cabinet in 1997 signed its first cooperation pact with the Hungarian Association of Multinational Companies (*Magyar Hírlap*, May 16, 1997, p. 5). There is no evidence that multinational corporations have exerted direct influence on social policy. Typically, they are more concerned with trade regulations and currency stability. But indirectly, foreign investors have influenced social policy by refusing to honor unionization and invoking the threat of exit should the cost of employer contributions to social insurance become too high.

CHANGES IN SOCIAL POLICY

Overall spending on the principal benefit systems—pensions, health insurance and unemployment insurance—declined from 30 percent in 1991 to 22 percent of GDP in 1996, despite a falling GDP and greater needs imposed on all these programs (OECD, 1997, p. 93). As Table 9.1 illustrates, reductions have hit all areas hard, but especially family support and unemployment. An important acceleration in spending reductions took place in 1995 with an aggressive package of changes. As previously mentioned, some of these measures were thwarted by public outrage or declared unconstitutional. The surviving provisions included many social spending cuts and greater targeting, a currency devaluation that diminished Hungarians' buying power while encouraging exports, and wage reductions, especially in the public sector.

To best understand the extended processes of growth and retrenchment, we must look more closely at specific program changes. New social programs for unemployment and poverty relief have been created. The post-communist institutions that regulate unemployment are virtually all new because, as noted, socialist planning had officially eradicated unemployment. Thus, newly elected post-communist governments found themselves

Table 9.1
Real Social Spending, 1991–1996 (Constant Billion Hungarian Forints)

	1991	1992	1993	1994	1995	1996	Percent Change
Social insurance (pension and health)		445.0	426.1	424.7	375.9	345.3	–22.4
Unemployment		63.8	62.2	42.5	34.9	31.8	–50.2
Family Support		93.4	86.9	80.9	59.1	44.6	–52.2
Social assistance, personal, and institutional care		125.1	138.6	137.3	138.5	102.1	–18.4
TOTAL	750.0	727.3	713.8	685.4	608.4	523.8	–30.1

Source: OECD (1997) using data from the Ministries of Finance and Welfare. Data do not include local government spending, except as financed through central expenditures.

without appropriate institutions for combating, compensating, or even counting unemployment in a market economy. They originally created generous benefits that paid 90 percent of wages and could continue for two years. Over time, as unemployment became more widespread and longer-lasting, the benefits were greatly reduced, and long-term relief was delegated to local residual aid.

A large number of new active labor market programs were also created to help move the unemployed into work. These measures include training, start-up business loans, work-sharing through part-time employment, and tax incentives for hiring the long-term unemployed. Total spending in these programs has, however, remained relatively modest. Perhaps this is because it is widely acknowledged that most unemployed persons, in fact, do some informal work to supplement their benefits, just as it is normal for Hungarians with full-time jobs to supplement their salaries with additional jobs. In an economy where informal work and multiple jobholding are the norm, programs such as those to move people into part-time work or start their own businesses are barely distinct from general wage supplements.

Local government acquired a new layer of social administration in 1990 and was given responsibility for general social assistance. This aid is discretionary and highly residual, picking up those who have exhausted other benefits or otherwise fallen through the social safety net, especially those who have exhausted their unemployment insurance benefits. The strain on local governments to perform this role immediately grew as the number of cases receiving regular and occasional social assistance almost quadrupled between 1990 and 1995 (UNICEF, 1997). Local governments in poor neighborhoods get some funds from the central government, but, unlike wealthier localities that are able to supplement their budgets by privatizing apartments and other holdings, the poorer neighborhoods also have less valuable real estate to privatize. Applicants for emergency aid must be far below the poverty line to receive aid. Much of the screening process is self-selecting because the payments are so small that people with adequate means do not bother to be interviewed. Despite their residual nature and inadequate funding, from a purely institutional point of view, these local programs represent an important addition to the development of the Hungarian welfare state.

CHANGES IN MAJOR SOCIAL WELFARE PROGRAMS

Pensions

The nature of welfare state changes can be seen not only in spending levels but also in the specific policies that have altered the most expensive programs like pensions, unemployment, and health. Major reforms have taken place in pensions. As mentioned earlier, the value of pensions has been allowed to fall with the minimum wage to which they are indexed, and they are below the subsistence minimum. In the new pension scheme about 60 percent of average wages are replaced. Pensioners who under Communism used to work part-time at their old jobs to supplement their pensions can no longer do so because these positions were mostly eliminated in post-communist downsizing. As a result, they are typically living on smaller pensions and no supplements.

The other big changes have been an increase in the retirement age and the introduction of a three-tier, privately subsidized pension system. Both of these measures were originally recommended by the World Bank and formulated in 1991 but were delayed until later in the decade (Gedeon, 1995). Legislation passed in 1996 will gradually raise the minimum pension ages from 55/60 years (women/men) to a uniform 62 years for both men and women by 2009. Legislation passed the following year mandated a three-pillar pension system: (1) the previous flat-rate, universal pension, (2) a pension based on lifetime earnings and employee–employer contributions, and (3) an individual supplementary insurance scheme. From 1998 on, anyone entering the workforce must be provided with a personal pension. Employees are required to contribute at least 6 percent of their earnings (up to a maximum salary of twice the national average) into a mandatory private pension fund. Various banks and insurance companies are establishing schemes, as may some large employers. Regulations will try to ensure that pension funds are invested relatively safely, and only a small proportion may be invested abroad. The long-term importance of this third pillar is the political effect that it will have on the future of the first two pillars.

Means-Tested Social Spending

Recent changes to better "target" social spending by making it more selective are likely to erode the long-term political prospects for these programs. It is a well-established fact of welfare state policy making that separating the fortunes of the more wealthy and the middle class from those of the poor inevitably leads to an erosion of the latter programs (Korpi, 1989; Korpi and Palme, 1998). The politically more influential middle class is much less inclined to identify its interests with the basic pensions. Over the long term, reliance on means-tested programs for the poor also tends to undermine their popularity because the "moral logic" of their procedural implementation is more difficult to legitimate (Rothstein, 1996). Unlike universally administered policies that give citizens simple and easy-to-defend decision criteria, selective programs are required to justify the exact line between the needy and non-needy. Because means-tested programs give administrators discretion over particular cases and hold them accountable for their judgment over whether or not specific individuals are "deserving," the programs are inherently vulnerable to bureaucratic abuse of power and client fraud. They also tend to be viewed as less competent because they must expend a greater portion of resources on control, rather than on actual provision. In Hungary, the moral logic of means testing is bound to be particularly destructive of long-term support for social programs because social norms reflect decades of evading communist authorities, and petty corruption is endemic to the coping strategies of economic life. Even more than in the West, the movement from universal to means-tested programs is bound to make Hungarians cynical about whether fellow citizens are paying their fair share of taxes and whether benefits are going to the truly deserving.

Health Care

Health care was made less universal in 1992. Access to health care was transformed into an earned right based on employment, with separate provisions for those without a source of earned income. The effective price of health care has also increased for citizens. "Gratuity money," or the ubiquitous system of tipping doctors and staff (their main source of income), has increased much faster than inflation because it has become more open, and medical salaries have stagnated. Universal health care has also been eroded by the growth of private health care for the very rich. In the absence of a nursing home network, the health system is further burdened by relatives who pay their doctors to have long-term hospital care prescribed, an expensive and inefficient alternative to elder care. The socialist government saved money by closing many regional hospitals and clinics, thereby achieving economies of scale but reducing availability in the process.

Unemployment Benefits

Unemployment benefits have seen reductions in eligibility, duration, and benefit levels, with an increasing emphasis on means testing. There are three kinds of unemployment benefits for which applicants might be eligible. Unemployment insurance (UI) payments are more generous than the benefits that go to those just leaving school or who have exhausted their other benefits and apply for means-tested local unemployment assistance (UA). Means-tested UA benefits are available to those whose UI eligibility has expired and whose total per capita family income is less than 80 percent of the minimum old age pension. Any income earned up to the maximum benefit is currently deducted from the benefit, although prior to 1996 no benefit penalty had been imposed on earnings up to the minimum wage. The school-leavers allowance is equivalent to benefits in the UA scheme and is available for a maximum of six months. Due to tightened eligibility criteria, the share of the unemployed receiving some form of benefits was cut in half, from 65 percent in 1992 to 31 percent in 1994. The maximum duration of UI benefits was cut in 1993 from two years to one year, less if the individual has been contributing to the benefit fund for less than four years. Prior to 1996 the UA benefits were of unlimited duration, but a two-year maximum was subsequently imposed. Before 1993, UI benefit levels remained constant throughout the eligibility period. Subsequently, a two-phase system was introduced with benefits reduced after the first three months.

As of 1997, the one-phase system was reinstated but with benefits at a reduced level. Benefits must fall within a prescribed band that has been falling. The ceiling in 1997 was 1.24 times the very low minimum wage. Because of high inflation and the fact that benefits are calculated on the previous year's unindexed earnings, the replacement rate in real terms is less than 50 percent for the majority of UI recipients. Because of various floors on replacement rates at all but the minimum level, only 10 percent of the workforce in 1994 received even the nominal statutory replacement rates of 75 and 60 percent. A majority of the benefits were below the official minimum subsistence level, not surprising considering that the minimum wage represented a benefit ceiling and that the minimum wage was significantly below the subsistence minimum. Before 1996, beneficiaries were permitted earnings up to the minimum wage without losing benefits; the limit has since been reduced to half the minimum wage. Until the creation of the residual UA system there were repeated temporary extensions of UI benefits as the government realized that the long-term unemployed were not finding jobs. As of 1996, over 45 percent of the registered unemployed received these lower benefits. Under the UA system, maximum benefits are set at 80 percent of the minimum old age pension, with all other earned income deducted from benefits. UA benefits are income-tested, with eligibility (but not amount) determined according to household per capita income.

Housing

A final area where we can see retrenchment is in the long-term trends in housing policy. The commitment to public provision of housing largely ended in the 1980s, when, despite urgent housing shortages, the state essentially abdicated responsibility for housing provision in favor of various schemes to help people take out loans and obtain material for building their own homes. Moreover, public housing provision was distributed in such a way that it increased, rather than decreased, inequality. After 1990, the decaying public housing stock was then placed under the stewardship of local governments, which were encouraged to sell units to their current residents at less-than-market rates. These measures were popular but nonetheless constitute a form of welfare state retrenchment because housing inequalities are increased, and the future capacity for housing policy to respond to social needs is undercut.

CONCLUSIONS: THE "RETURN TO NORMALCY" AND GENERALIZABILITY

The overall picture of recent Hungarian social policy developments is one of retrenchment mixed with the introduction of new programs that have subsequently undergone their own retrenchment. Eligibility and payment levels have been curtailed. Hungary's social policy arrangements will be less likely to maintain equality in the future because institutionalized political solidarities have been largely dismantled by the introduction of means testing and programs for privatized provision of pensions, health care, and housing. This conclusion considers two arguments about how generalizable Hungary's experience might be for comparative analysis. The first argument to be considered is whether, given Hungary's peculiar path of modernization, recent changes constitute more of a "return to normalcy" than retrenchment. The second considers whether Hungarian retrenchment can be attributed to the peculiar politics of post-Communism.

Given the evidence regarding spending curtailment and program redesign, recent Hungarian changes appear clearly to constitute welfare state retrenchment. However, a common alternative interpretation is that the reduced policy commitments should be viewed as part of a larger modernizing transition from an aberrant command economy to a more normal market equilibrium. This argument is particularly influential in Eastern Europe because reforms have been conceived as a "return to normalcy." Larger welfare states are viewed as unsustainable deviations in a competitive global market because of labor market inflexibility, excessive fiscal burdens, and disincentives to foreign capital investment. Only wealthy countries are viewed as able to afford the burdensome luxury of high social spending. By this logic Hungary's social spending was abnormally excessive for its low level of GDP. This "normal trajectory" type of argument is, however, contradicted by a wide and diverse literature that demonstrates how market economies have themselves followed very different developmental trajectories (Gershenkron, 1962; Shonfield, 1965; Piore and Sabel, 1984; Albert, 1992; Berger and Dore, 1996).

There are four reasons to suggest that relatively high levels of total spending might be a normal equilibrium for Hungary. First, the relationship between income and social spending is mediated by other relationships in which Hungary appears normal. An extensive previous literature tried to test competing theories of welfare state expansion by examining how different factors correlate across countries. These studies had trouble establishing clear causation for their theories but came to several interesting conclusions. When both developing and industrialized economies are considered, GDP per capita is the strongest predictor of welfare spending, but among industrialized nations, welfare state expansion correlates most closely with an aging population and union density (Wilensky, 1975; Stephens, 1979). Hungary has an aging population, and union density, while falling, was still relatively strong in 1990. Seen in the light of Hungary's demographics and union density, its sizable, but by no means lavish, welfare state seems normal.

Second, the size of Hungary's welfare state relative to GDP is a result, but not necessarily a cause, of its economic woes. Hungary's welfare state looks larger because of the increased need and decreased GDP since 1989. When Hungary's economy was healthier in 1980–1981, its various forms of social security expenditures consumed 20.1 percent of GDP, the same portion as in the United States, a notorious welfare state laggard by European standards. In areas where needs have remained relatively constant, such as education and health, Hungary still spends a very low portion of its GDP (Gács, 1986).

Third, standard measures of social transfers, such as those applied by the World Bank, ignore the indirect redistributive transfers in Western economies through such fiscal measures as, for instance in the United States, housing mortgage subsidies. These types of indirect transfers are ignored because of the difficulties of international comparison, but leaving them out biases the data.

Last, we should see Hungarian social spending in the context of the political process of democratization. In international comparison the other countries whose social spending is larger than expected for their level of development are Spain, Portugal, and Greece—all countries that have also emerged from authoritarian rule. Perhaps both the so-called model transitions of Southern Europe and those in Eastern Europe require large-scale redistribution to ensure political consensus. The years of democratic consolidation from 1976 to 1983 are when Spanish public spending increased by more than half, from 25 to 38 percent (Rhodes, 1997). In their current political context, Eastern European spending levels cannot be viewed as abnormally high.

The politics of post-communist transformation is distinct from retrenchment in the West. The strong hand of outside international lenders facilitates blame avoidance, and interest group networks are poorly developed to defend social programs. While the values of the population still strongly support egalitarian and active government, there is little capacity for collective action in defense of social protection. Perhaps steady growth and admittance to the European Union will undergird future generosity in social policies, but the changes since 1990 have made such a course far less likely.

NOTES

1. High social spending is generally found in countries with higher per capita income, such as the Scandinavian countries, but Hungary's income level is below that of Portugal and Ireland. Hungary's social expenditures grew by 29 percent from 1981 to 1987, while the GDP grew by only 3 percent (Bartlett, 1997, p. 200).

2. The Hungarian forint was worth about a penny in 1997, but was much higher during the mid-1980s when its exchange rate was controlled by the government and the currency was not convertible on world markets.

3. In the same poll, only 17 percent of Americans and 22 percent of West Germans responded thus. Similarly, "government provision of a basic income for all" was strongly favored by 51 percent of Hungarians, compared to 10 percent of Americans and 19 percent of West Germans (Freeman and Blanchflower, 1997). Other polls, however, have found higher support in the United States for full employment (see, for example, evidence cited by Skocpol, 1995).

REFERENCES

Albert, M. (1992). *Capitalism against Capitalism*. London: Whurr.

Amsden, A. H., K. Jacek, and L. Taylor. (1994). *The Market Meets Its Match*. Cambridge, MA: Harvard University Press.

Andorka, R. (1994). "Social changes and social problems in Hungary since the 1930s: Economic, social and political causes of the collapse of the socialist system." In A. B. Seligman, ed., *Comparative Social Research*, vol. 14. Greenwich, CT: JAI Press, pp. 49–96.

Árvay, J., and A. Vértes. (1995). *The Share of the Private Sector and the Hidden Economy in Hungary*. Budapest: GKI Economic Research.

Bartlett, D. (1997). *The Political Economy of Dual Transformations: Market Reform and Democratization in Hungary*. Ann Arbor: University of Michigan Press.

Berger, S., and R. Dore, eds. (1996). *National Diversity and Global Capitalism*. Ithaca, NY: Cornell University Press.

Bruszt, L. (1988). "Without us but for us? Political orientation in Hungary in the period of late paternalism." *Social Research* 55(1–2): 43–76.

CESTAT. (1997, first quarter). *CESTAT Statistical Bulletin.* Budapest: Central Statistical Office.

Clayton, R., and J. Pontusson. (1998). "Welfare-state retrenchment revisited: Entitlement cuts, public sector restructuring, and inegalitarian trends in advanced capitalist societies." *World Politics* 51 (October): 67–98.

Deacon, B., and H. Michelle. (1997). "The making of post-communist social policy: The role of international agencies." *Journal of Social Policy* 26(1): 43–62.

Ellingstad, M. (1997). "The Maquiladora syndrome: Central European prospects." *Europe-Asia Studies* 49(1): 7–21.

Elster, J. (1993). "Constitution-making in Eastern Europe: Rebuilding the boat in the open sea." *Public Administration* 71(1/2): 169–217.

Ferge, Z. (1979). *A Society in the Making.* White Plains, NY: M. E. Sharpe.

———. (1993). "Magyar szociálpolitika, 1992." In P.S.S. Kurtán and L. Vass, eds., *Magyarország Politikai Évkönyve.* Budapest: Demokrácia Kutatások Magyar Központja Alapítvány.

Freeman, R., and D. Blanchflower. (1997). "The attitudinal legacy of Communist labor regulations." *Industrial and Labor Relations Review* 50(3): 438–459.

Gábor, I. R. (1991). "Prospects and limits to the second economy." *Acta Oeconomica* 43(3–4): 349–352.

Gács, E. (1986). "Hungary's social expenditures in international comparison." *Acta Oeconomica* 36(1): 141–154.

Gedeon, P. (1995). "Hungary: Social policy in transition." *East European Politics and Societies* 9(3): 433–458.

Gershenkron, A. (1962). *Economic Backwardness in Historical Perspective.* Cambridge, MA: Harvard University Press.

Godfrey, M. (1994). "Are Hungarian labour costs really so high?" *ILO/Japan Project on Employment Policies for Transition in Hungary.* Geneva: ILO.

Goven, J. (1993). "The gendered foundations of Hungarian socialism: State, society, and the anti-politics of anti-feminism." Unpublished Ph.D. dissertation, Department of Sociology, University of California, Berkeley.

ILO. (1996). *Labour Market and Economic Transition.* Geneva: Author.

Institute for World Economics. (1995). *Human Resources and Social Stability during Transition in Hungary.* San Francisco: Author.

International Monetary Fund. (1998). "Hungary: Economic policies for sustainable growth." Occasional Paper 159. Washington, DC: Author.

Kolosi, T., and M. Sági. (1996). *Társadalmi Riport 1996.* Budapest: TARKI.

Kornai, J. (1992). "The post-Socialist transition and the state: Reflections in the light of Hungarian fiscal policy." *American Economic Review* 82(2): 1–21.

Korpi, W. (1989). "Power, politics, and state autonomy in the development of social citizenship: Social rights during sickness in eighteen OECD countries since 1930." *American Sociological Review* 54 (June): 309–328.

Korpi, W., and J. Palme. (1998). "The paradox of redistribution and strategies of equality: Welfare state institutions, inequality, and poverty in the Western countries." *American Sociological Review* 63 (October): 661–687.

Kovács, I. (1994). "Did we indeed consume too much?" *Acta Oeconomica* 46(1–2): 143–162.

Lipton, D., and J. Sacks. (1990). *Privatization in Eastern Europe: The case of Poland* (Brookings Papers). Washington, DC: Brookings Institution.

Milanovic, B. (1992). "Income distribution in late socialism: Poland, Hungary, Czechoslovakia, Yugoslavia and Bulgaria Compared." 2nd draft. Washington, DC: Socialist Economies Unit, The World Bank.

———. (1994). "Cash social transfers, direct taxes, and income distribution in late socialism." *Journal of Comparative Economics* 18 (April): 175–197.

Neumann, L. (1997). "Circumventing trade unions in Hungary: Old and new channels of wage bargaining." *European Journal of Industrial Relations* 3(2): 183–202.

OECD. (1995). *Social and Labour Market Policies in Hungary*. Paris: Author.

———. (1997). *OECD Economic Surveys: Hungary*. Paris: Author.

Ollman, B. (1997). "Market mystification in capitalist and market socialist societies." *Socialism and Democracy* 11(2): 35–45.

Örkeny, A., and G. Csepoli. (1994). "Perceptions of social inequality in Hungarian society." *Comparative Social Research* 14: 173–192.

Pierson, P. (1996). "The new politics of the welfare state." *World Politics* 48 (January): 143–179.

Piore, M., and C. Sabel. (1984). *The Second Industrial Divide*. New York: Basic Books.

Rhodes, M. (1997). "Spain." In H. Compston, ed., *The New Politics of Unemployment: Radical Policy Initiatives in Western Europe*. New York and London: Routledge.

Rose, R., and C. Haerpfer. (1993). "Adapting to transformation in Eastern Europe." In *Studies in Public Policy*. Glasgow: University of Strathclyde.

Rothstein, B. (1996). *Administration and Legitimacy: A Comparative Perspective*. Paper delivered at annual meeting of the American Political Science Association, Boston, September.

Shonfield, A. (1965). *Modern Capitalism: The Changing Balance of Public and Private Power*. London: Oxford University Press.

Skocpol, T. (1995). " 'Brother, can you spare a job?' Work and welfare in the United States." In T. Skocpol, *Social Policy in the United States: Future Possibilities in Historical Perspective*. Princeton, NJ: Princeton University Press, pp. 228–249.

Standing, G., and G. V.-W. Guy, eds. (1995). *Minimum Wages in Central and Eastern Europe: From Protection to Destitution*. New York: Central European University Press.

Stephens, J. D. (1979). *The Transition from Capitalism to Socialism*. London: Macmillan.

Szelenyi, I. (1978). "Social inequalitites under state socialist redistributive economies." *International Journal of Comparative Sociology* 61: 67–87.

UNICEF. (1997). *Children at Risk in Central and Eastern Europe: Perils and Promises*. Florence: Author.

Weaver, K. (1986). "The politics of blame avoidance." *Journal of Public Policy* 6 (October–December): 371–398.

Wilensky, H. (1975). *The Welfare State and Equality*. Berkeley: University of California Press.

World Bank. (1995). *Hungary: Structural Reforms for Sustainable Growth*. Washington, DC: Author.

Chapter 10

Is the Japanese-Style Welfare Society Sustainable?

Masami Nomura and Kimiko Kimoto

This chapter explores the question of how a modern, industrial nation manages to spend relatively little on social welfare and nonetheless maintains political and social stability. Japan has consistently achieved official unemployment rates much lower than most other capitalist countries, and this should reduce the need for social welfare. These low unemployment rates, however, do not mean that Japan has true full employment or more vacant jobs at fair wages than job seekers. Japan has high rates of latent or hidden unemployment, particularly among married women, but such unemployment is not compensated by direct provision of social welfare. We find that the explanation of the spare Japanese welfare state is in family structure, the role of women in the family and the labor market, and occupational benefits that take different forms for various groups of workers—from the privileged employees of large firms to workers in family businesses and the self-employed.

In this chapter we take up the political structure of Japan; demographic trends, such as the rapid aging of the population; labor market characteristics, including some of the changes in the last decade; the framework of social security; approaches to occupational welfare; and the persisting welfare functions of the Japanese family. Finally, we address the question of whether and to what extent Japanese exceptionalism is likely to continue. In this connection we take into account the effects of Japan's longest recession since World War II and the increasing tendency for hidden unemployment to become official unemployment.

POLITICAL RESHUFFLING IN THE 1990s

Japan, the second largest economic power in the world, is the only advanced industrial country outside Europe and North America. A latecomer to capitalism, Japan developed a system in which bureaucrats have had a dominant influence in politics and the economy since the Meiji Revolution in 1868. In the era of U.S. occupation after World War II, the Americans fundamentally reformed education, land-ownership, the corporate system, and labor relations but refrained from undermining the powerful bureaucracy in order to secure effective control over Japan.

Since 1955, when the conservative Liberal and Democratic Parties merged to form the Liberal Democratic Party (LDP), the Japanese power triangle has consisted of the LDP, the bureaucracy, and big business. The LDP controlled top bureaucrats by influencing promotion and assignment of key personnel. Top bureaucrats controlled big business through the use of industrial policies, administrative guidance, subsidies, and regulations. Big business supported the LDP by offering money and delivering votes. This power triangle collapsed in 1993, when, after critical groups left the party, the LDP lost its majority in Parliament. After being in opposition for nearly one year, the LDP regained power in 1994.

Since the LDP ended its single-party rule in 1993, the political constellation has been unpredictable. First, no one party can form a stable government, and that will be the case for the foreseeable future. The LDP regained the majority in the Lower House by poaching lawmakers from opposition parties and reestablished single-party government in May 1998. But voters felt that the LDP had become arrogant and that this might result in corruption. Furthermore, the LDP was thought to have lost the ability to tackle economic policy amid the deepening economic recession. The LDP was punished by voters in the election of the Upper House in July 1998. As a result, the LDP had only 104 of the total 252 seats in the Upper House. Despite the reduced power of the LDP, it is very unlikely that opposition parties will succeed in forming a new coalition government, because, with the exception of the Communist Party, the major opposition parties are far from being stabilized. The largest opposition party, founded in 1997, the Democratic Party, is suffering from power struggles within the party. Other opposition parties are now being reorganized.

The second reason for this unpredictability is the radical reshuffling of political parties since 1992 that brought the end of single-party rule the following year. Among the major political parties, only the LDP and the Japanese Communist Party remain. The Japanese Socialist Party, the largest opposition party for many years and traditionally representative of left-wing labor unions, is nearly dead. In 1994, the Japanese Democratic Socialist Party, representative of right-wing labor unions, merged with Komeito, the political wing of a powerful religious group, Soka Gakkai, to found the largest opposition party, Shinshinto. Shinshinto suffers from intraparty power struggles and, in fact, split apart at the end of 1997. In this process of political reshuffling, the traditional linkages between political parties and social movements have nearly diminished.

The third reason for unpredictability is that at the time of the political reshuffling, the bureaucracy came under attack from political parties and the public because of bribery and other scandals involving its top leaders in policy-making processes behind the scenes. Not only the Ministry of Health and Welfare but also the more powerful Ministries of International Trade and Industry (MITI) and Finance have lost public trust due to these scandals. Consequently, long-term policy making has become difficult.

THE POWER OF LABOR

Almost all Japanese labor unions are enterprise unions, usually one for each company. The membership and the full-time officers are strictly limited to the regular employees of the company. Enterprise unions exclude from membership the peripheral or contingent workforce such as part-timers, temporary workers, and dispatched workers (i.e., workers who are hired by a company but dispatched to another company to work). In small and medium-sized companies there are no enterprise unions. Working conditions of the peripheral workforce in big companies and of all employees in small or medium-sized companies—all of whom have no collective bargaining power—are less favorable than those of regular employees in big companies. The very employees who need unions to improve their poor working conditions are not organized. This is one important reason for big differences in working conditions between big companies and small and medium-sized enterprises and between peripheral and regular employees.

So-called industrial unions, such as the Japan Federation of Steel Workers' Unions, are federations of independent enterprise unions that coordinate their actions. However, they are not able to negotiate with companies on behalf of the individual enterprise unions.

Industrial unions were once powerful in political election campaigns. However, since the drastic political reshuffling in 1993, unions have fallen into a political identity crisis. They no longer have political parties that represent their interests. The unionization rate had declined to 23.8 percent of the workforce in 1995, in part due to the expansion of the historically non-unionized service sector and in part to the soaring numbers of peripheral workers who are not eligible for membership in an enterprise union. As a consequence, increasing numbers of workers lack power in relation to their employers and government.

DEMOGRAPHIC TRENDS

With a population of about 125 million (1995), Japan is the seventh most populous country in the world. Until 1988, Japan was the youngest among the industrial countries in terms of the proportion of persons over 65 years in the total population. However, owing partly to a declining birthrate and partly to the world's highest life expectancy rate, Japan is a rapidly aging society and is expected to be the society with the largest proportion of elderly people in the world by the year 2010—22.0 percent, compared to 13.2 percent in the United States, 20 percent in Germany, and 18.0 percent in Sweden (Management and Coordination Agency, 1997a).

Between 1975 and 1995, the total fertility rate in Japan declined from 1.91 to 1.42, and it is expected to continue declining. The present fertility rate is already below the 2.1 level, the rate at which the population remains constant.

In contrast to other industrialized societies, Japan has not experienced a significant increase in single parenthood. Estimates of single parenthood vary, depending on the definition used. Defining single-parent households as ones with a mother age 20–60 only and children under 20 years old, the Ministry of Health and Welfare estimates that the number was 452,000 (1.3 percent of all households) in 1980, 540,000 (1.3 percent) in 1990, and 547,000 (1.2 percent) in 1996. Divorce is responsible for 64.3 percent of single-mother households, widowhood for 24.6 percent, and non-marriage for 4.7 percent (Health and Welfare Statistics Association, 1997).

There are several reasons that single motherhood is not increasing. First, though the divorce rate has been increasing gradually in recent years, it is still low, 1.45 per 1,000 population in 1996. In contrast, it was 2.95 per 1,000 in the United Kingdom in 1989 and 4.70 in the United States (Inoue and Ehara, 1995). Second, nearly 60 percent of the divorced women remarry. Third, single motherhood resulting from non-marriage is much less common in Japan than in other countries, particularly the United States. In Japan in 1993, non-married single mothers accounted for only 4.7 percent of all the single mothers, a small group to begin with (Health and Welfare Statistics Association, 1997).

One major reason for the low rate of single motherhood resulting from non-marriage is that nearly all pregnant teenagers obtain abortions voluntarily or under pressure from their parents. Abortion is legal in Japan when the partners agree to allege that there are possible genetic defects, that the pregnancy is the result of rape, or that marriage is contraindicated for "economic reasons." Through the use of a loose definition of "economic reasons," abortion is de facto liberalized. The number of unmarried single mothers is only gradually increasing. Single motherhood, because it is limited in size, has never been a welfare topic in Japan.

ETHNIC COMPOSITION

Ethnically, Japan is a homogeneous country. After a 100-year assimilation policy, the aboriginal Ainu are mostly integrated into Japanese society. Yet, there still exists social discrimination against them.

In 1995, about 1.4 million foreigners were legal residents of Japan, nearly half of whom had permanent residence rights. They are mainly Koreans who were abducted to work in Japan during World War II and their descendants. Japan has rejected multiculturalism and endorsed assimilation policies, though not with equality among ethnic groups. There are severe restrictions on immigration so that only foreigners with special skills can legally find jobs. In the late 1980s, when manufacturing industries suffered serious labor shortages due to unfavorable working conditions, the government permitted immigrants and their offspring to take unskilled work in Japan.

Foreign workers, both legal and illegal, were estimated by the Ministry of Labor to number 260,000 in 1990, jumping to 610,000 in 1993 and then remaining at about 670,000 in 1998, or 1.0 percent of the total workforce. Illegal foreigners have no access to social welfare. Legal, foreign workers are classified in six groups. Each group has different access to social welfare. Koreans are legally classified in seven groups.

THE LABOR MARKET AND UNEMPLOYMENT

In the late 1980s, a time later termed the "bubble boom," there was an excessive demand for labor, which, in turn, led to a flood of legal and illegal foreign workers, mainly from other Asian countries. Optimism over full employment during the bubble boom was followed by fear of massive unemployment in the 1990s, after the burst of the bubble. In November 1998, the unemployment rate was 4.4 percent, the worst record after the war. However, by international standards, 4.4 percent is still low. At the same time, France and Germany suffered nearly 11 percent unemployment, and in 1997, the United States proclaimed its 5 percent unemployment rate as "full employment" (Ministry of Labor, 1997; Economic Report of the President, 1997, ch. 1). Although Japan's 4.4 percent unemployment rate is comparatively low, it is thought to be dangerously high by Japanese authorities. The United States continued to proclaim unemployment rates in the 4 percent range as full employment.

It is important to determine whether, in fact, Japan's unemployment rate is as low as it seems. Foreign social scientists have insisted that Japan's low unemployment rate is a function of its definition of who is or is not employed. Japan counts as unemployed those who are seeking a job and who have not worked more than one hour in the last week of the month that is being considered. According to this definition, part-timers who work over one hour in the week are not considered unemployed. To respond to international observers who doubted Japan's low unemployment rate, the Japanese Ministry of Labor and the Economic Planning Agency recalculated the nation's unemployment rate, using the standard international definition. They concluded that Japan's unemployment rate would be only slightly higher by international standards (Ono 1994, pp. 119–120); this measure, developed by the Organisation for Economic Co-operation and Development (OECD), includes discouraged workers who are jobless, want work, and are presumably available for work but who stop seeking a job. In 1993, the official unemployment rate was 2.6 percent in Japan and 6.9 percent in the United States, a difference of 4.3 percent. Adding discouraged workers brings the unemployment rate to 4.8 percent in Japan and 7.8 percent in the United States, a smaller difference of 3 percent (OECD, 1995). This means Japan has more latent unemployment than does the United States.

The U.S. Bureau of Labor Statistics publishes seven indices of unemployment (U1 to U7) in order to standardize the measurement of unemployment among countries. The U5 measurement in this series is identical to the Japanese and U. S. official unemployment rates. In 1993, U5 was 2.2 percent in Japan and 6.8 percent in the United States, more than three times as high. The Japanese government publishes only the figure corresponding to U5. (The United States, although it publishes figures on involuntary part-time and discouraged workers, also does not include them in its official measures of unemployment.) Another definition of unemployment, the U7, includes discouraged workers who are jobless, want work, and are presumably available for work but who stop seeking a job. The U7 rates in the two countries are closer: 7.0 percent in Japan and 10.2 percent in the United States (Sorrentino, 1995). Latent unemployment is much higher in Japan than in the United States.

In Japan, latent unemployment is distributed unequally between men and women. In 1993, the official unemployment rate was 2.5 percent for men and 2.8 percent for women. Including discouraged workers, however, brought the rate to 3.4 percent for men and 6.8 percent for women, just double (OECD, 1995).

In our view, Japan's flexible peripheral workforce is the main factor in its low official or U5 rate of unemployment First, the family-employed workforce is relatively high in Japan, accounting for 6.3 percent of the entire workforce in 1993, compared to 1.6 percent in Germany and only 0.3 percent in the United States (Shakai Keizai Seisansei Honbu, 1996, p. 188). A member of the family-employed workforce leaves the labor market when a family business declines and stays home until it recovers. Because these workers in family businesses do not seek jobs outside the home, they are not unemployed, according to the official definition. Similarly, married women who lose part-time jobs have tended to drop out of the labor market until employment that fits their household responsibilities becomes available.

There is still another reason that official unemployment of women is low in Japan. Official female labor force participation forms an M-curve; that is, a high ratio of young, unmarried women work, then quit in their late twenties and early thirties, returning to work in their forties. Thus, the labor market does not need to accommodate most women in these age groups. Among industrial countries, the M-curve of female labor force participation is unusual.

Although Japan's official unemployment rate remains comparatively low, it has been rising, albeit slowly, since the 1970s (with the exception of the economic boom of the late 1980s). As discussed, considerable amounts of unemployment have remained latent in the past because most of those affected were married women working as part-timers or family workers who depended on the incomes of their husbands when they lost their jobs. However, during the recession of the past decade the wages of men in small and medium-sized firms began to decrease, and housewives, needing additional income, were staying in the labor market instead of dropping out when they lost their jobs. In other words, married women are beginning to cease being employment buffers, and that is one reason that the official unemployment rates have increased.

FRAMEWORK OF SOCIAL POLICY

The public social welfare system of Japan is composed of three types of coverage: medical care insurance, pension insurance, and social welfare. In fiscal year 1995, social welfare expenditures were allocated as follows: 51.8 percent for pensions; 37.2 percent for medical care; and 11 percent for the others, including public assistance for the poor and child welfare. After describing the various types of coverage, we explain both the generally low level of total social security spending in Japan and the very small proportion of it that goes for public assistance.

Medical Care

All Japanese people are required to insure themselves for medical care. Altogether, there are seven insurance organizations for different social groups: regular employees of big firms; employees of small and medium-sized firms; seamen; national civil servants; local civil servants; teachers and other employees of private schools; and farmers and self-employed persons. Insurance contributions and benefits are different among the seven institutions. Benefits are high for civil servants and employees of big firms. Subsidies are provided by the government to the insurance institutions with the exception of those for national and local civil servants and private school teachers. Integration of these diversified organizations is not on the agenda.

Pensions

Until 1985, similar to the medical care insurance, each occupational group had its own pension scheme. In fear of soaring expenditures, the LDP government reformed pension insurance fundamentally in 1985. By integrating some parts of the different pension schemes, wealthy groups have to subsidize nearly bankrupt groups. In the so-called three-floor system, the ground or first floor is a basic pension for all insured persons. The second floor is an additional benefit for all employees in the private sector and all civil servants. The self-employed have their own second floor benefit, if they are willing to pay voluntarily. At the third floor, regular employees of big firms and national and local civil servants have additional benefits in relation to before-retirement income. One-third of the basic pension expenditure of the first floor is a subsidy from the state. In 1985, for the first time in history, full-time housewives gained the right to receive benefits, though they do not contribute.

Although a description of the public social security system as a whole sounds comprehensive, its most distinctive feature is its low level of expenditures. Social expenditures amounted to 14.6 percent of national income in 1992, compared to 19.4 percent in the United States, 26.9 percent in the United Kingdom, 31.5 percent in Germany, 35.6 percent in France, and 52.5 percent in Sweden (Social Insurance Agency, 1997, p. 260). The relatively low rate of expenditure in the United States can be explained partly by lack of public medical care insurance, which is not the case in Japan. Compared to the countries that also provide public medical care insurance, Japan's low level of social security expenditure is striking.

ACCOUNTING FOR THE LOW LEVEL OF SOCIAL EXPENDITURES

It is generally thought that a social security system is needed for political and social stability in a modern industrial society. If the society is stable despite insufficient public social security, it is very likely that something substitutes for this public institution. We show that this is the case in Japan.

There are three reasons explaining the coexistence of political stability in Japan and its low levels of spending on public social security. First, for nearly one-third of the labor force, those who are employed in large firms and the public sector, welfare facilities and services are provided by these firms or by national or local governments as their employers and thus substitute for public social security. The system of occupational welfare arose following World War II, when Japan experienced miserable economic conditions. At that time, the public social security system did not function at all.

For maintaining and improving living conditions, labor unions demanded that welfare systems be developed by business firms. Management gave in to these demands, expecting in return high loyalty to the company. The provision of welfare to employees resulted from negotiations between individual companies and the enterprise unions that are characteristic of Japanese labor. Because of the underdeveloped public social security system, company-run facilities and services became comprehensive: supplying company dormitories and housing as a way of recruiting young workers from rural areas during the period of high economic growth that began in 1955 and assisting in the purchase of private homes; providing medical care, life insurance, saving-incentive schemes, and company savings plans; and developing support facilities such as canteens, company cooperatives, home help, cultural and sports facilities, and so on. The wage system included allowances for housewives and for children. Furthermore, big firms paid substantial retirement allowances to long-term employees. Retirement allowances were so huge that firms began to introduce pension schemes instead of lump-sum retirement allowances.

Second, as previously stated, self-employed and family employees were and still are a considerable proportion of the total labor force. Together, they accounted for over one-third (35.0 percent) of the workforce in 1970. Although these forms of employment are declining gradually, they still accounted for nearly one-fifth (18.6 percent) of the labor force in 1994. These highly organized self-employed and family employees are very important politically and are the mainstay of the ruling LDP. In return for political support in election campaigns, the LDP has protected them from cutthroat capitalistic competition in various ways. First of all, in the service sector, which includes nearly half of all self-employed and family workers, the government has intervened in favor of family businesses. For example, the 1974 "act regulating large-scale retail chains" blocked large-scale retailers from establishing stores freely in order to protect small, local retailers. Similarly, gas stations, rice sellers, liquor sellers and other small retailers were protected by law for many years. In other cases, occupational groups such as barbers organized associations to regulate business by themselves, a strategy for which they have the support of the government bureaucracies.

The third reason for the coexistence of political stability and low levels of social expenditures pertains to the agricultural sector. Farmers were important in politics not only because they were well organized but also because the election system favored voters in rural areas at the cost of citizens in big cities (a situation that continues, but to a lesser extent). By strict import restrictions on agricultural products and government subsidies, the ruling LDP has protected an agricultural sector that has long been unable to compete on the world market. The construction industry, in which there are many family businesses, enjoyed prosperity by virtue of large government investments in public works. Not by social security, then, but by investment and protection the government has successfully maintained an adequate standard of living for the self-employed and employees in family businesses. Under such favorable conditions they have been better able to save for their old age and sustain family workers who become unemployed.

Employees of small and medium-sized companies enjoyed less favorable company welfare than did regular employees of big firms. They have tried to sustain themselves through self-help efforts: making extra money by working long hours overtime and by the employment of wives. For them, low rates of unemployment were important. Much the same could be said for temporary and part-time workers in the larger firms.

"PROGRESSIVE LOCAL GOVERNMENTS" AND "THE FIRST YEAR OF WELFARE"

In the long history of LDP rule, the government moved to expand welfare substantially only once—in the late 1960s–early 1970s. In those years, the ruling party faced a challenge from "progressive local governments." Many people thought that their lives had certainly improved, but at a much slower tempo than the nation's economic development would warrant. Furthermore, in big cities, living conditions as a whole deteriorated rapidly as evidenced by overpopulation, serious traffic jams, pollution, scarce social facilities such as schools and parks, and soaring inflation. Due to an electoral system of the Upper and the Lower Parliament that favors conservative rural areas, there was little chance to upset the conservative LDP. But, at the local level, especially in big cities such as Tokyo and Osaka, grumbling citizens succeeded in electing left-wing mayors or governors. One of the slogans of these mayors and governors was "welfare first." They established many nursery schools, introduced free medical care for the aged, paid children's allowances, and supported schooling for the handicapped. In short, progressive local governments were local welfare states. Faced with competition that threatened its rule, the LDP began to support more welfare in the early 1970s. In 1971, the children's allowance was introduced. The year 1973 was proclaimed by the government as the "first year of welfare"; free national medical care for people over 70 was introduced, and pension benefits were raised (Jinno, 1992).

Retreat from Welfare First: The Japanese Welfare Society

The LDP's turn toward welfare was soon suspended. The first oil crisis in 1973 triggered a panic in a nation now accustomed to high economic growth. Social movements promoting welfare lost influence amid general fear of a declining national economy. How greatly the Japanese were shocked by the oil crisis was revealed by the "toilet paper panic." Responding to a widespread rumor that toilet paper would no longer be produced, housewives rushed to supermarkets to buy as much toilet paper as they could; this, in turn, reduced the stock of toilet paper. The reduced stock of toilet paper led them to believe in the rumor and to buy more toilet paper, only exacerbating the problem. The Japanese fell into deep pessimism about the future and became especially aware that they had no resources except human ones. We have to work hard, they concluded; otherwise, we will fall behind. This implied that the country could not afford to enlarge its welfare programs. Such sentiments were almost a national consensus.

Four factors contributed to the shift from "welfare first" principles to "reexamining welfare." First, revenues of the progressive local governments that had been financing the increases in welfare fell seriously into the red. The LDP denounced progressive local governments for throwing around money for welfare. As for progressive mayors and governors, they could not present concrete plans for reducing their deficits. Second, it soon became obvious that the 1973 reform of social security would cause expenditures to soar. The LDP feared that the national government would follow the "bad" fiscal examples of the progressive local governments. Third, "welfare first" exacted a heavy toll on firms. Big firms had previously provided welfare programs voluntarily for their employees. But progressive welfare policies at the local level as well as the national level increased taxes for social expenditures; inevitably, firms reduced their voluntary welfare spending. Firms believed that it would be difficult to inspire loyalty to the firm without the company welfare benefits.

A fourth factor was that in other industrial countries, "excessive welfare" had been under discussion, and the Japanese inferred that other industrial countries were suffering the "industrial country disease," meaning low productivity and budget deficits resulting from heavy welfare burdens. To avoid the "industrial country disease," the LDP argued, Japan had to cut social spending, thereby making people help themselves instead of depending on public welfare programs.

This LDP campaign was very effective. Many Japanese became frightened when they heard about the dismal social conditions in Europe or in the United States, as if they were imminent in Japan. The LDP and the bureaucrats conducted their campaign against welfare by linking it to divorce, crime, drugs, and other problems that have been assumed to drain the public treasury. In the deafening chorus against welfare, progressive mayors and governors were replaced by conservative politicians, one after another: Kyoto Prefecture, Yokohama City, and Okinawa Prefecture in 1978; Tokyo and Osaka Prefecture in 1979.

Despite deep pessimism, the Japanese economy recovered from the first oil recession after several years, owing to increased exports of automobiles and other machinery to the United States and Western Europe. Nevertheless, public opinion against social welfare remained unchanged. In the late 1970s, the LDP proposed a plan for a "Japanese-style welfare society" in which public social security played a complementary, but secondary, role to the Japanese spirit of self-help, warm human relations, and a mutual aid system. The family should be the main pillar of the Japanese-style welfare society. The LDP stated definitely that "the main caretaker of the aged parent and children is the family," which really meant women. The Japanese family is stable and sound, different from the collapsed Western family. The family is a "hidden" welfare asset. The role of the government should be limited to supporting the family in its role as the primary provider of care. In the Japanese-style welfare society, married women should not work full-time, only part-time, so that they have time to take care of their families, including sick or infirm older people. Implicit in this model is a fixed, traditional division of labor between the sexes. Only with a Japanese-style welfare society, the LDP argued, could Japan avoid the "industrial country disease" (LDP, 1979).

In the early 1980s, the public social security system was reviewed in the context of this model of a Japanese-style welfare society. To curb soaring expenditures for medical care of aged people, which had risen from 867 billion yen in 1975 to 1.9 trillion yen in 1979, free medical care for persons over 70 was abolished in 1983. Thereafter, patients over 70 had to pay a part of the fees for medical care—outpatients, 400 yen per day, and inpatients, 30 yen per day. In 1985, the pension insurance system was reformed to curb steeply rising expenditures by reducing benefits and increasing contributions.

LOW LEVEL OF PUBLIC ASSISTANCE

What makes public assistance in Japan so meager? The most important reason is that most persons eligible for public assistance do not receive it. According to one estimate, 6.4 million households (nearly 16 percent of all households) had incomes below the level of public assistance in the early 1990s (Shoji, Sugimura, and Fujimura, 1997, p. 79). If this estimate is correct, the take-up rate for public assistance is only 9 percent. In an estimate for 1982, the take-up rate was 24.3 percent (Sohara, 1985)—a precipitous decline in less than a decade.

The low take-up rate is attributed to policies of the Ministry of Health and Welfare (MHW) and local governments, weak rights-consciousness of persons eligible for assistance, poor knowledge of the public assistance system, and the stigma of being on relief (Soeda, 1995, pp. 239–251). Of these, the most important are the MHW policies that tend to discourage the needy from utilizing public assistance, for example, by investigating applicants very carefully. In the late 1970s, national antagonism against welfare was fueled when the mass media reported that some members of Yakuza, the

Japanese Mafia, were receiving public assistance. Ignoring the plain fact that receipt of public assistance was not widespread, the government used this rumor to campaign against welfare.

In 1981, the MHW issued guidelines for "promoting appropriate implementation of public assistance." These included a more severe means test for applicants and income checking during the time when public assistance is received. In the next year, to make applications more difficult, the ministry again reformed the procedure for public assistance application and approval. In the campaign against welfare, civil servants who had once treated welfare benefits as social rights began to regard their clients as welfare bums and to stigmatize them (Furukawa, Shoji, and Sadato, 1993, pp. 377–379). In the strenuous efforts by the government to limit public assistance, the number of households receiving it dropped by 123,000 in a decade, from 747,000 in fiscal year 1980 to 624,000 in fiscal year 1990. These efforts of the government to cut back public assistance were supported not only by business leaders who feared that high taxes would undermine competitiveness but also by many working people, including the working poor, who firmly believed in self-help by working.

Although there has been heated discussion of whether the level of public assistance is enough to maintain the "healthy, cultural, minimum standard of living" that is prescribed by Article 25 of Japan's Constitutional Law, there are many of the working poor whose living standard is nearly the same as that of those on public assistance. Moreover, the working poor have to pay taxes. From their viewpoint, people receiving public assistance are unfairly favored. The working poor therefore stigmatize public assistance (Mizushima, 1994).

Before World War II, only those persons whose disabilities prevented them from working were eligible for public assistance. After the war, under the strong influence of the American Occupational Army, those who were able to work but getting less income than the poverty line became eligible for public assistance. To distinguish "able-to-work" and "idle poor" from the "honest working poor," the "idle poor" have been more strongly stigmatized (Shoji, Sugimura, and Fujimura, 1997, pp. 172–173).

By encouraging work, not welfare, the government upholds work norms. Aged people, too, are often forced to find jobs. In 1995, nearly 5 million people over 65 years old, one-fourth of all people that age, were working, mainly for economic reasons (Management and Coordination Agency, 1997a). Single mothers who are capable of being employed and who receive public assistance are stigmatized and marginalized.

The Japanese welfare system is characterized by work and marginalization of the poor, meaning that the problem of poverty tends to be minimized. However, the aged who are unable to work are increasing rapidly, and for them the government has to make large expenditures. To hold down the expenses of income support, the government expects much from family members. The principle is that the aged should be taken care of by their families, not by the state. Since the wife of the oldest son cares for the elderly, a married-couple family is the foundation of Japan's minimal welfare state. The Japanese family has a limited number of single mothers; childless, married couples; and co-habiting couples. Homosexuality is discouraged through oppression. The question that arises and that we take up later in this chapter is: How stable and how just are these conditions that limit the need for social welfare?

FEMINIZATION OF POVERTY?

In Japan, as Axinn (1990) points out, there is no explicit feminization of poverty. Single mothers are limited in number. One reason for this is that the Ministry of Health and Welfare imposes a severe means test on single mothers that, in effect, forces single mothers to find a job. In case of divorce, MHW staff strongly urge that single mothers should be supported by their former spouses, who, in many cases, refuse to pay. According to the survey by the MHW in 1993, only 14.9 percent of all divorced single mothers were receiving money for child care from their former husbands (Nakada, Sugimoto, and Morita, 1997, p. 35). As a result of this administrative "guidance," about 87 percent of all single mothers have jobs, usually low-paid ones. Their incomes are about 30 percent of the income of the average married-couple household (p. 35). Single mothers are poor, but feminization of poverty does not occur because there are too few of them to predominate among all poor families with children. Single-mother families are estimated to account for 2.6 percent of all poor families (Shoji, Sugimura, and Fujimura, 1997, p. 79).

THE "MODERN FAMILY" IN WESTERN COUNTRIES

Since the late 1960s, there has been concern over the "crisis in the family" in Europe and North America. The "modern family," composed of a male breadwinner, a full-time housewife caring for the household, and children, was once thought to be the "typical family" but is no longer the norm. The "modern family" was first accepted as a model by the British middle class in the early nineteenth century and subsequently by the working class (Seccombe, 1993). The idea of the "modern family" was coupled with the idea of the "family wage," which implied that the husband should earn enough money to sustain the family so that the wife could engage exclusively in work in the home.

By the end of 1970s, this "modern family" lost its relevance. A variety of family forms had evolved, including unmarried couples, childless couples, single mothers, homosexual couples, and singles. Around 1980, the "typical family" with a married, full-time housewife with children accounted for only about 10 percent of all families in the United Kingdom and the United States. Further, the "family wage" tended to diminish as the women's movement arose with its strong support of women's economic independence, and consumption needs expanded as well. By comparison, Japan has never experienced the "crisis of the family."

Some figures suffice to show the stability of the Japanese family. The Japanese divorce rate was 1.45 per 1,000 population in 1992, while it was 4.70 in the United States (1990) and 2.95 in the United Kingdom (1989). The newborn babies of unmarried mothers accounted for 1.0 percent of all new babies in 1989, while the figures were 47.0 percent in Sweden (1990), 28.2 percent in France (1989), and 25.7 percent in the United States (1989) (Inoue and Ehara, 1995). (It should be noted that many of the unmarried Swedish parents to whom these children are born are, in fact, co-habiting and often marry subsequently.)

EMPLOYEES OF BIG FIRMS AND THE "MODERN FAMILY"

Japan, the last among the industrialized countries to adopt capitalism, was also the last to accept the idea of the "modern family." By the end of World War II, white-collar workers living in big cities could accept and form families that conformed to this model. They received higher education, which provided a chance to be hired as privileged white-collar workers, and their salaries were high enough to support this family model. But the working class, the overwhelming majority of the employed population, could not afford the "modern family."

After World War II, with the economy ruined and factories destroyed, the working class needed wage and welfare facilities to sustain themselves. The ailing economy recovered as a result of military orders from the U.S. military forces during the Korean War. From 1955 on, the Japanese economy began the high growth known as the "Japanese economic miracle." The "family wage" or "*nenko*-based wage," along with company welfare, played a decisive role in forming the "modern family" among the Japanese working class.

The *nenko*-wage is often translated as seniority-based pay. But this is not a good translation and might lead to misunderstanding. Seniority pertains simply to length of service. *Nenko* is more ambiguous and includes the categories of age, length of service, and/or length of job experience. Under the *nenko*-wage, the individual wage increases as *nenko* increases. However, the *nenko*-wage does not mean equal pay for the same *nenko*. Assessments of individuals' performances, conducted by management three times a year, also affect pay. While the individual gets pay increases every year, the amounts depend on an assessment of the worker's performance.

Nenko-pay was demanded by enterprise unions. Immediately after World

War II, labor unions exerted a strong influence on the management of big firms. The powerful Workers' Union of the Electric Power Industry (Densan) created a wage system and succeeded in implementing it in 1946. This is the famous Densan wage system, and it has become a model for many companies. The Densan wage system included a family allowance, a typical family wage for a male breadwinner.

Expecting high loyalty to the company, big firms, as already noted, provided comprehensive welfare benefits to their employees, either voluntarily or based on collective agreements with their enterprise unions. The Densan system included a family allowance and pension scheme that might substitute for insufficient public social security. Big firms contributed to the establishment of the "modern family," not only by providing company welfare and a family wage but also by organizing a campaign to encourage this "modern family" pattern. By intensifying competition among workers, *nenko*-pay also functioned very effectively for management. The family wage enabled the management to mobilize employees on behalf of company goals. While the housewife was occupied in housekeeping, the husband devoted himself to his job for the whole day.

Another aspect of company-based welfare was the "New Life Movement," which originated in the 1950s in rural areas. This was designed to reform traditional rural regulations such as the huge expenses of marriage and funeral ceremonies, and it, too, was organized by big firms. For example, in 1953, NKK, the second biggest steelmaker, started the movement in cooperation with its enterprise union to encourage "happy homes" for employees. The management provided a training course for housewives on housekeeping and family planning, including birth control. A "happy home" was defined as one in which the housewife governs the family life, and the husband recovers his vitality for the company by enjoying a comfortable family life (Orii, 1973, pp. 112–113). The wife performs so-called reproductive work. This campaign helped to establish the "modern family" in the Japanese working class.

With firms' rapid development, the wage of the husband increased, and family life was enriched, at least materially. The wife encouraged her husband to compete hard in the firm for higher positions and better wages. Division of labor by gender thus separated the spouses' time clearly, the wife's time for housekeeping and the husband's for the company. This is how the *Kaisha Ningen* (company man) was created. Under this model, the wife tries to avoid divorce because she knows exactly what to expect. She will not only be stigmatized as a single mother but will face a severe daily struggle to support herself. At best she will find a part-time job. As for the husband, he also has reason to avoid divorce because he will be assessed negatively by management and will lose chances for promotion. This "modern family" is deeply rooted in Japanese management, and one who deviates from this model is interpreted as having some personal problems. In this division of labor by gender, the *Kaisha Ningen*, who is frequently absent from the home, and the stable family are considered fully compatible. This is the family in the company-centered society (Kimoto, 1995, 1997).

THE SELF-EMPLOYED AND THE "MODERN FAMILY MODEL"

The world of the big firm is, of course, important, but it is not the only one in Japanese society. Indeed, big firms accounted for about one-third of total employment and have been contracting during the 1990s. The world of the self-employed is never negligible in Japan.

As a process, capitalistic development undermines traditional, small establishments. However, since Japan is a latecomer to capitalism, this process was delayed. The self-employed and family employees accounted for over one-third (35.0 percent) of the workforce in 1970 and, although declining, were still nearly one-fifth (17.7 percent) in 1996. Among self-employed persons and family employees one-half were in tertiary industries in 1994, with the remainder nearly equally split between primary and secondary industries (Management and Coordination Agency, 1997b, p. 130). The households of these workers are inseparable from their businesses. Usually, their workplaces are homes. The family model of these self-employed workers is not that of the "modern family" but traditional patriarchy. In contrast to the "modern family," the traditional family can sustain itself by putting family members to work.

In these traditional families, however, the idea of the "modern family" began to attract the younger generation in the 1960s. It was then that traditional families sent their sons to senior high school and, if possible, to universities, where the "modern family" model was taken for granted. A better-educated son could decide whether to stay in the family business as a successor to his father or to find a job in a big firm. Only when he thought his family business would have a good chance to grow substantially did he become a successor. Consequently, family business retailers in big cities began to suffer from an absence of successors in the mid-1960s (Amano, 1994, p. 187). Many self-employed persons continue to utilize family members for their businesses, even though they are strongly affected by the "modern family" model.

In the pyramidal hierarchy of Japanese firms, there are many small and medium-sized firms. The "modern family" is a model for the employees of upper medium-sized firms, though they provide less favorable pay and fringe benefits to support the model. Small firms come closer to the self-employed in their family patterns. Employees of these firms are poorer, and wives are obliged to work part-time in order to make ends meet.

"MODERN FAMILY" BUT NOT SO MODERN

The "modern family" is a Japanese-style family in two ways. First, it is Japanese because it does not depend on romantic love between the husband and wife. Before World War II, 70 percent of all marriages were arranged by parents or relatives. With a decline in arranged marriages, love marriages have become the majority since the mid-1960s. According to the latest survey by the Institute of Population Problems of the MHW (1993), love marriages account for 82.8 percent of marriages, and arranged marriages for 15.2 percent. But, this does not mean a victory for love marriage. After marriage, couples think more of parent–child relations than of husband–wife relations.

According to a survey (Seimei Hoken Bunka Senta, 1992, p. 93), over half (53.2 percent) of married women followed the pattern of child-centered marriages, and nearly half (46.0 percent) of husbands adhered to the wife-centered pattern. These results suggest that the Japanese-style modern family is not necessarily based on romantic love between the husband and wife. That married couples do not require or expect romantic love contributes to their low divorce rates. For the children's sake, economic reasons, and the stigma, couples do not divorce, even if their love has become weak.

A second, traditional norm—that the eldest son and his wife should take care of the aged parents—is still strong. More than half (54.7 percent) of all persons over 65 were living with their children in 1995, though this percentage had declined from 64.5 percent in 1985 and 59.4 percent in 1990. These two features of the Japanese-style modern family are thought by bureaucrats and the government to be "hidden assets" that are functional substitutes for social welfare.

This "hidden asset" is sustained exclusively by women who are largely engaged in housekeeping. To strengthen the position of full-time housewives, who were expected to be a main pillar of the "welfare society," and to encourage this pattern, the government reformed the tax and social security systems in the 1980s. For example, since 1985, full-time housewives can receive a pension without having made a financial contribution. When housewives have jobs, they are expected to be part-timers. Roughly speaking, an income of 1 million yen per year is the upper limit for part-timers. Beyond this income, the husband of a working woman loses the housewife's tax deduction and wage benefits. Women employed for more than part-time, moreover, have to contribute to the public pension system. Women's labor force participation rate was 50 percent in 1996, and among married women, part-timers accounted for 30 percent, self-employed and family workers, 31 percent, regular employees, 28 percent, and others, 11 percent (Management and Coordination Agency, 1997b). With these tax policies the government is trying to maintain the tradition of married women's taking care of their husbands' aged parents.

GOVERNMENT PLANS FOR SOCIAL SECURITY REFORM

To curb expenses, the government has planned social security reforms, some of which have already been legislated; the rest are scheduled for the near future. The government argues that:

- public finance is suffering from a huge deficit
- social security expenditures account for 19 percent of the national budget
- according to a projection, by the year 2010, Japan will be the society with the highest proportion of people over age 65 in the world
- the rapidly increasing number of the aged will inevitably make medical expenditures soar
- the public pension system will collapse due to the increase in the aged population and the diminishing number of children to support them
- the present public social security system is not sustainable
- to maintain the social security system, a new medical care system and a new pension scheme are necessary (Ishi, 1996; MHW, 1997)

In May 1997, a new bill for nursing care insurance was passed without noteworthy discussion by the Lower House of the Japanese Parliament, although some technical difficulties and uncertain effectiveness of this new insurance were pointed out by specialists. All Japanese people over 40 years old have to contribute an average of nearly 3,000 yen a month to the system, which began to operate in 2000. Exact insurance fees and bases of taxation depend on demographic situation and service level of each city or town. Under certification by city or town, patients receive nursing care while they themselves pay 10 percent of the costs. To calm anxious aged people over 65, the government decided immediately before implementation of the program in April 2000 to excempt their insurance fees for six months and further to reduce them by half for the following year. With the continuous reshuffling of political parties that we have described earlier, no opposition parties except the minor Japan Communist Party are ready to oppose these new government policies.

Acknowledging that family care of the rapidly increasing population of the very old will no longer be sufficient, the government has introduced a new insurance program aimed at helping families. Already in 1989 the government announced the "Gold Plan" to improve home-help service and to increase the number of special nursing homes and other facilities for the aged. With the "New Gold Plan," introduced in 1994, the government set up a new target to enlarge service and facilities. The new insurance program is in this direction. But neither the "New Gold Plan" nor the new insurance program is designed to substitute public welfare for family care. Symbolically, the White Paper on Health and Welfare for 1996 was entitled "Fam-

ily and Social Security for Social Assistance of the Family." The government
acknowledged the need to supplement family care but maintained its basic
policy of holding down expenditures for social security at the expense of
the family.

THE FUTURE OF THE JAPANESE-STYLE WELFARE SOCIETY

Is the Japanese-style welfare society sustainable? In our view, it is not
sustainable in the long run. Company-run welfare programs are facing a
difficult future. The pension schemes of the big companies are suffering
huge deficits, owing to the lowest interest rates in history following the
burst of the bubble boom. In fact, some pension funds have already collapsed. Nikkeiren, the Federation of Employers' Associations, published a
strategic paper in 1995 predicting that "under severe economic and social
environments, public welfare expenses will soar, but in-company welfare
expenses will decrease" (Nikkeiren, 1995, p. 54). Nikkeiren further suggested that firms should limit and, if possible, reduce the number of regular
employees while increasing those with limited employment contracts. This
means that the number of regular employees in big firms who are eligible
for company welfare will decrease. In fact, large firms, which have reduced
their core male employees from 10.2 million in 1993 to 9.8 million in 1997
(Management and Coordination Agency, 1998), have been moving middle-
aged and older white-collar employees and managers into the status of
"specialists" with limited contracts instead of "lifetime employment." This
trend is expected to continue and will mean that the number of regular
employees in big firms who are eligible for company welfare will decrease.

Under strong pressure from other countries, especially the United States,
Japan will be opening up its markets, and this deregulation will hurt small
business. The long-term trend toward declining numbers of the self-
employed will be accelerated by deregulation. Employees in small and
medium-sized firms will have no hope of improving working and living
conditions. The number of part-timers will increase still more, with no
improvement in their working conditions.

But this will be a slow process. Big firms will reduce the number of
regular employees, but only gradually. Large-scale downsizing, such as in
American companies in the late 1980s and early 1990s, is not likely in
Japan, where the first social responsibility of firms is thought to be to maintain employment of regular, though not other, employees. The decrease in
occupational welfare will also be gradual, for management recognizes its
function of cementing employees' loyalty to the firm.

Deregulation might increase, but it will proceed slowly because it is likely
to have negative effects on political support for the ruling LDP. The LDP
has to assure the World Trade Organization (WTO) and the other indus-

trial economies that it will deregulate the Japanese market. However, the LDP has to protect small business and farmers in order to secure their political support. The government promised to open up the agricultural market as a result of the Uruguay Round of the General Agreement on Tariffs and Trade (GATT). Because Japanese agriculture is no longer competitive on the world market, it will lose ground if importation of food is liberalized. Typically, Japanese rice, the mainstay of the Japanese diet, is 8 to 10 times the price of rice on the world market. While promising free import of food and agricultural products, the LDP decided to invest about 6 trillion yen (about $52 billion) on agriculture, allegedly to improve competitiveness but, in fact, to calm angry farmers. In other industries, too, similar political compromises will be made. The labor market structure, which conceals considerable amounts of unemployment, will not change soon. Gender differences in labor market behavior will not change quickly, as the stable M-curve of female workforce participation suggests. The resilience of the Japanese labor market structure has already been proven by the fact that despite the longest recession since World War II, its unemployment rate of 4.7 percent in 1999 was still lower than in other advanced industrial economies except that of the United States.

Compared to other industrial countries, Japan is still very stable: relatively low unemployment and divorce rates, many three-generation households, and the strong modern family norm. Further, there are few political forces demanding the expansion of welfare. The left-wing labor movement and its political representative, the Japanese Socialist Party, were eager to defend and enrich social security. In the wake of the oil shock, we have shown the coalition of the LDP, big business, and right-wing labor based in large firms campaigned successfully for administrative reforms to reduce government expenditures and against both progressive local governments and welfare. In the late 1970s, political groups defending welfare nearly disappeared (Shinkawa, 1993, ch. 6).

Although it is still not costly by international standards, the Japanese social security system is seen domestically as money-eating and, as a result, receives severe criticism. As a latecomer to capitalism, Japan has looked at the experiences of Europe and America. For more than 100 years—from the mid-nineteenth century until the first oil crisis in 1973—European capitalism and American capitalism were good models to emulate. After the first oil crisis, Japan, exhibiting the "best economic performance" in the world, began to think of itself as "number one." Now "advanced Europe and America" are still models for Japan, but in the negative sense. From Japan's view, they suffer from low productivity and high welfare costs. They provide the worst models for tomorrow's Japan. Always trying to catch up with Europe and America, Japan feared that it would also catch the "industrial country disease." So, Japan has tried to ward off that crisis before it occurs. Even the present downturn of the Japanese and the world economy will not, in our opinion, evoke social unrest in Japan such as strikes or protests from poor people. There is a decoupling of economic and social or political crisis. The oil crisis in the 1970s aborted the drive for welfare, and with the fear of negative economic growth and massive unemployment, advocates of welfare receded and have not returned.

In Japan, interest groups consisting of beneficiaries of social programs (Pierson, 1994) have not developed. The first reason for this is that meager welfare programs not only limited the number receiving income support but also strongly stigmatized recipients, as demonstrated in the cases of single mothers and the aged. In a society in which work is the highest moral norm, these non-employed population groups were unable to defend their rights. A second reason why beneficiary groups have not developed is that pension and health insurance are not integrated so that its recipients are not united. Moreover, related to political fragmentation is the fact that different pension insurance systems provide different benefits. It is difficult to organize the pensioners as one interest group. Although Japan has a well-established bureaucracy and although bureaucrats play important policy-making roles in some countries, the Health and Welfare Ministry has very low prestige and, in any case, has not wanted to establish a welfare state. The most prestigious ministry, the Finance Ministry, has never accepted social security schemes that have the potential for increasing government expenditures.

One reason that we anticipate that social welfare will not expand is that since the early 1990s, political parties have been in a process of constant reshuffling. New parties are born and soon fade. Even if strong welfare interest groups were formed, they would have difficulties in finding political parties to represent their interests. For example, Shinshinto, the biggest opposition party, did have a welfare agenda, but, established in December 1994 and dissolved after a three-year existence of endless party struggles, it had little influence on government policy. The ruling LDP, one of two stable political parties, has been against a costly welfare state, and the other stable party, the Japan Communist Party, does not have strong influence on policy.

In the era of lasting political reshuffling, no political party has hegemony in social policy. Even the governing LDP, the majority in the Lower Parliament, needs junior coalition parties because it remains a minority in the Upper Parliament, and the LDP no longer has solid supporters among the electorate. The election of the Upper House in July 1998 exemplified the LDP's situation.

During the 50-year, post-war history, Japan was said several times to be in a crucial transitional stage and likely to abandon the "Japanese style" or its exceptionalism in areas such as employment policies, political decision making, and the welfare system. This was predicted in the recession following the 1964 Tokyo Olympics, after the first oil crisis in 1973, in the recession over the high price of the yen in the mid-1980s, and finally in the post-bubble recession in the 1990s. However, the 1990s were particularly challenging because of changes at all three levels of the labor market: large firms, self-employment or family businesses, and small or medium-sized firms. At each level, unemployment has either increased or become official rather than latent. Deregulation, the solution being imposed on Japan by international pressures, is both increasing unemployment and failing to stimulate consumption because working people, feeling insecure about future employment, are saving rather than spending. Nonetheless, the Japanese-style welfare state has been resilient to date, albeit with minor changes.

In the long run, the current Japanese style of social security is not sustainable. Japanese society is rapidly becoming an aging society, and the labor force participation of women is gradually increasing. These changes threaten the ability of families to care for the aged. Furthermore, young women are beginning to prefer a single life or later marriage, which accelerates the decreasing birthrate. These elements, especially changes in women's behavior and the labor market, might alter Japanese society.

REFERENCES

Amano, M. (1994). "Kinrin shotengai" (Shopping districts in cities). In H. Hazama, ed., *Kodo Keizai Seichoka no Seikatsu Sekai* (Life in the High Economic Growth Period). Tokyo: Bunshindo, pp. 173–203.

Axinn, June. (1990). "Japan: A special case." In G. S. Goldberg and E. Kremen, eds., *The Feminization of Poverty. Only in America?* New York: Praeger, pp. 91–105.

Berggren, C., and M. Nomura. (1997). *The Resilience of Corporate Japan: New Competitive Strategies and Personnel Practices*. London: Paul Chapman Publishing.

Economic Report of the President. (1997). Washington, DC: U.S. Government Printing Office.

Fujin Kyoiku Kenkyu Kai. (1996). *Tokei ni Miru Josei no Genjo: 1996* (Women in Statistics 1996). Tokyo: Kakiuchi Shuppan.

Furukawa, K., Y. Shoji, and T. Sadato. (1993). *Shakai Fukushi Ron* (Social Welfare). Tokyo: Yuhikaku.

Health and Welfare Statistics Association. (1997). *Kokumin no Fukushi no Doko 1997* (Trends in National Welfare 1997). Tokyo: Health and Welfare Statistics Association.

Inoue, T., and Y. Ehara. (1995). *Josei no Deta Bukku* (Women's Data Book), 2nd ed. Tokyo: Yuhikaku.

Institute of Population Problems of the Ministry of Health and Welfare. (1993). *Dai 10 kai Kekkon to Shussan ni Kansuru Zenkoku Chosa 1992* (The Tenth Japanese National Fertility Survey in 1992), vol. 1. Tokyo: Institute of Population Problems.

————. (1993b). *Dai 10 kai Shussei Doko Kihon Chosa dai 1 Hokokusho* (The 10th Report of Basic Birth Trends, no. 1). Tokyo: Institute of Population Problems.

Ishi, M. (1996). *Zaisei Kozo Kaikaku Hakusho* (White Paper on Public Finance Reform). Tokyo: Toyo Keizai Shinposha.

Jinno, N. (1992). "Nihongata fukushi kokka zaisei no Tokushitsu" (Some features of the Japanese-style welfare-state finance). In T. Hayashi and E. Kato, eds., *Fukushi Kokka Zaisei no Kokusai Hikaku* (International Comparison of Welfare-State Finance). Tokyo: University of Tokyo Press, pp. 217–238.

Kimoto, K. (1995). *Kazoku, Jenda, Kigyo Shakai* (Family, Gender and Company-Centered Society). Kyoto: Minerva Shobo.

————. (1997). "Company man makes family happy: Gender analysis of the Japanese family." *Hitotsubashi Journal of Social Studies* 29(1): 15–28.

Liberal Democratic Party (LDP). (1979). *Nihongata Fukushi Shakai* (The Japanese-style Welfare Society). Tokyo: Author.

Management and Coordination Agency. (1997a). *Suuji de Miru Korei Shakai 1997* (Aging Society in Figures 1997). Tokyo: Author.

————. (1997b). *Annual Report on the Labor Force Survey 1996*. Tokyo: Author.

————. (1998). *Labor Force Survey*. Tokyo: Author.

Ministry of Health and Welfare (MHW). (1997). *Kosei Hakusho 1997* (White Paper on Health and Welfare 1997). Tokyo: Author.

————. (2001). *Kosei Tokei Yoran 2000* (Basic Statistics on Welfare for 2000). Tokyo: Author.

Ministry of Labor. (1997). *White Paper on Labor for 1997*. Tokyo: Author.

Mizushima, H. (1994). *Kasan Ga Shinda* (A Mother Has Died). Tokyo: Shakai Shisosha.

Nakada, T., K. Sugimoto, and A. Morita. (1997). *Nichibei No Singuru Maza Tachi. Seikatsu to Fukushi No Feminisuto Chosa Hokoku* (Single mothers in Japan and America. A feminist research report on living and welfare). Kyoto: Minerva Shobo.

Nikkeiren. (1995). *Shinjidai No Nihonteki Keiei* (Japanese Management in a New Era). Tokyo: Author.

OECD. (1995). *Employment Outlook: July 1995*. Paris: Author.

Ono, A. (1994). *Rodo Keizaigaku* (Labor Economics), 2nd ed. Tokyo: Keizai Shinposha.

Orii, H. (1973). *20 Years of Labor Management*. Tokyo: Toyo Keizai Shinposha.

Pierson, P. (1994). *Dismantling the Welfare State? Reagan, Thatcher, and the Politics of Retrenchment*. Cambridge: Cambridge University Press.

Seccombe, W. (1993). *Weathering the Storm. Working-Class Families from the Industrial Revolution to the Fertility Decline*. London: Verso.

Seimei Hoken Bunka Senta (Life Insurance Culture Center). (1992). *Josei no Seikatsu Ishiki ni Kansuru Chosa* (Survey on Life Consciousness of Women). Tokyo: Author.

Shakai Keizai Seisansei Honbu. (1996). *Katsuyo Rodo Tokei 1996* (Statistical Handbook of Labor 1996). Tokyo: Author.

Shinkawa, T. (1993). *Nihongata Fukushi no Seiji Keizaigaku* (Political Economy of Japanese-Style Welfare). Tokyo: Sanichi Shobo.

Shoji, Y., H. Sugimura, and M. Fujimura, eds. (1997). *Hinkon, Hubyodo to Shakai Fukushi* (Poverty, Inequality, and Social Welfare). Tokyo: Yuhikaku.

Social Insurance Agency. (1997). *Suuji de Miru Nenkin 1997* (Pensions in Figures 1997). Tokyo: Kosei Shuppansha.

Soeda, Y. (1995). *Seikatsu Hogo Seido no Shakaishi* (Social History of Public Assistance). Tokyo: University of Tokyo Press.

Sohara, M. (1985). "Teishotoku setai to seikatsu hogo" (Low-income households and public assistance). In S. H. Kenkyusho, ed., *Fukushi Seisaku no Kihon Mondai* (Fundamental Problems of Welfare Policy). Tokyo: University of Tokyo Press, pp. 183–200.

Sorrentino, C. (1995). "International unemployment indicators, 1983–93." *Monthly Labor Review* (August): 31–47.

Uzuhashi, T. (1997). *Gendai Fukushi Kokka no Kokusai Hikaku: Nihon Moderu no Ichizuke to Tenbo* (International Comparison of Modern Welfare States: Position of the Japanese Model and Its Future). Tokyo: Nihon Hyoronsha.

Chapter 11

Diminishing Welfare: Convergence toward a Liberal Model?

Gertrude Schaffner Goldberg

To what extent has social welfare diminished in nine capitalist countries with different levels and paths of welfare state development? This chapter supplements the preceding, separate studies of the nine countries with cross-national data on national economic resources; the proportion of these resources spent on social welfare; unemployment and labor participation rates; inequality and poverty; and the reduction of poverty and inequality by social welfare. The summary of findings is a synthesis of the chapter studies and these cross-national data.

The chapter concludes with a discussion of whether and how models of the welfare state have been altered over the last 20 years. Is retrenchment as modest as Pierson concluded? Have welfare states continued to spend as much or more on benefits but nonetheless changed their structures? Have they shrunk but kept their basic structures? Does the prominence of neoliberal ideology signal a convergence toward the liberal model? What political factors determine the extent and patterns of retrenchment? Finally, can we anticipate the future of these welfare states from our knowledge of their past and present?

ECONOMIC RESOURCES AND SOCIAL EXPENDITURES

With the exception of post-communist Hungary, the nations in this study are wealthy and have grown more so since 1980 (see Table 11.1). Between 1980 and 1995, the gross domestic product (GDP) per capita of the eight countries for which data are available grew by an average of 30 percent, ranging from 18 percent in Sweden to 54 percent in Japan.

Did the countries spend their extra money on social welfare?[1] In fact, all

Table 11.1
Social Expenditures as Percent of GDP and GDP per Capita, 1980–1995

	1980		1985		1990		1995		% Increase, 1980–1995	
	Exp.[a]	GDP[b]	Exp.	GDP	Exp.	GDP	Exp.	GDP	Exp.	GDP
Canada	13.2	$19,116	16.4	$20,758	17.6	$22,308	18.2	$23,768	37.9	24.3
France	23.5	$17,251	27.0	$18,280	26.7	$20,914	30.1	$21,524	28.1	24.8
Germany	23.7	$17,883	24.8	$19,097	23.2	$21,739	28.0	$21,864[c]	18.1	22.3
Italy	18.4	$15,896	21.7	$16,871	23.1	$19,339	23.7	$21,224	28.8	33.6
Japan	9.9	$15,110	11.3	$17,244	11.2	$21,158	13.8	$23,334	39.4	54.4
Sweden	29.8	$17,010	31.1	$18,450	32.2	$20,152	33.0	$20,042	10.7	17.8
United Kingdom	18.3	$14,849	21.1	$16,310	19.5	$18,756	22.5	$19,416	23.0	30.8
United States	13.4	$22,007	13.0	$24,538	13.5	$27,504	15.8	$29,456	17.9	33.8
Average	18.8	$17,390	20.8	$18,943	20.9	$20,875	23.1	$22,590	25.5	30.2

[a]These expenditure data do not include education. Thus, in 1980, total U.S. expenditures would have been 18.0 percent of GDP rather than 13.4 percent, and Sweden's would have been 32.0 percent rather than 29.9 percent.

[b]1998 U.S. dollars.

[c]Figures for 1995 and 1998 are for Unified Germany. For former West Germany, the GDP per capita in 1995 was $23,904 instead of $21,864.

Sources: Author's calculation from OECD (1999b); U.S. Department of Labor (2000b), table 1.

except Hungary increased the proportion of GDP spent on social welfare, but in only two, Canada and France, did social spending increases equal or exceed GDP growth (Table 11.1). Sweden had the lowest increase in social expenditures, but with 33 percent of its GDP going for social welfare, it remained the highest spender. In the basement were Japan and the United States, both having spent less than half the proportion of resources on social welfare as Sweden. Figures for Hungary were not included in these data, but Baxandall (Chapter 9) reports that under post-Communism expenditures for social policy dropped much more than GDP—30 percent compared to 22 percent between 1991 and 1996.

When expenditures are broken down by purpose and population groups, there are large differences (Tables 11.2 and 11.3). Spending on cash benefits for the elderly rose in all these countries, but by 3 and 6 percent in Germany and the United States, compared to about 50 percent or more in Italy, Canada, and Japan. Three countries associated with the Conservative model, France, Germany, and Italy, continued to lead in the proportion of resources spent on cash benefits for the elderly. A different configuration emerges with cash benefits for families: with the exception of Canada, Sweden, and the United Kingdom, the proportion of GDP spent for this purpose fell, steeply in Italy and also significantly in Germany. (As noted in Tables 11.2 and 11.3, U.S. expenditures for cash benefits rose if the Earned Income Tax Credit is taken into account.) France, though slightly decreasing its effort on cash benefits for families, remained the highest in this group, continuing to be either an anomaly, if classified as Conservative, or something of a hybrid with attributes of both the Conservative and social democratic models.

Even with a reduction of effort, Sweden is the standout in expenditures for services. It spent more than twice as much on family services as Germany, the runner-up, and more than four times as much on services for elderly and disabled people as France, the second highest in that category. The familialism of Italy and Japan and the penchant of the latter for meager provision are illustrated by their low expenditures for services. Canada and the United States are also very low in public services for the elderly and disabled. Whereas six of the eight countries decreased the proportion of GDP allotted to family services, only the United States reduced its commitment to services for the elderly and disabled as well. Japan and Sweden increased the proportion of GDP allotted to services for the elderly and disabled equally, but at the end of the period Sweden was spending more than 12 times as much of its resources for that purpose as Japan. Thus, from the standpoint of emphasis on services, Sweden remains structurally distinct from the other countries in this study.

The finding that effort on unemployment insurance nearly doubled in this 16-year period is a good example of how expenditure data can be misleading. As the various country studies revealed, unemployment benefits

Table 11.2
Social Expenditures (Excluding Education)[a] for Selected Social Programs as Percent of GDP, 1995

	Health	Old Age Cash	Unemployment	Labor Market	Family Cash	Family Service	Eld./Dis. Service	Housing	Other	Total
Canada	6.58	4.34	1.30	.57	.80	x[b]	a[c]	a[c]	3.09	18.24
France	7.98	10.36	1.79	1.31	2.23	.37	.78	.92	.49	30.07
Germany	8.13	10.29	2.37	1.36	1.23	.78	.58	.15	.63	28.01
Italy	5.38	10.99	.87	1.13	.43	.10	.20	m[d]	m[d]	23.71
Japan	5.57	5.49	.39	.13	.20	.22	.27	a[c]	.18	13.80
Sweden	5.90	8.17	2.30	2.40	2.13	1.72	3.37	1.20	1.03	33.01
United Kingdom	5.73	6.46	.89	.45	1.87	.48	.68	1.85	.27	22.52
United States	6.33	5.36	.35	.20	.33[e]	.31	.05	a[c]	.63	15.76
Average[f]	6.45	7.68	1.28	.94	1.15	.57	.85	1.03	.90	23.14

[a]These expenditure data do not include education. Thus, in 1980, total U.S. expenditures would have been 18.0 percent of GDP rather than 13.4 percent, and Sweden's would have been 32.0 percent rather than 29.9 percent.

[b]Included in another category of social expenditures.

[c]Data are not applicable, but this does not mean there are no relevant expenditures.

[d]Data are not available because not yet collected or because of non-response.

[e]The U.S. Earned Income Tax Credit is included in other contingencies instead of family cash benefits. If added to family cash benefits, it would bring expenditures up to .62 percent of GDP.

[f]Averages based on categories for which data are available.

The category "Other" includes social expenditures (both in cash and in kind) for those persons who for various reasons fall outside the scope of the relevant program covering a particular contingency, or if this other benefit is insufficient to meet their needs. Social expenditures related to immigrants/refugees and indigenous persons are included in this category. Finally, any social expenditure which is not attributable to other categories is included in this category.

Source: Author's calculation from OECD (1999b).

Table 11.3
Total Social Expenditures as Percent of GDP and Percent Changes in Expenditures for Selected Social Programs

| | Social Expenditures, 1980–1995 | | | | Changes in Expenditures, 1980–1995 | | | | | | | |
	1980	1985	1990	1995	Total	Health	Old Age Cash	Unempl. Benefit	Labor Market[a]	Family Cash	Family Service	Eld./Dis. Service
Canada	13.2	16.4	17.6	18.2	37.9	26.8	55.6	6.6	96.6	25.0	-27.3[b]	—
France	23.5	27.0	26.7	30.1	28.1	34.1	33.0	36.6	184.8	-4.5	27.6	23.8
Germany	23.7	24.8	23.2	28.0	18.1	16.8	3.0	200.0	70.0[c]	-33.5	50.0	75.8
Italy	18.4	21.7	23.1	23.7	28.8	-4.6	49.3	45.0	151.1[c]	-56.1	-16.7	5.3
Japan	9.9	11.3	11.2	13.8	39.4	22.4	56.9	18.1[c]	0[d]	-13.0	-12.0	92.9
Sweden	29.8	31.1	32.2	33.0	10.8	-31.9	19.6	489.7	92.0	19.0	-25.5	91.5
United Kingdom	18.3	21.1	19.5	22.5	22.9	17.2	27.4	-16.0	-19.6	5.6	-7.7	28.3
United States	13.4	13.0	13.5	15.8	17.9	64.4	6.1	-49.3	25.0	-28.3[e]	-8.8	-61.5
Average[f]	18.8	20.8	20.9	23.1	25.5	18.2	31.4	101.8	75.8	-10.7	1.0	36.6

[a]Includes active labor market programs such as retraining, job placement, public employment as compared with passive programs, that is, cash unemployment benefits.
[b]1980–1990.
[c]1985–1995.
[d]1990–1995.
[e]If the Earned Income Tax Credit (classified as other contingencies by the OECD) is included in family cash benefits, then U.S. expenditures for that program category rise between 1980 and 1995 by 14.8 percent instead of fall 28.3 percent.
[f]Average for countries for which data from 1980–1995 are available.

Source: Author's calculation from OECD (1999b).

deteriorated in coverage and adequacy as need increased. Countries are spending more but meeting the increased need for protection against job loss less well.

The lineup on active labor market programs exemplifies defining differences. Sweden spent more on active than passive programs for the unemployed, in contrast to the conservative countries, which, particularly in the case of France, spent considerably on these programs but less than on cash unemployment benefits. In 1995, Canada had a somewhat higher unemployment rate than Germany but spent much less on both active and passive programs for the unemployed. Similarly, the United Kingdom, with an unemployment rate only about a point lower than Germany's, was also spending very much less in both categories.

Whether these social expenditures were sufficient to overcome the decline in market shares for lower-income groups and to have continued the progress against poverty is explored in a later section. Referring to the United States, Frances Fox Piven (1999) maintained that social expenditures have increased and that the welfare state has been restructured rather than cut back. However, we have argued that retrenchment occurs if spending does not keep pace with social need. Nonetheless, trends in social welfare expenditures do not lead us to compose a requiem for the welfare state—at least not yet.

UNEMPLOYMENT

The declining commitment to full employment preceded program cutbacks in most countries. Since the mid-1970s, one country after another abandoned full employment or a policy of keeping unemployment low. On average unemployment rates have climbed in every five-year interval since the first half of the 1970s (Table 11.4). By the last five years of the century, the average unemployment rate for the eight countries for which annual, standardized data are available was over three times that of the 1970 to 1974 interval. Questions have been raised about the comparability of unemployment rates in different countries. Constance Sorrentino, an economist in the Division of Foreign Labor Statistics of the U.S. Bureau of Labor Statistics (BLS), investigated this question. Adjusted to U.S. concepts, Canada's average unemployment rate for 1995–1998 would have been nearly one percentage point (.83) lower than the rates used for Table 11.4, which are based on U.S. concepts, but the effect of adjustment would have been smaller for the European countries. An earlier BLS study covering the years 1984–1992 found the Japanese rate virtually unchanged under U.S. concepts (Sorrentino, 2000, p. 46).

Mass unemployment had become a European phenomenon by the closing years of the century. In 1997, 18 million people or 11 percent of the active population of the European Union (EU) were officially unemployed,

Table 11.4

Average Unemployment Rates (Approximating U.S. Concepts), 1960–1999, Five-Year Averages

	1960–1964	1965–1969	1970–1974	1975–1979	1980–1984	1985–1989	1990–1994	1995–1999
Canada	5.7	3.9	5.8	7.5	9.9	8.9	10.3	8.8
France	1.4	2.1	2.8	5.1	8.2	10.4	10.6	11.9
West Germany	0.6	0.6	0.8	3.3	5.3	6.4	6.7	9.1
Italy	3.0	3.5	3.4	4.0	5.3	7.4	8.5	11.8
Japan	1.4	1.2	1.3	2.1	2.4	2.6	2.4	3.8
Sweden	1.6	1.8	2.3	1.9	2.8	2.2	5.9	8.9
United Kingdom	2.5	2.8	3.5	5.7	10.5	9.7	9.2	7.3
United States	5.7	3.8	5.4	7.0	8.3	6.2	6.6	4.9
Average	2.7	2.1	2.5	4.6	6.6	6.7	7.5	8.3

Source: Author's calculation from U.S. Department of Labor (2000a), table 2.

half of them were out of work for more than one year, and more than one-fifth of all young people in the EU were jobless (European Economists for Full Employment, 1997; see also ILO, 1995). Mass unemployment was also present in North America. Canada's unemployment rate, which exceeded the average for the eight countries during every five-year interval from 1960 to the end of the century, was at its highest in the first half of the 1990s (Table 11.4). Though down in the second half of the decade, two Canadian economists (Burke and Shields, 1999, p. 16) estimated that in May 1998, when official unemployment was 8.4 percent, 20.3 percent of the labor force experienced "structural exclusion" (unemployed, discouraged workers, involuntary part-time workers, etc.).

On average, labor force participation rates for the total population changed little in the years after 1980, but in every country men's rates went down, and in all but Sweden, women's increased (U.S. Department of Labor, 2000a, table 4). The participation rate of Swedish women peaked in 1990, before retrenchment began, and declined about 7 percent by 1999.[2] Of the eight countries, Sweden showed the largest decline in total labor force participation, and the United States, the largest increase. By the end of the century, Sweden had yielded its lead to the United States and Canada. Sweden's total participation rate in 1980 was greater than in any of the study countries in 1999.

The United States and Japan are the two countries that had relatively low unemployment rates in the last years of the century, but there are troubling attributes of both labor markets. With unemployment rates climbing slowly during each five-year interval, Japan had doubled its very low rates of the 1960s by the end of the 1980s. At the end of the century, its unemployment rate was four times what it had been 30 years earlier. Still, an unemployment rate considered a "crisis" in Japan is hailed as "full employment" by the U.S. government (Nomura, 2000).

While Japan was categorized as a full employment economy (Therborn, 1985), its policy was really "total employment." Whereas full employment means that there are more available jobs at fair wages than job seekers, total employment means that everyone who seeks work can find it but not always at fair wages (Nomura, 2000). However, many of the unemployed did not seek work. Japanese married women constituted a peripheral work-force whose members supplemented the earnings of their husbands and dropped out of the labor force when they lost a job, waiting until work that meshed with their family obligations became available. Thus, Japan had substantial latent unemployment during the period when it was considered a full employment economy. In the 1990s, women who lost work often could not afford to wait until a convenient job turned up, and so they were more likely to stay in the labor force and be counted as unemployed. This is a sign of deteriorating employment conditions for men and of women's unemployment becoming official rather than latent.

The United States, which never committed itself to full employment— and still has not—had relatively low unemployment rates in the last five years of the century. However, hidden employment and underemployment greatly exceeded official unemployment, which stood at 5.9 million in 1999. At the same time, there were 7.6 million involuntary part-time workers and non-job-seekers who wanted a job and an estimated 17 million full-time, year-round workers earning less than the paltry poverty level for a family of four in 1999, $17,028 (Ginsburg and Ayres, 2000). Furthermore, U.S. unemployment would be several points higher if the large prison population, many of whom would be unemployed if they were in the community, were counted.

The current U.S. labor market is closer to the total employment model that long prevailed in Japan. In both countries, very minimal public assistance for working-age men and women means that a low-wage job may be the only alternative to destitution. Full underemployment is another way of describing the model. However, the outcomes are different because of differences in family composition in the two countries. The pooled wages of family members can keep a family out of poverty in Japan, but the single woman's wage of many U.S. families leaves them poor. Total employment, it should be stressed, may be only a transient phase in the United States. It remains the policy of the Federal Reserve Board to slow the economy by raising interest rates at the slightest sign of wage growth. Thus, there is no commitment on the part of policymakers to maintaining current, American-style full employment, much less living-wage jobs for all.

Sweden was as much the full employment state as the quintessential welfare state. Its unemployment rates in the 1990s were not the highest among the countries in this study and were, in fact, falling as the century closed, but its 1990 announcement that price stability had replaced full employment as its main economic priority, reversing a 60-year commitment, symbolized retrenchment. In addition to unemployment rates that would have been political suicide for a Swedish regime only a decade ago, the numbers of involuntary part-timers and discouraged workers soared.

Even more of a policy reversal than Sweden's abandonment of full employment was the introduction of unemployment in countries where joblessness had not existed since the era of state socialism began. "Communist social policy was premised on full employment far more than any Western welfare state ever was" (Baxandall, Chapter 9). A market economy in Hungary has meant an enormous rise in unemployment, from less than 1 percent to 13.5 percent in the first four years of the 1990s, and it is still very high, if tapering somewhat. A shrinking labor force is a concomitant trend, with 20 percent of the working-age population resorting to parental and sick leave, disability, and early retirement benefits. Government policies and the increase of unemployment have depressed the wages of the employed. In East Germany, registered unemployment has been even higher—nearly 20 percent. Unification with a wealthy capitalist country, itself suffering from high unemployment, has not eased that part of the transition to capitalism, although the transfer of significant portions of the GDP of the former Federal Republic helped to pay for the costs of unemployment.

Work in a number of countries has become more contingent. Famous for long-term employment, large Japanese firms began to develop a new class of peripheral workers. Over the last two decades, full-time, permanent labor contracts fell by nearly one-fifth in France. According to one estimate, which included "nonstandard" work arrangements ranging from independent contracting and other forms of self-employment to work in temporary agencies or as day laborers, almost 30 percent of U.S. workers had jobs that were not regular, full-time employment in 1997 (Mishel, Bernstein, and Schmitt, 1999, p. 21); but when the definition is limited to wage and salaried workers who, for nonpersonal reasons, do not expect their jobs to last as long as they wish, the proportion is much smaller (Osterman, 1999, pp. 55–60). Germany has seen increased marginal employment that is not paying social insurance contributions. Temporary jobs became more common in Sweden during the 1990s, affecting nearly one in six employees.

In contrast to those who looked at earlier data, Franco Peracchi's (1999) study of the early and mid-1990s concluded that the United States is not unique in earnings inequality. In most developed countries, male wages at the bottom of the distribution have been falling relative to the median, while the top has been rising relative to the median. Among our countries, this is the case for bottom and top quartiles in Canada, Germany, Italy, and the United Kingdom, along with the United States. This was not true for Sweden between 1975 and 1992 but may have been the case later in the 1990s. Indeed, one study of income inequality found that between the mid-1980s and the mid-1990s, inequality increased more than 15 percent in Sweden (Burniaux et al., 1998, table 2.2).

INCREASING POVERTY AND INEQUALITY

Assessing trends in poverty is complicated by the fact that available data often pertain to different years for different countries, and most income studies do not include all of the countries in this study.[3] In addition, standardized, cross-national data for the second half of the 1990s are not available at this writing, and standardized data for 1980 to the mid-1990s are incomplete. Demographic trends such as increase in the elderly and single-parent populations and persisting low wages, high unemployment, or both have meant extra burdens for welfare systems in most countries. Thus, poverty and inequality grew, despite the pattern of increased welfare expenditures.

Inequality

Between the mid-1980s and mid-1990s, economic inequality increased in all the countries in this study but in quite different degrees—significantly in three countries, Hungary, Sweden, and the United Kingdom, less so in the United States, and modestly in Canada, France, Germany, Italy, and Japan (Table 11.5). In the previous decade, by contrast, there were no significant increases in inequality, and in six of the nine countries, inequality either decreased or stayed the same. The exceptions were Hungary, the United States, and the United Kingdom, which are also among the countries in which inequality increased in the subsequent decade.

In the case of the United States, inequality was substantial to begin with and increased in the 20-year period from the mid-1970s to the mid-1990s. At the beginning of the interval, the share of aggregate income of the top quintile of households was 9.8 times that of the bottom fifth, compared to a ratio of 13.2 in 1998, and the Gini ratio in 1997 was the highest recorded since 1967, when the series began, 15.6 percent higher than in 1975 (U.S. Bureau of the Census, 1998, table B-3, p. B-6).

The study by Burniaux and colleagues (1998) did not provide detailed inequality figures for the United Kingdom. However, Bradshaw and Chen's research on 20 countries used the Gini coefficient as the indicator of inequality and found that after taxes and income transfers the United Kingdom ranked second in inequality, along with the United States, and behind Russia (1996, p. 13).

Changing patterns of taxation can contribute to increased inequality. The

Table 11.5
Trends in Income Distribution Based on Several Income Inequality Indicators:
Summary Results from National Studies

	Mid-1970s to mid-1980s	Mid-1980s to mid-1990s
Canada	-	0
France	-	+
Germany	-	+
Hungary	+	+++
Italy	--	+
Japan	0	+
Sweden	-	+++
United Kingdom	++	+++
United States	++	++

Legend:
+++ significant rise in income inequality (more than 15 percent increase).
++ rise in income inequality (7 to 15 percent increase).
+ modest rise in income inequality (2 to 7 percent increase).
0 no change (–2 to +2 percent change).
- modest decrease in income inequality (2 to 7 percent decrease).
-- decrease in income inequality (7 to 15 percent decrease).
--- significant decrease in income inequality (more than 15 percent decrease).

Source: Burniaux et al. (1998), table 2.2.

countries in this study grew richer, and tax revenues were, on average, about the same proportion of GDP in 1996 as in 1985 (calculated from OECD, 1999a, pp. 38–39; 1988, pp. 32–33). Total tax receipts as a proportion of GDP either stayed the same or changed slightly in France, Germany, the United States, and Japan. Three countries, Italy, Canada, and Sweden, increased their total taxation, Italy by nearly one-fourth. The largest decrease was 5.5 percent in the United Kingdom.

Tax structures were more likely to change than the ratio of tax receipts to GDP. The big turns away from more progressive forms of taxation were in Germany and Japan where income taxes declined significantly as proportions of total tax revenues (about 20 percent). In Germany, payroll taxes on employees and sales taxes grew the most, and in Japan, payroll taxes increased by more than one-fourth. For the United States, the 1985–1996 interval is misleading because individual income taxes as percent of GDP had dropped between 1980 and 1985, but by the end of the century were a higher percent than in 1980; corporate income taxes dropped more steeply than individual income taxes in the first half of the 1980s and had increased by the late 1990s but were still not up to their 1980 mark.

In a cross-national study that looked particularly at the United States, the United Kingdom, and Sweden, economist Sven Steinmo concluded that marginal tax rates were dramatically reduced in the 1980s. The United Kingdom dropped its top individual rates from 93 to 40 percent and its corporate rates less precipitously, from 52 to 35 percent; these were even bigger tax cuts than in the United States, which lowered its top individual rate from 70 to 33 percent and its top corporate rate from 46 to 34 percent. Steinmo considers Sweden's 1990 tax cuts the "most striking" example of increased regressivity with its large reductions for upper-income groups, modest cuts for those with earnings closer to the average industrial wage, and increase in the indirect taxes paid mostly by lower- and middle-income groups (Steinmo, 1994, p. 15). The actions of the British and American governments put pressure on other governments to reduce their taxes, and every Organisation for Economic Co-operation and Development (OECD) country either proposed or enacted major restructuring of tax systems during the 1980s. Although the changes are quite complex, and countries have not conducted the distributional studies that are available in the United States, Britain, and Sweden, Steinmo writes that government statements announcing the reforms indicate that the cuts in tax rates were not being distributed progressively.

In the 1990s, the United States increased its top marginal tax rate twice, leading the Congressional Budget Office (CBO) to estimate that once these laws were fully implemented, the *effective* tax rate on the four lowest income quintiles would be lower than in 1977, and the rate for the top quintile, about the same as then (U.S. Congress, Congressional Budget Office, 1994, p. 54).[4] Nonetheless, for more than a decade, decreased marginal tax rates for the wealthy contributed to an increase in economic inequality that was already large. France, Kesselman reported (Chapter 6), took some steps to increase the progressivity of its tax structure in the late 1990s. On the other hand, in 2000, Germany, with a Social Democrat as chancellor, reduced its top marginal tax rate by about 18 percent and its corporate taxes even more steeply (Schmid, 2000, pp. 1, 14).

Poverty

Most of the cross-national data on poverty are based on the relative standard used by the Luxembourg Income Study (LIS) which is less than half a country's median disposable income, adjusted for family size. However, some figures based on the absolute standard of the United States ($17,028 for a family of four in the 1999) and on the real value of countries' relative thresholds in the previous decade are also given. Because the latest cross-national data for most of the countries in this study are from the mid-1990s, these will be used in the tables that follow. However, I will also refer to some later data that may alter or confirm impressions concerning trends. The data on relative poverty (Tables 11.6 and 11.7) should be viewed with some caution; although both are from LIS datasets, some figures on total poverty in the two differ, in the case of Germany, considerably (although both show an upward trend, albeit of different magnitudes). Morever, trends in a country's poverty level can be influenced considerably by relatively small changes in the time intervals considered. For example, between 1986 and 1991, childhood poverty decreased slightly in Italy, but increased dramatically and more than in any other country in the study between 1986 and 1995 (Japan not shown) (Bradbury and Jäntii, 1999, figure 3.2).

Relative poverty rose in six of the eight countries for which data are available, and nowhere were there significant gains against the poverty of the total population (Table 11.6). The increase in poverty was greatest in the United Kingdom, Germany, and Italy. Sweden's poverty rate rose from a very low base, and the United States rose less markedly but from a starting point almost three times that of Sweden. The U.S. relative poverty rate of 16.9 percent in 1997 (LIS, 2000) would register a somewhat smaller increase since 1979 but was still almost one-fifth higher than any of the other countries in the mid-1990s. The poverty of the total population fell slightly in Canada and stayed virtually the same in France. (The Canadian poverty rate had risen to 11.9 percent in 1997, and compared with 1981 was a decrease of only 4 percent, less than 1.0 percentage point or virtually no change.)

Trends in elderly poverty were the most promising. Five of the eight countries registered declines of one-fourth or more in poverty rates, and none showed an increase. In the middle 1980s and early 1990s, elderly poverty in Sweden rose to the 6–7 percent range but was still low by international standards (LIS, 2000). In the early 1990s, elderly poverty was very high in Britain (23.9 percent in 1991) but had fallen considerably by 1995. Poverty was still the lot of one out of five elderly Amerians (1994 and 1997), even though the rate had been reduced by one-fourth since 1979.

Childhood poverty presents a bleak picture and a much darker one that that of the elderly. In the mid-1990s, childhood poverty was, on average, almost three-fourths greater than elderly poverty in six of the eight countries for which data are available. By contrast, Sweden and France, the largest spenders on income support for families, did about equally well or better for children than for the elderly.

What about trends in child poverty? According to a 1999 report on 20 countries that also used LIS data, "the dominant trend is one of increasing relative child poverty" (Bradbury and Jäntti, 1999, p. 22). Bucking the trend were Sweden, which rescued significantly more of its children from

Table 11.6
Trends in Relative Poverty

		Poverty Rates			Percentage Point Change*			Percent Change		
		Total	Children	Elderly	Total	Children	Elderly	Total	Children	Elderly
Canada	1981	12.4	14.8	22.1	-	0	---	-8.9	6.1	-76.0
	1994	11.3	15.4	4.7						
France	1979	8.2	7.2	10.3	0	0	0	-2.4	9.7	-4.9
	1994	8.0	7.9	9.8						
Germany	1981	5.3	2.8	14.4	++	+++	---	41.5	278.6	-51.4
	1994	7.5	10.6	7.0						
Hungary	1991	8.2	6.9	14.0	+	+++	---	23.2	60.9	-37.1
	1994	10.1	11.4	8.8						
Italy	1986	10.4	11.4	13.1	++	+++	0	36.5	77.2	-6.9
	1995	14.2	20.2	12.2						
Sweden	1981	5.3	4.8	2.9	+	--	0	24.5	-45.8	-6.9
	1995	6.6	2.6	2.7						
United Kingdom	1979	9.2	9.0	21.6	+++	+++	---	45.7	120.0	-36.6
	1995	13.4	19.8	13.7						
United States	1979	15.8	20.4	27.3	++	+++	---	12.7	20.1	-24.5
	1994	17.8	24.5	20.6						

*Legend:
0   within +/- 1.0 points
+   increase of 1.0 to 1.9 points   -   decrease of 1.0 to 1.9 points
++   increase of 1.9 to 3.9 points   --   decrease of 1.9 to 3.9 points
+++ increase of 4.0 points or more   ---   decrease of 4.0 points or more

Source: Author's calculation from LIS (2000).

Table 11.7

Changes in Pre-Tax and Transfer and Post-Tax and Transfer Poverty Rates and in Poverty Reduction by Taxes and Transfers, ca. 1980 (Time I) and ca. 1994 (Time II), Percent

	Pre-Tax and Transfer			Post-Tax and Transfer			Poverty Reduction		
	I	II	% diff.	I	II	% diff.	I	II	% diff.
Canada[a]	25.8	32.8	27.1	12.5	10.6	−15.2	51.6	67.7	31.2
France[b]	37.3	46.0	23.3	7.9	8.4	6.3	78.8	81.7	3.7
Germany[c]	34.4	38.9	13.1	6.1	11.4	86.9	82.3	70.7	−14.1
Hungary[d]	45.5	51.9	14.1	6.3	11.0	74.6	86.2	78.8	−8.6
Italy[e]	36.9	..	..	9.8	12.8	30.6	72.9	..	..
Japan[f]	..	..	..	..	11.8	..	..	..	..
Sweden[g]	47.0	45.5	−3.2	5.6	8.7	55.4	88.1	80.9	−8.2
United Kingdom[h]	33.2	39.8	19.9	5.7	10.6	86.0	82.8	73.4	−11.4
United States[i]	27.5	31.4	14.2	16.4	17.9	9.1	40.4	43.0	6.4
Average*	34.2	39.1	15.7	9.0	11.3	38.1	70.7	69.6	1.3

[a]1981–1994; [b]1979–1994; [c]1981–1994; [d]1991–1994; [e]1986–1995; [f]1992; [g]1981–1995; [h]1979–1995; [i]1979–1994.

*Averages calculated for the six countries with complete data at Times I and II.

Source: Author's calculation from Smeeding (1997), table 1 (Japan) and Vlaminckx (1998).

poverty in 1995 than in 1981, and Canada and France, both of which held the line. Sweden's accomplishment is all the more noteworthy when one considers that its rate of childhood poverty in 1981 was already below 5 percent. By contrast, Germany, Britain, Hungary, and Italy were doing much less well by their children than before. Whereas child poverty rates in Germany were much lower than those of the elderly in 1981, the reverse was true in 1994. Britain, though not increasing its child poverty rate as greatly as Germany, more than doubled it. The picture for the United States had brightened slightly by 1997, further along in its economic boom, but even so over one-fifth (22.3 percent) of the children in the world's richest country were poor.

Single mothers continued to have high risks of poverty despite the fact that the ratio of women's to men's wages has been climbing in the countries that were capitalist at the start of this period (Peracchi, 1999, table 2). Rough comparison of the poverty rates of solo parents (largely single mothers) between the 1980s and early to middle 1990s reveals that solo-parent poverty increased sharply in Germany and the United Kingdom, remained about the same in Canada, dropped but remained very high in the United States, and fell significantly in Sweden (as of 1992). Solo-parent poverty rose in France between 1984 and 1989 (Smeeding and Rainwater, 1991, table 7; Smeeding and Ross, 1999, table 2). Data, largely from the early to mid-1990s, reveal poverty rates for single-mother families of almost two-fifths or more in Germany, Canada, and the United States; from about one-fourth to nearly one-third in France (1989) and Britain; and under 4 percent in Sweden[5] (Christopher et al., 1999, table 1). Ginsburg and Rosenthal (Chapter 4) report higher rates of solo-parent poverty (LIS standard) later in the decade—5.1 percent in 1994 and 5.7 percent in 1998; still very low by international standards.

Whereas relative poverty for the total population rose or stayed the same in most countries, it fell in all but one when a constant threshold (the equivalent of the relative poverty line at the earlier date) was used (Burniaux et al., 1998, table 5.1, p. 52; table 5.2, p. 53). This implies that larger proportions of people in these countries are experiencing impoverishing inequality (less than half the median disposable income), but only in Italy are more people poor by the relative standard of the earlier decade. However, the constant threshold may understate economic hardship, for if out-of-pocket costs for health increase or the real cost of housing rises, then the same income is worth less. Moreover, except in France and Canada, the income-gap ratio or the difference between the average income of the poor and the poverty line rose whichever measure was used, indicating that the poor were becoming poorer in both relative and absolute terms.

Using the absolute poverty standard of the United States instead of the LIS relative measure changes the picture somewhat. Japan's relative poverty rate, like that of all the other countries, was considerably below that of the United States, but much higher than Sweden's. However, when the U.S.

standard was applied, Japan's rate of 3.7 percent in 1992 was even below that of Sweden (4.6 percent) and Canada (5.9 percent), and less than one-third that of France, Germany, Britain, and the United States (Smeeding, 1997, table 5). In the early 1990s, Japan had the lowest absolute poverty rate among 16 countries for which LIS data were available, but given the continuing recession, Japanese poverty probably increased subsequently.

What do the LIS data tell us about trends in market poverty and the extent to which it is offset by taxes and income transfers? Between Times I and II, market or pre-tax and transfer poverty rose in six of the seven countries for which data are available (Table 11.7). In Sweden, the exception, the rate rose between 1981 and 1992, when it was 51.9 percent, but had fallen slightly below the 1981 rate by 1995 (Vlaminckx, 1998). Interestingly, in the mid-1990s, the U.S. pre-tax and transfer or market poverty rate was the lowest in the sample. It is in offsetting poverty with taxes and transfers or in income redistribution that the U.S. performance differs so markedly from European nations and its North American neighbor, none of which is as rich.

When it came to poverty after taxes and transfers (disposable income poverty), Canada was the exception to the general trend, and it also differed in significantly increasing its anti-poverty effort (by nearly one-third) between Times I and II. The other countries either reduced their efforts (between 9 percent and 14 percent) or, in the case of France and the United States, showed minimal improvement. Whereas Canada increased its effort in the face of deteriorating market conditions, Britain, which had a lesser increase in market poverty, decreased its effort, with a resultant steep rise in disposable income poverty. A slightly improved U. S. anti-poverty effort was not sufficient to overcome a larger increase in market poverty, leaving about 18 percent of American households with disposable incomes less than half the medium, the highest in the sample. With unemployment more than double what it was at the beginning of the interval, France experienced a substantial rise in market poverty, and although it increased its social welfare expenditures more than the average for the sample (Table 11.1), that was not enough to offset the market decline. The absence of data makes it impossible to determine trends in poverty reduction in both Italy and Japan.

Some of the preceding chapters provide more recent and detailed data than these cross-national figures. Evans, using Canada's absolute poverty standard, points to increasing poverty in that country after the mid-1990s. According to Canada's low-income cutoff or poverty standard, its poverty rates in the 1990s were all above a 13.6 percent low in 1989. However, the average poverty rate for the 1980s was virtually the same as that for the 1990s. The steadiness of the overall rate, however, conceals two opposite trends: a fall in elderly poverty, which was nearly cut in half between 1980 and 1998, and rising childhood poverty (an average of 19.3 in the

1990s, through 1998, compared to 16.0 percent in the 1980s [calculated from National Council of Welfare, 2000, tables 2.10, 2.2, and 2.3]). Better, recent news comes from Millar's (Chapter 5) report of a decline of more than 1 million in child poverty in Britain in the last years of the century.

SUMMARY OF THE FINDINGS

This summary combines the findings of the country studies and the cross-national data. It identifies the general trends that are discernible as well as modifications of policies or models specific to one or more of the nine countries. Inasmuch as retrenchment and restructuring are ongoing, this summary should be read as an interim report.

- Programmatic retrenchment has occurred in varying degrees in all nine countries. This has happened even though, with the exception of post-Communist Hungary, the countries are spending larger proportions of increased resources on social welfare.

- These rich capitalist nations have increased their wealth in the last 20 years. Although growth has slowed since the 1960s, they, nonetheless, have the fiscal capacity to reduce poverty and inequality if they choose to use their resources that way.

- All but two of the countries increased the proportion of GDP spent on social welfare by a smaller proportion than the increase in their economic resources (GDP per capita). Much less wealthy than the other countries and declining in resources since the fall of Communism, Hungary cut social spending by a larger percent than the decline in its resources.

- Retrenchment of the employment commitments that were integral to the post-war welfare state were, on the whole, greater than programmatic retrenchment (with notable exceptions like repeal of the partial entitlement to public assistance in the United States). Increased market (pre-tax and transfer) poverty was the result of retrenchment in the employment sphere that was itself largely the result of changed government policies. Even though the countries in this study (except for Hungary) increased their social expenditures, the rise was not sufficient to compensate for market failures. As a result, the poverty of the non-elderly populations rose.

- Welfare state "reform" is usually a euphemism for retrenchment. But expansion and innovation are discernible, along with the more prevalent pattern of contraction. Examples of innovation are initiation of Care Insurance in Germany and Japan; income support for long-term unemployed persons and youth in France, Sweden (youth), and Italy (on an experimental basis); and supplementation of low wages through the Earned Income Tax Credit in the United States and in-work benefits and family credits in Britain.

- The eight countries for which data were available were devoting larger proportions of their resources to cash benefits for the elderly at the end of the period. Seven of them increased their efforts on services to the elderly and disabled but not necessarily in proportion to increasing need. The United States was the lone dissenter.

- No country in the sample increased its effort in both family cash and family service expenditures. On average, declines in cash expenditures exceeded increases, but not by much. When it came to support of family services, only France and Germany spent more at the end of the period than at the beginning.

- Increased selectivity or means testing is a prominent trend. Rationalized as an efficiency measure or as concentrating resources on the needier, which it has done with positive anti-poverty results in some countries, targeting is typically driven by cost-cutting. When targeting excludes only the better-off (Canada), as compared with including only the poor (e.g., United States), its threat to solidarity is minimized but not eliminated.

- Benefits are more closely tied to past and present employment or denied altogether. Moreover, this recommodification—or commodification in the case of women—is concurrent with deteriorating employment opportunities.

- Cutbacks in unemployment insurance (e.g., reduced coverage and earnings replacements) have occurred in all countries and concurrently with increased unemployment. This increases the labor pool and exerts downward pressure on wages.

- Wages have been falling in some of the countries where unemployment is high. This reaffirms the traditional relationship between loose labor markets and downward pressure on wages and casts doubt on the proposition that countries have a choice between high unemployment and high wages (Germany, France) and lower unemployment and lower wages (United States). Some countries (Canada and the United Kingdom) have both low wages and high unemployment, and so did the United States prior to its economic boom in the 1990s.

- Institutional factors such as the reduced scope of Wages Councils in Britain and the steep decline in the statutory minimum wage in the United States contributed to deterioration in wages. The policy appears to have been reversed in Britain but not in the United States.

- Devolution or reduced financial and standard-setting functions of central governments are evident, resulting in increased financial pressures on lesser units of government (states, counties, municipalities) to pay for services and social assistance and greater disparity in provision. Since these governments are under financial constraints, the result is often a reduction in services, increased fees for consumers, or both. This trend is not confined to the federalized nation-states.

- Privatization in its several manifestations occurred in all of the countries studied. Usually, it has taken the form of retrenchment and contributed, in turn, to declines in solidarity and stakes in public provision, lower wages for service workers, and weakening of public service unions. In some cases (France, Italy), however, it is also associated with increased public responsibility for a social welfare function.

- Full, maximum, or total employment policies have been abandoned, disregarded, or at best temporarily laid aside in all sample countries. The United States has a low unemployment rate (through early 2001) but much underemployment, and, in any case, no official commitment to keeping it low. Sweden's unemployment declined but in 2000 it was still more than twice its rate a decade earlier. "Worklessness," a growing problem in Britain under Coservative rule, is being attacked by the Labour government through a number of policies.

• High unemployment reduces national resources and revenues and increases the need for public expenditures. This undermines the fiscal basis of the welfare state—particularly if a high proportion of revenues is derived from payroll taxes.

• Victims of unemployment and their families, particularly in the former Communist countries, are among those whose welfare diminished most in recent years. Youth are particularly hard hit in France, Germany, Sweden, Italy, and Britain (although youth unemployment declined under Labour), and immigrants and minorities of color are either losing ground or continuing to be disproportionately disadvantaged (United States, Britain, Germany, Hungary, France, Sweden) and are less welcome as economies suffer.

• Women lost the relatively privileged labor market position afforded to them under Communism and have suffered both job and child-care loss, resulting in much higher unemployment rates than men (former German Democratic Republic [GDR]) or departure from the labor market (especially Hungary).

• Reflecting unemployment and/or declining wages, along with changes in family composition, market or pre-transfer poverty rates increased. This occurred in different degrees and in all except one (and even there, the decline was very slight) of the countries for which data were available.

• Along with increased pre-transfer poverty, the poverty reduction rates of income transfers declined. The exceptions are Canada and, to a much lesser extent, the United States (which still had the lowest poverty reduction rate in the sample), and France.

• Between about 1980 and the mid-1990s, relative poverty (disposable income) increased in varying degrees in six of the eight countries for which comparable data were available. It stayed about the same in France and declined modestly in Canada, but may have increased there after mid-decade. Relative poverty grew substantially in Britain, Germany, and Italy, and sizably, though not as much in Sweden and Hungary (1990s data only). The United States lost some ground, but more noteworthy is its consistent, dismal record—the highest, not only in total poverty, but in elderly and childhood poverty as well.

• Progress against poverty of older people continued in all eight countries (ranging from decreases of under 5 percent in France to about 75 percent in Canada). France, Sweden, and Italy, although increasing cash expenditures for older persons, reduced their poverty only slightly, illustrating that if need increases countries have to run harder just to stay in place. Changes in pension policy that take effect in the future, along with increased out-of-pocket costs for services, are likely to reverse the trend.

• Reflecting unemployment, increasing single motherhood, and declining wages, the dominant trend was toward an increase in child poverty. The most dramatic rises were in Germany, the United Kingdom, Italy, and Hungary. Two of these countries, along with the United States, had childhood poverty rates around 20 percent or more in the mid-1990s. Canada ended the period with about 15 percent of its young in relative poverty. Sweden and France, the countries with the highest expenditures on family cash benefits, had the lowest childhood poverty rates.

- Higher unemployment and lower wages have increased men's vulnerability to poverty.

- Women, despite reductions in the wage gap, experience new disadvantages—loss of public sector jobs, extra care burdens resulting from service cuts, and the stress and struggle of making do on less household income.

- Women are increasingly and disproportionately consigned to the growing numbers of marginal, part-time, contingent forms of work. They have been downsized by cutbacks in both social welfare and employment and, in the case of those previously in Communist regimes, lost their relatively advantaged position.

- Liberal and conservative approaches have treated women's employment differently. The former, which devalue women's work in the home, limit their access to public assistance and force them into a low-wage labor market (e.g., U.S. welfare "reform"). The latter, which reinforce patriarchy, discourage employment by means of increased benefits for family care and tax and pension disincentives (e.g., Germany).

- Single mothers had high rates of poverty in all but one of the countries of this study. The exception is Sweden, even with a rising rate in the 1990s. The poverty of single mothers increased sharply in Germany and Britain and remained very high in the United States and Canada. In France, nearly one of four single mothers was poor, even though it had the second-lowest rate of single-mother poverty among the countries in this study.

- Economic inequality increased everywhere from the mid-1980s to the mid-1990s, though to different degrees. The increases were significant in the United Kingdom, Sweden, and Hungary, less but adding to already great inequality in the United States, and modest in Canada, France, Germany, Italy, and Japan.

- The United Kingdom is among the countries where social welfare declined most. Increased means testing, service cutbacks, privatization, moderately high unemployment, and more poverty and inequality are hallmarks of Britain's post-Beveridge welfare state. Despite some promising signs, it remains unclear whether the "new" Labour government will significantly alter the course set by the neoliberal rule that preceded it.

- Germany's welfare state suffers from sustained, high unemployment, a dramatic reversal of its post-war record. Germany uses a substantial amount of its resources on cash benefits for the elderly and is also biased toward income transfers. Nonetheless, it is the second highest spender on both family and elderly/disabled services. While unification drains its resources, Germany's problems were evident before annexing the GDR.

- Italy is the low spender on services and is second only to Japan in bias toward the elderly. Even though pensions have provided disguised forms of aid to the non-elderly, expenditures for people of working age are insufficient to compensate for chronic, high unemployment in the south. The system's pervasive patriarchy manifests itself in labor market and social service policies that deny women employment and burden them with family responsibilities.

- The United States, the richest of these wealthy countries, continues to be the poorest in preventing poverty and inequality. Whereas some European countries offer "welfare without work," cutbacks in income support, decline in the value of the minimum wage, and anti-labor policies approximate a policy of welfare only if one works. The growth of the Earned Income Tax Credit and replacement of the entitlement to welfare with a temporary assistance program epitomize the restructuring of a semiwelfare state that was always scantily decommodified.

- Japan is losing some of its alternatives to social welfare. The reasons include prolonged recession, more women needing to stay in the labor market to supplement family incomes, and fewer available to care for the increasing elderly population. Adoption of Care Insurance is a sign that, with demographic and economic pressures, the Japanese family cannot substitute entirely for the services of the welfare state. Minimum welfare, combined with low rates of unemployment, resulted in Japan's average ranking in relative poverty and low rates of absolute poverty (U.S. standard) and inequality, but partly owing to a level of gender inequality that makes it difficult for women to be economically independent.

- Canada and, to a lesser degree, France were alone in increasing social expenditures at a higher rate than the growth of their economic resources or per capita GDP. They thus maintained commitments to social welfare in the face of sustained, high rates of unemployment ("welfare without work"). France seems to be continuing in this policy as well as starting to address the problem of unemployment and its consequences, but Canada began to retrench after 1993.

- Sweden was advanced enough to remain a leader in a world of diminishing or, at best, stagnating welfare—even though it has reduced and restructured its generous, universal social programs and temporarily or permanently laid aside its full employment policies.

CONVERGENCE, DIVERGENCE, CONTINUITY?

Convergence toward the liberal model of social welfare is predictable, given the resurgence of classical liberalism or neoliberalism and its dominance in much of the capitalist world today. Our findings suggest that we have not only heard the rhetoric of retrenchment but also seen the reality of it. This is true of the two countries that Pierson (1994) used to prove his point that the welfare state is hard to cut back and had not been significantly retrenched. The trend in most countries, including those associated with the liberal model, is toward reduction of whatever employment guarantees there were, as well as toward greater selectivity or means testing, more restrictive unemployment insurance policies, tightening of work requirements, privatization, and lower benefits. In short, there are indications not only of retrenchment but also of convergence toward a liberal model that puts fewer brakes on capitalism than either the conservative or social democratic approaches. At the same time important distinctions remain, and there is still great variety in social provision and employment opportunity.

In two of the three countries that exemplify the liberal model, retrenchment results in further intensification of the characteristics identified with that approach. Contrast the new liberals with the old. The New Deal, which inaugurated the U.S. welfare state, was once said to have a "social democratic tinge" (Hofstadter, 1955). Before Britain's Right turn, there was a post-war consensus for social democratic collectivism along the lines of Keynes and Beveridge (Crewe, 1991). Full employment policies seemed well entrenched in Britain in the 1960s. Canadian conservatism was more in the Tory tradition than the rough-edged American version. At times, the left wing of the Canadian Liberal Party, which has recently spearheaded retrenchment, "succeeded in pulling that party quite close to the positions of 'right-wing social democracy' " (Bradford and Jenson, 1991, p. 192).

Writing before Britain's sharp turn to the Right, political scientists Furniss and Tilton (1977) classified the United Kingdom as a "social-security state" because it assured a basic minimum as a right to every citizen. Furniss and Tilton (p. 16) placed "the social-security state" between an "affirmative state" like the United States and a "social-welfare state" like Sweden. Whereas the former did not "guarantee surrogate forms of property for all citizens," the latter not only made that guarantee but also strove for equality and solidarity. Similarly, Millar (Chapter 5) writes explicitly that the goal of the British welfare state was never to promote equality. The change, she observes, is that the Conservative policies of the 1980s and 1990s threatened what had been the aim of the Beveridge model, namely, assuring a minimum living standard to all. In the United Kingdom, significant retrenchment also occurred in the labor market, where, in contrast to its Liberal cohorts, it had, as noted, once achieved full employment and, short of that, consistently low rates of unemployment.

The United States, though it made significant progress toward a welfare state in the 1930s and again in the 1960s, nonetheless defeated a second presidential proposal for universal coverage in health care in the early 1990s, repealed or severely curtailed its always meager public assistance programs later in the decade, hovered on the brink of privatization of its once-unassailable social security program, and continued to take a booby prize in poverty prevention and reduction of inequality. Perhaps we should simply follow popular discourse and refer to "the U.S. model"—an extreme example of the liberal approach.

The countries categorized as conservative welfare states continue to exhibit some of the characteristics associated with that model. They favor the aged over children or families (except for France), spend generously for the elderly, and, especially in the case of Italy, put less emphasis on services than Sweden and other Scandinavian countries. Despite the continuing generosity of their pension systems, France and Germany tightened the rules for eligibility and benefit determination precisely when labor conditions were deteriorating and when it had become more difficult to qualify for adequate benefits. Their pension systems continue to maintain and solidify status distinctions, although the privileged may be losing some of their lead in Italy. Japan, sometimes placed in the conservative camp, is a low spender generally, but what it does provide is biased toward the elderly, even more so than the European conservatives. France differs from the others in its generosity to families, and, as Kesselman (Chapter 6) made clear, none of the models fits it well. It continues to be a hybrid and to reflect the different values of the varied parties that support the welfare state but disagree on other policies.

Hungary has aspired toward the "social market," a term by which the Germans describe their model. This is in contrast to other post-communist states that want the market without any modifiers. However, it seems premature to characterize Hungary, which is clearly in transition, though it is not clear toward what. The use of the term "social market" is less an aspiration toward Germany's model per se than an indication that Hungarians want to hold onto the social protections that were theirs under Communism. The international lending organizations on which Hungary is highly dependent for loans have put pressure on it to move toward the U. S. model, and similarly, foreign businessmen make holding down unions and wages a condition for their investment. At the same time, the former subjects of state socialism evidently retain some egalitarian values.

Nomura and Kimoto (Chapter 10) emphasize stability and slow change in Japan, where women traditionally carried the burden of family service and, for all but the beneficiaries of large-firm occupational welfare, supplementary income as well. Benefits, with the important exception of health care, continue to be highly commodified and minimal, and in this respect Japan resembles the liberal welfare states, particularly the United States. Women are the bulwark of a system in which the family is the major provider of social welfare, but they are also its victims, so lacking in personal autonomy from marriage that they seldom risk economic independence (Axinn, 1990). Demography, women's aspirations, and the prolonged recession that is bringing some of Japan's latent unemployment into the open are potential forces for increased social provision. But the politics that would translate need into deed—government policies and programs—are missing under what is essentially one-party, conservative rule. As power resources theory (PRT) posits, without politics, there is nothing to compel rich nations to commit resources to the development of the welfare state (Olsen and O'Connor, 1998, p. 7).

To what extent can we still speak of the social democratic model in

Sweden? Full employment was the bedrock on which the generous benefits of Sweden's welfare state rested. Sweden allowed its unemployment rate to soar for the first time in 50 years but was reducing it by the end of the 1990s. Sweden's commitment to full employment, however, remains ambiguous. The Scandinavian star retains the lead in active labor market programs and is the only country to spend more on these than on passive labor market programs. Once an integral component of Sweden's policy of creating an efficient and highly trained labor market along with providing some employment, active labor market programs are now addressing a problem that they are not equipped to handle—mass unemployment.

Sweden remains a leader in services. Even if it were to continue to cut back family services at the rate that it did from 1990 to 1995, it would take many years for Sweden to reduce its effort to the level of conservative Germany, the second largest spender on family services, and even longer to sink to the level of the liberal United Kingdom, the next in line. Sweden's effort on family cash benefits has increased and in 1995 was only slightly less than that of France, the leader by a wider margin in 1980. Although Sweden was a standout in the area of services for the elderly and disabled in 1995 and had grown very significantly, it has subsequently cut back here, too. Interestingly, Sweden is forcing the less frail elderly to pay for services, whereas the United States cutbacks are leading home-care providers to "cream" or avoid the neediest.

The biggest pension spender in 1980, Sweden has fallen behind France, Germany, and Italy but much more importantly has changed the structure of its system from a defined benefit to a defined contribution. This is something that even U.S. conservatives or neoliberals have not succeeded in accomplishing, although they relentlessly try. Social assistance was more frequently used in Sweden than the social democratic model implies, and there is a move toward more income testing than in the past.

The survival of the social democratic model in Sweden depends on whether it has stopped hemorrhaging and begun to recover or whether slippage will continue. The distinctive interrelationship between full employment and public service employment, particularly of women, is central to the social democratic model and a defining characteristic that separates it from both the service poor and patriarchal approach of the conservatives and the privatized approach to service provision and employment of the United States.[6] The shape and size of Sweden's welfare state have changed, although not enough to blur the distinction between its model and that of the others. But the story is not over. It is thus unclear whether Sweden will continue to exemplify the model of a social democratic welfare state that significantly reduces poverty and inequality, decommodifies human beings, and fosters women's economic independence through employment and social services.

CUTTING BACK WORK

High unemployment is a great threat to the developed welfare states, but, as the French example of high unemployment and maintenance of extensive social benefits implies, not necessarily a fatal one—at least not so far. It is, however, misleading to speak of France as having resisted retrenchment. That is substantially true for income support and services but not for employment policies, where retrenchment has been substantial. One of the reasons that social welfare has held steady in France is the wide consensus in its favor, which is, to a considerable extent, beyond party and politics. Full employment enjoys no such support, perhaps not even in Sweden, where it reigned longest.

An apparent policy paradox is that work requirements in some countries have become stiffer as employment and labor market conditions have worsened, and benefits have become more closely tied to labor market status precisely as employment security has diminished. In Germany, where unemployment has been high for more than a decade, the motivation for diminishing social protection is not, Bäcker and Klammer (Chapter 7) contend, simply fiscal austerity: "[S]ocial protection is being diminished so that workers will be obliged to accept whatever job is available." Welfare "reform" in the United States exemplifies this approach, and those forced to leave the rolls are among the millions who find themselves in a condition of "poverty despite work" (Center on Budget and Policy Priorities, 1999).

What have been some of the other responses to rising unemployment? Under President Lionel Jospin, France has created 750,000 jobs for the unemployed in public services, but unemployment, which numbered over 3 million in 1997, remains very high. Sweden has nearly doubled the proportion of its resources spent on active labor market programs, and so have Germany, France, and Italy. France and Italy's programs include subsidizing employment for groups especially disadvantaged in the labor market. Such policies may provide work to some of the unemployed but chiefly contribute to efficiency and reduce inflationary pressures when the economy has been expanded by other means (Meidner, 1997). Germany has intervened in the labor law to deregulate its labor market with the hope of expanding employment. Derugulatory policies such as weakening dismissal laws, decentralizing wage bargaining, or eliminating automatic wage indexation have also been tried in the United Kingdom, Belgium, France, the Netherlands, and Italy but without reducing overall unemployment—thus casting doubts on the theory that labor market rigidities are causing high unemployment in Europe (Blank, 1997, pp. 81–82).

Some countries have developed means of spreading and subsidizing work. Germany has approached the unemployment crisis not by increasing total employment but by sharing available work through the reduction of work time. This reduction of the workweek by about two hours did decrease the unemployment effects of austerity measures, but declining union power and falling wages limit the extent to which this policy can be expanded. Studies project that France's policy of reducing the workweek from 39 to 35 hours will have only a marginal effect on its high joblessness (Molloy and Shields, 1998, p. 14). A review of research on work-time reductions concludes that the results are likely to be limited as well as industry-sensitive and that technological and organizational changes as well as globalization and macroeconomic policy are more important factors in job creation (Molloy and Shields, 1998). There are, of course, good reasons to reduce work time other than spreading available employment—less job-related stress and more time for family, leisure, and community, to name a few. The United States and Britain are spreading employment by subsidizing low-wage work.

Unemployment decreases revenues even more than it increases costs and renders it more difficult to finance the kinds of benefits—family allowances, paid parental leave, and family support services—that make the welfare state popular with non-poor majorities. The costs of unemployment are not only the direct ones of unemployment insurance but the indirect ones such as social exclusion (Paugam, 1996)[7] and increased physical and mental illness, family breakdown, crime, and other forms of social deviance (Brenner, 1995; Jin, Shah, and Svoboda, 1995). M. Harvey Brenner, who has conducted extensive research on the effects of unemployment, observes that many epidemiological and national-level studies demonstrate conclusively that not working bears a considerably greater risk of illnesses (heart disease, cancer, stroke, suicide, accidents, homicide, infant diseases, mental disorder) and early mortality than the very great majority of jobs (1996). Nonetheless, there is some evidence that the stability and quality of work—not work on any terms—inhibit criminal behavior or stress (Crutchfield and Pitchford, 1997; Wilson, 2000, pp. 152–154). There is considerable impressionistic evidence that the restructuring of work, so-called lean production, has put enormous stress on workers and increased rates of job-related injury and illness (Moody, 1997, pp. 191–193). These ominous side effects of contemporary employment notwithstanding, high unemployment has special significance for women, for it is a barrier to participation in the labor market and to full liberation.

High unemployment is a major reason that social expenditures and poverty have increased concurrently. Nonetheless, faith in the market has risen at the very time when market income leaves more people impoverished. As the growth of inequality and poverty shows, the market is providing very well for those who tout its virtues but less well for those who may perhaps pout but, on the whole, do not shout—or have not done so enough yet.

Lower unemployment would also mitigate the problems of increased need caused by demographic changes. As pointed out in Chapter 2, lower unemployment extended the solvency of the U.S. social security system by six years between 1997 and 1999. The best insurance for social security or payroll-financed social insurance is full employment or an economy with abundant jobs at living wages. High rates of single motherhood in the United States, another demographic change that adds to welfare state costs, have been associated with chronic, high unemployment among black males (Wilson, 1987), and there is reason to infer that sustained joblessness in other parts of the world could have that effect. Additionally, unemployment means a loss of national output and of potential resources to meet human need. For example, the U.S. Congressional Budget Office estimated that a sustained rise of only one percentage point in unemployment from 1995 through 2000 would cost the treasury a cumulative loss—in revenues and benefits—of more than $400 billion (Ginsburg, 1995).

The deterioration in employment conditions is often treated as a force beyond the control of nations. The current exogenous explanation of economic woes is the "global economy." What Ramesh Mishra (1996, pp. 316–317) has to say about the global economy as an excuse for cutting back social expenditures applies as well to retrenchment of the full employment dimension of the welfare state:

Globalization provides a far more powerful justification than neo-conservative ideology for retrenching the welfare state. For neo-conservatism at least appears to be a matter of political and ideological choice. . . . Globalization, on the other hand, appears as an *external* constraint—not a matter of political choice at all, but rather of economic necessity.

But the necessity to subordinate economic policy to the requirements of globalization is itself a neoliberal doctrine. Pierson (1994) has written that since social welfare is popular with the population, those who would cut it back must seek "blame avoidance." Hiding behind globalism is a form of "blame avoidance" in the sphere of labor-market policy. As Linda Weiss (1998, p. 193) observes, governments rationalize policies of retrenchment by claiming that they are responses to global trends beyond the control of the nation-state.

How exogenous is the global economy? How important? How new? Nation-states have done much to encourage globalization through treaties like the North American Free Trade Agreement (NAFTA) and the World Trade Organization (WTO), the primary purpose of which is not simply to eliminate tariffs but to clear the way for capital to invest freely across borders without being restrained by social protections and financial regulations. Most of the trade of the wealthy capitalist nations, however, is not with poor countries but with other rich ones with comparable wages. For example, Paul Krugman and Robert Lawrence (1994) point out that the United States continues to buy the bulk of its imports not from developing countries with cheaper labor but from other advanced countries whose workers have similar skills and wages. Because countries that have been more export-dependent, for example, Sweden, were able to maintain low unemployment rates in earlier decades, Vicente Navarro (1999) argues that high unemployment rates did not coincide with a change in integration into world markets, as globalization theory holds, and that the causes of un-employment must be sought elsewhere. One of these may be that in an economy in which exports had displaced domestic consumption, the inter-nationalist sector of capital did, in time, recognize that, so to speak, Sweden needed them, but they did not need Sweden. Once more supportive of employment and welfare policies that expanded domestic consumption, capital came to believe that lower taxes and lower inflation were more in its interest than full employment and income-boosting welfare.

There has long been tension between what Heilbroner (1989) aptly calls "the border-blind view of merchantdom and the border-bound view of dukedom," and technological advances in transportation and communi-cations have given merchantdom new advantages in its quest for higher profits. Nation-states and labor, being less mobile, have lost power as a result of what is really an *increased* globalization of capital rather than an altogether new phenomenon. As chief economist of the World Bank, Lawrence Summers suggested that many of the world's largest firms were transnational since birth, steamship transport did more for world trade than digitalized data transmission through fiber-optic cables, and people are "just incrementally better at doing things they've always done" (1991, cited by Henwood, 1996, p. 5).

Eddy Lee, a research economist with the International Labour Organi-zation (ILO), points his finger at a culprit much closer to home than glob-alization (ILO, 1995; Lee, 1997). Slow growth, he argues, is the source of employment problems. A group of distinguished European economists who favor alternatives to current economic policies takes a similar position and puts globalization theory in its place:

While accepting that there have been external factors which contributed to the build-up of unemployment we nevertheless insist that the main responsibility for the scale and persistence of mass unemployment in the EU rests . . . with a coun-terproductive and harmful economic policy conducted over a generation by gov-ernments and finance ministers and influenced by powerful vested interests and neoliberal political and scientific advisers. The result is the current macro-economic regime of the EU which consists of a centralized and very tight monetary policy, narrow restrictions on European and national fiscal policies and the absence of any coordinated fiscal policy or effective union-wide employment strategy. (European Economists for an Alternative Economic Policy, 1998, pp. 7–8)[8]

Economist Robert Solow, a Nobel laureate, has also argued that most of Europe's problem is macroeconomic and that labor market rigidity has been an alibi for policymakers in Europe. Solow points instead to the European shift to tight macroeconomic policies that put expansionary approaches off-limits (Solow, 1994; see also Blank, 1997).

In a study for the United Nations, Isabella Bakker (1999) reviewed a number of studies of globalization of trade and financial markets. Although the latter have the capacity to restrict the power of governments to influence interest rates, foreign exchange rates, and fiscal policies, Bakker, nonetheless, concludes that "a more skeptical approach to globalization begins with the assumption that there exists a degree of state autonomy and that governments do have the power to sustain differences in fiscal and monetary policies" (p. 35). Similarly, Linda Weiss' (1998) studies have led her to conclude that nation-states differ considerably in their ability to coordinate industrial restructuring to meet the changes in international competition.

When pressure is put on government, as in Seattle in 1999, or as 2 million protestors did in France in a mobilization against cutbacks, politicians may alter their domestic policies, defy supranational bodies, or perhaps begin to push for reform and restructuring of the regional and international organizations to which they have ceded power. The response to the Seattle demonstrations of WTO-supporter Bill Clinton may indicate the latter approach: "I think it is imperative that the W.T.O. become more open and accessible. . . . If the W.T.O. expects to have public support grow for our endeavors, the public must see and hear, and in a very real sense, actually join in the deliberations" ("Clinton's Plea," 1999, p. A17). That the WTO is hardly alone in operating behind closed doors is revealed in a scathing account of the undemocratic and reckless actions of the International Monetary Fund by the former chief economist of the World Bank (Stiglitz, 2000).

When politicians have to choose between important constituencies and global pressures, which way are they likely to bend? Japan's ruling Liberal Democratic Party (LDP) faces this dilemma, whether to yield to the WTO and the General Agreement on Tariffs and Trade (GATT) which are pushing it to deregulate, or to farmers and small business, important LDP constituencies that stand to lose from such a policy.

Technological advance is also blamed for employment problems. Productivity stemming from technological advance can reduce employment. It has done so in European economies that are often charged with rigidity but that have very substantial rates of both job growth and job destruction (Blank, 1997; Navarro, 1998). When productivity growth is high, job loss can result unless economies expand sufficiently. Once again, the culprit is restrictive monetary and fiscal policies.

The two public mechanisms that have the most to do with levels of employment, fiscal and monetary policy, are out of direct popular control at this time. The Maastricht Treaty obligates the newly created European Central Bank, which has total authority for monetary policy in the European Union, to strict austerity and subordinates all other goals, including employment, to price stability. Although Maastricht does not set fiscal policies of member nations, the strict deficit and debt limits that it establishes have kept governments from expanding their economies. The European Monetary Union, as Ginsburg and Rosenthal (Chapter 4) point out, requires a member country to maintain low inflation, exchange rate stability, low interest rates, low public deficits and debts—but not low unemployment. The semiautonomous "Fed," which controls the U.S. money supply and interest rates and whose chairman is appointed by the president with congressional approval every four years, is independent of elected representatives between the terms of its chair. Balanced budget agreements established in response to budgetary "crises" that are believed to have been contrived to reduce social spending (e.g., Wicker, 1984; Schlesinger, 1986, p. 241) have crippled fiscal policy. The tight fiscal and monetary policies that have much to do with high unemployment are exogenous only to the extent that nations have abdicated authority over these economic policies to supranational organizations and agreements.

The employment policies that create problems for workers and the social welfare policies that fail to compensate for these problems and force workers to take any job at any pay are parallel efforts that enhance the power of capital at the expense of labor. In other words, the two spheres of retrenchment, economic and social policy, are interrelated. Of the two, the pullback has been more pronounced in employment. No country has undertaken fiscal and monetary policies sufficiently expansionary to have achieved very low rates of unemployment *and* living wages.

How do we explain the lapse or even demise of the full employment component of welfare statism? One reason is that capitalism occupies a monopoly position and no longer has to compete with a system that provided full employment and a modicum of economic security, if not freedom and prosperity. The latter two have been billed as preferable to the economic guarantees of Communism but have bypassed many of these newcomers to capitalism. Another reason for its fall from grace is that full employment has had few defenders. In the absence of depression-level unemployment, a strong threat of it, or recent memory of its devastating consequences (as in the years after the Great Depression or in Germany at the first hint of increased unemployment in the 1960s), few think of themselves as beneficiaries of full employment. Consequently, those who advocate full employment are mainly doing so on behalf of others or for the public interest. This is generally true of selective social welfare programs in contrast to universal programs like social security, whose advocates are defending their own present or future benefits or those of their families.

Most workers remain employed and consider themselves unaffected when full employment policies are abandoned or ignored. This is the case even though full employment advocates argue that it strengthens the bargaining position of all workers and makes many other serious problems easier to solve. These include the fiscal problems of the welfare state that lead to cutbacks that injure a much larger population than the unemployed. Even when it reaches the 10 percent level, unemployment remains the problem of smaller minorities than the beneficiaries of universal programs. Its casualties may not see themselves as permanently in that state—in which case they may opt for adequate unemployment benefits. On the other hand, if the unemployed include the underemployed, the working poor, the sporadically or unstably employed and come to view themselves in this way, then the constituency for full employment becomes larger.

Labor unions with nearly universal or very high densities may be expected to have a larger stake in full employment since their constituencies include the more vulnerable as well as the more privileged workers (Western, 1997, p. 193).[9] However, Sweden, with its 90 percent density in the mid-1990s, though committed to full employment for decades, did not strongly or effectively resist its lapse. French labor, with very low density, led a nationwide strike against cutbacks not in employment but in a welfare state that provides very widely, though not universally (ILO, 1997, pp. 236–240 for union densities).

RETRENCHMENT: POLICY AND POLITICS

The fact that welfare states continue to be costly even as they provide less well implies that they will become less popular and less supportable. The restructuring that pulls welfare states in the direction of poor-law states implies a different and more adversarial relationship between recipient— less citizen than supplicant—and provider. It also means diminished stakes in public provision on the part of the non-poor and less solidarity, all of which could contribute to a decline in popular support. Reductions in pensions, which often escaped the public's eye or scorn because they will affect future retirees, will ultimately reduce commitment to social insurance and increase dependence on private provision. The neglect of children also bodes poorly for the future of the welfare state, for they will be less well equipped to produce, earn, and contribute to revenues and perhaps be grudging as well toward the generations that deprived them. If the social and economic policies of the post-war years created politics or interest groups to defend the welfare state, some policies of the past two decades are creating politics that reduce its defenders.

THE TIMING OF CHANGE

In addition to providing some insight about the change process, differences in timing lead us to be cautious in drawing conclusions about the extent and future of retrenchment. During the 1980s, when countries with less social welfare and more unemployment were cutting back, Sweden's politics continued to look as different as its policies. Only a few years before changes in government policy led to unemployment rates of 9 and even 10 percent in the former full employment state, Göran Therborn, author of a cross-national study of employment policies (1986), wrote, "Sweden's transition to post-industrialism is occurring without unemployment and with a historical upward turn of the job supply curve" (1991, p. 106). Canada appeared to be offsetting the rise in pre-transfer poverty caused by its high unemployment rates, but in the mid-1990s social welfare ceased to hold the fort.

France found itself unable to establish socialism in one country in the early 1980s, partly because the expansionary policies of the Mitterrand government collided with a worldwide recession. George Ross (1991) describes as "the reshaping of popular power" the "vastly less redistributive" approach to regenerating national economic capacity that emerged in the 1980s after the first Mitterrand government ran into economic trouble. Yet, the French version was to protect the welfare state even if, in the interest of flexibility, changes were made. Full employment policies were a casualty of these changes but not social protection.

German retrenchment, in contrast to that in Sweden and Canada, began early and stealthily, hitting the most vulnerable and least able to mobilize and protest and co-opting the more powerful constituencies, like the trade unions, which were largely shielded from unemployment (Offe, 1991; Ginsburg, 1993). According to Morlicchio and colleagues (Chapter 8), "the reduction of welfare expenditures in Italy has been a slow, long-term, moderate process that has been going on at least a decade and has accelerated in recent years." By contrast, war against the welfare state was the unabashed domestic policy in the United States and Britain in the early 1980s but, as noted, not in their liberal cohort Canada. Japan's ruling LDP and its bureaucratic partners in the social ministry were also not subtle; they used the Organization of Petroleum Exporting Countries (OPEC) crisis in the 1970s to disparage welfare expansion in the socialist-led big cities and then proceeded to cut back benefits that were low to begin with.

What about the process of change in Washington? Recent events suggest there is a sequel to the heavy storm of neoliberalism in the 1980s and to the absorption and co-opting of some of that agenda on the part of New Democrats. Bill Clinton's narrowly elected successor ran as a moderate with his conservative backers distinctively sotto voce, but, despite getting a minority of the popular vote, George W. Bush is pursuing an unabashedly neoliberal or conservative agenda in office that may well deal a serious blow to social security if his privatization plan is adopted. Cutbacks in social services, including child-care subsidies, are already threatened, environmental protection is giving way to a new deregulation drive, and a conservative approach to judicial appointments is in the offing. Tax cuts that favor the wealthy will not only lead to greater inequality, but will also likely result in further cuts in social services. Bush's opponent, Vice President Al Gore, was another New Democrat. His narrow loss or narrow win was, in either case, a poor showing for the heir to an economic boom. Although Gore's showing may be less political than personal, it is nonetheless clear that the path that started with a neoliberal Republican has not ended with a New Democrat.

In Britain, long Conservative rule, stridently neoliberal under Margaret Thatcher, has been followed by New Labour. Under Prime Minister Tony Blair, Labour seems to be developing a different welfare state, one that rewards the working poor and that includes some firsts for Britain like a national minimum wage and government responsibility for child care. A leaner, restructured welfare state with an emphasis on rewarding work has been seen as a way of gaining the support of an electorate that is unwilling to support universalism (Glennerster, 1999). The inference is that limited altruism in some political contexts is more supportable than universalism. This position, however, bows to neoliberal thinking, particularly the view that full employment is incompatible with price stability and hence not a feasible means of supporting a more generous welfare state. It also seems to overlook the ways that electorates have been manipulated, the subject of the next section in this chapter. Whether restructuring is an alternative to retrenchment in Britain and whether its proponents will last longer than New Democrats in Washington is open to question—particularly since issues other than social welfare, such as the handling of the U.K. cattle disease crisis suggests, could influence the political fortunes of a regime.

SELLING AND BUYING NEOLIBERALISM

Political scientists Charles Lindblom and Edward Woodhouse attribute the failure of democracies to significantly reduce economic inequality to "a powerful uniform social indoctrination, coupled with vigorous efforts to choke off a genuine competition of ideas" (1993, p. 122). Such manipulation, which Lindblom and Woodhouse regard as endemic in capitalist, democratic societies, was in high gear as political and economic elites sought to convince the beneficiaries of the post-war social contract that less—especially less government—is more. Yet, the intensity of selling and the propensity of populations to buy differed among these capitalist countries.

Neoliberal discourse appears to have predominated only in the United Kingdom and the United States and even there with reservations that will be discussed. Laissez-faire, Kesselman (Chapter 6) observed, is a French phrase but not a popular concept in France. This is not to say that France has escaped neoliberal policies. However, France has a statist tradition, as its post-war dirigiste approaches imply (Shonfield, 1965), and, as noted, support of the welfare state is shared by a wide spectrum of political parties, albeit for different reasons. Indeed, the post-war expansion of the welfare state was, as Kesselman emphasized, exceptional in that it occurred under governments of the Right, not the Left. In Germany, observed Claus Offe (1991, p. 143), "the neo-conservative populist approach has constituted a noticeable ingredient of the political discourse of the 1970s and 1980s without assuming anything like the hegemonic role it enjoys in Britain." Similarly, writes Evans (Chapter 3), "Canadian politics in the 1980s did not produce the strong neo-liberal discourse that was spearheaded by Thatcher in Britain or Reagan in the United States."

Selling neoliberalism was big business. Chapter 2 called attention to the political mobilization of the business community in the 1970s and its results, especially the greatly increased power of capital in Washington. This vigorous campaign to relegitimate laissez-faire, to elevate the free market, and to blame labor, the welfare state, and "big government" for mounting economic and social problems made it harder for lower- and middle-income groups to understand and define their real interests. Once in office, Ronald Reagan, a powerful ideologue for ideas that had been banned from the White House since the 1930s, used the presidency to promulgate the idea that government is "the problem," not the solution.

Propaganda generated by organizations aiming to prevent expansion of government responsibility for health care in the United States—such as the National Association of Manufacturers, the U.S. Chamber of Commerce, and pharmaceutical trade groups—is reported in the Canadian media. These messages serve to undermine public confidence in a universal health insurance system that, according to the Canadian Institute for Health Information, is structurally sound and largely satisfies its users (Marmor, 2000). Canadian business, however, has delivered its own messages. The Business Council on National Issues was organized not only with the express purpose of influencing policy or being consulted on specific legislation, but with the more ambitious goals of redesigning the state (Wilson, 2000, citing Clarke, 1997). Although neoliberalism is not nearly so strong in Canada as in the United States, Evans (Chapter 3) nonetheless observes that Canadians have changed their expectations of their governments.

Capital was on the march elsewhere as well. In Chapter 4 Ginsburg and Rosenthal call attention to a move to the Right on the part of the Swedish Employers' Association (SAF) and its well-funded, multifaceted campaign to turn the public against the welfare state that had served the nation, including business, so well. Claus Offe, though pointing out the limits of neoliberal discourse in Germany (1991, p. 143), gives an example of the "politics of interpretation": the assertion by the chief analyst of the Federation of German Employers' Associations that about half the unemployed were not, in fact, unemployed but unemployable because of irreversible physical, mental, or skill deficiencies, inferring that their handicaps would not be overcome by collectivist measures like full employment. Evidently, they did not need to explain the sudden outbreak of such individual deficiencies or why so many of these people held jobs when they were available.

Joel Krieger (1991, p. 51) writes that in the United Kingdom conservative think tanks like the Institute for Economic Affairs "colonized the press" with anti-statist, anti-collectivist themes. The institute, for example, sponsored visits to Britain by Charles Murray, whose book, *Losing Ground* (1984*)*, was said to be a bible for the Reagan administration and who warned that the British welfare system was creating an "underclass" as a consequence of generous welfare and would go the way of the United States if nothing were done about it (Millar, 2000). Joel Krieger (1991, p. 53) holds that "with Thatcher's rise to the leadership of the Conservative Party, Hayek and Friedman and these loosely identified new right currents received powerful institutional backing." Thatcher didn't stop with discrediting government but declared, "There is no such thing as society, only individual men and women and their families" (Krieger, 1991, p. 54, citing Hall and Held, 1989, p. 16). In explaining national differences, the role of militant and forceful conservative leadership should be counted.

Citizens of the capitalist democracies have been encouraged to believe that accepting cuts in wages and welfare benefits and loosening of labor market regulations and environmental standards in order to assure their country's victory in world markets would reward them in the long run. The German case illustrates the illusion of such promises. Between 1980 and 1990 the German share of world exports rose 14 percent, and the profit rate of German corporations rose by one-third, but at the same time both the official unemployment rate and the number of poor people more than doubled, and the proportion of GDP going to wages was down 8 percent (Huffschmid, 1997, p. 74). "Trickle-down" concepts such as what was sold to the Germans were integral to the approach of Ronald Reagan, a conservative who was popular among white, working-class voters. Freeing the market in order to create more wealth that would, in turn, benefit all was central to the ideology of British conservatives.

The term welfare "reform" to describe what is usually retrenchment is another form of manipulation. Progressive intellectuals and scholars in Italy refer to welfare "reform" instead of retrenchment, even though, Mingione points out, it is motivated or promoted not by social justice but by budgetary restrictions (cited by Morlicchio, Puglies,e and Spinella in Chapter 8). In the United States, welfare "reform" was almost universally applied to what turned out to be the repeal of the nation's 60-year-old public assistance program for single mothers and their children.

Leaders in Japan's LDP capitalized on the anxiety created by the first OPEC crisis to undermine new, expansive social welfare initiatives and then to pursue a policy of retrenchment. As Nomura and Kimoto (Chapter 10) recount, the LDP and government bureaucrats conducted an effective, chauvinistic campaign against these initiatives by linking welfare expenditures to the "industrial country disease"—low productivity, budget deficits, and problems like crime, divorce, and drugs. The campaign that lionized the Japanese "welfare society" paved the way for reduction of pensions, termination of free medical care to persons over 70, and a harshly deterrent approach to public assistance.

Offe (1984, pp. 150–151) points out that even if capitalists and conservative political elites exaggerate the profit squeeze or the harm imposed on them by the welfare state, they are in a position to define "reality" in the sense that they have the power to apply economic sanctions. But capital's power to enact its reality should not be confused with public acceptance of the economic necessity of retrenchment. The motivation to resist retrenchment hinges on rejection of that premise. In calling attention to the selling of neoliberal ideas, then, it is important to question the extent to which the public bought the message.

Even where neoliberalism was vigorously and widely expounded by elites and the media, the general population may not have bought the message. Jane Millar (Chapter 5) reports that support for the welfare state remains widespread in Britain. Ginsburg and Rosenthal (Chapter 4) point out that the Swedish middle class actually increased its preference for public over private services during the period of retrenchment.

In the United States, despite the relentless attacks on welfare recipients, public opinion polls taken in the latter part of the 1980s indicated some softening in attitudes toward the poor and toward welfare (Reischauer, 1989, p. 12, citing Shapiro et al., 1987). Reagan's successor, George Bush, president from 1989 to 1992, even tried to promote a "kinder, gentler" conservatism. Study of a random sample of adults in the late 1980s, again following the onslaught, found that although public assistance programs like food stamps and Aid to Families with Dependent Children (AFDC) enjoyed less wide support than insurance and means-tested programs for the elderly, three-fourths of the respondents favored maintaining or increasing expenditures for AFDC, and 65 percent voted aye for food stamps. Fifty percent opposed spending cuts for AFDC, and slightly over one-third expressed willingness to write a letter or sign a petition against spending cuts or were willing to pay more taxes to avoid cuts. Members of Congress, also surveyed in this research, gave more support for social programs than the public (Cook and Barrett, 1992). Of course, such stated support on the part of the general public, even expressed commitment to action, does not mean that large numbers of people would, in fact, mobilize to defend these programs or that they would strongly resist legislation to cut back or repeal them. Clearly, they did not, perhaps because mobilizing mechanisms were absent. A different Congress, the most right-wing in nearly a half century, presided over the retrenchment of both AFDC and food stamps.

Political change occurred but was not necessarily a reflection of the ideological campaign to which the public had been subjected. On the other hand, it is hard to estimate the long-term effects on public attitudes and voting behavior of the sustained ideological campaigns of militant capital.

Capital stepped up its effort to manipulate the masses and political leaders, but the relative absence of countervailing forces also played a part in capital's victory. One reason that neoliberal ideas and policies became more acceptable is that the events that influenced the post-war order were long over and receding from the collective memory. This may be one of the reasons that Britain slipped back into the liberal camp or, to put it another way, World War II brought the "upstairs" and the "downstairs" closer together than ever.

The experience of mass unemployment in a skeletal or nearly non-existent welfare state no longer influenced policy. Those who had never known such insecurity, due in part to the accomplishments of the welfare state and full employment, were perhaps more troubled by the minor inconveniences of the present than the major evils of the past. Neither was the success of expansive government in financing the war and creating full employment in their ken. The demise of Communism left capitalism, like all monopolies, with scant motivation to please its clientele, and, where the welfare state and full employment were associated with the Left, it may have discredited these policies. Legitimacy in the post-communist world came cheap, at least for a few years. As Bäcker and Klammer (Chapter 7) put it, "international developments in recent years show that social peace has become a 'bargain,' gained without paying for it in social welfare."

Emphasis on the decline of labor movements may itself be a form of neoliberal ideology. However, union density fell off in some of the countries between the mid-1980s and mid-1990s and, with it, some capacity to wage the war of ideas—or to counter capital's campaign to convince workers that elite interests coincide with their own. Here, too, there are differences among countries, with labor gaining numbers in Sweden, staying the same in Canada, and losing in France, the United Kingdom, Germany, and the United States (ILO, 1997). Even so, as Ginsburg and Rosenthal (Chapter 4) point out, Sweden's larger numbers included few activists and a less effective Swedish Trade Union Confederation (LO). By contrast, French unions, despite the big drop in what was always a low density, sparked Europe's most important popular uprising since the 1960s, and reportedly, rank-and-file activists pushed the less militant leadership into action (Moody, 1997, pp. 15–18; Wilson, 2000, pp. 207–212). Union density may be a poor or certainly incomplete indication of labor's political strength. France, with a density of only 9 percent in 1995, was covering 90 percent of wages earners de facto under collective bargaining agreements—about the same as Sweden—whereas the figures were much lower in the liberal countries (Esping-Andersen, 1999, p. 20, using Visser, 1996, as a source).

Labor's troubles stem from both agency and structure—the economic changes that reduced its power base in the industrial sector and its failure to recoup these losses through innovative approaches to a different sex and occupational sector. (Canadian labor's successful drive to unionize women with the result that women's density and men's density are about equal is one exception [Wilson, 2000, p. 221].) Organized labor has often concentrated narrowly on members' interests rather than the working class generally, and it has sometimes acquiesced in retrenchment that did not directly threaten unionists. In Italy, where the basic principle of solidarity is said to obtain, "the system of industrial relations has always had at its core the defense of the positions of workers who were already employed in steady jobs" (Chapter 8). An encouraging move in a labor movement characterized by a narrow focus on its own members is the campaign of the U.S. national labor federation (AFL-CIO): "America Needs a Raise," a drive to raise the minimum wage, which would directly benefit non-members rather than its higher-paid membership. On the side of structure rather than agency are the ascendancy of blatantly anti-union regimes, particularly in the United States and Britain, the increased hostility of employers, and the decline and decreasing commitment to labor of social democrats or what were once working-class parties (Piven, 1991; Western, 1997; Wilson, 2000, pp. 198–202). On the other hand, a weakened labor movement was easier prey for a hostile or less friendly state and for stronger and more antagonistic capital.

An important task of organized labor is to provide political education to its members specifically and workers generally, to counter what the mainstream, elite-dominated media have to say. A weakened labor movement may lack the will as well as the resources and the influence with workers to neutralize and overcome the messages of the mainstream. Crewe, for example, observed that by the 1980s unions in Britain were no longer agents of class or partisan socialization. Indeed, he wrote that "the educational institutions of the labor movement have almost all disappeared" (1991, pp. 31, 36).

PARTIES TO RETRENCHMENT

What generalizations, if any, can be made about the political persuasion of the government officials who broke the social contract? The business agenda found a home in both camps. A decline of class politics is one way to describe the change; another is that the capitalist class won.

While conservatives Margaret Thatcher and Ronald Reagan conducted an open and holy—if not victorious—war against the welfare state, their counterparts in Germany and Canada proceeded less openly because, as discussed, in neither country was there a dominant neoliberal discourse such as the ones that Thatcher and Reagan joined and intensified. Conservative Brian Mulroney made incursions on the welfare state while referring to social programs as a "sacred trust." Similarly, Christian Democrat Helmut Kohl continued to praise Germany's "social market," not to bury it, but at the same time diminished it. Here we have four examples: two liberal welfare states where neoliberalism predominated, and the attack on the welfare state was patent, and two others, one liberal and the other an exemplar of the conservative model, where neoliberalism was weaker, and retrenchment real but more subtle.

Moderate and leftist governments were often the agents of retrenchment. If neoliberalism was militant under Margaret Thatcher, full employment received its first blow under Labour. Bowing to International Monetary Fund (IMF) pressures, Labour abandoned Keynesianism for monetarism and presided over a doubling of the unemployment rate between 1974 and 1979 (Crewe, 1991). Unemployment surged in the last years of the Democratic administration of Jimmy Carter, who also began the deregulation drive and, having initially increased public service employment for the unemployed, later cut it back when unemployment was still high. In 1979, Paul Volcker, appointed by Carter as chairman of the Federal Reserve Board, announced his intention to fight inflation at whatever price it might cost, and the price of the board's high interest rates was the worst recession of the post-war period and double-digit unemployment (Galbraith, 1998, pp. 217–218).

Bill Clinton, a New Democrat, affixed his signature to the repeal of AFDC, the public assistance entitlement for single-mother families. The first Republican-controlled House of Representatives in 50 years and the radical Right leadership in that House were factors, but so were Clinton's promise four years earlier to "end welfare as we know it" and his administration's own policy of permitting state waivers that contravened the existing statute and anticipated its replacement. Although Clinton's campaign promise in 1992 was to make NAFTA, a Republican initiative then in draft form, more friendly to labor and the environment, he did not do so and went against some leaders in his own party and organized labor in signing it. In Italy, Morlicchio, Pugliese, and Spinelli (Chapter 8) point out, welfare retrenchment is taking place not under conservative government but in a political climate that is moderately progressive, with the parties of the Left in power.

Baxandall (Chapter 9) considers it ironic that Hungarian socialists were the most aggressive in imposing austerity and slashing social programs (although they did not get away with it and went down to defeat in 1998 to a right-wing Populist coalition that began with more generous policies toward some programs than those of their predecessors). A more recent example of conservatism under leftist rule comes from Germany in 2000, where Social Democrat Gerhard Schröder achieved very significant tax reductions for the highest earners and the corporations.

The phrase "Nixon in China" was applied by conservative policy wonk Douglas Besharov to Bill Clinton's signing the repeal of Aid to Families with Dependent Children, meaning that it would have been harder or even impossible for a Republican to have done it (Kilborn and Verhovek, 1996, p. A18). Besharov held that if Clinton had been a Republican, Democrats in Congress would have stopped the state welfare waivers that paved the way to welfare repeal in their tracks. Similarly, Evans (Chapter 3) points out that despite their record on social programs, Liberals at the federal level have not attracted the organized opposition that occurred against the neoconservative government of Ontario. George Ross (1991, p. 92) maintains that the deindexing of wages by French socialists would not have been possible under the Right. Swedish protest against the policies of the Social Democratic Party (SAP) was far more muted than under the non-socialists, and the powerful, blue-collar workers' federation (LO), was reluctant to openly attack its longtime ally the SAP, even when it disagreed with its policies. Thus, the forces that would defend welfare statism were less likely to attack moderate and left-leaning governments than the declared conservatives.

Wilson, who points out that "business groups have played an enlarged role in developing labor and social policies across the OECD," writes that it made sense for capital to target progressive parties (2000, pp. 146–147). Wilson cites Clarke's (1997, pp. 36–37) observation that when Conservative Brian Mulroney became unpopular, it was necessary to consolidate support for the business agenda in Canada's Liberal Party.

DEFENDING WELFARE STATISM

Does this volume lend support for the view that the welfare state creates its own defenders in the person of its beneficiaries or for the position, implied by PRT, that retrenchment politics is a reverse mirror of welfare state development? The latter proves to be a very complicated question, indeed, since the development trajectories of these countries are diverse, and not necessarily explained by PRT.

Both theories should lead us to expect that Sweden would be well defended. The Social Democratic Party (SAP) enjoyed near hegemony and was in close alliance with a labor movement that had one of the highest densities in the world and even increased in numbers between 1985 and 1995. However, as Ginsburg and Rosenthal (Chapter 4) described, there was an ideological change and a split in the SAP, cooler relations between labor (LO) and the party of labor, and dissension in both the LO and SAP ranks over the neoliberal turn of some of the leadership. Both this example and that of the role of French labor in the 1995 uprising imply a critique of PRT. As Olsen and O'Connor (1998, p. 22) write, "PRT's quantitative measures of labor strength, such as unionization rates or the electoral durability of parties of the Left, can mask potentially serious rifts and fractures to the labor movement and consequently provide a misleading reading of labor strength."

The Swedish welfare state continued to be a rousing success into the 1990s—reducing poverty and inequality to what is probably the lowest level of any country in modern history, maintaining full employment in the face of successive economic shocks, and even achieving a budget surplus. The international pressures, the defection of Swedish capital, and a capital-financed ideological campaign caused the political leaders of a small, export-driven economy to change their longtime independent course and their commitment to the welfare state. The leadership and economic advisors of the ruling Social Democrats (SAP) became more conservative, no longer imbued with the ideology of their predecessors. Moreover, LO and SAP had established their power not only because of their considerable political acumen but because their opponents were weak and divided (Garrett, 1993). In the years preceding retrenchment, Swedish capital itself moved to the Right, became stronger, and enjoyed the support of a militant, international movement.

Pierson's theory that the welfare state creates its own defenders should have applied to Sweden, if anywhere. Programs that are both universal and generous, even from a middle-income perspective, should attract widespread support. Swedish regimes lost elections three times in the 1990s, and unemployment and cutbacks have been heavily implicated in their defeat. Retrenchment may have been slowed, but it nonetheless occurred. Potential defenders of the welfare state have to be mobilized, but the likely organizer in Sweden, the labor movement, has been reluctant to move against its ally (the SAP) and, perhaps like other bureaucracies, to stir up its rank and file. Finally, some changes like pension restructuring are complicated, poorly understood, and mostly not felt until the future, hence unlikely to be strongly resisted. In other words, they utilize some of the "strategies of obfuscation" identified by Pierson (1994, pp. 19–22).

Neither this study nor any that we know of has carefully analyzed the interests of welfare state defenders. Kesselman (2000) points out that some influential social scientists in France have argued that those who protested in 1995 were self-interested—and somewhat self-centered—since they were relatively privileged civil servants with high job security and good pay, early retirement, and so on. Other influential scholars claimed that many of those who participated in the protests were not direct beneficiaries but were demonstrating out of solidarity and that the fact that those slated for benefit reductions were not the worst-off members of French society did not mean that they were privileged. Indeed, proposed cutbacks were possibly the opening salvo in a series of cutbacks—so it was rational to hold the line at the first opportunity. They may have defined themselves as beneficiaries of the welfare state rather than of a specific program under siege. As one

French writer put it, "It quickly became apparent that the strikers were fighting on everyone's behalf" (Daniel Bensaid, 1996, cited by Moody, 1997, p. 16).

In Hungary, taxi and truck drivers met a sudden gasoline price hike with nationwide blockades crippling transportation for three days. They were not alone. The police showed solidarity with the demonstrators by refusing to remove them by force.

In the United States the elderly are certainly not alone in their resistance to changes in the structure of social security. Indeed, the AFL-CIO overlooked Vice President Gore's position on trade agreements with China or, in any case, did not withdraw its support over an issue that directly affects some of its membership, but it made maintenance of the current structure of social security a condition for organized labor's support of a presidential candidate.

What are the potential gains from resistance? It is true that politicians have to be elected and must respond to aroused electorates or lose their jobs. "In 1997 and 1998," writes German economist Jörg Huffschmid (1999, p. 4), "the conservative governments of Italy, Great Britain, France and Germany were voted out because of frustration and opposition to the downward wage pressure, social cuts and deregulation, sold as the only way to more employment and European unity." Indeed, by the end of 1998, 12 out of 15 European Union member states were led by Social Democrats. Yet, how different will their responses be? Or, given external pressures, can they be? With the exception of France, the Social Democrats or Laborites or New Democrats were, as the latter designation implies, different from their predecessors. Is their "third way"—like the path of the New Democrats in Washington—more like the old capitalism than the old democratic socialism? How likely are the protesters to take aim at the Left of Center?

France, as Huffschmid (1999, p. 4) points out, is exceptional, for it has pursued a macroeconomic policy with public programs for new jobs in services, reduction of the workweek in the private sector, and, after two years, the creation of 750,000 jobs. "Though not enough," he adds, "the direction is right." At the Socialist International World Congress in Paris early in 2000, Premier Lionel Jospin declared, "Our first priority as socialists is to work for full employment" (Mason, 2000, p. 5). Whether France under Jospin will adopt that priority remains to be seen. President Jacques Chirac's campaign promise to combat the "enemy," which he said was unemployment, was not kept.

The level of protest over proposed cuts in France was a mark of French exceptionalism. It is perhaps the reason that French policy has been responsive to popular mobilizations, that Jospin has refused to join the "Third Way" of his counterparts in Germany and Britain who were under the influence of the New Democrat in Washington, and that he has taken the initiative at the level of the EU to put the fight against unemployment back on the agenda. Such a widespread mobilization—2 million people in Paris alone—is very much in the French tradition. Washington is the scene of many demonstrations, and there have been boasts of Million Man or Million Moms' Marches, but even the great civil rights March for Jobs and Freedom in 1963 was only one-fourth the size of the 1995 protest in Paris in a country with a much smaller population than that of the United States. What the French example does show is that with enough protest, a government, even a medium-sized power, will respond on both the domestic and international levels, in the latter case encouraging other nations to join in reducing the exogenous pressures toward retrenchment.

This book reports protests elsewhere, albeit not so large as in France. Baxandall (Chapter 9) holds that Hungary has little capacity for collective action in defense of social protection and that, overall, there have been few mass protests. Nonetheless, he reports some large demonstrations over cutbacks in family benefits, introduction of tuition for higher education, and the gasoline hikes already mentioned. Canada and Germany have also been host to some large demonstrations. As Baxandall points out, it is hard to gauge the effects of popular protest, and it is also hard to know how much retrenchment is tempered by politicians' anticipation that the response will be negative and damaging. There seems to be a relationship between protests and concessions in France (Borrel, cited by Kesslman, Chapter 6). However, a few months after the massive outpouring in 1995, Premier Juppé proposed some far-reaching cuts in health benefits. While politicians will respond to widespread resistance, they may do so only temporarily or symbolically. Despite an election platform that promised gradual deficit reduction, the government of Liberal Jean Chrétien was more successful in promoting a radical and rapid deficit-reduction agenda than could have been imagined during the years of his Conservative predecessor (Chapter 3).

In some countries, politicians who blame retrenchment on external forces like the Maastricht Treaty with its strict convergence criteria for entry into the European Monetary Union are engaging in political manipulation or obfuscation. Bäcker and Klammer (Chapter 7) consider this to be true of Germany: "[T]he Federal Republic . . . is the initiator and driving force of this disastrous devaluation race in the field of state welfare, not merely its helpless victim." On the other hand, Hungary's indebtedness makes it dependent on the international organizations, like the International Monetary Fund, that put pressure on it to adapt an American-style residual welfare state. Convergence criteria are another force to be reckoned with in Europe. Unfortunately, the United States, potentially the most independent, is the most constrained by a neoliberal ideology that has a strong hold on the elites of both parties, though not necessarily on the electorate.

Will the mobilization of capital evoke a popular countermobilization? It is possible to argue that "globalization has generated new political constituencies for left-of-center parties among the increasing ranks of the economically insecure" (Garrett, 1998, p. 10). But it seems that the organization of these potential constituencies is, at best, in its infancy and that there has been little pressure on governments to restructure the undemocratic international organizations that they have helped to create and to which they have ceded power over their domestic policies. Such an initiative to restructure the blatantly non-democratic organizations that set the anti-labor, anti-environmental rules for the global economy is more likely to succeed if it is taken by a group of nations, preferably including one or more of the principal economic powers (Chorney, 2000).

But who will mobilize the people? Labor, as Seattle showed, is a candidate. In the United States, labor is a more progressive force than it has been in decades. Environmental groups, often at odds with labor, are natural opponents of international agreements and organizations that abrogate environmental regulations in the name of free trade. As one of the Seattle slogans, "Teamsters and Turtles: Together at Last," suggests, labor and environmentalists joined forces against the WTO. Women's movements are potential movers, given the losses that women are suffering in both work and welfare, but their commitment to social services is likely to vary, among other things, according to levels of privatization in their countries. Organizations representing minority racial and ethnic groups as well as immigrants are still other candidates. The elderly have been a potent force in some countries and are a potential partner for those who face future cuts in pensions. Minority parties, progressively oriented, strategically located, and out to expand their constituencies, are another prospect. Religious organizations have countenanced inequality but have also made social justice their mission and can certainly claim to transcend national boundaries, but their strength, salience, and social stance vary from country to country. Social movements are often led by new organizations that arise and arouse constituencies that have not been sufficiently stirred by long-standing efforts to achieve the same goals.

Given the wide range in welfare state development and decline and the diversity in political structures and traditions, movement strategies need to vary from country to country. Nonetheless, the basic job description for this movement would be reinforcing and uniting the diverse progressive forces in many countries and putting pressure on both national governments and international bodies—in short, a global movement for economic justice with branch offices in many countries.

NOTES

1. See Chapter 1 on limitations of social expenditure as measures of social welfare effort. Expressing social welfare effort in terms of social expenditures per capita

would control for population increases, but not for the larger shifts in the composition of the populations such as higher proportions of the elderly or single-mother families.

2. The OECD participation rates are based on the population between 15 and 64 years old, whereas the U.S. Department of Labor's (DOL) are for persons 16 and over. Labor force participation rates are naturally higher using the OECD approach. Moreover, if a country's elderly population were growing, the U.S. measurement might reflect that rather than a change in the participation of persons of working age. Like the DOL figures, the OECD's for Sweden show a decline in female participation rates from 81.7 at their peak in 1990 to 74.5 percent in 1997, a drop of almost 9 percent (OECD, 1991, 1995, 1999a).

3. Japan and, to a lesser extent, Italy are usually not included in the reports of the Luxembourg Income Study (LIS), the major source of standardized, cross-national data on poverty and inequality or, if they are, for less than the complete set of variables observed. Data for Hungary are only for the 1990s. An OCED study of income distribution and poverty (Burniaux et al., 1998) has very little data on the United Kingdom.

4. In figuring effective tax rates, the Congressional Budget Office includes the effect of the Earned Income Tax Credit, which it acknowledges is not a tax credit but a benefit that is budgeted like other income support programs. The CBO incudes the EITC because it was enacted as part of the tax code.

5. Also using LIS data but specifically on single mothers (as opposed to all solo parents), Christopher et al. (1999, table 1) reported the following actual rates: Canada, 40.5 (1994); France, 24.7 (1989); Germany, 39.1 (1994); Sweden, 3.4 (1992); United Kingdom, 31.9 (1995); United States, 47.1 (1994).

6. The United States spends almost as small a portion of GDP on public social services as Italy, but it invests heavily in private services. Percentages of private household expenditures that go for health, education, pensions, and day care are similar in the United States and Sweden (39.6 percent vs. 41.2 percent), but 73 percent of these expenditures are private in the United States, compared to 11 percent in Sweden. U.S. households spend about three times as much on private as on public expenditures, compared to nearly eight times more on public than private in Sweden (Bakker, 1999, table 12, p. 67).

7. Social exclusion is a broader concept than poverty and incorporates not only the traditional focus on disposable income or expenditure at a given time but the duration of disadvantage; local community as well as individual or household resources; relational issues such as inadequate social participation, lack of social integration, and lack of power; and catastrophic discontinuity in relationships with the rest of society (Room, 1999). Paugam (1996) found that precariousness in the labor market (i.e., lack of job security or short- and long-term unemployment) was correlated with weak family connections or the non-availability of a private support network in France, Germany, and Great Britain but not in Spain, Netherlands, Italy, and Denmark.

8. Among these economists are Miren Etxezarreta, University of Barcelona; John Grahl, University of North London; Jörg Huffschmid, University of Bremen; and Jacques Mazier, University of Paris.

9. The Ghent system, in which unemployment insurance is administered by

unions, has been an important factor in high union density in countries where it is practiced (Western, 1997, pp. 50–65; Rothstein, 1998).

REFERENCES

Axinn, J. (1990). "Japan: A special case." In G. S. Goldberg and E. Kremen, eds., *The Feminization of Poverty: Only in America?* New York: Praeger, pp. 91–105.

Bakker, I. (1999). "Globalization and human development in the rich countries: Lessons from labour markets and welfare states." In *Globalization with a Human Face*, Background Papers, vol. 2. *Human Development Report 1999*. New York: United Nations Development Programme, pp. 29–80.

Bensaid, D. (1996). "Neo-liberal reform and popular rebellion." *New Left Review* 215 (January/February): 109–116.

Blank, R. M. (1997). "The misdiagnosis of Eurosclerosis." *American Prospect* (January–February): 81–85.

Bradbury, R., and M. Jäntti. (1999). *Child Poverty across Industrialized Nations.* Working Paper no. 205, Luxembourg Income Study. Florence: UNICEF International Child Development Centre; Syracuse, NY: Maxwell School of Citizenship and Public Affairs, Syracuse University.

Bradford, N., and J. Jenson. (1997). "Facing economic restructuring and constitutional renewal: Social democracy adrift in Canada." In F. F. Piven, ed., *Labor Parties in Postindustrial Societies*. New York: Oxford University Press, pp. 190–211.

Bradshaw, J., and J. R. Chen. (1996). *Poverty in the UK: A Comparison with Nineteen Other Countries.* Working Paper no. 147, Luxembourg Income Study. Syracuse, NY: Maxwell School of Citizenship and Public Affairs, Syracuse University, October.

Brecher, J. (1998). "Popular movements and economic globalization." In Frank Bonilla, Edwin Meléndez, Rebecca Morales, and María de los Angles Torres, eds., *Borderless Borders: U.S. Latinos, Latin Americans, and the Paradox of Interdependence*. Philadelphia: Temple University Press.

Brenner, M. H. (1995). "Political economy and health." In B. C. Amick III, S. Levine, A. R. Tarlov, and D. C. Walsh, eds., *Society and Health*. New York: Oxford University Press.

———. (1996). Letter to the author. April 10.

Burke, M., and J. Shields. (1999). *The Job Poor Recovery: Social Cohesion and the Canadian Labour Market.* Ryerson Social Reporting Network. Toronto: Ryerson Polytechnic University, May.

Burniaux, J. M., T. T. Dang, D. Fore, M. Förster, M. M. d'Ercole, and H. Oxley. (1998). *Income Distribution and Poverty in Selected OECD Countries*. Economics Department Working Paper no. 189. Paris: OECD.

Center on Budget and Policy Priorities. (1999). *The Poverty despite Work Handbook*, 2nd ed. Washington, DC: Author.

Chorney, H. (2000). Personal communication with the author, June 21, 2000. (Harold Chorney is Professor of Public Policy, Concordia University, Montreal.)

———. (1999). *Unemployment in Canada, 1974 to 1999: A Case Study of Monetarism in Action.* Paper presented at the Columbia University Seminar on Full Employment, New York, December 6.

Christopher, K., P. England, S. McLanahan, K. Ross, and T. Smeeding. (2000). *Gender Inequality in Poverty in Affluent Nations: The Role of Single Motherhood and the State.* Philadelphia: University of Pennsylvania Population Studies Center, January 5.

Clarke, T. (1997). *Silent coup: Confronting the Big Business Takeover of Canada.* Ottawa: Canadian Centre for Policy Alternatives.

"Clinton's Plea: 'Open the Meetings.' " (1999). *New York Times*, December 2, p. A17.

Cook, F. L., and E. J. Barrett. (1992). *Support for the American Welfare State: The Views of Congress and the Public.* New York: Columbia University Press.

Crewe, I. (1991). "Labor force changes, working class decline, and the Labour vote: Social and electoral trends in postwar Britain." In F. F. Piven, ed., *Labor Parties in Postindustrial Societies.* New York: Oxford University Press, pp. 20–46.

Crutchfield, R. D., and S. R. Pitchford. (1997). "Work and crime: The effects of labor stratification." *Social Forces* 76 (September): 93–118.

Esping-Andersen, G. (1999). *Social Foundations of Postindustiral Economies.* New York: Oxford University Press.

European Economists for an Alternative Economic Policy. (1998). "Full employment, solidarity, and sustainability in Europe." Contact: Miren Etxezarreta, Departmento de Economía Aplicada, Universitat Autónoma de Barcelona, November.

European Economists for Full Employment, Social Cohesion and Equity. (1997). *Full Employment, Social Cohesion and Equity for Europe: Alternatives to Competitive Austerity: A Declaration and Memorandum of European Economists.* Circulated by Jörg Huffschmid, Universität Bremen, Bremen, Germany, May.

Furniss, N., and T. Tilton. (1977). *The Case for the Welfare State.* Bloomington: Indiana University Press.

Galbraith, J. G. (1998). *Created Unequal: The Crisis in American Pay.* New York: Free Press.

Garrett, G. (1993). "The politics of structural change: Swedish social democracy and Thatcherism in comparative perspective." *Comparative Political Studies* 25 (January): 521–547.

———. (1998). *Partisan Politics in the Global Economy.* Cambridge: Cambridge University Press.

Ginsburg, H. (1993). "With jobs for all: Rhetoric and reality in the United States, Germany, and Sweden." Unpublished manuscript, Department of Economics, Brooklyn College, City University of New York.

———. (1995). "Unemployment means lost output and human deficits." *Uncommon Sense* 2. New York: National Jobs for All Coalition.

Ginsburg, H. L., and B. Ayres (2000). "Employment statistics: Let's tell the whole story." *Uncommon Sense* 4. New York: National Jobs for All Coalition, February.

Glennnester, H. (1999). "Which welfare states are most likely to survive?" *International Journal of Social Welfare* 8: 2–13.

Hall, S., and D. Held. (1989). "Left and rights." *Marxism Today* (June): 16–23.

Heilbroner, R. (1989). "The triumph of capitalism." *New Yorker*, January 23.

Henwood, D. (1996). "Post what? Economics in the Postmodern Era." *Monthly Review* 48 (September): 1–11.

Hofstadter, R. (1955). *The Age of Reform.* New York: Vintage Press.

Huffschmid, J. (1997). "Economic policy for full employment: Proposals for Germany." *Economic and Industrial Democracy* 18 (February): 67–86.

——— (1999). "Back to austerity? The scene from Europe." *Good Jobs for All* (Fall): 4–5. [*Good Jobs for All* is the newsletter of the National Jobs for All Coalition, New York]

ILO (International Labour Organization). (1995). *World Employment 1995: An ILO Report.* Geneva: Author.

———. (1997). *World Labour Report: Industrial Relations, Democracy, and Social Stability.* Geneva: Author.

Jin, R. L., C. P. Shah, and T. J. Svoboda. (1995). "The impact of unemployment on health: A review of the evidence." *Canadian Medical Association Journal* 153: 529–540.

Kesselman, M. (2000). Personal communication to the author, February 2.

Kilborn, P. T., and S. H. Verhovek. (1996). "Clinton's welfare shift ends tortuous journey." *New York Times*, August 2, pp. A1, A18–19.

Krieger, J. (1991). "Class, consumption, and collectivism: Perspectives on the Labour Party and electoral competition in Britain." In F. F. Piven, ed., *Labor Parties in Postindustrial Societies.* New York: Oxford University Press, pp. 47–70.

Krugman, P. (1997). "We are not the world." *New York Times*, February 13, p. A33.

Krugman, P., and R. Z. Lawrence. (1994). "Trade, jobs, and wages." *Scientific American* 270 (April): 44–49.

Lee, E. (1997). "Is full employment still desirable and feasible?" *Economic and Industrial Democracy* 18 (February): 35–54.

Lindblom, C. E., and E. J. Woodhouse. (1993). *The Policy-Making Process*, 3rd ed. Englewood Cliffs, NJ: Prentice-Hall.

Luxembourg Income Study (2000). Relative Poverty Rates for the Total Population, Children and the Elderly. Available on the Internet at http://lisweb.ceps.lu.keyfigures/povertytable.htm (visited March 6, 2001).

Marmor, T. T. (2000). "If it ain't broke, don't fix it." *Toronto Globe and Mail*, Metro Edition, May 15, p. 1A.

Mason, J. G. (2000). "DSA and the Socialist International: A report from the XXI World Congress in Paris." *Democratic Left* 27(4): 4–6.

Meidner, R. (1997). "The Swedish model in an era of mass unemployment." *Economic and Industrial Democracy* 18 (February): 87–98.

Millar, J. (2000). Personal communication to the author, June 2.

Mishel, L., J. Bernstein, and J. Schmitt. (1999). *The State of Working America, 1998–99.* Ithaca, NY: ILR Press of Cornell University Press.

Mishra, R. (1996). "The welfare of nations." In R. Boyer, ed., *States against Markets: The Limits of Globalization.* London: Routledge, pp. 316–333.

Molloy, A., and J. Shields. (1998). "Tackling unemployment through working time reduction: A cautionary tale." *Window on Work*, No. 2 (May/June): 12–15.

Moody, K. (1997). *Workers in a Lean World: Unions in the International Economy.* New York: Verso.

Murray, C. (1984). *Losing Ground: American Social Policy, 1950–1980*. New York: Basic Books.

National Council of Welfare. (2000). *Poverty Profile 1998*. Ottawa: Minister of Public Works and Government Services Canada, Autumn.

Navarro, V. (1998). "Eurosclerosis versus U.S. dynamism." *Challenge* 41 (July–August): 66–75.

———. (1999). "The political economy of the welfare state in developed capitalist countries." *International Journal of Health Services* 29(1): 1–50.

Nomura, M. (2000). *Full Employment or "All Employment?" Japan's Labor Market Structure for Low Unemployment*. Paper presented to the Third Latin American Congress on the Sociology of Work, Buenos Aires, May 17–20.

OECD. (1988). *OECD in Figures: 1988 Edition*. Paris: Author.

———. (1991). *OECD in Figures: 1991 Edition*. Paris: Author.

———. (1995). *OECD Historical Statistics*. Paris: Author.

———. (1999a). *OECD in Figures: 1999 Edition*. Paris: Author.

———. (1999b). *OECD Social Expenditure Database, 1980–1996*. Paris: Author.

Offe, C. (1991). "Smooth consolidation in the West German welfare state: Structural change, fiscal policies, and populist politics." In F. F. Piven, ed., *Labor Parties in Postindustrial Societies*. New York: Oxford University Press, pp. 124–146.

Olsen, G. M., and J. S. O'Connor. (1998). "Introduction: Understanding the welfare state: Power resources theory and its critics. In J. S. O'Connor and G. M. Olsen, eds., *Power Resource Theory and the Welfare State: A Critical Approach*. Toronto: University of Toronto Press, pp. 3–33.

Osterman, P. (1999). *Securing Prosperity*. Princeton, NJ: Princeton University Press.

Paugam, S. (1996). "Poverty and social disqualification: A comparative analysis of cumulative social disadvantage in Europe." *Journal of European Social Policy* 6(4): 287–303.

Peracchi, F. (1999). *Earnings Inequality in International Perspective*. Working Paper no. 208. Syracuse, NY: Maxwell School of Citizenship and Public Affairs, Syracuse University, June.

Pierson, P. (1994). *Dismantling the Welfare State? Reagan, Thatcher, and the Politics of Retrenchment*. Cambridge: Cambridge University Press.

Piven, F. F. (1991). *Labor Parties in Postindustrial Societies*. New York: Oxford University Press.

———. (1999). *The Market-Friendly American Welfare State*. 12th Annual Robert J. O'Leary Memorial Lecture. Columbus: College of Social Work, Ohio State University, October 27.

Reischauer, R. D. (1989). "The welfare reform legislation: Directions for the future." In P. H. Cottingham and D. T. Ellwood, eds., *Welfare Policy for the 1990s*. Cambridge, MA: Harvard University Press.

Room, G. J. (1999). "Social exclusion, solidarity and the challenge of globalization." *International Journal of Social Welfare* 8: 166–174.

Ross, G. (1992). "The changing face of popular power in France." In F. F. Piven, ed., *Labor Parties in Postindustrial Societies*. New York: Oxford University Press.

Rothstein, B. (1998). "Labour-maket institutions and working-class strength." In J. S. O'Connor and G. M. Olsen, eds., *Power Resources Theory and the*

Welfare State: A Critical Approach. Toronto: University of Toronto Press, pp. 283–311.

Schlesinger, A. M., Jr. (1986). *The Cycles of American History*. Boston: Houghton Mifflin.

Schmid, J. (2000). "Schroeder triumphs in battle over taxes." *International Herald Tribune*, July 15–16, pp. 1, 14.

Shapiro, R. Y., K. D. Patterson, J. Russell, and J. T. Young. (1987). "The polls: Public assistance." *Public Opinion Quarterly* 51 (Spring): 120–130.

Shonfield, A. (1965). *Modern Capitalism: The Changing Balance of Public and Private Power*. New York: Oxford University Press.

Smeeding, T. M. (1997). *Financial Poverty in Developed Countries: The Evidence from LIS*. Luxembourg Income Study, Working Paper no. 155. Syracuse, NY: Maxwell School of Citizenship and Public Affairs, Syracuse University.

Smeeding, T. M. and L. Rainwater. (1991). *Cross National Trends in Income Poverty and Dependency: The Evidence for Young Adults in the Eighties*. Working Paper no. 67. Syracuse, NY: Maxwell School of Citizenship and Public Affairs, Syracuse University, August.

Smeeding, T. M. and K. Ross. (1999). *Social Protection for the Poor in the Developed World: The Evidence from LIS*. Working Paper no. 204. Syracuse, NY: Maxwell School of Citizenship and Public Affairs, Syracuse University, March.

Solow, R. (1996). "Is all that European unemployment necessary?" In R. Hinshaw, ed., *The World in Transition: What Leading Economists Think*. Cheltenham: Edward Elgar, pp. 164–178.

Sorrentino, C. (2000). "International unemployment rates: How comparable are they?" *Monthly Labor Review* 123 (June): 3–20.

Steinmo, S. (1994). "The end of redistribution? International pressures and domestic tax policy choices." *Challenge* 24 (November/December): 9–17.

Stiglitz, J. (2000). "The insider: What I learned at the world economic crisis: The insider." *New Republic* (April 17): 56–60.

Summers, L. (1991). Memo on a draft of the World Bank's annual *Global Economic Prospects and the Developing Countries*, December.

Therborn, G. (1986). *Why Some Peoples Are More Employed Than Others: The Strange Paradox of Growth and Unemployment*. London: Verso.

———. (1991). "Swedish social democracy and the transition from industrial to postindustrial politics." In F. F. Piven, ed., *Labor Parties in Postindustrial Societies*. New York: Oxford University Press, pp. 101–123.

U.S. Bureau of the Census. (1998). *Money Income in the United States: 1997*. Current Population Reports, P60–200. Washington, DC: U.S. Government Printing Office.

U.S. Congress, Congressional Budget Office. (1994). *The Economic and Budget Outlook: Fiscal Years 1995–1999*. Washington, DC: U.S. Government Printing Office.

U.S. Department of Labor, Bureau of Labor Statistics. (2000a). "Comparative civilian labor force statistics: Ten countries, 1959–1999." Unpublished data. Washington, DC, April 17. Available on the Internet at ftp://ftp.bls.gov/pub/special.requests/ForeignLabor/flslforc.txt (visited July 7, 2000).

———. (2000b). "Comparative real gross domestic product per capita and per employed persons: Fourteen countries, 1960–1998." Unpublished data. Washington, DC, March 30. Available on the Internet at ftp://ftp.bls.gov/pub/special.requests/ForeignLabor/flsgdp.txt (visited May 2, 2000).

Visser, J. (1996). "Union trends revisited." Mimeo, University of Amsterdam.

Vleminckx, K. (1998). "LIS Low Income Measures." Luxembourg Income Study. Available on the Internet at http://www.lis.ceps.llu/LISLowincomemeasures.htm (visited June 6, 2000).

Weiss, L. (1998). *The Myth of the Powerless State*. Ithaca, NY: Cornell University Press.

Western, B. (1997). *Between Class and Market Power: Postwar Unionization in Capitalist Democracies*. Princeton, NJ: Princeton University Press.

Wicker, T. (1984). "The other Fritz." *New York Times*, February 3, p. A29.

Wilson, S. (2000). "The struggle over work: Conflict & debate over the distribution of employment, income & power." Unpublished doctoral dissertation, University of New South Wales, Sydney.

Wilson, W. J. (1987). *The Truly Disadvantaged: The Inner City, the Underclass, and Public Policy*. Chicago: University of Chicago Press.

Wood, A. (1994). *North-South Trade, Employment, and Inequality*. Oxford: Clarendon Press.

Bibliographical Essay

Marguerite G. Rosenthal

Diminishing Welfare: A Cross-National Study of Social Provision is designed to be a contribution to the growing body of scholarship that examines social welfare policy from a comparative perspective. These studies have had somewhat varying foci, but in recent years many have sought to explain the reasons for variations in welfare state comprehensiveness and have examined and questioned whether or not the welfare state is beginning to wither away and, if so, why. This brief essay will point the reader to some of the most significant of these works. We suggest, however, that the reader also consult the chapter reference lists for information about the specific countries in this book.

CLASSIC SOURCES

Beginning in the 1930s, political theorists and economists were formulating policies that sought to provide for the economic well-being, health, and social inclusion of citizens in the Western industrialized nation-states. These included, famously, John Maynard Keynes' *The General Theory of Employment, Interest and Money* (1936), Alva and Gunnar Myrdal's *Nation and Family* (published in Sweden in 1934 and in English in 1941). Sir William Beveridge (1942, 1944), whose significance is discussed in the Introduction of this book, emphasized the importance of full employment and social insurance. T. H. Marshall (*Citizenship and Social Development*, 1947/1973) and Richard M. Titmuss (*Essays on the "Welfare State"* [1958]), "The Role of Redistribution in Social Policy" [1965], and *Commitment to Welfare* [1968/1976] were two other British writers who had a strong influence on welfare state theory.

By the late 1950s, there were a few studies that compared social welfare provisions across national boundaries. Very influential in the United States was Harold L. Wilensky and Charles N. Lebeaux's *Industrial Society and Social Welfare* (1958/1965). The authors argued that industrialization was the primary factor that required countries to adopt welfare policies. In an introductory chapter for their 1965 edition, Wilensky characterized the United States as a "reluctant welfare state" and posed explanations for its comparatively weak social welfare efforts, including traditions of economic individualism, the historical preference for private charity, its decentralized and fragmented political structure, and racial and ethnic diversity, which served to divide the working class population that elsewhere was the engine of welfare state development.

WELFARE STATE EXPANSION AND WELFARE STATE "REGIMES" THEORIES

The analysis of welfare state types was undertaken in a concerted way in the late 1970s and 1980s. In 1971, Frances Fox Piven and Richard A. Cloward published their influential and controversial book, *Regulating the Poor*, which posited that welfare expansion in the United States—and earlier in Britain in its Poor Law iterations—followed episodes of social disorder and was used to pacify protests from the lower classes. An important line of inquiry was developed by Walter Korpi (1978, 1983, 1989) and his colleagues at the Swedish Institute of Social Research (e.g., Korpi and Palme, 1998); the "power resources" theory attributed the development of the comprehensive welfare state to a mobilized working class with strong ties to a dominant social democratic political party. The importance of union strength as the engine behind both social welfare expansion and resistance to retrenchment was the theme of a 1992 book edited by Frances Fox Piven, *Labor Parties in Postindustrial Societies*. Bruce Western's *Between Class and Market* (1997) examines in comparative perspective the labor movement, its relationship to political parties, and the decline in its political influence in recent years. *Power Resources Theory and the Welfare State*, edited by Julia S. O'Connor and Gregg M. Olsen (1998), examines this theory cross-nationally from the perspectives of several disciplines.

In an article written with Walter Korpi (1984) and especially in a series of books, Gøsta Esping-Andersen has been responsible for developing a theoretical approach to categorizing and understanding the differences in three types of welfare state "regimes." Perhaps the most influential, *The Three Worlds of Welfare Capitalism* (1990), distinguished among regimes depending on their "decommodification" or the extent to which benefits are provided on the basis of citizenship rather than market status. Esping-Andersen probed the different trajectories and alliances of working-class movements to explain variations in the comprehensiveness and conditions of eligibility for a variety of social welfare benefits in three categories of countries: (1) conservative (most of Western Europe), where benefits are tied to employment; (2) liberal (English-tradition countries) that are market-driven and where meager means-tested benefits are a primary instrument of social welfare distribution; and (3) social democratic (Scandinavian countries) where citizenship is the qualification for a host of universal benefits. Esping-Andersen's later works (1996 and 1999) have sought to answer his critics, to place more emphasis on family and demographic factors, and to examine changes in welfare state provisions in light of economic difficulties experienced by much of Europe and Asia in the 1990s.

A theorist in the British tradition, Anthony Giddens (e.g., 1982, 1994) is both analytical and prescriptive. Articulating the importance of political struggle for extending citizenship rights and thus critiquing Marshall (see Chapter 1), Giddens recognized early that welfare states can contract as well as expand, and he exphasized the importance of historical context for the development of welfare programs. Giddens has demonstrated a concern with the rigidities of many welfare state programs and the passivity among recipients they sometimes engender; and more than most writers, he has discussed the negative impact of welfare programs imposed on developing countries by the industrialized ones. A self-styled welfare state reformer, Giddens has written extensively and provocatively about the "third way" by reformulating the social compact between state and citizen, where the private sector is admitted as the engine of economic growth and the state ensures the active participation of the citizen/recipient (1999, 2000). He is considered a major contributor to the social philosophy of Britain's "New" Labour Party.

STRUCTURAL THEORIES

One line of Esping-Andersen's critics are those who argue, not unlike Wilensky and Lebeaux, that governmental structures and capacity are highly influential in determining the extent and quality of a country's welfare state provisions. Federalist structures not only impede development of uniform policies, but also inhibit labor and citizen groups from mobilizing to promote changes (Castles, 1998). Castles (1994) has also examined the role that religious difference has played in developing or inhibiting welfare provision and has challenged the Esping-Andersen paradigm of three regime types (1993).

Theda Skocpol and her colleagues (Weir, Orloff, and Skocpol, 1988) have been prominent advocates of the position that governmental and institutional structures, including bureaucratic capacities, affect the development of welfare provisions. Interested primarily in the phenomenon of "American exceptionalism" (i.e., the U.S. welfare laggard phenomenon).

Skocpol (1992) argued that the American state, its locally based political party system, and the courts have been crucial elements in limiting the development of social provision; on the other hand, elites, rather than the working class, have had an important role in developing policy frameworks in the United States. However, Skocpol (1992) questions American exceptionalism in at least one historical period, arguing that widespread provision of pensions to Civil War veterans and their dependents in the late nineteenth century compared favorably with European social insurance provision.

WELFARE STATE RETRENCHMENT

Recent studies of the welfare state, including this one, have been concerned with reductions in welfare state programs and provisions, although they have different perspectives on the extent and reasons for retrenchment. Many employ the term coined by Esping-Andersen (1996) that the "Golden Age" of the welfare state is behind us. As our introduction discusses in some detail, Paul Pierson (1994) was an early investigator of the extent to which the conservative governments of Margaret Thatcher in Great Britain and Ronald Reagan in the United States were able to curtail welfare activities. While he concluded that these two political leaders were unable to undo welfare state programs to the degree that they intended, others have been less sanguine about the long-term trends of welfare state programs. This book can be counted among those works.

One thread of this discussion has concentrated on Western Europe, where high levels of unemployment have contributed to the perception that the generous welfare state is no longer sustainable. The so-called jobs/equality tradeoff has dominated this discussion, reflecting neoliberal arguments that generous social welfare benefits, based on high levels of taxation, curtail private sector investment and economic growth. These arguments are reviewed and critiqued by A. B. Atkinson (1999). The role that the European Union, and particularly the European Monetary Union (EMU), have played in eroding national policies has been studied by Andrew Martin (1999), who cites the weakened position of labor as crucial for understanding welfare state retrenchment. The edited volume by Stefan Leibfried and Paul Pierson (1995) presents varying perspectives on the extent to which the European Union affects national sovereignty in social policy development and implementation, concluding that nation-states still have primary responsibility in this area but are more restricted than previously.

"Globalization" is Ramesh Mishra's (1996, 1999) explanation for the decline of welfare state activities. He cites greatly relaxed restrictions controlling the free flow of capital beyond national boundaries, capital's preference for cheap industrial labor in third world or developing countries, and the collapse of communism—which served as an alternative social and economic structure and therefore a political threat—as the primary economic changes that are weakening labor's strength and capital's willingness to pay for the welfare state. Gary Teeple (1995) provides a Marxist analysis of many of the same issues but holds that the post–World War II welfare state amounted to concessions from capital, not resolutions to fundamental class conflicts, and he emphasizes the loss of the nation-state's ability to control its economy. These arguments are countered by Linda Weiss (1998), who posits that states, in fact, retain their importance as political and economic actors. Isabella Bakker (1999) provides an excellent overview of many of these issues, including their relationship to unemployment, inequality and poverty, different economic and social policy responses, and a call for more attention to human investment policies. Also recommended is "The Challenge of Full Employment in the Global Economy," a special issue of the journal *Economic and Industrial Democracy*, edited by Helen Ginsburg and her colleagues (1997) at the Columbia University Seminar on Full Employment.

FEMINIST VIEWPOINTS

Until the 1980s, analysts paid little attention to the impact of the welfare state on women, but since then a growing body of literature has been concerned with this topic. Hilda Scott, a journalist, examined approaches to facilitating or thwarting women's participation in the paid labor force in two countries, Czechoslovakia and Sweden (1974, 1982). Mary Ruggie (1984) compared social policies, and particularly child care policies, in Britain and Sweden. Alice Cook, an influential analyst of women workers in comparative perspective, co-edited *Women and Trade Unions in Eleven Countries* (1984). See also *Women Workers in Fifteen Countries*, edited by Jennie Farley (1985). Goldberg and Kremen's 1990 book, *The Feminization of Poverty*, examined social welfare, employment, and demographic policies pertaining to women in seven countries and found that feminization of poverty was most marked in the United States and was the least marked in Sweden and Japan, but for different reasons. Diane Sainsbury and her colleagues (1994, 1996, 1999) have been particularly concerned with examining the welfare "regimes" paradigm in light of policies affecting women. Her work has prompted Esping-Andersen to attend more carefully to policies that encourage women's participation in paid employment as well as the importance of family-maintenance roles—usually performed by women—and their variations in his later work. A book co-edited by Julia S. O'Connor, Ann Shola Orloff, and Sheila Shaver (1999) examines benefit structures for and labor force participation of women in four liberal (English-speaking) countries. *Poverty, Social Assistance, and the Employability of Mothers*, by Maureen Baker and David Tippin (1999), examines welfare state restructuring and its impact on low-income mothers and their families in Canada, Australia, New Zealand, and Britain.

POVERTY, INEQUALITY, AND FAMILY POLICY

A number of publications have focused on the impact that different countries' economic and social policies have had on reducing poverty and inequality. These studies often discuss family policy, since women and children—especially families headed by single mothers—and the elderly are disproportionately likely to be poor. Alfred Kahn and Sheila Kamerman's *Income Transfers for Families with Children* (1983) was an early and influential examination of policies affecting family poverty. Analyzing data compiled by the Luxembourg Income Study (LIS), Timothy Smeeding, with various colleagues, has published numerous analyses (e.g., Palmer, Smeeding, and Torrey, 1988; Smeeding, O'Higgins, and Rainwater, 1990; Smeeding, 2000) of poverty in specific demographic categories, especially children, in comparative perspective. A volume edited by Katharine Mc-Fate, Roger Lawson, and William Julius Wilson (1995) examined work force participation, economic stress, and social and economic policies for specific demographic groups (e.g., youth, minorities, single parents) in the United States, Canada, and Europe. These books consistently conclude that the poor in the United States are more disadvantaged than in other industrialized countries.

An interesting approach to studying persistent poverty has recently been published by Robert E. Goodin and his colleagues. *The Real Worlds of Welfare Capitalism* (1999) compares poverty spells, reliance on income maintenance programs, inequality, and related phenomena among subjects from the United States, the Netherlands, and Germany (countries chosen to represent the three welfare "regimes") over a 10-year period of time. In this study, too, American families have the highest percentage of poor families, and they remain poor for longer stretches of time than do their European counterparts.

A few books have focused on the social service sector in comparative perspective. Ruggie's 1984 comparative study of child care has been mentioned above. Kahn and Kamerman also examined child-care policy (1987), and they have published a number of subsequent studies of comparative social policy related to child and family well-being. Goldberg and Kremen and their contributors (1990) analyzed the economic status of social and economic policies for single-parent families in seven countries. Marianne A. Ferber and Brigid O'Farrell's edited book, *Work and Family* (1991), has a useful comparative summary of family-oriented policies for working women. Jane Lewis, whose interest is women workers and relevant social policies, has examined changes in care work resulting from policy shifts in Europe (1998). *Comparative Social Policy*, edited by Jochen Clasen (1999), is recommended for researchers interested in particular social welfare programs (including social assistance, long-term care, unemployment insurance), and themes (including lone motherhood and migrants); the book's chapters summarize past research, pose methodological issues, and give extensive bibliographic references. A related work, edited by Anna Kwak and Robert Dingwall (1998), looks at changes in European social policy and social work.

COMPENDIUMS AND JOURNALS

Finally, two recent compendiums provide seminal articles and selections from important welfare state researchers and theorists. These are Robert E. Goodin and Deborah Mitchell's two-volume set, *The Foundations of the Welfare State* (2000) and Christopher Pierson and Francis G. Castles' *The Welfare State: A Reader* (2000).

The International Journal of Social Welfare (formerly the *Scandinavian Journal of Social Welfare*) is an excellent source for articles concerning social welfare problems and programs from a cross-national perspective.

WORKS CITED

Atkinson, A. B. (1999). *The Economic Consequences of Rolling Back the Welfare State*. Cambridge, MA: MIT Press.

Baker, M., and D. Tippin (1999). *Poverty, Social Assistance, and the Employability of Mothers: Restructuring Welfare States*. Toronto: University of Toronto Press.

Bakker, I. (1999). "Globalization and human development in the rich countries: Lessons from labour markets and welfare states." In *Globalization with a Human Face*, Background Papers, vol. 2, *Human Development Report 1999*. New York: United Nations Development Programme, pp. 29–80.

Beveridge, W. H. (1942). *Social Insurance and Allied Services*. New York: Macmillan.

———. (1944). *Full Employment in a Free Society*. London: Allen and Unwin.

Castles, F. G., ed. (1993). *Families of Nations: Patterns of Public Policy in Western Democracies*. Aldershot: Dartmouth.

———. (1994). "On religion and public policy: Does Catholicism make a difference?" *European Journal of Political Research* 25: 19–40.

———. (1998). *Comparative Public Policy*. Cheltenham, UK and Northampton, MA: Edward Elgar.

Clasen, J., ed. (1999). *Comparative Social Policy: Concepts, Theories and Methods*. Oxford and Malden, MA: Blackwell.

Cook, A. H., V. R. Lorwin, and A. K. Daniels, eds. (1984). *Women and Trade Unions in Eleven Industrialized Countries*. Philadelphia: Temple University Press.

Esping-Andersen, G. (1990). *Three Worlds of Welfare Capitalism*. Princeton, NJ: Princeton University Press.

————. (1995). *The Equality-Employment Trade-Off: Europe's Welfare States at the End of the Century*. Trento, Italy: University of Trento and Instituto Juan March.

————, ed. (1996). *Welfare States in Transition: National Adaptations in Global Economies*. London: Sage Publications.

————. (1999). *Social Foundations of Postindustrial Economies*. Oxford: Oxford University Press.

Esping-Andersen, G., and W. Korpi. (1984). "Social policy as class politics in post-war capitalism: Scandinavia, Austria and Germany." In J. H. Goldthorpe, ed., *Order and Conflict in Contemporary Capitalism*. Oxford: Clarendon Press, pp. 179–208.

Farley, J., ed. (1985). *Women Workers in Fifteen Countries: Essays in Honor of Alice Hanson Cook*. Ithaca, NY: Cornell University Press.

Ferber, M. A., and B. O'Farrell, eds. (1991). *Work and Family: Policies for a Changing Work Force*. Washington, DC: National Academy Press.

Giddens, A. (1982). *Profiles and Critiques in Social Theory*. Berkeley: University of California Press.

————. (1994). *Beyond Left and Right: The Future of Radical Politics*. Stanford, CA: Stanford University Press.

————. (1999). *The Third Way: The Renewal of Social Democracy*. Oxford: Polity Press.

————. (2000). *The Third Way and Its Critics*. Oxford: Polity Press.

Ginsburg, H. L., J. Zaccone, G. S. Goldberg, S. D. Collins, and S. M. Rosen. (1997). "The challenge of full employment in the global economy." *Economic and Industrial Democracy: An International Journal* 18(1): 5–34.

Goldberg, G. S. and E. Kremen, eds. (1990). *The Feminization of Poverty: Only in America?* New York: Praeger.

Goodin, R. E., B. Heady, R. Muffels, and H-J. Dirven. (1999). *The Real Worlds of Welfare Capitalism*. Cambridge: Cambridge University Press.

Goodin, R. E., and D. Mitchell. (2000). *The Foundations of the Welfare State*. Northampton, MA: Edward Elgar.

Kahn, A. J., and S. B. Kamerman. (1983). *Income Transfers for Families with Children: An Eight-Country Study*. Philadelphia: Temple University Press.

————. (1987). *Child Care: Facing the Hard Choices*. Dover, MA: Auburn House.

Keynes, J. M. (1936). *The General Theory of Employment, Interest and Money*. New York: Harcourt, Brace and World.

Korpi, W. (1978). *The Working Class in Welfare Capitalism: Work, Unions and Politics in Sweden*. London: Routledge and Kegan Paul.

————. (1983). *The Democratic Class Struggle*. London: Routledge.

————. (1989). "Power, politics, and state autonomy in the development of social citizenship." *American Sociological Review* 54: 309–328.

Korpi, W., and J. Palme. (1998). "The paradox of redistribution and strategies of equality: Welfare state institutions, inequality, and poverty in the Western countries." *American Sociological Review* 63 (October): 661–687.

Kwak, A., and R. Dingwall. (1998). *Social Change, Social Policy and Social Work in the New Europe*. Aldershot, UK: Ashgate.

Leibfried, S., and P. Pierson, eds. (1995). *European Social Policy: Between Fragmentation and Integration*. Washington, DC: Brookings Institution.

Lewis, J., ed. (1998). *Gender, Social Care and Welfare State Restructuring in Europe.* Aldershot: Ashgate.

Marshall, T. H. (1947/1973). *Citizenship and Social Development.* Westport, CT: Greenwood Press.

Martin, A. (1999). *Wage Bargaining under EMU: Europeanization, Renationalization, or Americanzation?* Cambridge, MA: Center for European Studies, Harvard University.

McFate, K., R. Lawson, and W. J. Wilson, Eds. (1995). *Poverty, Inequality, and the Future of Social Policy: Western States in the New World Order.* New York: Russell Sage.

Mishra, R. 1996. "The welfare of nations." In R. Boyer and D. Drache, eds., *States against Markets: The Limits of Globalization.* London: Routledge, pp. 316–333.

———. (1999). *Globalization and the Welfare State.* Cheltenham, UK and Northampton, MA: Edward Elgar.

Myrdal, A., and G. Myrdal. (1941). *Nation and Family: The Swedish Experiment in Democratic Family and Population Policy.* New York: Harper.

O'Connor, J. S., and G. M. Olsen, eds. (1998). *Power Resources Theory and the Welfare State: A Critical Approach.* Toronto: University of Toronto Press.

O'Connor, J. S., A. S. Orloff, and S. Shaver. (1999). *States, Markets, Families: Gender, Liberalism, and Social Policy in Australia, Canada, Great Britain, and the United States.* Cambridge: Cambridge University Press.

Palmer, J. L., T. M. Smeeding, and B. B. Torrey, eds. (1988). *The Vulnerable.* Washington, DC: The Urban Institute Press.

Pierson, P. (1994). *Dismantling the Welfare State? Reagan, Thatcher and the Politics of Retrenchment.* Cambridge: Cambridge University Press.

Pierson, C., and F. G. Castles, eds. (2000). *The Welfare State: A Reader.* Cambridge and Malden, MA: Polity Press and Blackwell Publishers.

Piven, F. F., ed. (1992). *Labor Parties in Postindustrial Societies.* New York: Oxford University Press.

Piven, F. F., and R. A. Cloward. (1971). *Regulating the Poor: The Functions of Public Welfare.* New York: Random House.

Ruggie, M. (1984). *The State and Working Women: A Comparative Study of Britain and Sweden.* Princeton, NJ: Princeton University Press.

Sainsbury, D., ed. (1994). *Gendering Welfare States.* London: Sage.

———. (1996). *Gender, Equality, and Welfare States.* Cambridge: Cambridge University Press.

———, ed. (1999). *Gender and Welfare State Regimes.* Oxford: Oxford University Press.

Scott, H. (1974). *Does Socialism Liberate Women? Experiences from Eastern Europe.* Boston: Beacon Press.

———. (1982). *Sweden's "Right to Be Human"—Sex-Role Equality: The Goal and the Reality.* Armonk, NY: M.E. Sharpe.

Skocpol, T. (1992). *Social Policy in the United States: Futures Possibilities in Historical Perspective.* Princeton, NJ: Princeton University Press.

Smeeding, T. M. (2000). *Child Well-being, Child Poverty and Child Policy in Modern Nations.* Toronto: University of Toronto Press.

Smeeding, T. M., M. O'Higgins, and L. Rainwater, eds. (1990). *Poverty, Inequality and Income Distribution in Comparative Perspective: The Luxembourg Study.* Washington, DC: Urban Institute Press.

Teeple, G. (1995). *Globalization and the Decline of Social Reform.* Toronto: Garamond Press; Atlantic Highlands, NJ: Humanities Press.

Titmuss, R. M. (1958). *Essays on the "Welfare State."* London: Allen and Unwin.

———. (1965). "The Role of Redistribution in Social Policy." *Social Security Bulletin* 18 (June): 14–20.

———. (1968/1976). *Commitment to Welfare.* London: Allen and Unwin.

Weir, M., A. S. Orloff, and T. Skocpol, eds. (1988). *The Politics of Social Policy in the United States.* Princeton, NJ: Princeton University Press.

Weiss, L. (1998). *The Myth of the Powerless State.* Ithaca, NY: Cornell University Press.

Western, B. (1997). *Between Class and Market: Postwar Unionization in the Capitalist Democracies.* Princeton, NJ: Princeton University Press.

Wilensky, H. L., and C. N. Lebeaux. (1958/1965). *Industrial Society and Social Welfare.* New York: Free Press.

Index

Index

About the Contributors

GERHARD BÄCKER is Professor of Social Policy at the University of Applied Sciences, Lower-Rhineland, Mönchengladbach. His key areas of research and lecturing are the welfare state and the social security system, financing social welfare, social security and the labor market, income distribution and poverty, and family policy. He is the author of *Sozialpolitik und soziale Lage in Deutschland: Ein Lehr- und Studienbuch* (Social Policy and Social Legislation in Germany: A Teaching and Study Book), 2 vols. (with R. Bispinck, K. Hofemann, and G. Naegele, 2000), and he has contributed chapters to *La exclusion social* (Social Exclusion) (J. Hernandez and M. Olza, eds., 1998) and *Kinder in Armut* (Children in Poverty) (C. Butterwegge and D. Ruiss, eds., 2000).

PHINEAS BAXANDALL is a lecturer at the Harvard University Social Studies program, specializing in comparative politics of unemployment. He taught at the Budapest University of Economic Sciences in 1990–1991. His publications include "The Communist Taboo against Unemployment: Ideology, Soft-Budget Constraints, or the Politics of de-Stalinization?" in *East European Politics and Societies* (Fall 2000) and "When Is Unemployment Politically Important? Explaining Differences in Political Salience across European Countries," in *West European Politics* (January 2001), as well as numerous popular articles on political economy for *Dollars & Sense*, where he serves on the editorial board.

PATRICIA M. EVANS is Associate Professor (Emerita) and a former Associate Dean of Graduate Studies at York University in Toronto. Her many publications on income security place Canada in a comparative perspective, and she writes with particular attention to gender issues. Recently she co-edited *Women's Caring* (1998) and *Women and the Canadian Welfare State* (1997), and she contributed to *Restructuring Caring Labour* (2000).

HELEN LACHS GINSBURG is Professor Emerita of Economics, Brooklyn College, City University of New York. She was the recipient of a Swedish Bicentennial Fund research grant to study employment policy in Sweden and the Lawrence Klein Award of the U.S. Bureau of Labor Statistics for her work on comparative employment. She is the author of *Unemployment, Subemployment, and Public Policy* (1975), *Full Employment and Public Policy: The United States and Sweden* (1983), and *Jobs for All: A Plan for the Revitalization of America* (with Sheila D. Collins and Gertrude Schaffner Goldberg, 1994), and the editor of *Poverty, Economics, and Society* (1972, 1981). In January 1997 she was the chief guest editor of a special issue, "The Challenge of Full Employment in the Global Economy," in the international journal *Economic and Industrial Democracy*. Professor Ginsburg is a co-founder of the National Jobs for All Coalition and co-chair of the Columbia University Seminar on Full Employment.

GERTRUDE SCHAFFNER GOLDBERG is Professor of Social Policy, Adelphi University School of Social Work. For a number of years she served as the director of its Center for Social Policy. Her areas of interest are full employment, public assistance, the feminization of poverty, comparative social welfare systems, and social administration. She is the author of *Jobs for All: A Plan for the Revitalization of America* (with Sheila D. Collins and Helen Lachs Ginsburg, 1994) and *Washington's New Poor Law: Welfare "Reform" and the Roads Not Taken, 1935 to the Present* (with Sheila D. Collins, 2001), and the editor of *The Feminization of Poverty: Only in America?* (with Eleanor Kremen, 1990). She is a co-founder and Chair of the National Jobs for All Coalition.

MARK KESSELMAN is Professor of Political Science at Columbia University, specializing in the political economy of Western Europe and comparative labor movements. Since 1998 he has been co-director of the Columbia University Seminar on Labor and Popular Struggles. He is the author of *The Politics of Power: A Critical Introduction to American Politics*, 4th ed. (with Alan Draper and Ira Katznelson, 2001) and the editor of *A Century of Organized Labor in France: A Union Movement for the Twenty-First Century?* (with Herrick Chapman and Martin Schain, 1998), *An Introduction to Comparative Politics: Political Challenges and Changing Agendas* (with Joel Krieger and William A. Joseph, 1999), and *European Politics in Transition*, 4th ed. (with Joel Krieger, 2001).

KIMIKO KIMOTO is Professor of Sociology of the Family and Work at the Graduate School of Sociology, Hitosubashi University. Based on her research on the families of employees of the Toyota Automobile Company, Professor Kimoto's book, *Family, Gender and Company-Centered Society in Japan*, was awarded a prize from the Society for the Study of Social Policy in Japan in 1996. Since then she has co-edited several books, the most recent of which is *Women and Working World* (with T. Kamada and S. Yazawa, 2000). Professor Kimoto's recent research on job segregation by gender in the retail industry was conducted at one of the largest department stores in Japan.

UTE KLAMMER is Senior Researcher at the Institute of Economic and Social Research (WSI), Germany. Dr. Klammer lectures at the Universities of Frankfurt am Main and Cologne. Her key areas of research are pension systems, European and comparative social policy, social protection and justice, social protection and labor market participation of women, and the financing of social security. Among her recent publications are "Soziale Sicherung in Europa: Welche Strategien verfolgen unterschiedliche Länder bei vergleichbarer Krisensymptomatik?" (in *Von den Nachbarn lernen, Wirtschafts- und Beschäftigungspolitik in Europa, Schüren Scherrer*, Marburg, 1998), "Restructuring Germany's Pension System" (in *Pension Reform and Aging Populations: North American and European Perspectives, Looking Ahead*, April 1999), and "Les différences de salaire entre hommes et femmes en Allemagne: Un rattrapage limité et fragile" (in *Travail et emploi*, April 2000, with C. Ochs).

JANE MILLAR is Professor of Social Policy and Director of the Centre for the Analysis of Social Policy at the University of Bath. Her research interests include family policy and the policy implications of family change, income support and labor market policies for unemployed people and lone parents, poverty, inequality, and social exclusion, gender and social policy, and comparative social policy. She is the author of *Evaluation of the New Deal for Lone Parents: Synthesis Report* (with J. Hales et al., 2000) and editor of *The Politics of the Family* (with H. Jones, 1996) and *Private Lives and Public Costs: Lone Parents and the State* (with R. Ford, 1998).

ENRICA MORLICCHIO is Senior Research Associate in the Department of Sociology at the University of Naples "Federico II," where she also teaches Sociology of Development. She has been involved in a series of studies including poverty, social polarization, and immigration. Professor Morlicchio is presently involved in a project on Spatial Dimensions of Urban Social Exclusion and Integration, sponsored by the European Commission. Her most recent book is *Povertà ed excluusione sociale: La prospettiva del mercato del lavoro* (Poverty and Social Exclusion: The Perspective of the Labor Market) (2000).

MASAMI NOMURA is Professor of Labor Economics and Japanese Economy in the Graduate School of Economics at Tohoku University. His first book on the history of industrial relations in the Ruhr received the prize for the "Best Book on Labor" from the Japan Institute of Labor. A subsequent focus was on the mutual relationship between the production system and the labor market, a point especially stressed his *Toyotism*, which also won a prize—from the Japan Association of Management in 1995. Since the early 1980s Professor Nomura has been collaborating with foreign researchers with whom he has produced several books, including *The Resilience of Corporate Japan* (with Christian Berggren, 1997). His book *Koyo Huan* (Insecure Employment) on the current problems in the Japanese labor market was ranked among the best-selling books in Japan in August 1998.

ENRICO PUGLIESE is Professor of Sociology of Work at the University of Naples "Federico II," where he has also been chairman of the Department of Sociology. He was director of the joint graduate school in sociology of the University of Naples and of Salerno. Professor Pugliese has been both a Harkness and a Fulbright fellow and visiting professor at several American universities. He has carried out research in the field of international migration, labor markets, and the social and economic implications of unemployment. Among his publications are *Gli immigrati in Italia* (Immigrants in Italy) (1995) and *Sociologia della disoccupazione* (Sociology of Unemployment) (1993, also published in French). He is currently involved in a series of research projects on international migration.

MARGUERITE G. ROSENTHAL is Professor of Social Policy in the School of Social Work at Salem State College. She specializes in the areas of social welfare history and child and family policy. Her previously published works are on the Swedish welfare state, juvenile delinquency policy, and privatization. She is active in a number of advocacy organizations.

ELENA SPINELLI is Senior Lecturer in Social Policy and Social Services at the School of Social Work, University "La Sapienza," Rome. She also works in public services for immigrants. Professor Spinelli has conducted research on social work and mental health, medical care, and social work and gender.